Readings on Logic

IRVING M. COPI
THE UNIVERSITY OF MICHIGAN

JAMES A. GOULD
THE UNIVERSITY OF SOUTH FLORIDA

The Macmillan Company, New York

Collier-Macmillan Limited, London

Fifth Printing, 1968

Library of Congress catalog card number: 64–15457
The Macmillan Company, New York
Collier-Macmillan Canada, Ltd., Toronto, Ontario

Printed in the United States of America

PREFACE

In the typical introductory logic course today logical techniques are presented and students are drilled in their application. These techniques are central to the study of logic and must be mastered. Most contemporary logic textbooks are devoted primarily to describing and illustrating these logical techniques. If the textbook does its task well, not all the classroom time available need be spent either on supplementing the textbook's exposition of these techniques or on drilling the students in them. Happily, there is more to the study of logic than the mastery of techniques.

Logic involves not only skills to be acquired but also insights to be achieved. There are logical principles and issues to be understood as well as techniques to be practiced. Fruitful classroom discussion must deal with the theory or philosophy of logic rather than with its techniques—which, as techniques, are scarcely debatable. But the typical logic textbook does not provide enough material for stimulating classroom discussion. So much space is required to present the techniques of logic that a textbook which performs this function adequately cannot do much else. It has no room to raise the exciting theoretical issues that have engaged the attention of great logicians from antiquity to the present. This book of readings is intended to satisfy the indicated need. It is designed to serve as a supplementary textbook in a first course in logic: its function is to furnish the bases for classroom discussion of logical issues.

Naturally it is not possible in a single book to consider every question of logical theory. Our selection of issues has been determined by the topics that are usually studied in elementary courses of logic. Most introductory logic courses include some work on deductive logic: the traditional syllogism, elementary symbolic logic, or both. Consequently, we have included theoretical discussions of issues in both of these areas of deductive logic. Most introductory logic courses contain some work on induction, so we have included lively discussions of still living issues in inductive logic. In distinguishing induction from deduction, as well as in studying deductive logic itself, the notion of logical truth arises. We have included discussions of the traditional "laws of thought," which are relevant to current investigations into the topic of logical necessity. And since any first course in logic must confront the question of what logic is, we have included discussions of the nature of logic. The five parts of this book deal, in order, with the nature of logic, the syllogism, the laws of thought, symbolic logic, and induction.

Each part contains essays by distinguished logicians. These essays have been written from widely divergent historical and theoretic points of view. Classical, medieval, idealist, pragmatist, and mathematical logicians have all been included. A glance at the table of contents will reveal the diversity of points of views herein expressed. Some of the essays are as vigorously polemical as any in philosophy. They should help to kindle the dialogue that many still believe to be the best way to teach it. And of course it is hoped that these essays will stimulate further reading in the great original works of logic from which they were selected.

The editors wish to thank many friends for helpful suggestions. They are particularly indebted to Professor Marx W. Wartofsky of Boston University and to Professor Julius R. Weinberg of the University of Wisconsin, who read an early version of the manuscript, and made very useful comments.

IRVING M. COPI

JAMES A. GOULD

CONTENTS

I The Nature of Logic

INTRODUCTION A textbook cannot linger over the problems that arise in defining its subject, for it must hasten on to develop that subject in detail. So textbooks often convey the impression that a standard, universally accepted definition of logic is easily given. But there are many different conceptions of logic, and books on logic written from different points of view have offered strikingly different definitions of it. As John Stuart Mill wrote in his *A System of Logic:* "It is not to be expected that there should be agreement about the definition of any thing until there is agreement about the thing itself." The following selections from the writings of great logicians reveal that the definition of logic, its scope, its proper method, its divisions, and its relation to the other fields of knowledge are all highly debatable issues.

The brief passage from Plato's *Republic* emphasizes the difference between the intellect and the senses, exalts the role of pure intelligence, and praises dialectic[1] as "the coping stone of the sciences."

A more prosaic discussion of reasoning is provided by Aristotle in our excerpts from three of the six books of his *Organon.* In the selection from the *Topics* Aristotle distinguishes different kinds of reasoning and explains the notions of "definition," "property," "genus," and "accident." In the selection from his *Posterior Analytics* Aristotle comes to grips with the question of the utility of logic in acquiring knowledge. If logic is used in deriving conclusions from premisses, then if logic is involved in all knowledge, these premisses must themselves be derived as conclusions from other premisses. Is regression or circularity inevitable? Aristotle develops his theory of logic further in answering this question. In the brief excerpt from *Sophistical Refutations* Aristotle records his claim to

---

[1] Although Plato uses the term "dialectic" in many different senses in his dialogues, here and fairly generally it signifies the art or practice of logical discussion as employed in the search for truth.

have originated the science of logic—a claim that has never been challenged.

The short selection from Boethius (a commentary on Porphyry's commentary on Aristotle's *Categories*) contains an account of the relation between logic and philosophy. The issue is whether logic is a part of philosophy or a mere instrument of philosophy.

The discussion is continued by Peter Abailard (also in a commentary on Porphyry). Abailard agrees with Boethius and goes on to distinguish two parts of logic, one appropriate to discovering, the other to judging. He also agrees with Boethius that logic is "composed of and reduced to certain rules of argumentation," a doctrine not accepted by all later logicians.

Radical innovations in logic were urged by Francis Bacon, who wrote (in 1620) that "the logic now in use . . . does more harm than good." Constructively, he proposed the adoption of new methods of inductive logic based upon close observation of nature (see the selection from Francis Bacon in Part Five). But he felt that criticism of the old must precede construction of the new, and in the present selection he exposes and condemns four "Idols," or types of errors, that infect men's thinking.

In the selection from his *Introduction to Logic,* Kant stresses the *a priori* and nonempirical character of logic, arguing that logic "cannot be an *organon* of the sciences" (though it is doubtful how much of his dispute here with Aristotle and Bacon is real and how much is merely verbal). He likens logic to ethics and contrasts it with aesthetics (the philosophy of art), asserting that logic furnishes *a priori* rules "by which to judge of every use of the understanding." In the brief passage reproduced from his *Critique of Pure Reason,* Kant asserts that since Aristotle "logic has not been able to advance a single step, and is thus to all appearances a closed and completed body of doctrine." Written more than a century after Bacon's vigorous proposals for logical change in his *Novum Organum,* this records a sharp difference in appraisal of Aristotle's logic.

In Hegel we see logic elevated from a mere science of which Aristotle was the founder, whose study (Hegel says patronizingly) "undoubtedly has its uses," to something much more grand. This follows the idealist[2] elevation of thought from the status of a subjective activity or faculty to coextensiveness and identity with the whole of reality. Despite the difficulty of this conception, Hegel has many interesting things to say about logic.

John Stuart Mill takes more than usual care in formulating a

[2] Idealism in philosophy is the doctrine that whatever is real must be in some sense mental or spiritual, and that all objects of perception consist of ideas.

definition of logic. In the empiricist[3] tradition he stresses the importance of induction. On the question of the possibility of progress in logic, Mill agrees more with Bacon than with Kant. He disagrees with Hegel's identification of logic with metaphysics.

Peirce's justly famous essay "The Fixation of Belief" is clearly in what philosophers call the empiricist tradition. Significant here is his remark that "each chief step in science has been a lesson in logic," which links the two and implies their joint growth and development. But his biological and psychological approach identifies him as a pragmatist.[4] His pragmatic notion of habit, or "guiding principle of inference," contrasts vividly with Kant's conception of logical rules that can be discerned "independently of all experience." And near the very end of his essay Peirce's characterization of truth is strikingly different from Hegel's reverent invocation of Truth as the object of Logic.

Dewey continues along the pragmatist path first taken by Peirce. He too insists that logic is "not purely formal" and assigns it the status of a descriptive science, which enables him to say that logic is both descriptive and prescriptive, both empirical and normative, both psychological and regulative (as is mathematics also). The last few pages of the selection from Dewey are devoted to explaining the pragmatist theory of truth that is "given by the experimental and functional type of logic."

Russell's famous essay "Logic as the Essence of Philosophy" sketches the development of logic and argues that all genuinely philosophical problems "reduce themselves . . . to problems of logic." Russell's own logico-philosophical position is not easily classified in terms of the older schools. Like Kant, he maintains that "in pure logic . . . we confine ourselves wholly to forms." He disagrees sharply with the older empiricists, whom he considers himself to have refuted; but he shares their emphasis on the value of science, praising the new logic for having "rendered a truly scientific discussion of many philosophical problems possible." Primarily a mathematical logician, Russell insists that "The old logic put thought in fetters, while the new logic gives it wings."

The following selections are given in historical order, but the reader may find it desirable to begin his readings in logical theory with the essays by Peirce, Mill, and Bacon.

[3] Empiricism in philosophy is the doctrine that all knowledge is derived from experience: that experience is the source of all our ideas and that experience alone provides a test for truth.

[4] Pragmatism in philosophy is the doctrine that their effects and consequences are what determine both the meanings of our terms and the truth or falsehood of our beliefs.

IN PRAISE OF

DIALECTIC*

PLATO (427–347 B.C.)   was a student of Socrates and a teacher of Aristotle. He left Athens to travel widely after his teacher was put to death in 399 B.C. Returning to Athens, he founded his school, the Academy, in 387 B.C. and taught there until his death. His universal genius is attested in an often quoted remark of the American philosopher and teacher Alfred North Whitehead, "the safest general characterization of the European philosophical tradition is that it consists of a series of footnotes to Plato." Since this is as true of logic as of the other branches of philosophy, it is appropriate that this book of readings should begin with a brief selection from Plato's most famous and influential work, the *Republic*.

And so, Glaucon, I said, we have at last arrived at the hymn of dialectic. This is that strain which is of the intellect only, but which the faculty of sight will nevertheless be found to imitate; for sight, as you may remember, was imagined by us after a while to behold the real animals and stars, and last of all the sun himself. And so with dialectic; when a person starts on the discovery of the absolute by the light of reason only, and without any assistance of sense, and perseveres until by pure intelligence he arrives at the perception of the absolute good, he at last finds himself at the end of the intellectual world, as in the case of sight at the end of the visible.

Exactly, he said.

Then this is the progress which you call dialectic?

True.

But the release of the prisoners from chains, and their translation from the shadows to the images and to the light, and the ascent from the underground den to the sun, while in his presence they are vainly trying to look on animals and plants and the light of the sun, but are able to perceive even with their weak eyes the images in the water [which are divine], and are the shadows of true existence (not shadows of images cast by a light of fire, which compared with the sun is only an image)—this power of elevating the highest principle in the soul to the contemplation of that which is best in existence, with which we may compare the raising of that faculty which is the very light of the body to the sight of that which is brightest in the material and vis-

* From Plato's *Republic,* Book 7, translated by Benjamin Jowett. Reprinted by permission of The Clarendon Press, Oxford.

ible world—this power is given, as I was saying, by all that study and pursuit of the arts which has been described.

I agree in what you are saying, he replied, which may be hard to believe, yet, from another point of view, is harder still to deny. This however is not a theme to be treated of in passing only, but will have to be discussed again and again. And so, whether our conclusion be true or false, let us assume all this, and proceed at once from the prelude or preamble to the chief strain, and describe that in like manner. Say, then, what is the nature and what are the divisions of dialectic, and what are the paths which lead thither; for these paths will also lead to our final rest.

Dear Glaucon, I said, you will not be able to follow me here, though I would do my best, and you should behold not an image only but the absolute truth, according to my notion. Whether what I told you would or would not have been a reality I cannot venture to say; but you would have seen something like reality; of that I am confident.

Doubtless, he replied.

But I must also remind you, that the power of dialectic alone can reveal this, and only to one who is a disciple of the previous sciences.

Of that assertion you may be as confident as of the last.

And assuredly no one will argue that there is any other method of comprehending by any regular process all true existence or of ascertaining what each thing is in its own nature; for the arts in general are concerned with the desires or opinions of men, or are cultivated with a view to production and construction, or for the preservation of such productions and constructions; and as to the mathematical sciences which, as we were saying, have some apprehension of true being—geometry and the like—they only dream about being, but never can they

behold the waking reality so long as they leave the hypotheses which they use unexamined, and are unable to give an account of them. For when a man knows not his own first principle, and when the conclusion and intermediate steps are also constructed out of he knows not what, how can he imagine that such a fabric of convention can ever become science?

Impossible, he said.

Then dialectic, and dialectic alone, goes directly to the first principle and is the only science which does away with hypotheses in order to make her ground secure; the eye of the soul, which is literally buried in an outlandish slough, is by her gentle aid lifted upwards; and she uses as handmaids and helpers in the work of conversion, the sciences which we have been discussing. Custom terms them sciences, but they ought to have some other name, implying greater clearness than opinion and less clearness than science: and this, in our previous sketch, was called understanding. But why should we dispute about names when we have realities of such importance to consider?

Why indeed, he said, when any name will do which expresses the thought of the mind with clearness?

At any rate, we are satisfied, as before, to have four divisions; two for intellect and two for opinion, and to call the first division science, the second understanding, the third belief, and the fourth perception of shadows, opinion being concerned with becoming, and intellect with being; and so to make a proportion:

As being is to becoming, so is pure intellect to opinion.
And as intellect is to opinion, so is science to belief, and understanding to the perception of shadows.

But let us defer the further correlation and subdivision of the subjects of opinion and of intellect, for it will be a long enquiry, many times longer than this has been.

As far as I understand, he said, I agree.

And do you also agree, I said, in describing the dialectician as one who attains a conception of the essence of each thing? And he who does not possess and is therefore unable to impart this conception, in whatever degree he fails, may in that degree also be said to fail in intelligence? Will you admit so much?

Yes, he said; how can I deny it?

And you would say the same of the conception of the good? Until the person is able to abstract and define rationally the idea of good, and unless he can run the gauntlet of all objections, and is ready to disprove them, not by appeals to opinion, but to absolute truth, never faltering at any step of the argument—unless he can do all this, you would say that he knows neither the idea of good nor any other good; he apprehends only a shadow, if anything at all, which is given by opinion and not by science;—dream-

ing and slumbering in this life, before he is well awake here, he arrives at the world below, and has his final quietus.

In all that I should most certainly agree with you.

And surely you would not have the children of your ideal State, whom you are nurturing and educating—if the ideal ever becomes a reality—you would not allow the future rulers to be like posts, having no reason in them, and yet to be set in authority over the highest matters?

Certainly not.

Then you will make a law that they shall have such an education as will enable them to attain the greatest skill in asking and answering questions?

Yes, he said, you and I together will make it.

Dialectic, then, as you will agree, is the coping-stone of the sciences, and is set over them; no other science can be placed higher—the nature of knowledge can no further go?

I agree, he said.

THE BEGINNINGS OF

LOGIC*

ARISTOTLE (384–322 B.C.) was one of the greatest philosophers of ancient
Greece. After studying for twenty years in Plato's Academy, he became tutor to Alexander the Great. Later he founded his own school,
the Lyceum, where he contributed to nearly every field of human
knowledge. After Aristotle's death his treatises on reasoning were
grouped together and came to be called the *Organon*. The word "logic"
did not acquire its modern meaning until the 2nd century A.D., but
the subject matter of logic was determined by the content of the
Organon.

FROM *Topics*

1

Our treatise proposes to find a line of
inquiry whereby we shall be able to reason from opinions that are generally accepted about every problem propounded
to us, and also shall ourselves, when
standing up to an argument, avoid saying
anything that will obstruct us. First, then,
we must say what reasoning is, and what
its varieties are, in order to grasp dialectical reasoning: for this is the object of
our search in the treatise before us.

Now reasoning is an argument in
which, certain things being laid down,
something other than these necessarily
comes about through them. (*a*) It is a
'demonstration', when the premisses from
which the reasoning starts are true and
primary, or are such that our knowledge

of them has originally come through
premisses which are primary and true:
(*b*) reasoning, on the other hand, is 'dialectical', if it reasons from opinions that
are generally accepted. Things are 'true'
and 'primary' which are believed on the
strength not of anything else but of themselves: for in regard to the first principles of science it is improper to ask any
further for the why and wherefore of
them; each of the first principles should
command belief in and by itself. On the
other hand, those opinions are 'generally
accepted' which are accepted by every
one or by the majority or by the philosophers—i. e. by all, or by the majority, or
by the most notable and illustrious of
them. Again (*c*), reasoning is 'contentious' if it starts from opinions that seem
to be generally accepted, but are not
really such, or again if it merely seems to
reason from opinions that are or seem to

* From *The Works of Aristotle*, Vol. I, translated under the editorship of W. D. Ross.
Reprinted by permission of The Clarendon Press, Oxford.

be generally accepted. For not every opinion that seems to be generally accepted actually is generally accepted. For in none of the opinions which we call generally accepted is the illusion entirely on the surface, as happens in the case of the principles of contentious arguments; for the nature of the fallacy in these is obvious immediately, and as a rule even to persons with little power of comprehension. So then, of the contentious reasonings mentioned, the former really deserves to be called 'reasoning' as well, but the other should be called 'contentious reasoning', but not 'reasoning', since it appears to reason, but does not really do so.

Further (*d*), besides all the reasonings we have mentioned there are the misreasonings that start from the premisses peculiar to the special sciences, as happens (for example) in the case of geometry and her sister sciences. For this form of reasoning appears to differ from the reasonings mentioned above; the man who draws a false figure reasons from things that are neither true and primary, nor yet generally accepted. For he does not fall within the definition; he does not assume opinions that are received either by every one or by the majority or by philosophers—that is to say, by all, or by most, or by the most illustrious of them —but he conducts his reasoning upon assumptions which, though appropriate to the science in question, are not true; for he effects his mis-reasoning either by describing the semicircles wrongly or by drawing certain lines in a way in which they could not be drawn.

The foregoing must stand for an outline survey of the species of reasoning. In general, in regard both to all that we have already discussed and to those which we shall discuss later, we may remark that that amount of distinction between them may serve, because it is not our purpose to give the exact definition of any of them; we merely want to describe them in outline; we consider it quite enough from the point of view of the line of inquiry before us to be able to recognize each of them in some sort of way.

2

Next in order after the foregoing, we must say for how many and for what purposes the treatise is useful. They are three—intellectual training, casual encounters, and the philosophical sciences. That it is useful as a training is obvious on the face of it. The possession of a plan of inquiry will enable us more easily to argue about the subject proposed. For purposes of casual encounters, it is useful because when we have counted up the opinions held by most people, we shall meet them on the ground not of other people's convictions but of their own, while we shift the ground of any argument that they appear to us to state unsoundly. For the study of the philosophical sciences it is useful, because the ability to raise searching difficulties on both sides of a subject will make us detect more easily the truth and error about the several points that arise. It has a further use in relation to the ultimate bases of the principles used in the several sciences.[1] For it is impossible to discuss them at all from the principles proper to the particular science in hand, seeing that the principles are the *prius* of everything else: it is through the opinions generally held on the particular points that these have to be discussed, and this task belongs properly, or most appropriately, to dialectic: for dialectic is a process of criticism wherein lies the path to the principles of all inquiries.

---

[1] Or . . . 'in relation to the ultimate bases of the several sciences'.

3

We shall be in perfect possession of the way to proceed when we are in a position like that which we occupy in regard to rhetoric and medicine and faculties of that kind: this means the doing of that which we choose with the materials that are available. For it is not every method that the rhetorician will employ to persuade, or the doctor to heal: still, if he omits none of the available means, we shall say that his grasp of the science is adequate.

4

First, then, we must see of what parts our inquiry consists. Now if we were to grasp (*a*) with reference to how many, and what kind of, things arguments take place, and with what materials they start, and (*b*) how we are to become well supplied with these, we should have sufficiently won our goal. Now the materials with which arguments start are equal in number, and are identical, with the subjects on which reasonings take place. For arguments start with 'propositions', while the subjects on which reasonings take place are 'problems'. Now every proposition and every problem indicates either a genus or a peculiarity or an accident— for the differentia too, applying as it does to a class (or genus), should be ranked together with the genus. Since, however, of what is peculiar to anything part signifies its essence, while part does not, let us divide the 'peculiar' into both the aforesaid parts, and call that part which indicates the essence a 'definition', while of the remainder let us adopt the terminology which is generally current about these things, and speak of it as a 'property'. What we have said, then, makes it clear that according to our present division, the elements turn out to be four, all told, namely either property or definition

or genus or accident. Do not let any one suppose us to mean that each of these enunciated by itself constitutes a proposition or problem, but only that it is from these that both problems and propositions are formed. The difference between a problem and a proposition is a difference in the turn of the phrase. For if it be put in this way, ' "An animal that walks on two feet" is the definition of man, is it not?' or ' "Animal" is the genus of man, is it not?' the result is a proposition: but if thus, 'Is "an animal that walks on two feet" a definition of man or no?' [or 'Is "animal" his genus or no?'] the result is a problem. Similarly too in other cases. Naturally, then, problems and propositions are equal in number: for out of every proposition you will make a problem if you change the turn of the phrase.

5

We must now say what are 'definition', 'property', 'genus', and 'accident'. A 'definition' is a phrase signifying a thing's essence. It is rendered in the form either of a phrase in lieu of a term, or of a phrase in lieu of another phrase; for it is sometimes possible to define the meaning of a phrase as well. People whose rendering consists of a term only, try it as they may, clearly do not render the definition of the thing in question, because a definition is always a phrase of a certain kind. One may, however, use the word 'definitory' also of such a remark as 'The "becoming" is "beautiful" ', and likewise also of the question, 'Are sensation and knowledge the same or different?', for argument about definitions is mostly concerned with questions of sameness and difference. In a word we may call 'definitory' everything that falls under the same branch of inquiry as definitions; and that all the above-mentioned examples are of this character is clear on the face of

be generally accepted. For not every opinion that seems to be generally accepted actually is generally accepted. For in none of the opinions which we call generally accepted is the illusion entirely on the surface, as happens in the case of the principles of contentious arguments; for the nature of the fallacy in these is obvious immediately, and as a rule even to persons with little power of comprehension. So then, of the contentious reasonings mentioned, the former really deserves to be called 'reasoning' as well, but the other should be called 'contentious reasoning', but not 'reasoning', since it appears to reason, but does not really do so.

Further (d), besides all the reasonings we have mentioned there are the mis-reasonings that start from the premisses peculiar to the special sciences, as happens (for example) in the case of geometry and her sister sciences. For this form of reasoning appears to differ from the reasonings mentioned above; the man who draws a false figure reasons from things that are neither true and primary, nor yet generally accepted. For he does not fall within the definition; he does not assume opinions that are received either by every one or by the majority or by philosophers—that is to say, by all, or by most, or by the most illustrious of them —but he conducts his reasoning upon assumptions which, though appropriate to the science in question, are not true; for he effects his mis-reasoning either by describing the semicircles wrongly or by drawing certain lines in a way in which they could not be drawn.

The foregoing must stand for an outline survey of the species of reasoning. In general, in regard both to all that we have already discussed and to those which we shall discuss later, we may remark that that amount of distinction between them may serve, because it is not our purpose to give the exact definition of any of them; we merely want to describe them in outline; we consider it quite enough from the point of view of the line of inquiry before us to be able to recognize each of them in some sort of way.

2

Next in order after the foregoing, we must say for how many and for what purposes the treatise is useful. They are three—intellectual training, casual encounters, and the philosophical sciences. That it is useful as a training is obvious on the face of it. The possession of a plan of inquiry will enable us more easily to argue about the subject proposed. For purposes of casual encounters, it is useful because when we have counted up the opinions held by most people, we shall meet them on the ground not of other people's convictions but of their own, while we shift the ground of any argument that they appear to us to state unsoundly. For the study of the philosophical sciences it is useful, because the ability to raise searching difficulties on both sides of a subject will make us detect more easily the truth and error about the several points that arise. It has a further use in relation to the ultimate bases of the principles used in the several sciences.[1] For it is impossible to discuss them at all from the principles proper to the particular science in hand, seeing that the principles are the *prius* of everything else: it is through the opinions generally held on the particular points that these have to be discussed, and this task belongs properly, or most appropriately, to dialectic: for dialectic is a process of criticism wherein lies the path to the principles of all inquiries.

[1] Or . . . 'in relation to the ultimate bases of the several sciences'.

primary premisses—some if not all of them—beforehand, but know them better than the conclusion: for the cause of an attribute's inherence in a subject always itself inheres in the subject more firmly than that attribute; e.g. the cause of our loving anything is dearer to us than the object of our love. So since the primary premisses are the cause of our knowledge—i. e. of our conviction—it follows that we know them better—that is, are more convinced of them—than their consequences, precisely because our knowledge of the latter is the effect of our knowledge of the premisses. Now a man cannot believe in anything more than in the things he knows, unless he has either actual knowledge of it or something better than actual knowledge. But we are faced with this paradox if a student whose belief rests on demonstration has not prior knowledge; a man must believe in some, if not in all, of the basic truths more than in the conclusion. Moreover, if a man sets out to acquire the scientific knowledge that comes through demonstration, he must not only have a better knowledge of the basic truths and a firmer conviction of them than of the connexion which is being demonstrated: more than this, nothing must be more certain or better known to him than these basic truths in their character as contradicting the fundamental premisses which lead to the opposed and erroneous conclusion. For indeed the conviction of pure science must be unshakable.

3

Some hold that, owing to the necessity of knowing the primary premisses, there is no scientific knowledge. Others think there is, but that all truths are demonstrable. Neither doctrine is either true or a necessary deduction from the premisses. The first school, assuming that there is no way of knowing other than by demonstration, maintain that an infinite regress is involved, on the ground that if behind the prior stands no primary, we could not know the posterior through the prior (wherein they are right, for one cannot traverse an infinite series): if on the other hand—they say—the series terminates and there are primary premisses, yet these are unknowable because incapable of demonstration, which according to them is the only form of knowledge. And since thus one cannot know the primary premisses, knowledge of the conclusions which follow from them is not pure scientific knowledge nor properly knowing at all, but rests on the mere supposition that the premisses are true. The other party agree with them as regards knowing, holding that it is only possible by demonstration, but they see no difficulty in holding that all truths are demonstrated, on the ground that demonstration may be circular and reciprocal.

Our own doctrine is that not all knowledge is demonstrative: on the contrary, knowledge of the immediate premisses is independent of demonstration. (The necessity of this is obvious; for since we must know the prior premisses from which the demonstration is drawn, and since the regress must end in immediate truths, those truths must be indemonstrable.) Such, then, is our doctrine, and in addition we maintain that besides scientific knowledge there is its originative source which enables us to recognize the definitions.

Now demonstration must be based on premisses prior to and better known than the conclusion; and the same things cannot simultaneously be both prior and posterior to one another: so circular demonstration is clearly not possible in the unqualified sense of 'demonstration', but only possible if 'demonstration' be extended to include that other method of argument which rests on a distinction between truths prior to us and truths without qualification prior, i. e. the method by which induction produces knowledge.[6] But if we accept this extension of its meaning, our definition of unqualified knowledge will prove faulty; for there seem to be two kinds of it. Perhaps, however, the second form of demonstration, that which proceeds from truths better known to us, is not demonstration in the unqualified sense of the term.[7]

The advocates of circular demonstration are not only faced with the difficulty we have just stated: in addition their theory reduces to the mere statement that if a thing exists, then it does exist—an easy way of proving anything. That this is so can be clearly shown by taking three terms,[8] for to constitute the circle it makes no difference whether many terms or few or even only two are taken. Thus by direct proof, if A is, B must be; if B is, C must be; therefore if A is, C must be. Since then—by the circular proof— if A is, B must be, and if B is, A must be, A may be substituted for C above. Then 'if B is, A must be' = 'if B is, C must be', which above gave the conclusion 'if A is, C must be': but C and A have been identified.[9] Consequently the upholders of cir-

cular demonstration are in the position of saying that if A is, A must be—a simple way of proving anything. Moreover, even such circular demonstration is impossible except in the case of attributes that imply one another, viz. 'peculiar' properties.

Now, it has been shown that the positing of one thing—be it one term or one premiss—never involves a necessary consequent: two premisses constitute the first and smallest foundation for drawing a conclusion at all and therefore a fortiori for the demonstrative syllogism of science. If, then, A is implied in B and C, and B and C are reciprocally implied in one another and in A, it is possible, as has been shown in my writings on the syllogism, to prove all the assumptions on which the original conclusion rested, by circular demonstration in the first figure. But it has also been shown that in the other figures either no conclusion is possible, or at least none which proves both the original premisses. Propositions the terms of which are not convertible cannot be circularly demonstrated at all, and since convertible terms occur rarely in actual demonstrations, it is clearly frivolous and impossible to say that demonstration is reciprocal and that therefore everything can be demonstrated.

---

[6] . . . Aristotle seems to mean that circular demonstration is impossible unless demonstration is taken to include a type of argument based on truths prior only in the sense of 'prior to us', such as induction, where we grasp the particular and recognize in it the universal . . . The next sentence . . . seems to confirm this interpretation, which does, however, involve a verbal contradiction . . .

[7] sc. 'and therefore our definition is not faulty'.

[8] sc. to constitute the valid syllogism which Aristotle sets up . . . to illustrate the tautology of the circular demonstration when reduced to explicit syllogism.

[9] . . . [this] seems to mean that 'B implies C' taken in conjunction with 'A implies B' gave the conclusion 'A implies C'. Aristotle

tries to show the circular proof tautologous by reducing it to syllogism, apparently arguing thus: 'B implies C', 'A implies B', ∴ 'A implies C' is valid syllogism (a schema for comparison): while according to the circular proof A necessitates B and B necessitates A. If A–B, B–A ('A implies B', 'B implies A') are to be made the premisses of a syllogism, there is nothing but A to take the place of C in the schema—no major term different from the minor: ∴ B–A is all we have to fill the place of the major premiss B–C. Now, in the schema, B–C (taken in conjunction with the minor premiss A–B, which is common to both syllogisms) gave the conclusion A–C. But C is now A (a restatement of the fact that B–C has become B–A). Therefore the conclusion is A–A.

FROM *Sophistical Refutations*

Our programme was, then, to discover some faculty of reasoning about any theme put before us from the most generally accepted premises that there are. For that is the essential task of the art of discussion (dialectic) and of examination (peirastic). Inasmuch, however, as it is annexed to it, on account of the near presence of the art of sophistry (sophistic), not only to be able to conduct an examination dialectically but also with a show of knowledge, we therefore proposed for our treatise not only the aforesaid aim of being able to exact an account of any view, but also the aim of ensuring that in standing up to an argument we shall defend our thesis in the same manner by means of views as generally held as possible. The reason of this we have explained; for this, too, was why Socrates used to ask questions and not to answer them; for he used to confess that he did not know. We have made clear, in the course of what precedes, the number both of the points with reference to which, and of the materials from which, this will be accomplished, and also from what sources we can become well supplied with these: we have shown, moreover, how to question or arrange the questioning as a whole, and the problems concerning the answers and solutions to be used against the reasonings of the questioner. We have also cleared up the problems concerning all other matters that belong to the same inquiry into arguments. In addition to this we have been through the subject of Fallacies, as we have already stated above.

That our programme, then, has been adequately completed is clear. But we must not omit to notice what has happened in regard to this inquiry. For in the case of all discoveries the results of previous labours that have been handed down from others have been advanced bit by bit by those who have taken them on, whereas the original discoveries generally make an advance that is small at first though much more useful than the development which later springs out of them. For it may be that in everything, as the saying is, 'the first start is the main part': and for this reason also it is the most difficult; for in proportion as it is most potent in its influence, so it is smallest in its compass and therefore most difficult to see: whereas when this is once discovered, it is easier to add and develop the remainder in connexion with it. This is in fact what has happened in regard to rhetorical speeches and to practically all the other arts: for those who discovered the beginnings of them advanced them in all only a little way, whereas the celebrities of to-day are the heirs (so to speak) of a long succession of men who have advanced them bit by bit, and so have developed them to their present form, Tisias coming next after the first founders, then Thrasymachus after Tisias, and Theodorus next to him, while several people have made their several contributions to it: and therefore it is not to be wondered at that the art has attained considerable dimensions. Of this inquiry, on the other hand, it was not the case that part of the work had been thoroughly done before, while part had not. Nothing existed at all. For the training given by the paid professors of contentious arguments was like the treatment of the matter by Gorgias. For they used to hand out speeches to be learned by heart, some rhetorical, others in the form of question and answer, each side supposing that their arguments on either side generally fall among them. And therefore the teaching they gave their pupils was ready but rough. For they used to suppose that they trained people by imparting to them not the art but its products, as though any one professing that he would impart a form of knowledge to obviate any pain in the feet, were then not to teach a man the art of shoe-making or the sources whence he can acquire anything of the kind, but were to present him with several kinds of shoes of all sorts: for he has helped him to meet his need, but has not imparted an art to him. Moreover, on the subject of Rhetoric there exists much that has been said long ago, whereas on the subject of reasoning we had nothing else of an earlier date to speak of at all, but were kept at work for a long time in experimental researches. If, then, it seems to you after inspection that, such being the situation as it existed at the start, our investigation is in a satisfactory condition compared with the other inquiries that have been developed by tradition, there must remain for all of you, or for our students, the task of extending us your pardon for the shortcomings of the inquiry, and for the discoveries thereof your warm thanks.

LOGIC AND PHILOSOPHY*

BOETHIUS (480–525)   was a Roman philosopher who translated into Latin, and
wrote commentaries on, Aristotle's logical treatises. He also translated,
and wrote a commentary on, Porphyry's *Isogogue*, itself a commentary
on Aristotle's *Categories*. Boethius is probably best known today for
his book *The Consolations of Philosophy*, written while he was in jail
awaiting execution on a trumped-up charge of treason.

2

Since the activity of the human soul is
such that it is always occupied in the
comprehension of present things, or in
the understanding of absent things, or in
the investigation and discovery of unknown things, there are two problems in
which the power of the reasoning soul
extends all its care: one, that it know the
natures of things by a sure method of inquiry, and the other, that that which
moral gravity may later perform, may
come to be known beforehand. In investigating these matters there must necessarily be many things which may lead the
inquiring mind not a little from progress
along the right road, as happened in
many points to Epicurus, who thinks the
world consists of atoms and who measures virtue by pleasure. It is clear, moreover, that this happened to him, and to
others, because they thought through in-

experience in logical argument that
everything they comprehended in reasoning occurred also in things themselves. This surely is a great error; for in
reasoning it is not as in numbers. For in
numbers whatever has come out in com-
puting the digits correctly, must without
doubt also eventuate in the things themselves, so that if by calculation there
should happen to be a hundred, there
must also be a hundred things subject
to that number. But this does not hold
equally in argumentation; nor, in fact, is
everything which the evolution of words
may have discovered held fixed in nature
too. Wherefore it was inevitable that they
fall into error who, having cast aside the
art of argument, made diligent search
into the nature of things. For unless one
have learned first the science that shows
which reasoning holds to the true path of
argument, and which holds to the path
like to the truth, and unless one have

learned to recognize what is trustworthy and what can be suspected, the uncorrupted truth of things can not be found by reasoning. Therefore, since the ancients often fell into a great many errors and brought together in argumentation many doctrines false and contrary to each other, and since it seemed impossible that this was done in order that, having come to contrary conclusions concerning the same thing, both conclusions which reasoning disagreeing with itself had formed should be true, and since it was ambiguous which line of thought should be believed, it seemed proper to consider the true and whole nature of argumentation itself first, and when that was known, what was discovered or what had been comprehended truly by argument could then be understood too. Hence started the knowledge of the logical discipline, which so contrives the modes of arguing and the ways of distinguishing reasonings themselves, that one can recognize what reasoning is now false, and now again true, what reasoning is always false, what never false. The power of this discipline, moreover, must be considered to be twofold, one in finding, the other in judging. This Cicero, too, expresses clearly in the book whose title is the *Topics,* saying:

Although all reason suited to discourse has two parts, one of discovering, the other of judging, the prince of both, it seems to me, was Aristotle. The Stoics, however, exerted themselves in only one, for they pursued the ways of judging carefully in the science which they call dialectic, but they left aside the whole art of discovering, which is called topic, and which was more excellent in use and certainly prior in order of nature. But since there is the greatest utility in both and since we think to pursue both if there will be leisure, we shall begin from that which is first.

Since, therefore, the fruit of this consideration is so great, the whole attention of the mind must be given to this so very in-

genious discipline, that we may be able, having been made steady in our first steps in the truth of arguing, to come easily to a sure comprehension of things themselves.

3

And since we have already stated what the beginning of the logical discipline is, the next question seems to follow: whether logic is absolutely a definite part of philosophy or, as others hold, an apparatus or instrument by which philosophy seizes on the knowledge and nature of things. I see that these opinions concerning this matter are diametrically opposed. For those who think the logical consideration a part of philosophy, use approximately the following arguments, saying, that philosophy doubtless has speculative and practical parts; the question concerning this third rational part is whether it is to be asserted to be a part; but it can not be doubted that it too is part of philosophy. For just as the investigation of philosophy alone is concerned with natural and other questions which are classed under the speculative part, and again as only philosophy deliberates concerning moral and other questions which fall under the practical part, so too only philosophy judges of this part of the inquiry, that is, concerning these questions which are subjects of logic. But if the speculative and practical are parts of philosophy because philosophy alone treats of them, then by the same reason logic will be part of philosophy, since this matter of arguing falls under philosophy alone. But then they say: since philosophy is concerned with these three, and since the subject matters distinguish the practical and speculative considerations, because the latter inquires concerning the nature of things, and the former concerning morals, there is no doubt that the logical discipline is distinct from the natural and the moral by the characteristic of its subject matter. For the consideration of logic is of propositions and syllogisms and other subjects of this sort, and neither that part of philosophy which speculates, not of discourse, but of things, nor the practical part which watches over morals, can take care of that too. But if philosophy consists in these three, that is, speculative, practical, and rational, which are set off from each other by their separate and triple ends, since the speculative and the practical are said to be parts of philosophy, there is no doubt that the rational, too, may be demonstrated to be part of philosophy.

Those on the other hand who think it is not a part but an instrument of philosophy, urge approximately the following arguments. They say, there is no end of logic similar to the end of the speculative and practical parts. For each of these is turned to its proper end, the speculative to work out the knowledge of things, and the practical to perfect morals and institutions; nor is the one referred to the other. The end of logic, however, can not be absolute, but is drawn and bound up in a certain manner with the other two parts. For what is there in the logical discipline which should be desired for its own worth; or was not the practise of this art undertaken for the investigation of things? For to know how an argumentation is to be concluded, or what is true, and what similar to the true, tends obviously to this, that this science of reasons is referred either to a knowledge of things or to discovering those things which produce happiness, having led to the exercise of morality. And therefore since the end of the speculative and the end of the practical

parts are their own and certain, whereas the end of logic is referred to the other two parts, it is clear that logic is not a part of philosophy but rather an instrument. There are, of course, many more arguments which may be stated on either part, of which it suffices that we have noted strictly these which have been stated.

We settle this controversy, however, with the following reasoning. We say that surely nothing prevents the same logic from serving at the same time the function of part and of instrument. For since it retains its own end, and this end is considered by philosophy only, it must be asserted to be a part of philosophy, but since that end of logic, which philosophy alone contemplates, promises its aid to the other parts of philosophy, we do not deny that it is the instrument of philosophy; but the end of logic is the discovery and judgment of reasons. Obviously it will not seem strange that the same thing should be called a part and a kind of instrument, if we turn our mind to the parts of the body, for something is done by them, so that we use them as a manner of instruments, and yet they hold the place of parts in the whole body. For the hand is for touching, the eyes for seeing, and the other parts of the body seem to have each a proper function. But still if the utility of the whole body be considered, these, which no one would deny are also parts, are judged to be certain instruments of the body. So too the logical discipline is a part of philosophy, since philosophy alone is mistress of it, but it is an instrument too because by it the sought-for truth of philosophy is investigated.

THE PARTS OF LOGIC*

PETER ABAILARD (1079–1142) was a French medieval philosopher and logician who rose in the church despite occasional lapses from orthodox church doctrine. Most famous today for his romantic affair with Heloise, from whom he was so brutally cut off by her uncle, Abailard influenced medieval philosophy deeply by his stand on the problem of universals.† What that stand was has been a continuing topic for controversy among philosophers.

We may open our introduction to logic by examining something of the characteristic property of logic in its genus which is *philosophy*. Boethius says that not any knowledge whatever is philosophy, but only that which consists in the greatest things; for we do not call all wise men philosophers, but only those whose intelligence penetrates subtle matters. Moreover, Boethius distinguishes three species of philosophy, *speculative,* which is concerned with speculation on the nature of things, *moral,* for the consideration of the honorableness of life, *rational,* for compounding the relation of arguments, which the greeks call logic. However, some writers separated logic from philosophy and did not call it, according to Boethius, a part of philosophy but an instrument, because obviously the other parts work in logic in a manner, when they use its arguments to prove their own questions. As, if a question should arise in natural or moral speculation, arguments are derived from logic. Boethius himself holds, against them, that there is nothing to prevent the same thing from being both an instrument and a part of a single thing, as the hand is both a part and an instrument of the human body. Logic moreover seems itself often its own instrument when it demonstrates a question pertaining to itself by its own arguments, as for example: *man is the species of animal.* It is none the less logic, however, because it is the instrument of logic. So too it is none the less philosophy because it is the instrument of philosophy. Moreover, Boethius distinguishes it from the other two species of philosophy by its proper end, which consists in compounding arguments. For although the physicist compounds arguments, it is not physics but only logic which instructs him in that.

---

* Extracts from *Selections from Medieval Philosophers,* Volumes I and II, edited by Richard McKeon, are used by permission of Charles Scribner's Sons. Copyright 1929 Charles Scribner's Sons; renewal copyright © 1957.

† In philosophy the problem of universals is the problem of the metaphysical status, or ultimate mode of being, of the referents of such general terms as "man" or "animal."

He noted too in regard to logic that it was composed of and reduced to certain rules of argumentation for this reason, namely, lest it lead inconstant minds into error by false inferences, since it seems to construct by its reasons what is not found in the nature of things, and since it seems often to infer things contrary in their conditions, in the following manner: *Socrates is body, but body is white, therefore Socrates is white.* On the other hand: *Socrates is body, but body is black, therefore Socrates is black.*

Moreover in writing logic the following order is extremely necessary that since arguments are constructed from propositions, and propositions from words, he who will write logic perfectly, must first write of simple words, then of propositions, and finally devote the end of logic to argumentations, just as our prince Aristotle did, who wrote the *Categories* on the science of words, the *On Interpretation* on the science of propositions, the *Topics* and the *Analytics* on the science of argumentations.

Porphyry himself moreover as the very statement of the title shows, prepares this introduction for the *Categories* of Aristotle, but later he himself shows that it is necessary to the whole art. The *intention* of it, the *matter,* the *manner of treatment,* the *utility* or *the part of dialectic to which the present science is to be subordinated,* will now be distinguished briefly and precisely.

The *intention* is particularly to instruct the reader in the *Categories* of Aristotle, that he may be able to understand more easily the things that are there treated. This makes necessary the treatment of the five subjects which are its materials, namely genus, species, difference, property, and accident. He judged the knowledge of these to be particularly useful to the *Categories* because the investigation is concerning them in almost the whole course of the *Categories.* That which we

spoke of as five, however, can be referred to the words, genus, species and the others and also in a certain sense to the things signified by them. For he appropriately makes clear the significance of these five words which Aristotle uses, lest one be ignorant, when one has come to the *Categories,* of what is to be understood by these words; and he is able, moreover, to treat of all the things signified by these words, as if of five things, since, although they are infinite taken singly, inasmuch as genera are infinite and likewise species and the others, nevertheless as has been said, all are considered as five, because all are treated according to five characteristics, all genera according to what constitutes genera, and the others in the same way, for in this same way the eight parts of speech are considered according to their eight characteristics, although taken singly they are infinite.

The *manner of treatment* here is the following: having first distinguished the natures of each singly in separate treatments of them, he proceeds then for further knowledge of them to their common properties and characteristics.

Its *utility,* as Boethius himself teaches, is principally as it is directed to the *Categories.* But it is spread in four directions which we shall disclose more carefully later when he himself takes it up.

If the parts of logic have first been distinguished carefully, it is seen at once what is the part through which the science of the present work leads to logic. On the authority of Cicero and Boethius there are two parts of which logic is composed, namely, the science of *discovering* arguments and of *judging* them, that is, of confirming and proving the arguments discovered. For two things are necessary to one who argues, first to find the arguments by which to argue, then if any should criticize the arguments as defective or as insufficiently firm to be able to confirm them. Wherefore Cicero says that discovery is by nature prior. The present science, however, is concerned with both parts of logic, but most of all with discovery. And it is a part of the science of discovering. For how can an argument be deduced from genus or species or the others, if the things which are here treated are not known? Wherefore Aristotle himself introduces the definition of the predicables into the *Topics,* when he treats of their places, as Cicero likewise does in his *Topics.* But since an argument is confirmed from the same considerations from which it is discovered, this science is not unrelated to judgment. For, as an argument is derived from the nature of genus and species, so, once derived, it is confirmed from the nature of genus and species. For considering the nature of species in man, so far as it is related to animal, I find at once from the nature of the species the argument for proving animal. But if any one should criticize the argument, I show that it is suitable immediately by indicating the nature of the species and the genus in both, so that from the same conditions of the terms the argument may be found and when it has been found it may be confirmed.

There are some nevertheless who separate this science [i.e., the *Isagoge*] and the science of the categories and of the divisions and of definitions and even of propositions completely from discovery and judgment, nor do they count it in any sense among the parts of logic, although, for all that, they think such subjects are necessary to the whole of logic. But authority as well as reason seems contrary to them. For Boethius *On the Topics of Cicero* asserts a double division of dialectic, both parts of which so include each other reciprocally that they each comprise the whole of dialectic. The first part is through the science of discovery and judgment; the second through the science of division, definition and collection. He reduces each of these to the other so that in the science of discovery (which is one of the two divisions of the above classification) he includes also the science of division or definition, for the reason that arguments are deduced from divisions as well as from definitions. Wherefore the science of genus and of species or of the others may also be adapted for a similar reason to discovery. Boethius himself says that the treatise on the *Categories* comes first among the books of Aristotle for those beginning logic. From this it is apparent that the *Categories,* in which the reader has his introduction to logic, are not to be separated from logic, particularly since the distinction of the categories supplies the greatest strength to the argumentation, since the nature, to which each thing pertains or does not pertain, can be established by it. The peculiar study of propositions [i.e., the *On Interpretation*] likewise is not unrelated to that of arguments, since it proves now this, now that, as contrary or contradictory or opposed in any other manner whatever. Therefore, since all treatises of logic converge to the end of logic, that is to argumentation, we separate the knowledge of none of them from logic.

IDOLS WHICH BESET

MEN'S MINDS*

FRANCIS BACON (1561–1626)   was an English statesman, essayist and philosopher. His most important philosophical writings deal with the advantages he anticipated would come from the *Advancement of Learning* and from general acceptance of the new inductive logic set forth in his *Novum Organum*. His emphasis on observation marks him as one of the early advocates of the empirical method in modern philosophy.

I

Man, being the servant and interpreter of Nature, can do and understand so much and so much only as he has observed in fact or in thought of the course of nature: beyond this he neither knows anything nor can do anything.

II

Neither the naked hand nor the understanding left to itself can effect much. It is by instruments and helps that the work is done, which are as much wanted for the understanding as for the hand. And as the instruments of the hand either give motion or guide it, so the instruments of the mind supply either suggestions for the understanding or cautions.

III

Human knowledge and human power meet in one; for where the cause is not known the effect cannot be produced. Nature to be commanded must be obeyed; and that which in contemplation is as the cause is in operation as the rule.

IV

Towards the effecting of works, all that man can do is to put together or put asunder natural bodies. The rest is done by nature working within.

V

The study of nature with a view to works is engaged in by the mechanic, the mathematician, the physician, the alchemist, and the magician; but by all (as things now are) with slight endeavor and scanty success.

VI

It would be an unsound fancy and self-contradictory to expect that things which have never yet been done can be done except by means which have never yet been tried.

* From Francis Bacon, *Novum Organum* (1620).

VII

The productions of the mind and hand seem very numerous in books and manufactures. But all this variety lies in an exquisite subtlety and derivations from a few things already known; not in the number of axioms.

VIII

Moreover the works already known are due to chance and experiment rather than to sciences; for the sciences we now possess are merely systems for the nice ordering and setting forth of things already invented; not methods of invention or directions for new works.

IX

The cause and root of nearly all evils in the sciences is this—that while we falsely admire and extol the powers of the human mind we neglect to seek for its true helps.

X

The subtlety of nature is greater many times over than the subtlety of the senses and understanding; so that all those specious meditations, speculations, and glosses in which men indulge are quite from the purpose, only there is no one by to observe it.

XI

As the sciences which we now have do not help us in finding out new works, so neither does the logic which we now have help us in finding out new sciences.

XII

The logic now in use serves rather to fix and give stability to the errors which have their foundation in commonly received notions, than to help the search after truth. So it does more harm than good.

XIII

The syllogism is not applied to the first principles of sciences, and is applied in vain to intermediate axioms; being no match for the subtlety of nature. It commands assent therefore to the proposition, but does not take hold of the thing.

XIV

The syllogism consists of propositions, propositions consist of words, words are symbols of notions. Therefore if the notions themselves (which is the root of the matter) are confused and overhastily abstracted from the facts, there can be no firmness in the superstructure. Our only hope therefore lies in a true induction.

. . .

XXXVIII

The idols and false notions which are now in possession of the human understanding, and have taken deep root therein, not only so beset men's minds that truth can hardly find entrance, but even after entrance obtained, they will again in the very instauration of the sciences meet and trouble us, unless men being forewarned of the danger fortify themselves as far as may be against their assaults.

XXXIX

There are four classes of Idols which beset men's minds. To these for distinction's sake I have assigned names,—calling the first class Idols of the Tribe; the second, Idols of the Cave; the third,

Idols of the Market-place; the fourth, *Idols of the Theatre.*

XL

The formation of ideas and axioms by true induction is no doubt the proper remedy to be applied for the keeping off and clearing away of idols. To point them out, however, is of great use; for the doctrine of Idols is to the Interpretation of Nature what the doctrine of the refutation of Sophisms is to common Logic.

XLI

The Idols of the Tribe have their foundation in human nature itself, and in the tribe or race of men. For it is a false assertion that the sense of man is the measure of things. On the contrary, all perceptions as well of the sense as of the mind are according to the measure of the individual and not according to the measure of the universe. And the human understanding is like a false mirror, which, receiving rays irregularly, distorts and discolours the nature of things by mingling its own nature with it.

XLII

The Idols of the Cave are the idols of the individual man. For everyone (besides the errors common to human nature in general) has a cave or den of his own, which refracts and discolours the light of nature; owing either to his own proper and peculiar nature; or to his education and conversation with others; or to the reading of books, and the authority of those whom he esteems and admires; or to the differences of impressions, accordingly as they take place in a mind preoccupied and predisposed or in a mind indifferent and settled; or the like. So that the spirit of man (according as it is meted out to different individuals) is in fact a

thing variable and full of perturbation, and governed as it were by chance. Whence it was well observed by Heraclitus that men look for sciences in their own lesser worlds, and not in the greater or common world.

XLIII

There are also Idols formed by the intercourse and association of men with each other, which I call Idols of the Market-place, on account of the commerce and consort of men there. For it is by discourse that men associate; and words are imposed according to the apprehension of the vulgar. And therefore the ill and unfit choice of words wonderfully obstructs the understanding. Nor do the definitions or explanations wherewith in some things learned men are wont to guard and defend themselves, by any means set the matter right. But words plainly force and overrule the understanding, and throw all into confusion, and lead men away into numberless empty controversies and idle fancies.

XLIV

Lastly, there are Idols which have immigrated into men's minds from the various dogmas of philosophies, and also from wrong laws of demonstration. These I call Idols of the Theatre; because in my judgment all the received systems are but so many stage-plays, representing worlds of their own creation after an unreal and scenic fashion. Nor is it only of the systems now in vogue, or only of the ancient sects and philosophies, that I speak: for many more plays of the same kind may yet be composed and in like artificial manner set forth; seeing that errors the most widely different have nevertheless causes for the most part alike. Neither again do I mean this only of entire systems, but also of many principles and axioms in science, which by tradition, credulity, and negligence have come to be received.

But of these several kinds of Idols I must speak more largely and exactly, that the understanding may be duly cautioned.

XLV

The human understanding is of its own nature prone to suppose the existence of more order and regularity in the world than it finds. And though there be many things in nature which are singular and unmatched, yet it devises for them parallels and conjugates and relatives which do not exist. Hence the fiction that all celestial bodies move in perfect circles; spirals and dragons being (except in name) utterly rejected. Hence too the element of Fire with its orb is brought in, to make up the square with the other three which the sense perceives. Hence also the ratio of density of the so-called elements is arbitrarily fixed at ten to one. And so on of other dreams. And these fancies affect not dogmas only, but simple notions also.

XLVI

The human understanding when it has once adopted an opinion (either as being the received opinion or as being agreeable to itself) draws all things else to support and agree with it. And though there be a greater number and weight of instances to be found on the other side, yet these it either neglects and despises, or else by some distinction sets aside and rejects; in order that by this great and pernicious predetermination the authority of its former conclusions may remain inviolate. And therefore it was a good answer that was made by one who when they showed him hanging in a temple a picture of those who had paid their vows as having escaped shipwreck, and would have him say whether he did not now acknowledge the power of the gods,— "Aye," asked he again, "but where are they painted that were drowned after their vows?" And such is the way of all superstition, whether in astrology, dreams, omens, divine judgments, or the like; wherein men, having a delight in such vanities, mark the events where they are fulfilled, but where they fail, though this happen much oftener, neglect and pass them by. But with far more subtlety does this mischief insinuate itself into philosophy and the sciences; in which the first conclusion colours and brings into conformity with itself all that come after, though far sounder and better. Besides, independently of that delight and vanity which I have described, it is the peculiar and perpetual error of the human intellect to be more moved and excited by affirmatives than by negatives; whereas it ought properly to hold itself indifferently disposed towards both alike. Indeed in the establishment of any true axiom, the negative instance is the more forcible of the two.

XLVII

The human understanding is moved by those things most which strike and enter the mind simultaneously and suddenly, and so fill the imagination; and then it feigns and supposes all other things to be somehow, though it cannot see how, similar to those few things by which it is surrounded. But for that going to and fro to remote and heterogeneous instances, by which axioms are tried as in the fire, the intellect is altogether slow and unfit, unless it be forced thereto by severe laws and overruling authority.

XLVIII

The human understanding is unquiet; it cannot stop or rest, and still presses onward, but in vain. Therefore it is that we cannot conceive of any end or limit to the world; but always as of necessity it occurs to us that there is something beyond. Neither again can it be conceived how eternity has flowed down to the present day: for that distinction which is commonly received of infinity in time past and in time to come can by no means hold; for it would thence follow that one infinity is greater than another, and that infinity is wasting away and tending to become finite. The like subtlety arises touching the infinite divisibility of lines, from the same inability of thought to stop. But this inability interferes more mischievously in the discovery of causes: for although the most general principles in nature ought to be held merely positive, as they are discovered, and cannot with truth be referred to a cause; nevertheless the human understanding being unable to rest still seeks something prior in the order of nature. And then it is that in struggling towards that which is further off it falls back upon that which is more nigh at hand; namely, on final causes: which have relation clearly to the nature of man rather than to the nature of the universe; and from this source have strangely defiled philosophy. But he is no less an unskilled and shallow philosopher who seeks causes of that which is most general, then he who in things subordinate and subaltern omits to do so.

XLIX

The human understanding is no dry light, but receives an infusion from the will and affections; whence proceed sciences which may be called 'sciences as one would.' For what a man had rather were true he more readily believes. Therefore he rejects difficult things from impatience of research; sober things, because they narrow hope; the deeper things of nature, from superstition; the light of experience, from arrogance and pride, lest his mind should seem to be occupied with things mean and transitory; things not commonly believed, out of deference to the opinion of the vulgar. Numberless in short are the ways, and sometimes imperceptible, in which the affections colour and infect the understanding.

L

But by far the greatest hindrance and aberration of the human understanding proceeds from the dullness, incompetency, and deceptions of the senses; in that things which strike the sense outweigh things which do not immediately strike it, though they be more important. Hence it is that speculation commonly ceases where sight ceases; insomuch that of things invisible there is little or no observation. Hence all the working of the spirits inclosed in tangible bodies lies hid and unobserved of men. So also all the more subtle changes of form in the parts of coarser substances (which they commonly call alteration, though it is in truth local motion through exceedingly small spaces) is in like manner unobserved. And yet unless these two things just mentioned be searched out and brought to light, nothing great can be achieved in nature, as far as the production of works is concerned. So again the essential nature of our common air, and of all bodies less dense than air (which are very many), is almost unknown. For the sense by itself is a thing infirm and erring; neither can instruments for enlarging or sharpening the senses do much; but all the truer kind of interpretation of nature is effected by instances and experiments fit and apposite; wherein the sense decides touching the experiment only, and the experiment touching the point in nature and the thing itself.

LI

The human understanding is of its own nature prone to abstractions and gives a substance and reality to things which are fleeting. But to resolve nature into abstractions is less to our purpose than to dissect her into parts; as did the school of Democritus, which went further into nature than the rest. Matter rather than forms should be the object of our attention, its configurations and changes of configuration, and simple action, and law of action or motion; for forms are figments of the human mind, unless you will call those laws of action forms.

LII

Such then are the idols which I call *Idols of the Tribe;* and which take their rise either from the homogeneity of the substance of the human spirit, or from its preoccupation, or from its narrowness, or from its restless motion, or from an infusion of the affections, or from the incompetency of the senses, or from the mode of impression.

LIII

The *Idols of the Cave* take their rise in the peculiar constitution, mental or bodily, of each individual; and also in education, habit, and accident. Of this kind there is a great number and variety; but I will instance those the pointing out of which contains the most important caution, and which have most effect in disturbing the clearness of the understanding.

LIV

Men become attached to certain particular sciences and speculations, either because they fancy themselves the authors and inventors thereof, or because they have bestowed the greatest pains upon them and become most habituated to them. But men of this kind, if they betake themselves to philosophy and contemplations of a general character, distort and colour them in obedience to their former fancies; a thing especially to be noticed in Aristotle, who made his natural philosophy a mere bond-servant to his logic, thereby rendering it contentious and well nigh useless. The race of chemists again out of a few experiments of the furnace have built up a fantastic philosophy, framed with reference to a few things; and Gilbert also, after he had employed himself most laboriously in the study and observation of the lodestone, proceeded at once to construct an entire system in accordance with his favourite subject.

LV

There is one principal and as it were radical distinction between different minds, in respect of philosophy and the sciences; which is this: that some minds are stronger and apter to mark the differences of things, others to mark their resemblances. The steady and acute mind can fix its contemplations and dwell and fasten on the subtlest distinctions; the lofty and discursive mind recognizes and puts together the finest and most general resemblances. Both kinds however easily err in excess, by catching the one at gradations the other at shadows.

LVI

There are found some minds given to an extreme admiration of antiquity, others to an extreme love and appetite for novelty; but few so duly tempered that they can hold the mean, neither carping at what has been well laid down by the ancients, nor despising what is well introduced by the moderns. This however turns to the great injury of the sciences and philosophy: since these affectations of antiquity and novelty are the humours of partisans rather than judgments; and truth is to be sought for not in the felicity of any age, which is an unstable thing, but in the light of nature and experience, which is eternal. These factions therefore must be abjured, and care must be taken that the intellect be not hurried by them into assent.

LVII

Contemplations of nature and of bodies in their simple form break up and distract the understanding, while contemplations of nature and bodies in their composition and configuration overpower and dissolve the understanding: a distinction well seen in the school of Leucippus and Democritus as compared with the other philosophies. For that school is so busied with the particles that it hardly attends to the structure; while the others are so lost in admiration of the structure that they do not penetrate to the simplicity of nature. These kinds of contemplation should therefore be alternated and taken by turns; that so the understanding may be rendered at once penetrating and comprehensive, and the inconveniences above mentioned, with the idols which proceed from them, may be avoided.

LVIII

Let such then be our provision and contemplative prudence for keeping off and dislodging the Idols of the Cave, which grow for the most part either out of the predominance of a favourite subject, or out of an excessive tendency to compare or to distinguish, or out of partiality for particular ages, or out of the largeness or minuteness of the objects contemplated. And generally let every student of nature take this as a rule,—

that whatever his mind seizes and dwells upon with peculiar satisfaction is to be held in suspicion, and that so much the more care is to be taken in dealing with such questions to keep the understanding even and clear.

LIX

But the *Idols of the Market-place* are the most troublesome of all: idols which have crept into the understanding through the alliances of words and names. For men believe that their reason governs words; but it is also true that words react on the understanding; and this it is that has rendered philosophy and the sciences sophistical and inactive. Now words, being commonly framed and applied according to the capacity of the vulgar, follow those lines of division which are most obvious to the vulgar understanding. And whenever an understanding of greater acuteness or a more diligent observation would alter those lines to suit the true divisions of nature, words stand in the way and resist the change. Whence it comes to pass that the high and formal discussions of learned men end oftentimes in disputes about words and names; with which (according to the use and wisdom of the mathematicians) it would be more prudent to begin, and so by means of definitions reduce them to order. Yet even definitions cannot cure this evil in dealing with natural and material things; since the definitions themselves consist of words, and those words beget others: so that it is necessary to recur to individual instances, and those in due series and order; as I shall say presently when I come to the method and scheme for the formation of notions and axioms.

LX

The Idols imposed by words on the understanding are of two kinds. They are either names of things which do not exist (for as there are things left unnamed through lack of observation, so likewise are there names which result from fantastic suppositions and to which nothing in reality corresponds), or they are names of things which exist, but yet confused and ill-defined, and hastily and irregularly derived from realities. Of the former kind are Fortune, the Prime Mover, Planetary Orbits, Elements of Fire, and like fictions which owe their origin to false and idle theories. And this class of idols is more easily expelled, because to get rid of them it is only necessary that all theories should be steadily rejected and dismissed as obsolete.

But the other class, which springs out of a faulty and unskillful abstraction, is intricate and deeply rooted. Let us take for example such a word as *humid,* and see how far the several things which the word is used to signify agree with each other; and we shall find the word *humid* to be nothing else than a mark loosely and confusedly applied to denote a variety of actions which will not bear to be reduced to any constant meaning. For it both signifies that which easily spreads itself round any other body; and that which in itself is indeterminate and cannot solidize; and that which readily yields in every direction; and that which easily divides and scatters itself; and that which easily unites and collects itself; and that which readily flows and is put in motion; and that which readily clings to another body and wets it; and that which is easily reduced to a liquid, or being solid easily melts. Accordingly when you come to apply the word,—if you take it in one sense, flame is humid; if in another, air is not humid; if in another, fine dust is humid; if in another, glass is humid. So that it is easy to see that the notion is taken by abstraction only from water and common and ordinary liquids, without any due verification.

There are however in words certain degrees of distortion and error. One of the least faulty kinds is that of names of substances, especially of lowest species and well-deduced (for the notion of *chalk* and of *mud* is good, of *earth* bad); a more faulty kind is that of actions, as *to generate, to corrupt, to alter;* the most faulty is of qualities (except such as are the immediate objects of the sense) as *heavy, light, rare, dense,* and the like. Yet in all these cases some notions are of necessity a little better than others, in proportion to the greater variety of subjects that fall within the range of the human sense.

LXI

But the *Idols of the Theatre* are not innate, nor do they steal into the understanding secretly, but are plainly impressed and received into the mind from the play-books of philosophical systems and the perverted rules of demonstration. To attempt refutations in this case would be merely inconsistent with what I have already said: for since we agree neither upon principles nor upon demonstrations there is no place for argument. And this is so far well, inasmuch as it leaves the honour of the ancients untouched. For they are no wise disparaged—the question between them and me being only as to the way. For as the saying is, the lame man who keeps the right road outstrips the runner who takes a wrong one. Nay it is obvious that when a man runs the wrong way, the more active and swift he is the further he will go astray.

But the course I propose for the discovery of sciences is such as leaves but little to the acuteness and strength of wits, but places all wits and understandings nearly on a level. For as in the drawing of a straight line or a perfect circle, much depends on the steadiness and practice of the hand, if it be done by aim of hand only, but if with the aid of rule or compass, little or nothing; so is it exactly with my plan. But though particular confutations would be of no avail, yet touching the sects and general divisions of such systems I must say something; something also touching the external signs which show that they are unsound; and finally something touching the causes of such great infelicity and of such lasting and general agreement in error; that so the access to truth may be made less difficult, and the human understanding may the more willingly submit to its purgation and dismiss its idols.

LXII

Idols of the Theatre, or of Systems, are many, and there can be and perhaps will be yet many more. For were it not that now for many ages men's minds have been busied with religion and theology; and were it not that civil governments, especially monarchies, have been averse to such novelties, even in matters speculative; so that men labour therein to the peril and harming of their fortunes,—not only unrewarded, but exposed also to contempt and envy: doubtless there would have arisen many other philosophical sects like to those which in great variety flourished once among the Greeks. For as on the phenomena of the heavens many hypotheses may be constructed, so likewise (and more also) many various dogmas may be set up and established on the phenomena of philosophy. And in the plays of this philosophical theatre you may observe the same thing which is found in the theatre of the poets, that stories invented for the stage are more compact and elegant, and more as one would wish them to be, than true stories out of history.

In general however there is taken for the material of philosophy either a great deal out of a few things, or a very little out of many things; so that on both sides philosophy is based on too narrow a foundation of experiment and natural history, and decides on the authority of too few cases. For the Rational School of philosophers snatches from experience a variety of common instances, neither duly ascertained nor diligently examined and weighed, and leaves all the rest to meditation and agitation of wit.

There is also another class of philosophers, who having bestowed much diligent and careful labour on a few experiments, have thence made bold to educe and construct systems; wresting all other facts in a strange fashion to conformity therewith.

And there is yet a third class, consisting of those who out of faith and veneration mix their philosophy with theology and traditions; among whom the vanity of some has gone so far aside as to seek the origin of science among spirits and genii. So that this parent stock of errors—this false philosophy—is of three kinds; the Sophistical, the Empirical, and the Superstitious.

LXIII

The most conspicuous example of the first class was Aristotle, who corrupted natural philosophy by his logic: fashioning the world out of categories; assigning to the human soul, the noblest of substances, a genus from words of the second intention; doing the business of density and rarity (which is to make bodies of greater or less dimensions, that is, occupy greater or less spaces), by the frigid distinction of act and power; asserting that single bodies have each a single and proper motion, and that if they participate in any other, then this results from an external cause; and imposing countless other arbitrary restrictions on the nature of things; being always more solicitous to provide an answer to the question and affirm something positive in words, than about the inner truth of things; a failing best shown when his philosophy is compared with other systems of note among the Greeks. For the Homœomera of Anaxagoras; the Atoms of Leucippus and Democritus; the Heaven and Earth of Parmenides; the Strife and Friendship of Empedocles; Heraclitus's doctrine how bodies are resolved into the indifferent nature of fire, and remoulded into solids; have all of them some taste of the natural philosopher,—some savour of the nature of things, and experience, and bodies; whereas in the physics of Aristotle you hear hardly anything but the words of logic; which in his metaphysics also, under a more imposing name, and more forsooth as a realist than a nominalist, he has handled over again. Nor let any weight be given to the fact that in his books on animals, and his problems, and other of his treatises, there is frequent dealing with experiments. For he had come to his conclusion before; he did not consult experience, as he should have done, in order to the framing of his decisions and axioms; but having first determined the question according to his will, he then resorts to experience, and bending her into conformity with his placets leads her about like a captive in a procession; so that even on this count he is more guilty than his modern followers, the schoolmen, who have abandoned experience altogether.

LXIV

But the Empirical school of philosophy gives birth to dogmas more deformed and monstrous than the Sophistical or Rational school. For it has its foundations not in the light of common notions (which, though it be a faint and superficial light, is yet in a manner universal, and has reference to many things) but in the narrowness and darkness of a few ex-

periments. To those therefore who are daily busied with these experiments, and have infected their imagination with them, such a philosophy seems probable and all but certain; to all men else incredible and vain. Of this there is a notable instance in the alchemists and their dogmas; though it is hardly to be found elsewhere in these times, except perhaps in the philosophy of Gilbert. Nevertheless with regard to philosophies of this kind there is one caution not to be omitted; for I foresee that if ever men are roused by my admonitions to betake themselves seriously to experiment and bid farewell to sophistical doctrines, then indeed through the premature hurry of the understanding to leap or fly to universals and principles of things, great danger may be apprehended from philosophies of this kind; against which evil we ought even now to prepare.

LXV

But the corruption of philosophy by superstition and an admixture of theology is far more widely spread, and does the greatest harm, whether to entire systems or to their parts. For the human understanding is obnoxious to the influence of the imagination no less than to the influence of common notions. For the contentious and sophistical kind of philosophy ensnares the understanding; but this kind, being fanciful and tumid and half poetical, misleads it more by flattery. For there is in man an ambition of the understanding, no less than of the will, especially in high and lofty spirits.

Of this kind we have among the Greeks a striking example in Pythagoras, though he united with it a coarser and more cumbrous superstition; another in Plato and his school, more dangerous and subtle. It shows itself likewise in parts of other philosophies, in the introduction of abstract forms and final causes and first causes, with the omission in most cases of causes intermediate, and the like. Upon this point the greatest caution should be used. For nothing is so mischievous as the apotheosis of error; and it is a very plague of the understanding for vanity to become the object of veneration. Yet in this vanity some of the moderns have with extreme levity indulged so far as to attempt to found a system of natural philosophy on the first chapters of Genesis, on the book of Job, and other parts of the sacred writings; seeking for the dead among the living: which also makes the inhibition and repression of it the more important, because from this unwholesome mixture of things human and divine there arises not only a fantastic philosophy but also an heretical religion. Very meet it is therefore that we be soberminded, and give to faith that only which is faith's.

LXVI

So much then for the mischievous authorities of systems, which are founded either on common notions, or on a few experiments, or on superstition. It remains to speak of the faulty subject-matter of contemplations, especially in natural philosophy. Now the human understanding is infected by the sight of what takes place in the mechanical arts, in which the alteration of bodies proceeds chiefly by composition or separation, and so imagines that something similar goes on in the universal nature of things. From this source has flowed the fiction of elements, and of their concourse for the formation of natural bodies. Again, when man contemplates nature working freely, he meets with different species of things, of animals, of plants, of minerals; whence he readily passes into the opinion that there are in nature certain primary forms which nature intends to educe, and that the remaining variety proceeds from hin-

drances and aberrations of nature in the fulfilment of her work, or from the collision of different species and the transplanting of one into another. To the first of these speculations we owe our primary qualities of the elements; to the other our occult properties and specific virtues; and both of them belong to those empty *compendia* of thought wherein the mind rests, and whereby it is diverted from more solid pursuits. It is to better purpose that the physicians bestow their labour on the secondary qualities of matter, and the operations of attraction, repulsion, attenuation, conspissation, dilatation, astriction, dissipation, maturation, and the like; and were it not that by those two compendia which I have mentioned (elementary qualities, to wit, and specific virtues) they corrupted their correct observations in these other matters,—either reducing them to first qualities and their subtle and incommensurable mixtures, or not following them out with greater and more diligent observation to third and fourth qualities, but breaking off the scrutiny prematurely,—they had made much greater progress. Nor are powers of this kind (I do not say the same, but similar) to be sought for only in the medicines of the human body, but also in the changes of all other bodies.

But it is a far greater evil that they make the quiescent principles, *wherefrom,* and not the moving principles, *whereby,* things are produced, the object of their contemplation and inquiry. For the former tend to discourse, the latter to works. Nor is there any value in those vulgar distinctions of motion which are observed in the received system of natural philosophy, as generation, corruption, augmentation, diminution, alteration, and local motion. What they mean no doubt is this: If a body, in other respects not changed, be moved from its place, this is *local motion;* if without change of place or essence, it be changed in quality, this is *alteration;* if by reason of the change the mass and quantity of the body do not remain the same, this is *augmentation* or *diminution;* if they be changed to such a degree that they change their very essence and substance and turn to something else, this is *generation* and *corruption.* But all this is merely popular, and does not at all go deep into nature; for these are only measures and limits, not kinds of motion. What they intimate is *how far,* not *by what means,* or *from what source.* For they do not suggest anything with regard either to the desires of bodies or to the development of their parts: it is only when that motion presents the thing grossly and palpably to the sense as different from what it was, that they begin to mark the division. Even when they wish to suggest something with regard to the causes of motion, and to establish a division with reference to them, they introduce with the greatest negligence a distinction between motion natural and violent; a distinction which is itself drawn entirely from a vulgar notion, since all violent motion is also in fact natural; the external efficient simply setting nature working otherwise than it was before. But if, leaving all this, anyone shall observe (for instance) that there is in bodies a desire of mutual contact, so as not to suffer the unity of nature to be quite separated or broken and a vacuum thus made; or if anyone say that there is in bodies a desire of resuming their natural dimensions or tension, so that if compressed within or extended beyond them, they immediately strive to recover themselves, and fall back to their old volume and extent; or if anyone say that there is in bodies a desire of congregating towards masses of kindred nature,—of dense bodies, for instance, towards the globe of the earth, of thin and rare bodies towards the compass of the sky; all these and the like are truly physical kinds of motion;—but those others are entirely logical and scholastic, as is abundantly manifest from this comparison.

Nor again is it a less evil, that in their philosophies and contemplations their labour is spent in investigating and handling the first principles of things and the highest generalities of nature; whereas utility and the means of working result entirely from things intermediate. Hence it is that men cease not from abstracting nature till they come to potential and uninformed matter, nor on the other hand from dissecting nature till they reach the atom; things which, even if true, can do but little for the welfare of mankind.

LXVII

A caution must also be given to the understanding against the intemperance which systems of philosophy manifest in giving or withholding assent; because intemperance of this kind seems to establish Idols and in some sort to perpetuate them, leaving no way open to reach and dislodge them.

This excess is of two kinds: the first being manifest in those who are ready in deciding, and render sciences dogmatic and magisterial; the other in those who deny that we can know anything, and so introduce a wandering kind of inquiry that leads to nothing; of which kinds the former subdues, the latter weakens the understanding. For the philosophy of Aristotle, after having by hostile confutations destroyed all the rest (as the Ottomans serve their brothers), has laid down the law on all points; which done, he proceeds himself to raise new questions of his own suggestion, and dispose of them likewise; so that nothing may remain that is not certain and decided: a practice which holds and is in use among his successors.

The school of Plato, on the other hand, introduced *Acatalepsia,* at first in jest and irony, and in disdain of the older sophists,

Protagoras, Hippias, and the rest, who were of nothing else so much ashamed as of seeming to doubt about anything. But the New Academy made a dogma of it, and held it as a tenet. And though theirs is a fairer seeming way than arbitrary decisions; since they say that they by no means destroy all investigation, like Pyrrho and his Refrainers, but allow of some things to be followed as probable, though of none to be maintained as true; yet still when the human mind has once despaired of finding truth, its interest in all things grows fainter; and the result is that men turn aside to pleasant disputations and discourses and roam as it were from object to object, rather than keep on a course of severe inquisition. But, as I said at the beginning and am ever urging, the human senses and understanding, weak as they are, are not to be deprived of their authority, but to be supplied with helps.

LXVIII

So much concerning the several classes of Idols, and their equipage: all of which must be renounced and put away with a fixed and solemn determination, and the understanding thoroughly freed and cleansed; the entrance into the kingdom of man, founded on the sciences, being not much other than the entrance into the kingdom of heaven, whereinto none may enter except as a little child.

LXIX

But vicious demonstrations are as the strongholds and defences of Idols; and

those we have in logic do little else than make the world the bond-slave of human thought, and human thought the bond-slave of words. Demonstrations truly are in effect the philosophies themselves and the sciences. For such as *they* are, well or ill established, such are the systems of philosophy and the contemplations which follow. Now in the whole of the process which leads from the sense and objects to axioms and conclusions, the demonstrations which we use are deceptive and incompetent. This process consists of four parts, and has as many faults. In the first place, the impressions of the sense itself are faulty; for the sense both fails us and deceives us. But its shortcomings are to be supplied, and its deceptions to be corrected. Secondly, notions are ill drawn from the impressions of the senses, and are indefinite and confused, whereas they should be definite and distinctly bounded. Thirdly, the induction is amiss which infers the principles of sciences by simple enumeration, and does not, as it ought, employ exclusions and solutions (or separations) of nature. Lastly, that method of discovery and proof according to which the most general principles are first established, and then intermediate axioms are tried and proved by them, is the parent of error and the curse of all science. Of these things however, which now I do but touch upon, I will speak more largely, when, having performed these expiations and purgings of the mind, I come to set forth the true way for the interpretation of nature.

THE FORMAL LAWS

OF THOUGHT*

IMMANUEL KANT (1724–1804)   is recognized as one of the greatest philosophers of all times. All of his well-ordered life was spent in Königsberg,
Germany, where he was a professor of philosophy. In *The Critique of
Pure Reason* (1781) Kant developed his Critical Philosophy, an ingen-
ious synthesis of rationalism† and empiricism.‡ He believed it to be a
revolution in the theory of knowledge as significant as that of Copernicus in astronomy. Kant made significant and highly original contributions to astronomy, ethics, aesthetics, jurisprudence, and philosophy
of religion, as well as theory of knowledge.

FROM *Introduction to Logic*

Everything in nature, whether in the
animate or inanimate world, takes place
according to rules, although we do not
always know these rules. Water falls according to laws of gravity, and in animals
locomotion also takes place according to
rules. The fish in the water, the bird in
the air, moves according to rules. All nature, indeed, is nothing but a combination
of phenomena which follow rules; and
nowhere is there *any irregularity.* When
we think we find any such, we can only
say that the rules are unknown.

The exercise of our own faculties takes
place also according to certain rules,
which we follow at first *unconsciously,*
until by a long-continued use of our faculties we attain the knowledge of them,
and at last make them so familiar, that it
costs us much trouble to think of them *in
abstracto.* Thus, *ex. gr.* general grammar
is the form of language in general. One
may speak, however, without knowing
grammar, and he who speaks without
knowing it has really a grammar, and
speaks according to rules of which, however, he is not aware.

Now, like all our faculties, the *understanding,* in particular, is governed in its
actions by rules which we can investigate.
Nay, the understanding is to be regarded
as the source and faculty of conceiving

* From Immanuel Kant, *Introduction to Logic,* translated by T. K. Abbott (London:
Longmans, Green, 1885), pp. 1–6; and from Immanuel Kant, *Critique of Pure Reason,*
translated by N. K. Smith (London: Macmillan & Company, Ltd., 1929), pp. 17–19. Reprinted by permission of Macmillan & Company, Ltd., and St. Martin's Press, New York.

† Rationalism in philosophy is the doctrine that experience is not necessary for knowledge, but that pure reason can provide us with substantial knowledge about the world.

‡ For empiricism, see footnote on p. 3.

rules in general. For just as the sensibility is the faculty of intuitions, so the understanding is the faculty of thinking, that is, of bringing the ideas of sense under rules. It desires, therefore, to seek for rules, and is satisfied when it has found them. We ask, then, since the understanding is the source of rules, What rules does it follow itself? For there can be no doubt that we cannot think or use our understanding otherwise than according to certain rules. Now these rules, again, we may make a separate object of thought, that is, we can conceive them, *without their application, or in abstracto*. What now are these rules?

All rules which the understanding follows, are either *necessary* or *contingent*. The former are those without which no exercise of the understanding would be possible at all; the latter are those without which some certain definite exercise of the understanding could not take place. The contingent rules which depend on a definite object of knowledge are as manifold as these objects themselves. For example, there is an exercise of the understanding in mathematics, metaphysics, morals, &c. The rules of this special definite exercise of the understanding in these sciences are contingent, because it is contingent that I think of this or that object to which these special rules have reference.

If, however, we set aside all knowledge that we can only borrow from *objects,* and reflect simply on the exercise of the understanding in general, then we discover those rules which are absolutely necessary, independently of any particular objects of thought, because without them we cannot think at all. These rules, accordingly, can be discerned *a priori,* that is, *independently of all experience,* because they contain merely the conditions of the use of the understanding in general, whether pure or empirical, without distinction of its objects. Hence, also, it follows that the universal and

necessary laws of thought can only be concerned with its *form,* not in anywise with its *matter.* The science, therefore, which contains these universal and necessary laws is simply a science of the form of thought. And we can form a conception of the possibility of such a science, just as of a *universal grammar* which contains nothing beyond the mere form of language, without words, which belong to the matter of language.

This science of the necessary laws of the understanding and the reason generally, or, which is the same thing, of the mere form of thought generally, we call *Logic.*

Since Logic is a science which refers to all thought, without regard to objects which are the matter of thought, it must therefore be viewed—

1. as the *basis* of all other sciences, and the *propaedeutic* of all employment of the understanding. But just because it abstracts altogether from objects—

2. it cannot be an *organon* of the sciences.

By an *organon* we mean an instruction how some particular branch of knowledge is to be attained. This requires that I already know the object of this knowledge which is to be produced by certain rules. An organon of the sciences is therefore not a mere logic, since it presupposes the accurate knowledge of the objects and sources of the sciences. For example, mathematics is an excellent organon, being a science which contains the principles of extension of our knowledge in respect of a special use of reason. Logic, on the contrary, being the general propaedeutic of every use of the understanding and of the reason, cannot meddle with the sciences, and anticipate their matter, and is therefore only a *universal Art of Reason (Canonica Epicuri),* the Art of making any branch of knowledge accord with the form of the understanding. Only so far can it be called an organon, one which serves not for the *enlargement,* but only for the *criticism and correction* of our knowledge.

3. Since Logic is a science of the necessary laws of thought, without which no employment of the understanding and the reason takes place, which consequently are the conditions under which alone the understanding can and should be consistent with itself—the necessary laws and conditions of its right use—Logic is therefore a *Canon.* And being a canon of the understanding and the reason, it cannot borrow any principles either from any science or from any experience; it must contain nothing but *a priori* laws, which are necessary, and apply to the understanding universally.

Some logicians, indeed, presuppose in Logic *psychological* principles. But it is just as inappropriate to bring principles of this kind into Logic as to derive the science of morals from life. If we were to take the principles from psychology, that is, from observations on our understanding, we should merely see *how* thought takes place, and *how* it is affected by the manifold subjective hindrances and conditions; so that this would lead only to the knowledge of *contingent* laws. But in Logic the question is not of *contingent,* but of *necessary* laws; not how we do think, but how we *ought* to think. The rules of Logic, then, must not be derived from the *contingent,* but from the *necessary* use of the understanding, which, without any psychology, a man finds in himself. In Logic we do not want to know how the understanding is and thinks, and how it has hitherto proceeded in thinking, but how it ought to proceed in thinking. Its business is to teach us the correct use of reason, that is, the use which is consistent with itself.

From the definition we have given of Logic, the other essential properties of this science may be deduced; namely—

4. That both as to its form and its *mat-*

ter, it is a rational science; since its rules are not derived from experience, and since, at the same time, it has reason as its object. Logic, therefore, is a self-cognition of the understanding and the reason, *not,* however, as to their power in respect of objects, but simply as to form. In Logic I do not ask *what* the understanding knows, and *how much* it can know, or *how far* its knowledge reaches; for that would be self cognition in respect of its *material* use, and therefore belongs to metaphysics. In Logic, the question is only: *How will the understanding know itself?*

5. Finally, being a science which is rational both in form and matter, Logic is a *Doctrine,* or *demonstrated theory.* For as it does not concern itself with the common and merely empirical use of the understanding and the reason, but solely with the universal and necessary laws of thought, therefore it rests on *a priori* principles, from which all its rules can be derived and proved, as rules to which all rational knowledge must conform.

By this character Logic is essentially distinguished from *Aesthetics,* which being a mere *criticism* of *Taste,* has no canon (law), but only *Form* (pattern or measure by which to judge), which consists in general agreement of opinion. Aesthetics, in fact, contains the rules of the agreement of knowledge with the laws of the sensibility; Logic, on the contrary, contains the rules of the agreement of knowledge with the laws of the understanding and the reason. The former have only empirical principles, and therefore can never be a science or doctrine, if we mean by doctrine a dogmatic instruction founded on *a priori* principles, in which we discern everything by the understanding, without any information obtained from experience, and which gives us rules by following which the desired completeness is secured. Many persons, especially orators and poets, have attempted to reduce taste to a rational system, but they have never been able to arrive at a decisive judgment upon it. The philosopher Baumgarten, in Frankfort, had constructed the plan of an Aesthetic regarded as a science. But Home[1] has more correctly called Aesthetics Criticism, because it does not, like Logic, furnish *a priori* rules, which are adequate to determine the judgment, but procures its rules *a posteriori,* and merely generalises by comparison the empirical laws by which we take knowledge of the more perfect (beautiful) and the more imperfect.

Logic, therefore, is more than mere criticism; it is a Canon which afterwards serves for the purpose of criticism, that is, serves as the principle by which to judge of every use of the understanding; although only as to its correctness in respect of form, since it is not an organon any more than universal grammar is such.

On the other side, general logic being a propaedeutic of every use of the understanding, is distinguished from *Transcendental* Logic, in which the object itself is conceived as an object of the understanding alone; whereas general Logic applies to all objects universally.

Now, if we collect together all the essential attributes which belong to the complete determination of the conception of Logic, we must exhibit the following definition of it:

Logic is a Rational Science, both as to its form, and also its matter; an *a priori* science of the necessary laws of thought, not, however, in respect to any particular objects, but to all objects generally: accordingly it is a science of the right use of the understanding and the reason generally, not subjectively, that is, not according to empirical (psychological)

[1] [Lord Kames, author of "Principles of Criticism."]

principles as to how the understanding actually thinks, but objectively, that is, according to *a priori* principles, as to how it ought to think.

FROM *Critique of Pure Reason*

Whether the treatment of such knowledge as lies within the province of reason does or does not follow the secure path of a science, is easily to be determined from the outcome. For if after elaborate preparations, frequently renewed, it is brought to a stop immediately it nears its goal; if often it is compelled to retrace its steps and strike into some new line of approach; or again, if the various participants are unable to agree in any common plan of procedure, then we may rest assured that it is very far from having entered upon the secure path of a science, and is indeed a merely random groping. In these circumstances, we shall be rendering a service to reason should we succeed in discovering the path upon which it can securely travel, even if, as a result of so doing, much that is comprised in our original aims, adopted without reflection, may have to be abandoned as fruitless.

That logic has already, from the earliest times, proceeded upon this sure path is evidenced by the fact that since Aristotle it has not required to retrace a single step, unless, indeed, we care to count as improvements the removal of certain needless subtleties or the clearer exposition of its recognised teaching, features which concern the elegance rather than the certainty of the science. It is remarkable also that to the present day this logic has not been able to advance a single step, and is thus to all appearance a closed and completed body of doctrine. If some of the moderns have thought to enlarge it by introducing *psychological* chapters on the different faculties of knowledge (imagination, wit, etc.), *meta-*

physical chapters on the origin of knowledge or on the different kinds of certainty according to difference in the objects (idealism, scepticism, etc.), or *anthropological* chapters on prejudices, their causes and remedies, this could only arise from their ignorance of the peculiar nature of logical science. We do not enlarge but disfigure sciences, if we allow them to trespass upon one another's territory. The sphere of logic is quite precisely delimited; its sole concern is to give an exhaustive exposition and a strict proof of the formal rules of all thought, whether it be *a priori* or empirical, whatever be its origin or its object, and whatever hindrances, accidental or natural, it may encounter in our minds.

That logic should have been thus successful is an advantage which it owes entirely to its limitations, whereby it is justified in abstracting—indeed, it is under obligation to do so—from all objects of knowledge and their differences, leaving the understanding nothing to deal with save itself and its form. But for reason to enter on the sure path of science is, of course, much more difficult, since it has to deal not with itself alone but also with objects. Logic, therefore, as a propaedeutic, forms, as it were, only the vestibule of the sciences; and when we are concerned with specific modes of knowledge, while logic is indeed presupposed in any critical estimate of them, yet for the actual acquiring of them we have to look to the sciences properly and objectively so called.

LOGIC AS METAPHYSICS*

GEORGE WILHELM FRIEDRICH HEGEL (1770–1831)   was a German philosopher who contributed to almost every branch of philosophy. Although his writings are very difficult, they contain many highly original and provocative ideas. Hegel was an enormously influential thinker. His works are still studied as philosophical classics in Europe, South America, and the Orient; some of his central doctrines have been infused with renewed vigor in contemporary Existentialist philosophy; and both his logical views and a somewhat modified version of his metaphysics and philosophy of history are accepted as gospel today in communist countries. Hegel's writings are considered outdated today only in the English-speaking philosophical world.

19

Logic is the science of the pure Idea; pure, that is, because the Idea is in the abstract medium of Thought.

This definition, and the others which occur in these introductory outlines, are derived from a survey of the whole system, to which accordingly they are subsequent. The same remark applies to the prefatory notions in general explanation of philosophy.

Logic might have been defined as the science of thought, and of its laws and characteristic forms. But thought, as thought, constitutes only the general medium, or qualifying circumstance, which renders the Idea distinctively logical. If we identify the Idea with thought, thought must not be taken in the sense of a method or form, but in the sense of the self-developing system of its laws and constituent elements. These laws are the work of thought itself, and not a fact which it finds and must submit to.

From different points of view, Logic is either the hardest or the easiest of the sciences. Logic is hard, because it has to deal not with perceptions, nor, like geometry, with abstract representations of the senses, but with pure abstractions; and because it requires a habit and faculty of abstraction, a firm apprehension of thought *per se,* and a facility of movement among these intangible realities. Logic is easy, because its facts are nothing but our own thought and its familiar terms: and these are the acme of simplicity, the *a b c* of everything else. They are also what we are best acquainted with:

* From *The Logic of Hegel,* translated from *The Encyclopaedia of the Philosophical Sciences* by William Wallace (Oxford, Eng.: The Clarendon Press, 1874), pp. 25–38.

such as, 'Is' and 'Is not': quality and magnitude: being potential and being actual: one, many, and so on. But such an acquaintance only adds to the difficulties of the study; for while, on the one hand, we naturally think it is not worth our trouble to occupy ourselves any longer with things so well known, on the other hand, the purpose is to become acquainted with them in a new way, quite opposite to that in which we know them already.

The utility of Logic is a matter which concerns its bearings upon the student, and the training it may give for other purposes. This logical training consists of the exercise in thinking which the student has to undergo (this science is the thinking of thinking): and in the fact that he stores his head with thoughts, in their native unalloyed character. It is true that Logic, being the absolute form of truth, and another name for abstract truth itself, is something more than merely useful. Yet if what is noblest, most liberal and most independent is also most useful, Logic has some claim to the latter character. Its value must then be estimated by some other standard than exercise in thought for the sake of the exercise.

(1) The first question is: What is the object of our science? The simplest and most intelligible answer to this question is that Truth is the object of Logic. Truth is a great word, and the thing is greater still. So long as man is sound at heart and in spirit, the search for truth must awake all the enthusiasm of his nature. But immediately there steps in the objection—Are *we* able to know truth? There seems to be an incommensurability between finite beings like ourselves and the truth which is absolute: and doubts suggest themselves whether there is any bridge between the finite and the infinite. God is truth: how shall we know Him? Such a claim appears to stand in contradiction with the graces of lowliness and humility. Others who ask whether we can know the truth have a different purpose. They want to justify themselves in living on contented with their petty, finite aims. And humility of this stamp does not count for much.

The time is past, when people asked: How shall I, a poor worm of the dust, be able to know the truth? And we have now to contend with the vanity and arrogance of those, who claim, without any trouble on their part, to breathe the very atmosphere of truth. The young have been flattered into the belief, that they possess a natural birthright of moral and religious truth. And in the same strain, our riper years are declared to be sunk, petrified, ossified in falsehood. Youth, say these teachers, sees the bright light of dawn: but the older generation lies in the slough and mire of the common day. They admit that the special sciences are something that certainly ought to be cultivated, but merely as the means to satisfy the needs of outer life. In all this there is none of the humility which shrinks in awe from the knowledge and study of the truth, but a conviction that we are already in full possession of the truth. It is an unquestionable fact that the young carry with them the hopes of their elder compeers; on them rests the advance of the world and science. But these hopes are set upon the young, only on the condition, that instead of remaining as they are, they undertake the hard work of thought.

This modesty in truth-seeking has still another phase: and that is the genteel indifference to truth, as we see it in Pilate's conversation with Christ. Pilate asked 'What is truth?' with the air of a man who had settled accounts with everything long ago, and concluded that nothing particularly matters:—he meant much the same as Solomon when he says: 'All is vanity.' When it comes to this, nothing is left but self-conceit.

The knowledge of the truth meets an additional obstacle in timidity. A slothful mind finds it easy to say: 'Don't let it be supposed that we mean to be in earnest with our philosophy. We shall be glad *inter alia* to study Logic: but Logic must be sure to leave us as we were before.' People have a feeling that, if thinking exceeds the ordinary limits in which our material conceptions are confined, it cannot but be on the evil road. They seem to be trusting themselves to a sea, on which they will be tossed to and fro by the waves of thought, till they again reach the sand-bank of this temporal scene, as empty as they left it. What comes of such a view, we see in the world. It is possible within these limits to gain varied information and many accomplishments, to become a master of official routine, and to be trained for special purposes. But, it is quite another thing to educate the spirit for the higher life and to devote our energies to its service. In our own day it may be hoped a longing for something better has sprung up among the young, so that they will not be contented with the empty straw of outer knowledge.

(2) It is universally agreed that thought is the object of Logic. Our opinion of thought may be very mean, or it may be very high. On one hand, people say: 'It is only a thought.' In their view thought is subjective, arbitrary and accidental—distinguished from the thing itself, and neither true nor real. On the other hand, a very high estimate may be taken of thought; when thought alone is held adequate to attain the highest of all things, the nature of God, of which the senses can tell us nothing. God is a spirit, it is said, and must be worshipped in spirit and in truth. But the objects of sense and feeling are different from the object of spirit—of which the innermost nature is thought: and only spirit can know spirit. Feeling is undoubtedly a mode of spiritual life (of which we have an instance in religion) : but mere feeling, as a mode of consciousness, is one thing, and its contents another. Feeling, as feeling, is the general form of the sensuous nature, which we have in common with the brutes. This form, viz. feeling, may possibly adopt and appropriate all the elements of religious truth: but the form has no real congruity with its contents. The form of feeling is the lowest in which spiritual truth can be expressed. The central idea of spiritual consciousness, that is, God himself, exists in his proper truth, only in thought and as thought. If this be so, therefore, thought, far from being a mere thought, is the highest, and in strict accuracy, the sole mode of apprehending the eternal and absolute being.

As of thought, so also of the science of thought, a very high or a very low opinion may be formed. Any man, it is supposed, can think without Logic, as he can digest without studying physiology. If he have studied Logic, he thinks afterwards as he did before, perhaps more methodically, but with little difference. If this were all, and if Logic had no more to do than make men acquainted with the action of thought as the faculty of comparison and classification, nothing would ensue which had not been done quite as well before. The position of previous Logic was substantially the same as this. Yet the knowledge of thought, even as a mere activity of the subject-mind, is honourable and interesting for man. It is in knowing what he is and what he does, that man is distinguished from the brutes. But we may take the higher estimate of thought. In that case, Logic as the science of thought occupies a high ground. Thought alone is capable of learning to know the highest of all things—Truth. If the science of Logic then considers thought in its activity and with reference to its productions (and thought being no resultless energy produces thoughts and the particular thought required), its facts may be generally said to constitute the supersensible world, and to deal with these facts is to dwell for a while in that world. Mathematics is concerned with the abstractions of time and space. But these are the object of sense, although the sensible is abstract and idealized. Thought bids adieu even to this last abstraction from the senses: and asserts its own native independence, while it renounces the field of the external and internal sense, and turns its back upon the interests and inclinations of the individual. When Logic takes this ground, it is a higher science than we are in the habit of supposing.

(3) The necessity of understanding Logic in a wider sense than as the science of the form of thought is enforced by the interests of religion and politics, of law and morality. At first men had no suspicions of thought; and they thought away freely and fearlessly. They thought about God, about Nature, and the State; and they felt sure that a knowledge of the truth was obtainable by thought only, and not by the senses or any occasional conception and opinion. But while they so thought, the principal ordinances of life began to be seriously affected by their conclusions. Thought deprived existing institutions of their force. Constitutions fell a victim to thought: religion was assailed by thought: firm religious beliefs which had been always looked upon in the light of revelations were undermined, and in many minds the old faith was overthrown. The Greek philosophers, for example, became the antagonists of the old religion, and annihilated the forms of popular belief. Philosophers were accordingly banished or put to death, as revolutionists who had subverted religion and the state, two things which were inseparable. Thought, in short, made itself a power in the real world, and exercised enormous influence. The matter ended by

drawing attention to the influence of thought and by a more rigorous scrutiny of its claims, in which the world would have been glad to find that thought arrogated too much to itself and was unable to perform what it had undertaken. It had not learned what was the essence of God, of Nature and Mind. It had not learned what the truth was. What it had done, was to overthrow religion and the state. It became imperative therefore to justify thought, with reference to the results it had produced: and it is this examination into the nature of thought and this justification which in modern times has constituted one of the main problems of philosophy.

20

When we examine the simplest popular conception of what is meant by Thought, we find several points worthy of remark. First (a) in its common subjective acceptation, thought is one out of many activities or faculties of the mind, co-ordinate with such others as sensation, perception, imagination, desire, volition, and the like. The product of this activity, the form or character peculiar to thought, is a UNIVERSAL, of which the nature is to be abstract. Thought, regarded as an activity of the mind, may be accordingly described as the active universal; and since the result produced by it is a repetition of the universal, thought may be called a self-actualising universal. Thought conceived as a subject is a thinker, and the subject existing as a thinker is simply denoted by the term 'I.'

The propositions giving an account of thought in this and the following sections are not offered as assertions or opinions of mine on the matter. But in these preliminary chapters any deduction or proof would be impossible, and the statements may be taken for facts. In other words, every man, when he thinks and considers his thoughts, will discover by the experience of his consciousness that they involve the character of universality as well as the other forms or characters of thought to be afterwards enumerated. We assume that his powers of attention and abstraction have undergone a previous training, enabling him to observe correctly the facts of his consciousness and his conceptions.

This introductory exposition has already alluded to the distinction between Sense, Conception, and Thought. As the distinction is of capital importance for understanding the nature and the different kinds of knowledge, it will help to explain matters if we here call attention to it. For the explanation of Sense, the easiest method certainly is, to refer to its external source—the organs of sense. But to give the name of the organ, does not help much to explain what is apprehended by it. The real distinction between sense and thought may be formulated as follows. The former is individual, and as the individual (which, reduced to its simplest terms, is the atom) is also a member of a series, sensible existence presents a number of mutually exclusive units,—a state of things which conforms to the more special abstract conditions of co-existence and succession. Conception or picture-thinking works with materials from the same sensuous source. But these materials when conceived are expressly characterised as in me and therefore mine: and secondly, as universal, or simple, because only referred to self. Nor is sense the only source of materialised conception. There are conceptions based upon materials emanating from self-conscious thought, such as those of right, morality, religion, and even of thought itself, and one does not immediately observe where the difference exists between such conceptions, and thoughts having the same scope. For it is a thought of which such conception is the vehicle, and

there is no want of the form of universality, without which no content could be in me, or be a conception at all. Yet here also the peculiarity of conception is the individualism or isolation of its contents. True it is that morality and moral ideas do not exist in the sensible world of space, mutually excluding one another. Nor as regards time, though they appear to some extent in succession, are their contents themselves conceived as affected by time, or as transient and changeable in it. The fault in conception lies deeper. These ideas, though they are properly due to the mind, stand isolated here and there on the broad field of the faculty of conception, which gives them only an inward and imperfect generality. Being thus reduced to separate entities, they are what we call simple: Justice, Duty, God. Conception in these circumstances either rests satisfied with declaring that Justice is justice, God is God: or in a higher grade of culture, it proceeds to enunciate the attributes; as, for instance, God is the Creator of the world, omniscient, almighty, &c. In this way several isolated, simple predicates are strung together: but in spite of the link supplied by their subject, the predicates never get beyond mere contiguity. In this point Conception coincides with Understanding: the only distinction being that the latter introduces relations of universal and particular, of cause and effect, &c., and in this way gives a necessary connexion to the isolated ideas of pictorial conception; which last has left them side by side in the vague background of imagination, connected only by a bare 'and.' The difference between conception and thought is of special importance: because philosophy may be said to do nothing but transform conceptions into thoughts,—though it works the further transformation of mere thought into the comprehensive notion.

Sensible existence has been characterised by the attributes of individuality, and a mutual exclusion of the members. It is well to remember that these very attributes are thoughts and general terms. It will be shown in the Logic that thought (and the universal) is not a mere opposite of sense: it comprehends its opposite, and, overlapping even that, lets nothing escape it. Now language is the work of thought: and hence all that is expressed in language must be universal. What I only mean or suppose is mine: it belongs to me as a particular individual. But language expresses nothing but universality; and so I cannot say what I merely mean or feel. And what cannot be uttered, feeling or sensation, far from being the highest truth, is the most unimportant and untrue. If I say 'The Unit,' 'This Unit,' 'here,' 'now,' all these are universal terms. Everything and anything is an individual, a 'this,' or if it be sensible, is here and now. Similarly when I say, 'I,' I *mean* my single self to the exclusion of all others: but what I *say*, viz. 'I,' is just every 'I,' which in like manner excludes all others from itself. In an awkward expression which Kant used, he said that the I is *associated* with our sensations, desires, and actions, as well as our conceptions. 'I' is the absolute universal: and community or association is one of the forms, though an external form of universality. All other men have it in common with me to be 'I:' just as it is common to all my sensations and conceptions to be mine. But 'I,' in the abstract, as such, is the mere act of concentration or reference to self, in which we make abstraction from all conception, and feeling, from every state of mind and every peculiarity of nature, talent, and experience. To this extent, 'I' means the existence of a wholly abstract universality, a principle of abstract freedom. Thought, viewed as a subject, is expressed by the word 'I:' and since I am at the same time in all my sensations, conceptions, and

states of consciousness, thought is everywhere present, and is a category that runs through all these modifications.

Our first conception when we use the term thought is of a subjective activity— one amongst many similar faculties, such as memory, imagination and will. Were thought merely an activity of the subject-mind and treated under that aspect by logic, logic would resemble the other sciences in possessing a well-marked object. The only wonder in that case would be, that any one should have imagined it necessary to devote a special science to thought, whilst will, imagination and the rest were denied the same privilege. The selection of one faculty however might even in this view be very well grounded on a certain authority acknowledged to belong to thought, and on its claim to be regarded as the true nature of man, in which consists his distinction from the brutes. Nor is it unimportant to study thought even as a subjective energy. A detailed analysis of its nature would exhibit rules and laws, a knowledge of which is derived from experience. A treatment of the laws of thought, from this point of view, used once to form the body of logical science. Of that science Aristotle was the founder. He succeeded in assigning to thought what properly belongs to it. Our thought is extremely concrete: but in its composite contents we must distinguish the part that belongs to thought, or the abstract mode of its action. A subtle spiritual bond, consisting in the agency of thought, knits all these contents into one, and it was this bond, the form as form, that Aristotle noted and described. Up to the present day, the logic of Aristotle continues to be the received system. It has indeed been spun out to greater length, especially by the labours of the medieval Schoolmen, who, without extending the material, merely worked it out in more detail. The moderns also have left their mark upon this logic, partly by omitting many points of logical doctrine due to Aristotle and the Schoolmen, and partly by foisting in a quantity of psychological matter. The purport of the science is to become acquainted with the procedure of finite thought (or of thought dealing with existing objects): and, if it is adapted to its pre-supposed object, the science is entitled to be styled correct. The study of this formal logic undoubtedly has its uses. It clears the head, as the phrase goes, and teaches us to collect our thoughts, and to abstract—whereas in common consciousness we have to deal with sensuous conceptions which cross and perplex one another. Abstraction moreover implies the concentration of the mind on a single point, and thus induces the habit of attending to our inward selves. An acquaintance with the forms of finite thought may be made a sort of introduction to the prosecution of the empirical sciences, since their method is regulated by these forms: and in this sense logic has been designated Instrumental. It is true, we may be still more liberal, and say: Logic is to be studied not for its utility, but for its own sake: the highest good is not to be sought for the sake of mere utility. In one sense this is quite correct: but it may be replied that the highest good is also the most useful: because it is the all-encompassing fact, which, having a subsistence of its own, may therefore serve as the vehicle of all the special ends which it furthers and secures. And thus, special ends, though they have no right to be set first, are still fostered by the presence of the highest good. Religion, for instance, has an absolute value of its own; yet at the same time other ends flourish and succeed in its train. As Christ says: 'Seek ye first the kingdom of God, and all these things shall be added unto you.' Particular ends can be attained only in the attainment of what absolutely is and exists in its own right.

21

(*b*) Thought has been shown to be active. We now, in the second place, consider this action in its bearings upon objects, or as Reflection upon something. In this case the universal or product of its operation is rated as equivalent to the fact, the essence, the intrinsic value, the truth.

In Sect. 5 the old belief was quoted that the reality in object, circumstance, or event, the intrinsic worth or essence, is the fact on which stress is to be laid— that this fact is not a self-evident datum of consciousness, or coincident with the first appearance and impression; that, on the contrary, Reflection is required in order to discover the real constitution of the object—and that by such Reflection it will be ascertained.

To reflect is a lesson which even the child has to learn. One of his first lessons is to join adjectives with substantives. This obliges him to attend and distinguish: he has to remember a rule and apply it to the particular case. This rule is nothing but a universal: and the child must see that the particular adapts itself to this universal. In life, again, we have ends to attain. And with regard to these we ponder which is the best way to secure them. The end here represents the universal or governing principle: and we have means and instruments whose action we regulate in conformity to the end. In the same way reflection is active in questions of conduct. To reflect here means to remember the law of righteousness, and duty,—the universal which serves as a fixed rule to guide our behaviour in the given case. Our particular act must imply and recognise the universal law. We find the same thing exhibited in our study of natural phenomena. For instance, we observe thunder and lightning. The phenomenon is a familiar one, and we often perceive it. But man is not content with a bare acquaintance, or with the fact as it appears to the senses; he would like to get behind the surface, to know what it is, and to comprehend it. This leads him to reflect: he seeks to find out the cause as something distinct from the mere phenomenon: he tries to know the inside in its distinction from the outside. Hence the phenomenon becomes double, it splits into inside and outside, into force and its manifestation, into cause and effect. Once more we find the inside or the force identified with the universal and permanent: not this or that flash of lightning, this or that plant—but that which continues the same in them all. The sensible appearance is individual and evanescent: the permanent fact contained in it is discovered by a process of reflection. Nature shows us a countless number of individual forms **and phenomena**. Into this variety we feel ourselves forced to introduce unity: we compare, consequently, and try to find the universal of each single case. Individuals are born and perish: the species abides and recurs in them all: and its existence is only visible to reflection. Under the same head fall such laws as those regulating the motion of the heavenly bodies. To-day we see the stars here, and to-morrow there: and our mind finds something incongruous in this chaos —something in which it can put no faith, because it believes in order, and in a simple, constant, and universal law. Inspired by this belief, our mind has directed its reflection towards the phenomena, and learnt their laws. In other words, it has established the movement of the heavenly bodies to be in accordance with a universal law, from which every change of position may be known and predicted. The case is the same with the influences which make themselves felt in the infinite complexity of human conduct. There, too, man has the belief in the sway of a general principle. From all these examples it

may be gathered how reflection is always seeking for something fixed and permanent, which has a certainty of its own, and governs the particulars. This universal principle cannot be apprehended by the senses; yet it alone can be esteemed true and essential. Thus, duties and rights are all-important in the matter of conduct: and an action is true when it conforms to those universal formulæ.

In thus characterising the universal, we become aware of its antithesis to something else. This something else is the merely immediate, outward and individual, as opposed to the mediate, inward and universal. The universal does not exist externally to the outward eye as a universal. The kind as kind cannot be perceived: the laws of the celestial motions are not written on the sky. The universal is neither seen nor heard, its existence is the secret known only to the mind. Religion leads us to a universal, which embraces all else within itself, to an Absolute by which all else is brought into being: and this Absolute is an object not of the senses but of the mind and of thought.

22

(c) By the act of reflection and meditation, a *change* comes over the import of our sensation, perception and material conceptions. The object of consciousness undergoes a transformation. Thus, as it appears, an alteration of the object must be interposed before its true nature can be discovered.

What reflection elicits, is a product of our thought. Solon, for instance, drew from his own judgment, the laws he gave to the Athenians. This is half of the truth: but we must not on that account forget that the universal (in Solon's case the laws) is the very reverse of merely subjective, or fail to note that it is the essential, true, and objective being of things. To discover the truth in things, mere attention is not enough; we must call in the action of our own faculties to transform what is immediately before us. Now, at first sight, this seems an inversion of the natural order, calculated to thwart the very purpose on which knowledge is bent. But the method is not so irrational as it seems. Every period of history has felt, that the only way of reaching the permanent substratum, was to transmute the given phenomenon by means of reflection. In modern times a doubt has for the first time been raised on this point in connexion with the difference alleged to exist between the results of our thought and the things in their own nature. This real nature of things, it is said, is very different from what we make out of them. The divorce between thought and thing is mainly the work of the Critical Philosophy and runs counter to the conviction of all previous ages, that their agreement was a matter of course. The antithesis between them is the hinge on which modern philosophy turns. Meanwhile the natural belief of men gives the lie to it. In common life we reflect, without particularly noting that this is the process of arriving at the truth, and we think without hesitation, and in the firm belief that thought coincides with thing. And this belief is of the greatest importance. It marks the diseased state of the age when we see it adopt the despairing creed that our knowledge is only subjective, and that this subjective result is final. Whereas, rightly understood, truth is objective, and ought so to regulate the conviction of every one, that the conviction of the individual is stamped as wrong, when it does not agree with this rule. Modern views indeed put great value on the mere fact of conviction; and hold that to be convinced is good for its own sake, whatever it may be applied to, there being no standard by which we can measure its truth.

We said above that, according to the old belief, it was the characteristic function of the mind to know the truth. We may go a step further and say, that everything we know both of outward and inward nature, in one word, the objective world, is in its own self the same as it is in thought, and that thought consequently expresses the truth of the objects of perception. The whole problem of philosophy is to bring into explicit consciousness what the world in all ages has believed about thought. Philosophy therefore advances nothing new; and our present discussion has led us to a conclusion which agrees with the natural belief of mankind.

23

(d) The real nature of the object is brought to light in reflection, but it is no less true that this exertion of thought is *my* act. If this be so, the real nature is a production of my mind, in its character of thinking subject. The Ego in its non-composite universality, self-collected and removed from extraneous influences,—in one word, our Freedom, is thus the source of this real nature.

Think for yourself, is a common remark, which people utter, as if it expressed something of importance. The fact is, no man can think for another, any more than he can eat or drink for him: and the expression savours of pleonasm. Freedom is obviously and intimately associated with thought, which as the action of the universal, puts us in relation only with a second self, since subject and object of thought are alike universal. Here we are at home with ourselves; yet there is no prominence allowed to any special aspect of the subject-mind, and the contents of our consciousness are entirely based upon the fact and the deliverances of the fact. If this be admitted, and if we apply the term humility to an attitude where no particular act or influence is ascribed to our own mental selves, it is easy to appreciate the question touching the humility or pride of philosophy. For in point of contents, thought is only true in proportion as it is absorbed in the facts; and in point of form it is no special or peculiar state or act of the mind. What thought implies is simply this. the mind as an Ego, in a mere point of its being, as it were, shakes itself free of all the special limitations to which its ordinary states or qualities are liable, and restricts itself to that universal action, in which it is identical with all individuals. In these circumstances philosophy may be acquitted of the charge of pride. And when Aristotle summons the mind to rise to the dignity of that action, the dignity he seeks is won by letting slip all our individual opinions and prejudices, and submitting to the sway of the fact.

24

With these explanations and qualifications, thoughts may be termed Objective Thoughts, among which we shall include the forms ordinarily discussed in the common logic, where they are believed to be forms of conscious thought only. *Logic in our sense coincides with Metaphysics, the science of things in a setting of thoughts;* which thoughts, it is allowed, express the essence of things.

THE SCIENCE OF
EVIDENCE*

JOHN STUART MILL (1806–1873) is one of the best known and most engaging figures in the history of British Empiricism. His general philosophical views are best stated in *An Examination of Sir William Hamilton's Philosophy* (1865); and his *On Liberty* (1859) and *Utilitarianism* (1863) are classic works in political theory and ethics. The selections included in this volume are from his encyclopaedic and influential *A System of Logic* (1843).

1

There is as great diversity among authors in the modes which they have adopted of defining logic, as in their treatment of the details of it. This is what might naturally be expected on any subject on which writers have availed themselves of the same language as a means of delivering different ideas. Ethics and jurisprudence are liable to the remark in common with logic. Almost every writer having taken a different view of some of the particulars which these branches of knowledge are usually understood to include; each has so framed his definition as to indicate beforehand his own peculiar tenets, and sometimes to beg the question in their favor.

This diversity is not so much an evil to be complained of, as an inevitable and in some degree a proper result of the imperfect state of those sciences. It is not to be expected that there should be agreement about the definition of any thing, until

there is agreement about the thing itself. To define, is to select from among all the properties of a thing, those which shall be understood to be designated and declared by its name; and the properties must be well known to us before we can be competent to determine which of them are fittest to be chosen for this purpose. Accordingly, in the case of so complex an aggregation of particulars as are comprehended in any thing which can be called a science, the definition we set out with is seldom that which a more extensive knowledge of the subject shows to be the most appropriate. Until we know the particulars themselves, we can not fix upon the most correct and compact mode of circumscribing them by a general description. It was not until after an extensive and accurate acquaintance with the details of chemical phenomena, that it was found possible to frame a rational definition of chemistry; and the definition of the science of life and organization is still a matter of dis-

* From John Stuart Mill, *A System of Logic* (New York: Harper & Bros., 1874) pp. 17–24.

pute. So long as the sciences are imperfect, the definitions must partake of their imperfection; and if the former are progressive, the latter ought to be so too. As much, therefore, as is to be expected from a definition placed at the commencement of a subject, is that it should define the scope of our inquiries: and the definition which I am about to offer of the science of logic, pretends to nothing more than to be a statement of the question which I have put to myself, and which this book is an attempt to resolve. The reader is at liberty to object to it as a definition of logic; but it is at all events a correct definition of the subject of this volume.

2

Logic has often been called the Art of Reasoning. A writer[1] who has done more than any other person to restore this study to the rank from which it had fallen in the estimation of the cultivated class in our own country, has adopted the above definition with an amendment; he has defined Logic to be the Science, as well as the Art, of reasoning; meaning by the former term, the analysis of the mental process which takes place whenever we reason, and by the latter, the rules, grounded on that analysis, for conducting the process correctly. There can be no doubt as to the propriety of the emendation. A right understanding of the mental process itself, of the conditions it depends on, and the steps of which it consists, is the only basis on which a system of rules, fitted for the direction of the process, can possibly be founded. Art necessarily presupposes knowledge; art, in any but its infant state, presupposes scientific knowledge: and if every art does not bear the name of a science, it is only because several sciences are often necessary to form the groundwork of a single art. So

[1] Archbishop Whately.

complicated are the conditions which govern our practical agency, that to enable one thing to be *done,* it is often requisite to *know* the nature and properties of many things.

Logic, then, comprises the science of reasoning, as well as an art, founded on that science. But the word Reasoning, again, like most other scientific terms in popular use, abounds in ambiguities. In one of its acceptations, it means syllogizing; or the mode of inference which may be called (with sufficient accuracy for the present purpose) concluding from generals to particulars. In another of its senses, to reason is simply to infer any assertion, from assertions already admitted: and in this sense induction is as much entitled to be called reasoning as the demonstrations of geometry.

Writers on logic have generally preferred the former acceptation of the term: the latter, and more extensive signification is that in which I mean to use it. I do this by virtue of the right I claim for every author, to give whatever provisional definition he pleases of his own subject. But sufficient reasons will, I believe, unfold themselves as we advance, why this should be not only the provisional but the final definition. It involves at all events, no arbitrary change in the meaning of the word; for, with the general usage of the English language, the wider signification, I believe, accords better than the more restricted one.

3

But reasoning, even in the widest sense of which the word is susceptible, does not seem to comprehend all that is included, either in the best, or even in the most current, conception of the scope and province of our science. The employment of the word Logic to denote the theory of Argumentation, is derived from the Aristotelian, or, as they are commonly termed, the scholastic, logicians. Yet even with them, in their systematic treatises, Argumentation was the subject only of the third part: the two former treated of Terms, and of Propositions; under one or other of which heads were also included Definition and Division. By some, indeed, these previous topics were professedly introduced only on account of their connection with reasoning, and as a preparation for the doctrine and rules of the syllogism. Yet they were treated with greater minuteness, and dwelt on at greater length, than was required for that purpose alone. More recent writers on logic have generally understood the term as it was employed by the able author of the Port Royal Logic; viz., as equivalent to the Art of Thinking. Nor is this acceptation confined to books, and scientific inquiries. Even in ordinary conversation, the ideas connected with the word Logic include at least precision of language, and accuracy of classification: and we perhaps oftener hear persons speak of a logical arrangement, or of expressions logically defined, than of conclusions logically deduced from premises. Again, a man is often called a great logician, or a man of powerful logic, not for the accuracy of his deductions, but for the extent of his command over premises; because the general propositions required for explaining a difficulty or refuting a sophism, copiously and promptly occur to him: because, in short, his knowledge, besides being ample, is well under his command for argumentative use. Whether, therefore, we conform to the practice of those who have made the subject their particular study, or to that of popular writers and common discourse, the province of logic will include several operations of the intellect not usually considered to fall within the meaning of the terms Reasoning and Argumentation.

These various operations might be brought within the compass of the sci-ence, and the additional advantage be obtained of a very simple definition, if, by an extension of the term, sanctioned by high authorities, we were to define logic as the science which treats of the operations of the human understanding in the pursuit of truth. For to this ultimate end, naming, classification, definition, and all other operations over which logic has ever claimed jurisdiction, are essentially subsidiary. They may all be regarded as contrivances for enabling a person to know the truths which are needful to him, and to know them at the precise moment at which they are needful. Other purposes, indeed, are also served by these operations; for instance, that of imparting our knowledge to others. But, viewed with regard to this purpose, they have never been considered as within the province of the logician. The sole object of Logic is the guidance of one's own thoughts: the communication of those thoughts to others falls under the consideration of Rhetoric, in the large sense in which that art was conceived by the ancients; or of the still more extensive art of Education. Logic takes cognizance of our intellectual operations only as they conduce to our own knowledge, and to our command over that knowledge for our own uses. If there were but one rational being in the universe, that being might be a perfect logician; and the science and art of logic would be the same for that one person as for the whole human race.

4

But, if the definition which we formerly examined included too little, that which is now suggested has the opposite fault of including too much.

Truths are known to us in two ways: some are known directly, and of themselves; some through the medium of other truths. The former are the subject of

Intuition, or Consciousness;[2] the latter, of Inference. The truths known by intuition are the original premises from which all others are inferred. Our assent to the conclusion being grounded on the truth of the premises, we never could arrive at any knowledge by reasoning, unless something could be known antecedently to all reasoning.

Examples of truths known to us by immediate consciousness, are our own bodily sensations and mental feelings. I know directly, and of my own knowledge, that I was vexed yesterday, or that I am hungry to-day. Examples of truths which we know only by way of inference, are occurrences which took place while we were absent, the events recorded in history, or the theorems of mathematics. The two former we infer from the testimony adduced, or from the traces of those past occurrences which still exist; the latter, from the premises laid down in books of geometry, under the title of definitions and axioms. Whatever we are capable of knowing must belong to the one class or to the other; must be in the number of the primitive data, or of the conclusions which can be drawn from these.

With the original data, or ultimate premises of our knowledge; with their number or nature, the mode in which they are obtained, or the tests by which they may be distinguished; logic, in a direct way at least, has, in the sense in which I conceive the science, nothing to do. These questions are partly not a subject of science at all, partly that of a very different science.

[2] I use these terms indiscriminately, because, for the purpose in view, there is no need for making any distinction between them. But metaphysicians usually restrict the name Intuition to the direct knowledge we are supposed to have of things external to our minds, and Consciousness to our knowledge of our own mental phenomena.

Whatever is known to us by consciousness is known beyond possibility of question. What one sees or feels, whether bodily or mentally, one can not but be sure that one sees or feels. No science is required for the purpose of establishing such truths; no rules of art can render our knowledge of them more certain than it is in itself. There is no logic for this portion of our knowledge.

But we may fancy that we see or feel what we in reality infer. A truth, or supposed truth, which is really the result of a very rapid inference, may seem to be apprehended intuitively. It has long been agreed by thinkers of the most opposite schools, that this mistake is actually made in so familiar an instance as that of the eyesight. There is nothing of which we appear to ourselves to be more directly conscious than the distance of an object from us. Yet it has long been ascertained, that what is perceived by the eye, is at most nothing more than a variously colored surface; that when we fancy we see distance, all we really see is certain variations of apparent size, and degrees of faintness of color; that our estimate of the object's distance from us is the result partly of a rapid inference from the muscular sensations accompanying the adjustment of the focal distance of the eye to objects unequally remote from us, and partly of a comparison (made with so much rapidity that we are unconscious of making it) between the size and color of the object as they appear at the time, and the size and color of the same or of similar objects as they appeared when close at hand, or when their degree of remoteness was known by other evidence. The perception of distance by the eye, which seems so like intuition, is thus, in reality, an inference grounded on experience; an inference, too, which we learn to make; and which we make with more and more correctness as our experience increases; though in familiar cases it takes place so rapidly as to appear exactly on a par with those perceptions of sight which are really intuitive, our perceptions of color.

Of the science, therefore, which expounds the operations of the human understanding in the pursuit of truth, one essential part is the inquiry: What are the facts which are the objects of intuition or consciousness, and what are those which we merely infer? But this inquiry has never been considered a portion of logic. Its place is in another and a perfectly distinct department of science, to which the name metaphysics more particularly belongs: that portion of mental philosophy which attempts to determine what part of the furniture of the mind belongs to it originally, and what part is constructed out of materials furnished to it from without. To this science appertain the great and much debated questions of the existence of matter; the existence of spirit, and of a distinction between it and matter; the reality of time and space, as things without the mind, and distinguishable from the objects which are said to exist *in* them. For in the present state of the discussion on these topics, it is almost universally allowed that the existence of matter or of spirit, of space or of time, is in its nature unsusceptible of being proved; and that if any thing is known of them, it must be by immediate intuition. To the same science belong the inquiries into the nature of Conception, Perception, Memory, and Belief; all of which are operations of the understanding in the pursuit of truth; but with which, as phenomena of the mind, or with the possibility which may or may not exist of analyzing any of them into simpler phenomena, the logician as such has no concern. To this science must also be referred the following; and all analogous questions: To what extent our intellectual faculties and our emotions are innate—to what extent the result of association: Whether God and duty are realities, the existence of which is manifest to us *a priori* by the constitution of our rational faculty; or whether our ideas of them are acquired notions, the origin of which we are able to trace and explain; and the reality of the objects themselves a question not of consciousness or intuition, but of evidence and reasoning.

The province of logic must be restricted to that portion of our knowledge which consists of inferences from truths previously known; whether those antecedent data be general propositions, or particular observations and perceptions. Logic is not the science of Belief, but the science of Proof, or Evidence. In so far as belief professes to be founded on proof, the office of logic is to supply a test for ascertaining whether or not the belief is well grounded. With the claims which any proposition has to belief on the evidence of consciousness—that is, without evidence in the proper sense of the word—logic has nothing to do.

5

By far the greatest portion of our knowledge, whether of general truths or of particular facts, being avowedly matter of inference, nearly the whole, not only of science, but of human conduct, is amenable to the authority of logic. To draw inferences has been said to be the great business of life. Every one has daily, hourly, and momentary need of ascertaining facts which he has not directly observed; not from any general purpose of adding to his stock of knowledge, but because the facts themselves are of importance to his interests or to his occupations. The business of the magistrate, of the military commander, of the navigator, of the physician, of the agriculturist, is merely to judge of evidence, and to act accordingly. They all have to ascertain certain facts, in order that they may afterward apply certain rules, either devised by themselves or prescribed for their guidance by others; and as they do this well or ill, so they discharge well or ill the duties of their several callings. It is the only occupation in which the mind never ceases to be engaged; and is the subject, not of logic, but of knowledge in general.

Logic, however, is not the same thing with knowledge, though the field of logic is co-extensive with the field of knowledge. Logic is the common judge and arbiter of all particular investigations. It does not undertake to find evidence, but to determine whether it has been found. Logic neither observes, nor invents, nor discovers; but judges. It is no part of the business of logic to inform the surgeon what appearances are found to accompany a violent death. This he must learn from his own experience and observation, or from that of others, his predecessors in his peculiar pursuit. But logic sits in judgment on the sufficiency of that observation and experience to justify his rules, and on the sufficiency of his rules to justify his conduct. It does not give him proofs, but teaches him what makes them proofs, and how he is to judge of them. It does not teach that any particular fact proves any other, but points out to what conditions all facts must conform, in order that they may prove other facts. To decide whether any given fact fulfills these conditions, or whether facts can be found which fulfill them in a given case, belongs exclusively to the particular art or science or to our knowledge of the particular subject.

It is in this sense that logic is, what it was so expressively called by the schoolmen and by Bacon, *ars artium;* the science of science itself. All science consists of data and conclusions from those data, of proofs and what they prove: now logic points out what relations must subsist between data and whatever can be concluded from them, between proof and every thing which it can prove. If there be any such indispensable relations, and if these can be precisely determined, every particular branch of science, as well as every individual in the guidance of his conduct, is bound to conform to those relations, under the penalty of making false inferences—of drawing conclusions which are not grounded in the realities of things. Whatever has at any time been concluded justly, whatever knowledge has been acquired otherwise than by immediate intuition, depended on the observance of the laws which it is the province of logic to investigate. If the conclusions are just, and the knowledge real, those laws, whether known or not, have been observed.

6

We need not, therefore, seek any further for a solution of the question, so often agitated, respecting the utility of logic. If a science of logic exists, or is capable of existing, it must be useful. If there be rules to which every mind consciously or unconsciously conforms in every instance in which it infers rightly, there seems little necessity for discussing whether a person is more likely to observe those rules, when he knows the rules, than when he is unacquainted with them.

A science may undoubtedly be brought to a certain, not inconsiderable, stage of advancement, without the application of any other logic to it than what all persons, who are said to have a sound understanding, acquire empirically in the course of their studies. Mankind judged of evidence, and often correctly, before logic was a science, or they never could have made it one. And they executed great mechanical works before they understood the laws of mechanics. But there are limits both to what mechanicians can do without principles of mechanics, and to what thinkers can do without principles of logic. A few individuals, by extraordinary genius, or by the accidental acquisition of a good set of intellectual habits, may work without principles in the same way, or nearly the same way, in which they would have worked if they had been in possession of principles. But the bulk of mankind require either to understand the theory of what they are doing, or to have rules laid down for them by those who have understood the theory. In the progress of science from its easiest to its more difficult problems, each great step in advance has usually had either as its precursor, or as its accompaniment and necessary condition, a corresponding improvement in the notions and principles of logic received among the most advanced thinkers. And if several of the more difficult sciences are still in so defective a state; if not only so little is proved, but disputation has not terminated even about the little which seemed to be so; the reason perhaps is, that men's logical notions have not yet acquired the degree of extension, or of accuracy, requisite for the estimation of the evidence proper to those particular departments of knowledge.

7

Logic, then, is the science of the operations of the understanding which are subservient to the estimation of evidence: both the process itself of advancing from known truths to unknown, and all other intellectual operations in so far as auxiliary to this. It includes, therefore, the operation of Naming; for language is an instrument of thought, as well as a means of communicating our thoughts. It includes, also, Definition, and Classification. For, the use of these operations (putting all other minds than one's own out of consideration) is to serve not only for keeping our evidences and the conclusions from them permanent and readily accessible in the memory, but for so marshalling the facts which we may at any time be engaged in investigating, as to enable us to perceive more clearly what evidence there is, and to judge with fewer chances of error whether it be sufficient. These, therefore, are operations specially instrumental to the estimation of evidence, and, as such, are within the province of Logic. There are other more elementary processes, concerned in all thinking, such as Conception, Memory, and the like; but of these it is not necessary that Logic should take any peculiar cognizance, since they have no special connection with the problem of Evidence, further than that, like all other problems addressed to the understanding, it presupposes them.

Our object, then, will be, to attempt a correct analysis of the intellectual process called Reasoning or Inference, and of such other mental operations as are intended to facilitate this: as well as, on the foundation of this analysis, and *pari passu* with it, to bring together or frame a set of rules or canons for testing the sufficiency of any given evidence to prove any given proposition.

With respect to the first part of this undertaking, I do not attempt to decompose the mental operations in question into their ultimate elements. It is enough if the analysis as far as it goes is correct, and if it goes far enough for the practical purposes of logic considered as an art. The separation of a complicated phenomenon into its component parts is not like a connected and interdependent chain of proof. If one link of an argument breaks, the whole drops to the ground; but one step toward an analysis holds good and has an independent value, though we should never be able to make a second. The results which have been obtained by analytical chemistry are not the less valuable, though it should be discovered that all which we now call simple substances are really compounds. All other things are at any rate compounded of those elements: whether the elements themselves admit of decomposition, is an important inquiry, but does not affect the certainty of the science up to that point.

I shall, accordingly, attempt to analyze the process of inference, and the processes subordinate to inference, so far only as may be requisite for ascertaining the difference between a correct and an incorrect performance of those processes. The reason for thus limiting our design, is evident. It has been said by objectors to logic, that we do not learn to use our muscles by studying their anatomy. The fact is not quite fairly stated; for if the action of any of our muscles were vitiated by local weakness, or other physical defect, a knowledge of their anatomy might be very necessary for effecting a cure. But we should be justly liable to the criticism involved in this objection, were we, in a treatise on logic, to carry the analysis of the reasoning process beyond the point at which any inaccuracy which may have crept into it must become visible. In learning bodily exercises (to carry on the same illustration) we do, and must, analyze the bodily motions so far as is necessary for distinguishing those which ought to be performed from those which ought not. To a similar extent, and no further, it is necessary that the logician should analyze the mental processes with which Logic is concerned. Logic has no interest in carrying the analysis beyond the point at which it becomes apparent whether the operations have in any individual case been rightly or wrongly performed: in the same manner as the science of music teaches us to discriminate between musical notes, and to know the combinations of which they are susceptible, but not what number of vibrations in a second correspond to each; which, though useful to be known, is use-

ful for totally different purposes. The extension of Logic as a Science is determined by its necessities as an Art: whatever it does not need for its practical ends, it leaves to the larger science which may be said to correspond, not to any particular art, but to art in general; the science which deals with the constitution of the human faculties, and to which, in the part of our mental nature which concerns Logic, as well as in all other parts, it belongs to decide what are ultimate facts, and what are resolvable into other facts. And I believe it will be found that most of the conclusions arrived at in this work have no necessary connection with any particular views respecting the ulterior analysis. Logic is common ground on which the partisans of Hartley and of Reid, of Locke and of Kant, may meet and join hands. Particular and detached opinions of all these thinkers will no doubt occasionally be controverted, since all of them were logicians as well as metaphysicians; but the field on which their principal battles have been fought, lies beyond the boundaries of our science.

It can not, indeed, be pretended that logical principles can be altogether irrelevant to those more abstruse discussions; nor is it possible but that the view we are led to take of the problem which logic proposes, must have a tendency favorable to the adoption of some one opinion, on these controverted subjects, rather than another. For metaphysics, in endeavoring to solve its own peculiar problem, must employ means, the validity of which falls under the cognizance of logic. It proceeds, no doubt, as far as possible, merely by a closer and more attentive interrogation of our consciousness, or more properly speaking, of our memory; and so far is not amenable to logic. But wherever this method is insufficient to attain the end of its inquiries, it must proceed, like other sciences, by means of evidence. Now, the moment this science begins to draw inferences from evidence, logic becomes the sovereign judge whether its inferences are well grounded, or what other inferences would be so.

This, however, constitutes no nearer or other relation between logic and metaphysics, than that which exists between logic and every other science. And I can conscientiously affirm that no one proposition laid down in this work has been adopted for the sake of establishing, or with any reference to its fitness for being employed in establishing, preconceived opinions in any department of knowledge or of inquiry on which the speculative world is still undecided.

THE FIXATION

OF BELIEF*

CHARLES SANDERS PEIRCE (1839–1914) is regarded by many as the most profound and original of American philosophers. His genius was not recognized in his own lifetime, and he never held a permanent university position. Peirce published a number of philosophical articles during his career, but no book on philosophy. Much of his best work remained unpublished until the publication of the *Collected Papers of C. S. Peirce* (8 volumes: 1931-58).

Few persons care to study logic, because everybody conceives himself to be proficient enough in the art of reasoning already. But I observe that this satisfaction is limited to one's own ratiocination, and does not extend to that of other men.

We come to the full possession of our power of drawing inferences the last of all our faculties, for it is not so much a natural gift as a long and difficult art. The history of its practice would make a grand subject for a book. The medieval schoolman, following the Romans, made logic the earliest of a boy's studies after grammar, as being very easy. So it was as they understood it. Its fundamental principle, according to them, was, that all knowledge rests on either authority or reason; but that whatever is deduced by reason depends ultimately on a premise derived from authority. Accordingly, as soon as a boy was perfect in the syllogistic procedure, his intellectual kit of tools was held to be complete.

To Roger Bacon, that remarkable mind who in the middle of the thirteenth century was almost a scientific man, the schoolmen's conception of reasoning appeared only an obstacle to truth. He saw that experience alone teaches anything— a proposition which to us seems easy to understand, because a distinct conception of experience has been handed down to us from former generations; which to him also seemed perfectly clear, because its difficulties had not yet unfolded themselves. Of all kinds of experience, the best, he thought, was interior illumination, which teaches many things about Nature which the external senses could never discover, such as the transubstantiation of bread.

Four centuries later, the more celebrated Bacon, in the first book of his

* Reprinted by permission of the publishers from Charles Hartshorne and Paul Weiss, editors, *Collected Papers of Charles Sanders Peirce*, Volume V (Cambridge, Mass.: Harvard University Press). Copyright 1932, 1960 by The President and Fellows of Harvard College. This essay was originally published in *Popular Science Monthly*, 1877.

"Novum Organum," gave his clear account of experience as something which must be opened to verification and re-examination. But, superior as Lord Bacon's conception is to earlier notions, a modern reader who is not in awe of his grandiloquence is chiefly struck by the inadequacy of his view of scientific procedure. That we have only to make some crude experiments, to draw up briefs of the results in certain blank forms, to go through these by rule, checking off everything disproved and setting down the alternatives, and that thus in a few years physical science would be finished up—what an idea! "He wrote on science like a Lord Chancellor," indeed.

The early scientists, Copernicus, Tycho Brahe, Kepler, Galileo and Gilbert, had methods more like those of their modern brethren. Kepler undertook to draw a curve through the places of Mars; and his greatest service to science was in impressing on men's minds that this was the thing to be done if they wished to improve astronomy; that they were not to content themselves with inquiring whether one system of epicycles was better than another but that they were to sit down by the figures and find out what the curve, in truth, was. He accomplished this by his incomparable energy and courage, blundering along in the most inconceivable way (to us), from one irrational hypothesis to another, until, after trying twenty-two of these, he fell, by the mere exhaustion of his invention, upon the orbit which a mind well furnished with the weapons of modern logic would have tried almost at the outset.

In the same way, every work of science great enough to be remembered for a few generations affords some exemplification of the defective state of the art of reasoning of the time when it was written; and each chief step in science has been a lesson in logic. It was so when Lavoisier and his contemporaries took up the study of Chemistry. The old chemist's maxim had been, "Lege, lege, lege, labora, ora, et relege." Lavoisier's method was not to read and pray, not to dream that some long and complicated chemical process would have a certain effect, to put it into practice with dull patience, after its inevitable failure, to dream that with some modification it would have another result, and to end by publishing the last dream as a fact: his way was to carry his mind into his laboratory, and to make of his alembics and cucurbits instruments of thought, giving a new conception of reasoning as something which was to be done with one's eyes open, by manipulating real things instead of words and fancies . . .

The object of reasoning is to find out, from the consideration of what we already know, something else which we do not know. Consequently, reasoning is good if it be such as to give a true conclusion from true premises, and not otherwise. Thus, the question of validity is purely one of fact and not of thinking. A being the premises and B being the conclusion, the question is, whether these facts are really so related that if A is, B is. If so, the inference is valid; if not, not. It is not in the least the question whether, when the premises are accepted by the mind, we feel an impulse to accept the conclusion also. It is true that we do generally reason correctly by nature. But that is an accident; the true conclusion would remain true if we had no impulse to accept it; and the false one would remain false, though we could not resist the tendency to believe in it.

We are, doubtless, in the main logical animals, but we are not perfectly so. Most of us, for example, are naturally more sanguine and hopeful than logic would justify. We seem to be so constituted that in the absence of any facts to go upon we are happy and self-satisfied; so that the effect of experience is continually to counteract our hopes and aspirations. Yet a lifetime of the application of this corrective does not usually eradicate our sanguine disposition. Where hope is unchecked by any experience, it is likely that our optimism is extravagant. Logicality in regard to practical matters is the most useful quality an animal can possess, and might, therefore, result from the action of natural selection; but outside of these it is probably of more advantage to the animal to have his mind filled with pleasing and encouraging visions, independently of their truth; and thus, upon unpractical subjects, natural selection might occasion a fallacious tendency of thought.

That which determines us, from given premises, to draw one inference rather than another, is some habit of mind, whether it be constitutional or acquired. The habit is good or otherwise, according as it produces true conclusions from true premises or not; and an inference is regarded as valid or not, without reference to the truth or falsity of its conclusion specially, but according as the habit which determines it is such as to produce true conclusions in general or not. The particular habit of mind which governs this or that inference may be formulated in a proposition whose truth depends on the validity of the inferences which the habit determines; and such a formula is called a *guiding principle* of inference. Suppose, for example, that we observe that a rotating disk of copper quickly comes to rest when placed between the poles of a magnet, and we infer that this will happen with every disk of copper. The guiding principle is, that what is true of one piece of copper is true of another. Such a guiding principle with regard to copper would be much safer than with regard to many other substances—brass, for example.

A book might be written to signalize all the most important of these guiding principles of reasoning. It would probably be, we must confess, of no service to a person whose thought is directed wholly to practical subjects, and whose activity moves along thoroughly beaten paths. The problems which present themselves to such a mind are matters of routine which he has learned once for all to handle in learning his business. But let a man venture into an unfamiliar field, or where his results are not continually checked by experience, and all history shows that the most masculine intellect will ofttimes lose his orientation and waste his efforts in directions which bring him no nearer to his goal, or even carry him entirely astray. He is like a ship on the open sea, with no one on board who understands the rules of navigation. And in such a case some general study of the guiding principles of reasoning would be sure to be found useful.

The subject could hardly be treated, however, without being first limited; since almost any fact may serve as a guiding principle. But it so happens that there exists a division among facts, such that in one class are all those which are absolutely essential as guiding principles, while in the other are all those which have any other interest as objects of research. This division is between those which are necessarily taken for granted in asking whether a certain conclusion follows from certain premises, and those which are not implied in that question. A moment's thought will show that a variety of facts are already assumed when the logical question is first asked. It is implied, for instance, that there are such states of mind as doubt and belief—that a passage from one to the other is possible, the object of thought remaining the same, and that this transition is subject to some rules which all minds are alike bound by. As these are facts which we must already know before we can have any clear conception of reasoning at all, it cannot be supposed to be any longer of much interest to inquire into their truth or falsity. On the other hand, it is easy to believe that those rules of reasoning which are deduced from the very idea of the process are the ones which are the most essential; and, indeed, that so long as it conforms to these it will, at least, not lead to false conclusions from true premises. In point of fact, the importance of what may be deduced from the assumptions involved in the logical question turns out to be greater than might be supposed, and this for reasons which it is difficult to exhibit at the outset. The only one which I shall here mention is, that conceptions which are really products of logical reflections, without being readily seen to be so, mingle with our ordinary thoughts, and are frequently the causes of great confusion. This is the case, for example, with the conception of quality. A quality as such is never an object of observation. We can see that a thing is blue or green, but the quality of being blue and the quality of being green are not things which we see; they are products of logical reflections. The truth is, that common-sense, or thought as it first emerges above the level of the narrowly practical, is deeply imbued with that bad logical quality to which the epithet *metaphysical* is commonly applied; and nothing can clear it up but a severe course of logic.

We generally know when we wish to ask a question and when we wish to pronounce a judgment, for there is a dissimilarity between the sensation of doubting and that of believing.

But this is not all which distinguishes doubt from belief. There is a practical difference. Our beliefs guide our desires and shape our actions. The Assassins, or followers of the Old Man of the Mountain, used to rush into death at his least command, because they believed that obedience to him would insure everlasting felicity. Had they doubted this, they would not have acted as they did. So it is with every belief, according to its degree. The feeling of believing is a more or less sure indication of there being established in our nature some habit which will determine our actions. Doubt never has such an effect.

Nor must we overlook a third point of difference. Doubt is an uneasy and dissatisfied state from which we struggle to free ourselves and pass into the state of belief; while the latter is a calm and satisfactory state which we do not wish to avoid, or to change to a belief in anything else. On the contrary, we cling tenaciously, not merely to believing, but to believing just what we do believe.

Thus, both doubt and belief have positive effects upon us, though very different ones. Belief does not make us act at once, but puts us into such a condition that we shall behave in a certain way, when the occasion arises. Doubt has not the least effect of this sort, but stimulates us to action until it is destroyed. This reminds us of the irritation of a nerve and the reflex action produced thereby; while for the analogue of belief, in the nervous system, we must look to what are called nervous associations—for example, to that habit of the nerves in consequence of which the smell of a peach will make the mouth water.

The irritation of doubt causes a struggle to attain a state of belief. I shall term this struggle *inquiry,* though it must be admitted that this is sometimes not a very apt designation.

The irritation of doubt is the only immediate motive for the struggle to attain belief. It is certainly best for us that our beliefs should be such as may truly guide our actions so as to satisfy our desires; and this reflection will make us reject any belief which does not seem to have been so formed as to insure this result. But it will only do so by creating a doubt in the place of that belief. With the doubt, therefore, the struggle begins, and with the cessation of doubt it ends. Hence, the sole object of inquiry is the settlement of opinion. We may fancy that this is not enough for us, and that we seek not merely an opinion, but a true opinion. But put this fancy to the test, and it proves groundless; for as soon as a firm belief is reached we are entirely satisfied, whether the belief be false or true. And it is clear that nothing out of the sphere of our knowledge can be our object, for nothing which does not affect the mind can be a motive for a mental effort. The most that can be maintained is, that we seek for a belief that we shall *think* to be true. But we think each one of our beliefs to be true, and, indeed, it is mere tautology to say so.

That the settlement of opinion is the sole end of inquiry is a very important proposition. It sweeps away, at once, various vague and erroneous conceptions of proof. A few of these may be noticed here.

1. Some philosophers have imagined that to start an inquiry it was only necessary to utter a question or set it down on paper, and have even recommended us to begin our studies with questioning everything! But the mere putting of a proposition into the interrogative form does not stimulate the mind to any struggle after belief. There must be a real and living doubt, and without this all discussion is idle.

2. It is a very common idea that a demonstration must rest on some ultimate and absolutely indubitable propositions. These, according to one school, are first principles of a general nature; according to another, are first sensations. But, in point of fact, an inquiry, to have that completely satisfactory result called demonstration, has only to start with propositions perfectly free from all actual doubt. If the premises are not in fact doubted at all, they cannot be more satisfactory than they are.

3. Some people seem to love to argue a point after all the world is fully convinced of it. But no further advance can be made. When doubt ceases, mental action on the subject comes to an end; and, if it did go on, it would be without a purpose.

If the settlement of opinion is the sole object of inquiry, and if belief is of the nature of a habit, why should we not attain the desired end, by taking any answer to a question, which we may fancy, and constantly reiterating it to ourselves, dwelling on all which may conduce to that belief, and learning to turn with contempt and hatred from anything which might disturb it? This simple and direct method is really pursued by many men. I remember once being entreated not to read a certain newspaper lest it might change my opinion upon free-trade. "Lest I might be entrapped by its fallacies and misstatements," was the form of expression. "You are not," my friend said, "a special student of political economy. You might, therefore, easily be deceived by fallacious arguments upon the subject. You might, then, if you read this paper, be led to believe in protection. But you admit that free-trade is the true doctrine; and you do not wish to believe what is not true." I have often known this system to be deliberately adopted. Still oftener, the instinctive dislike of an undecided state of mind, exaggerated into a vague dread of doubt, makes men cling spasmodically to the views they already take. The man feels that, if he only holds to his belief without wavering, it will be entirely satisfactory. Nor can it be denied that a steady and immovable faith yields great peace of mind. It may, indeed, give rise to inconveniences, as if a man should resolutely continue to believe that fire would not burn him, or that he would be eternally damned if he received his *ingesta* otherwise than through a stomach-pump. But then the man who adopts this method will not allow that its inconveniences are greater than its advantages. He will say. "I hold steadfastly to the truth and the truth is always wholesome." And in many cases it may very well be that the pleasure he derives from his calm faith overbalances any inconveniences resulting from its deceptive character. Thus if it be true that death is annihilation then the man who believes that he will certainly go straight to heaven when he dies, provided he have fulfilled certain simple observances in this life, has a cheap pleasure which will not be followed by the least disappointment. A similar consideration seems to have weight with many persons in religious topics, for we frequently hear it said, "Oh, I could not believe so-and-so, because I should be wretched if I did." When an ostrich buries its head in the sand as danger approaches, it very likely takes the happiest course. It hides the danger, and then calmly says there is no danger; and, if it feels perfectly sure there is none, why should it raise its head to see? A man may go through life, systematically keeping out of view all that might cause a change in his opinions, and if he only succeeds—basing his method, as he does, on two fundamental psychological laws—I do not see what can be said against his doing so. It would be an egotistical impertinence to object that his procedure is irrational, for that only amounts to saying that his method of settling belief is not ours. He does not propose to himself to be rational, and indeed, will often talk with scorn of man's weak and illusive reason. So let him think as he pleases.

But this method of fixing belief, which may be called the method of tenacity, will be unable to hold its ground in practice. The social impulse is against it.

The man who adopts it will find that other men think differently from him, and it will be apt to occur to him in some saner moment that their opinions are quite as good as his own, and this will shake his confidence in his belief. This conception, that another man's thought or sentiment may be equivalent to one's own, is a distinctly new step, and a highly important one. It arises from an impulse too strong in man to be suppressed, without danger of destroying the human species. Unless we make ourselves hermits, we shall necessarily influence each other's opinions; so that the problem becomes how to fix belief, not in the individual merely, but in the community.

Let the will of the state act, then, instead of that of the individual. Let an institution be created which shall have for its object to keep correct doctrines before the attention of the people, to reiterate them perpetually, and to teach them to the young; having at the same time power to prevent contrary doctrines from being taught, advocated, or expressed. Let all possible causes of a change of mind be removed from men's apprehensions. Let them be kept ignorant, lest they should learn of some reason to think otherwise than they do. Let their passions be enlisted, so that they may regard private and unusual opinions with hatred and horror. Then, let all men who reject the established belief be terrified into silence. Let the people turn out and tar-and-feather such men, or let inquisitions be made into the manner of thinking of suspected persons, and, when they are found guilty of forbidden beliefs, let them be subjected to some signal punishment. When complete agreement could not otherwise be reached, a general massacre of all who have not thought in a certain way has proved a very effective means of settling opinion in a country. If the power to do this be wanting, let a list of opinions be drawn up, to which no man of the least independence of thought can assent, and let the faithful be required to accept all these propositions, in order to segregate them as radically as possible from the influence of the rest of the world.

This method has, from the earliest times, been one of the chief means of upholding correct theological and political doctrines, and of preserving their universal or catholic character. In Rome, especially, it has been practised from the days of Numa Pompilius to those of Pius Nonus. This is the most perfect example in history; but wherever there is a priesthood—and no religion has been without one—this method has been more or less made use of. Wherever there is an aristocracy, or a guild, or any association of a class of men whose interests depend, or are supposed to depend, on certain propositions, there will be inevitably found some traces of this natural product of social feeling. Cruelties always accompany this system; and when it is consistently carried out, they become atrocities of the most horrible kind in the eyes of any rational man. Nor should this occasion surprise, for the officer of a society does not feel justified in surrendering the interests of that society for the sake of mercy, as he might his own private interests. It is natural, therefore, that sympathy and fellowship should thus produce a most ruthless power.

In judging this method of fixing belief, which may be called the method of authority, we must, in the first place, allow its immeasurable mental and moral superiority to the method of tenacity. Its success is proportionately greater; and, in fact, it has over and over again worked the most majestic results. The mere structures of stone which it has caused to be put together—in Siam, for example, in Egypt, and in Europe—have many of them a sublimity hardly more than rivalled by the greatest works of Nature. And, except the geological epochs, there are no periods of time so vast as those which are measured by some of these organized faiths. If we scrutinize the matter closely, we shall find that there has not been one of their creeds which has remained always the same; yet the change is so slow as to be imperceptible during one person's life, so that individual belief remains sensibly fixed. For the mass of mankind, then, there is perhaps no better method than this. If it is their highest impulse to be intellectual slaves, then slaves they ought to remain.

But no institution can undertake to regulate opinions upon every subject. Only the most important ones can be attended to, and on the rest men's minds must be left to the action of natural causes. This imperfection will be no source of weakness so long as men are in such a state of culture that one opinion does not influence another—that is, so long as they cannot put two and two together. But in the most priest-ridden states some individuals will be found who are raised above that condition. These men possess a wider sort of social feeling; they see that men in other countries and in other ages have held to very different doctrines from those which they themselves have been brought up to believe; and they cannot help seeing that it is the mere accident of their having been taught as they have, and of their having been surrounded with the manners and associations they have, that has caused them to believe as they do and not far differently. Nor can their candour resist the reflection that there is no reason to rate their own views at a higher value than those of other nations and other centuries; thus giving rise to doubts in their minds.

They will further perceive that such doubts as these must exist in their minds with reference to every belief which seems to be determined by the caprice either of themselves or of those who originated the popular opinions. The willful adherence to a belief, and the arbitrary forcing of it upon others, must, therefore. both be given up. A different new method of settling opinions must be adopted, that shall not only produce an impulse to believe, but shall also decide what proposition it is which is to be believed. Let the action of natural preferences be unimpeded, then, and under their influence let men, conversing together and regarding matters in different lights, gradually develop beliefs in harmony with natural causes. This method resembles that by which conceptions of art have been brought to maturity. The most perfect example of it is to be found in the history of metaphysical philosophy. Systems of this sort have not usually rested upon any observed facts, at least not in any great degree. They have been chiefly adopted because their fundamental propositions seemed "agreeable to reason." This is an apt expression; it does not mean that which agrees with experience, but that which we find ourselves inclined to believe. Plato, for example, finds it agreeable to reason that the distances of the celestial spheres from one another should be proportional to the different lengths of strings which produce harmonious chords. Many philosophers have been led to their main conclusions by considerations like this; but this is the lowest and least developed form which the method takes, for it is clear that another man might find Kepler's theory, that the celestial spheres are proportional to the inscribed and circumscribed spheres of the different regular solids, more agreeable to *his* reason. But the shock of opinions will soon lead men to rest on preferences of a far more universal nature. Take, for example, the doctrine that man only acts selfishly— that is, from the consideration that acting in one way will afford him more pleasure than acting in another. This rests on no fact in the world, but it has had a wide acceptance as being the only reasonable theory.

This method is far more intellectual and respectable from the point of view of reason than either of the others which we have noticed. But its failure has been the most manifest. It makes of inquiry something similar to the development of taste; but taste, unfortunately, is always more or less a matter of fashion, and accordingly metaphysicians have never come to any fixed agreement, but the pendulum has swung backward and forward between a more material and a more spiritual philosophy, from the earliest times to the latest. And so from this, which has been called the *a priori* method, we are driven, in Lord Bacon's phrase, to a true induction. We have examined into this *a priori* method as something which promised to deliver our opinions from their accidental and capricious element. But development, while it is a process which eliminates the effect of some casual circumstances, only magnifies that of others. This method, therefore, does not differ in a very essential way from that of authority. The government may not have lifted its finger to influence my convictions; I may have been left outwardly quite free to choose, we will say, between monogamy and polygamy, and, appealing to my conscience only, I may have concluded that the latter practice is in itself licentious. But when I come to see that the chief obstacle to the spread of Christianity among a people of as high culture as the Hindoos has been a conviction of the immorality of our way of treating women, I cannot help seeing that, though governments do not interfere, sentiments in their development will be very greatly determined by accidental causes. Now, there are some people, among whom I must suppose that my reader is to be found, who, when they see that any belief of theirs is determined by any circumstance extraneous to the facts, will from that moment not merely admit in words that that belief is doubtful, but will experience a real doubt of it, so that it ceases in some degree to be a belief.

To satisfy our doubts, therefore, it is necessary that a method should be found by which our beliefs may be caused by nothing human, but by some external permanency—by something upon which our thinking has no effect. Some mystics imagine that they have such a method in a private inspiration from on high. But that is only a form of the method of tenacity, in which the conception of truth as something public is not yet developed. Our external permanency would not be external, in our sense, if it was restricted in its influence to one individual. It must be something which affects, or might affect, every man. And, though these affections are necessarily as various as are individual conditions, yet the method must be such that the ultimate conclusion of every man shall be the same. Such is the method of science. Its fundamental hypothesis, restated in more familiar language, is this: There are Real things, whose characters are entirely independent of our opinions about them; those realities affect our senses according to regular laws, and, though our sensations are as different as are our relations to the objects, yet, by taking advantage of the laws of perception, we can ascertain by reasoning how things really are; and any man, if he have sufficient experience and he reason enough about it, will be led to the one True conclusion. The new conception here involved is that of Reality. It may be asked how I know that there are any realities. If this hypothesis is the sole support of my method of inquiry, my method of inquiry must not be used to support my hypothesis. The reply is this: (1) If investigation cannot be regarded

as proving that there are Real things, it at least does not lead to a contrary conclusion; but the method and the conception on which it is based remain ever in harmony. No doubts of the method, therefore, necessarily arise from its practice, as is the case with all the others. (2) The feeling which gives rise to any method of fixing belief is a dissatisfaction at two repugnant propositions. But here already is a vague concession that there is some *one* thing to which a proposition should conform. Nobody, therefore, can really doubt that there are realities, for, if he did, doubt would not be a source of dissatisfaction. The hypothesis, therefore, is one which every mind admits. So that the social impulse does not cause men to doubt it. (3) Everybody uses the scientific method about a great many things, and only ceases to use it when he does not know how to apply it. (4) Experience of the method has not led us to doubt it, but, on the contrary, scientific investigation has had the most wonderful triumphs in the way of settling opinion. These afford the explanation of my not doubting the method or the hypothesis which it supposes; and not having any doubt, nor believing that anybody else whom I could influence has, it would be the merest babble for me to say more about it. If there be anybody with a living doubt upon the subject, let him consider it. . . .

This is the only one of the four methods which presents any distinction of a right and a wrong way. If I adopt the method of tenacity, and shut myself out from all influences, whatever I think necessary to doing this, is necessary according to that method. So with the method of authority: the state may try to put down heresy by means which, from a scientific point of view, seem very ill-calculated to accomplish its purposes; but the only test *on that method* is what the state thinks; so that it cannot pursue the method wrongly. So with the *a priori* method. The very essence of it is to think as one is inclined to think. All metaphysicians will be sure to do that, however they may be inclined to judge each other to be perversely wrong. The Hegelian system recognizes every natural tendency of thought as logical, although it is certain to be abolished by counter-tendencies. Hegel thinks there is a regular system in the succession of these tendencies, in consequence of which, after drifting one way and the other for a long time, opinion will at last go right. And it is true that metaphysicians get the right ideas at last; Hegel's system of Nature represents tolerably the science of that day; and one may be sure that whatever scientific investigation has put out of doubt will presently receive *a priori* demonstration on the part of the metaphysicians. But with the scientific method the case is different. I may start with known and observed facts to proceed to the unknown; and yet the rules which I follow in doing so may not be such as investigation would approve. The test of whether I am truly following the method is not an immediate appeal to my feelings and purposes, but, on the contrary, itself involves the application of the method. Hence it is that bad reasoning as well as good reasoning is possible; and this fact is the foundation of the practical side of logic.

It is not to be supposed that the first three methods of settling opinion present no advantage whatever over the scientific method. On the contrary, each has some peculiar convenience of its own. The *a priori* method is distinguished for its comfortable conclusions. It is the nature of the process to adopt whatever belief we are inclined to, and there are certain flatteries to the vanity of man which we all believe by nature, until we are awakened from our pleasing dream by rough facts. The method of authority will always govern the mass of mankind; and those who wield the various forms of organized force in the state will never be convinced that dangerous reasoning ought not to be suppressed in some way. If liberty of speech is to be untrammelled from the grosser forms of constraint, then uniformity of opinion will be secured by a moral terrorism to which the respectability of society will give its thorough approval. Following the method of authority is the path of peace. Certain nonconformities are permitted; certain others (considered unsafe) are forbidden. These are different in different countries and in different ages; but, wherever you are, let it be known that you seriously hold a tabooed belief, and you may be perfectly sure of being treated with a cruelty less brutal but more refined than hunting you like a wolf. Thus, the greatest intellectual benefactors of mankind have never dared, and dare not now, to utter the whole of their thought; and thus a shade of *prima facie* doubt is cast upon every proposition which is considered essential to the security of society. Singularly enough, the persecution does not all come from without; but a man torments himself and is oftentimes most distressed at finding himself believing propositions which he has been brought up to regard with aversion. The peaceful and sympathetic man will, therefore, find it hard to resist the temptation to submit his opinions to authority. But most of all I admire the method of tenacity for its strength, simplicity, and directness. Men who pursue it are distinguished for their decision of character, which becomes very easy with such a mental rule. They do not waste time in trying to make up their minds what they want, but, fastening like lightning upon whatever alternative comes first, they hold it to the end, whatever happens, without an instant's irresolution. This is one of the splendid qualities which generally accompany brilliant, unlasting success. It is impossible not to envy the man who can dismiss reason, although we know how it must turn out at last.

Such are the advantages which the other methods of settling opinion have over scientific investigation. A man should consider well of them; and then he should consider that, after all, he wishes his opinions to coincide with the fact, and that there is no reason why the results of those three methods should do so. To bring about this effect is the prerogative of the method of science. Upon such considerations he has to make his choice —a choice which is far more than the adoption of any intellectual opinion, which is one of the ruling decisions of his life, to which, when once made, he is bound to adhere. The force of habit will sometimes cause a man to hold on to old beliefs, after he is in a condition to see that they have no sound basis. But reflection upon the state of the case will overcome these habits, and he ought to allow reflection its full weight. People sometimes shrink from doing this, having an idea that beliefs are wholesome which they cannot help feeling rest on nothing. But let such persons suppose an analogous though different case from their own. Let them ask themselves what they would say to a reformed Mussulman who should hesitate to give up his old notions in regard to the relations of the sexes; or to a reformed Catholic who should still shrink from reading the Bible. Would they not say that these persons ought to consider the matter fully, and

clearly understand the new doctrine, and then ought to embrace it, in its entirety? But, above all, let it be considered that what is more wholesome than any particular belief is integrity of belief, and that to avoid looking into the support of any belief from a fear that it may turn out rotten is quite as immoral as it is disadvantageous. The person who confesses that there is such a thing as truth, which is distinguished from falsehood simply by this, that if acted on it will carry us to the point we aim at and not astray, and then, though convinced of this, dares not know the truth and seeks to avoid it, is in a sorry state of mind indeed.

Yes, the other methods do have their merits: a clear logical conscience does cost something—just as any virtue, just as all that we cherish, costs us dear. But we should not desire it to be otherwise. The genius of a man's logical method should be loved and reverenced as his bride, whom he has chosen from all the world. He need not contemn the others; on the contrary, he may honour them deeply, and in doing so he only honours her the more. But she is the one that he has chosen, and he knows that he was right in making that choice. And having made it, he will work and fight for her, and will not complain that there are blows to take, hoping that there may be as many and as hard to give, and will strive to be the worthy knight and champion of her from the blaze of whose splendours he draws his inspiration and his courage.

THE APPLICATION OF
INTELLIGENCE*

JOHN DEWEY (1859–1952)   has had a greater influence upon the world of
practical affairs in the United States than any other professor of
philosophy. This is not accidental, for in all his writings Dewey regards philosophy as a human activity whose value lies in its social
impact. Greatly influenced by C. S. Pierce and William James, Dewey
developed his own type of pragmatism† that has become known as
instrumentalism, and wielded his instrumentalism to create new approaches to and new insights into all branches of philosophy, psychology, and educational theory.

Logic—like philosophy itself—suffers
from a curious oscillation. It is elevated
into the supreme and legislative science
only to fall into the trivial estate of
keeper of such statements as A is A and
the scholastic verses for the syllogistic
rules. It claims power to state the laws of
the ultimate structure of the universe, on
the ground that it deals with the laws of
thought which are the laws according to
which Reason has formed the world.
Then it limits its pretensions to laws of
correct reasoning which is correct even
though it leads to no matter of fact, or
even to material falsity. It is regarded by
the modern objective idealist as the adequate substitute for ancient ontological
metaphysics; but others treat it as that
branch of rhetoric which teaches profi-
ciency in argumentation. For a time a
superficial compromise equilibrium was
maintained wherein the logic of formal
demonstration which the Middle Ages extracted from Aristotle was supplemented
by an inductive logic of discovery of
truth that Mill extracted from the practice of scientific men. But students of
German philosophy, of mathematics, and
of psychology, no matter how much they
attacked one another, have made common cause in attack upon the orthodox
logics both of deductive proof and inductive discovery.

Logical theory presents a scene of
chaos. There is little agreement as to its
subject-matter, scope or purpose. This
disagreement is not formal or nominal
but affects the treatment of every topic.
Take such a rudimentary matter as the
nature of judgment. Reputable authority
can be quoted in behalf of every possible
permutation of doctrine. Judgment is the

* From John Dewey, *Reconstruction in Philosophy,* pp. 132–138, 155–166. Copyright 1920
by Henry Holt and Co., and reprinted by permission of Holt, Rinehart and Winston, Inc.
    † See footnote on page 3.

central thing in logic; and judgment is not logical at all, but personal and psychological. If logical, it is the primary function to which both conception and inference are subordinate; and it is an after-product from them. The distinction of subject and predicate is necessary, and it is totally irrelevant; or again, though it is found in some cases, it is not of great importance. Among those who hold that the subject-predicate relationship is essential, some hold that judgment is an analysis of something prior into them, and others assert that it is a synthesis of them into something else. Some hold that reality is always the subject of judgment, and others that "reality" is logically irrelevant. Among those who deny that judgment is the attribution of predicate to subject, who regard it as a relation of elements, some hold that the relation is "internal," some that it is "external," and others that it is sometimes one and sometimes the other.

Unless logic is a matter of some practical account, these contrarieties are so numerous, so extensive, and so irreconcilable that they are ludicrous. If logic is an affair of practical moment, then these inconsistencies are serious. They testify to some deep-lying cause of intellectual disagreement and incoherency. In fact, contemporary logical theory is the ground upon which all philosophical differences and disputes are gathered together and focussed. How does the modification in the traditional conception of the relation of experience and reason, the real and ideal affect logic?

It affects, in the first place, the nature of logic itself. If thought or intelligence is the means of intentional reconstruction of experience, then logic, as an account of the procedure of thought, is not purely formal. It is not confined to laws of formally correct reasoning apart from truth of subject-matter. Neither, on the contrary, is it concerned with the inherent

thought structures of the universe, as Hegel's logic would have it; nor with the successive approaches of human thought to this objective thought structure as the logic of Lotze, Bosanquet, and other epistemological logicians would have it. If thinking is the way in which deliberate reorganization of experience is secured, then logic is such a clarified and systematized formulation of the procedures of thinking as will enable the desired reconstruction to go on more economically and efficiently. In language familiar to students, logic is both a science and an art; a science so far as it gives an organized and tested descriptive account of the way in which thought actually goes on; an art, so far as on the basis of this description it projects methods by which future thinking shall take advantage of the operations that lead to success and avoid those which result in failure.

Thus is answered the dispute whether logic is empirical or normative, psychological or regulative. It is both. Logic is based on a definite and executive supply of empirical material. Men have been thinking for ages. They have observed, inferred, and reasoned in all sorts of ways and to all kinds of results. Anthropology, the study of the origin of myth, legend and cult; linguistics and grammar; rhetoric and former logical compositions all tell us how men have thought and what have been the purposes and consequences of different kinds of thinking. Psychology, experimental and pathological, makes important contributions to our knowledge of how thinking goes on and to what effect. Especially does the record of the growth of the various sciences afford instruction in those concrete ways of inquiry and testing which have led men astray and which have proved efficacious. Each science from mathematics to history exhibits typical fallacious methods and typical efficacious methods in special subject-matters. Logical theory has thus a large, almost inexhaustible field of empirical study.

The conventional statement that experience only tells us how men have thought or *do* think, while logic is concerned with norms, with how men *should* think, is ludicrously inept. Some sorts of thinking are shown *by* experience to have got nowhere, or worse than nowhere—into systematized delusion and mistake. Others have proved in manifest experience that they lead to fruitful and enduring discoveries. It is precisely in experience that the different consequences of different methods of investigation and ratiocination are convincingly shown. The parrot-like repetition of the distinction between an empirical description of what is and a normative account of what should be merely neglects the most striking fact about thinking as it empirically is—namely, its flagrant exhibition of cases of failure and success—that is, of good thinking and bad thinking. Any one who considers this empirical manifestation will not complain of lack of material from which to construct a *regulative* art. The more study that is given to empirical records of actual thought, the more apparent becomes the connection between the specific features of thinking which have produced failure and success. Out of this relationship of cause and effect as it is empirically ascertained grow the norms and regulations of an art of thinking.

Mathematics is often cited as an example of purely normative thinking dependent upon *a priori* canons and supraempirical material. But it is hard to see how the student who approaches the matter historically can avoid the conclusion that the status of mathematics is as empirical as that of metallurgy. Men began with counting and measuring things just as they began with pounding and burning them. One thing, as common speech profoundly has it, led to another. Certain ways were successful—not merely in the immediately practical sense, but in the sense of being interesting, of arousing attention, of exciting attempts at improvement. The present-day mathematical logician may present the structure of mathematics as if it had sprung all at once from the brain of a Zeus whose anatomy is that of pure logic. But, nevertheless, this very structure is a product of long historic growth, in which all kinds of experiments have been tried, in which some men have struck out in this direction and some in that, and in which some exercises and operations have resulted in confusion and others in triumphant clarifications and fruitful growths; a history in which matter and methods have been constantly selected and worked over on the basis of empirical success and failure.

The structure of alleged normative *a priori* mathematics is in truth the crowned result of ages of toilsome experience. The metallurgist who should write on the most highly developed method of dealing with ores would not, in truth, proceed any differently. He too selects, refines, and organizes the methods which in the past have been found to yield the maximum of achievement. Logic is a matter of profound human importance precisely because it is empirically founded and experimentally applied. So considered, the problem of logical theory is none other than the problem of the possibility of the development and employment of intelligent method in inquiries concerned with deliberate reconstruction of experience. And it is only saying again in more specific form what has been said in general form to add that while such a logic has been developed in respect to mathematics and physical science, intelligent method, logic, is still far to seek in moral and political affairs.

. . .

Little time is left to speak of the account of the nature of truth given by the experimental and functional type of logic. This is less to be regretted because this account is completely a corollary from the nature of thinking and ideas. If the view held as to the latter is understood, the conception of truth follows as a matter of course. If it be not understood, any attempt to present the theory of truth is bound to be confusing, and the theory itself to seem arbitrary and absurd. *If ideas, meanings, conceptions, notions, theories, systems are instrumental to an active reorganization of the given environment, to a removal of some specific trouble and perplexity, then the test of their validity and value lies in accomplishing this work. If they succeed in their office, they are reliable, sound, valid, good, true. If they fail to clear up confusion, to eliminate defects, if they increase confusion, uncertainty and evil when they are acted upon, then are they false. Confirmation, corroboration, verification lie in works, consequences.* Handsome is that handsome does. By their fruits shall ye *know* them. That which guides us truly is true—demonstrated capacity for such guidance is precisely what is meant by truth. The adverb "truly" is more fundamental than either the adjective, true, or the noun, truth. An adverb expresses a way, a mode of acting. Now an idea or conception is a claim or injunction or plan to *act* in a certain way as the way to arrive at the clearing up of a specific situation. When the claim or pretension or plan is acted upon *it guides us truly or falsely;* it leads us to our end or away from it. Its active, dynamic function is the all-important thing about it, and in the quality of activity induced by it lies all its truth and falsity. The hypothesis that works is the *true* one; and *truth* is an abstract noun applied to the collection of cases, actual, foreseen and desired, that receive confirmation in their works and consequences.

So wholly does the worth of this conception of truth depend upon the correctness of the prior account of thinking that it is more profitable to consider why the conception gives offence than to expound it on its own account. Part of the reason why it has been found so obnoxious is doubtless its novelty and defects in its statement. Too often, for example, when truth has been thought of as satisfaction, it has been thought of as merely emotional satisfaction, a private comfort, a meeting of purely personal need. But the satisfaction in question means a satisfaction of the needs and conditions of the problem out of which the idea, the purpose and method of action, arises. It includes public and objective conditions. It is not to be manipulated by whim or personal idiosyncrasy. Again when truth is defined as utility, it is often thought to mean utility for some purely personal end, some profit upon which a particular individual has set his heart. So repulsive is a conception of truth which makes it a mere tool of private ambition and aggrandizement, that the wonder is that critics have attributed such a notion to sane men. As matter of fact, truth as utility means service in making just that contribution to reorganization in experience that the idea or theory claims to be able to make. The usefulness of a road is not measured by the degree in which it lends itself to the purposes of a highwayman. It is measured by whether it actually functions *as* a road, as a means of easy and effective public transportation and communication. And so with the serviceableness of an idea or hypothesis as a measure of its truth.

Turning from such rather superficial misunderstandings, we find, I think, the chief obstacle to the reception of this notion of truth in an inheritance from the classic tradition that has become so deeply engrained in men's minds. In just the degree in which existence is divided into two realms, a higher one of perfect being and a lower one of seeming, phenomenal, deficient reality, truth and falsity are thought of as fixed, ready-made static properties of things themselves. Supreme Reality is true Being, inferior and imperfect Reality is false Being. It makes claims to Reality which it cannot substantiate. It is deceitful, fraudulent, inherently unworthy of trust and belief. Beliefs are false not because they mislead us; they are not mistaken ways of thinking. They are false because they admit and adhere to false existences or subsistences. Other notions are true because they do have to do with true Being—with full and ultimate Reality. Such a notion lies at the back of the head of every one who has, in however an indirect way, been a recipient of the ancient and medieval tradition. This view is radically challenged by the pragmatic conception of truth, and the impossibility of reconciliation or compromise is, I think, the cause of the shock occasioned by the newer theory.

This contrast, however, constitutes the importance of the new theory as well as the unconscious obstruction to its acceptance. The older conception worked out practically to identify truth with authoritative dogma. A society that chiefly esteems order, that finds growth painful and change disturbing, inevitably seeks for a fixed body of superior truths upon which it may depend. It looks backward, to something already in existence, for the source and sanction of truth. It falls back upon what is antecedent, prior, original, *a priori,* for assurance. The thought of looking ahead, toward the eventual, toward consequences, creates uneasiness and fear. It disturbs the sense of rest that is attached to the ideas of fixed Truth already in existence. It puts a heavy burden of responsibility upon us for search, unremitting observation, scrupulous development of hypotheses and thoroughgoing testing. In physical matters men have slowly grown accustomed in all specific beliefs to identifying the true with the verified. But they still hesitate to recognize the implication of this identification and to derive the definition of truth from it. For while it is nominally agreed upon as a commonplace that definitions ought to spring from concrete and specific cases rather than be invented in the empty air and imposed upon particulars, there is a strange unwillingness to act upon the maxim in defining truth. To generalize the recognition that the true means the verified and means nothing else places upon men the responsibility for surrendering political and moral dogmas, and subjecting to the test of consequences their most cherished prejudices. Such a change involves a great change in the seat of authority and the methods of decision in society.

LOGIC AS THE ESSENCE
OF PHILOSOPHY*

BERTRAND RUSSELL was born in 1872. John Stuart Mill was his godfather. Many consider him to be the greatest philosopher of the twentieth century. Russell has made many contributions to logic, epistemology, history of philosophy, and philosophy of science. He is the only philosopher to have received both the Order of Merit and the Nobel Prize. His *Principia Mathematica* (1910–1913), coauthored with A. N. Whitehead, is one of the monumental works in the history of logic. His other significant books dealing with logic are: *The Principles of Mathematics* (1903), *Introduction to Mathematical Philosophy* (1918), *An Inquiry into Meaning and Truth* (1940). His *Human Knowledge* (1948) is a major contribution to epistemology and the philosophy of science. In addition Russell has written scores of other books dealing with philosophy, social and political issues, and education.

The topics we discussed in our first lecture, and the topics we shall discuss later, all reduce themselves, in so far as they are genuinely philosophical, to problems of logic. This is not due to any accident, but to the fact that every philosophical problem, when it is subjected to the necessary analysis and purification, is found either to be not really philosophical at all, or else to be, in the sense in which we are using the word, logical. But as the word "logic" is never used in the same sense by two different philosophers, some explanation of what I mean by the word is indispensable at the outset.

Logic, in the Middle Ages, and down to the present day in teaching, meant no more than a scholastic collection of technical terms and rules of syllogistic inference. Aristotle had spoken, and it was the part of humbler men merely to repeat the lesson after him. The trivial nonsense embodied in this tradition is still set in examinations, and defended by eminent authorities as an excellent "propædeutic," *i.e.* a training in those habits of solemn humbug which are so great a help in later life. But it is not this that I mean to praise in saying that all philosophy is logic. Ever since the beginning of the seventeenth century, all vigorous minds that have concerned themselves with inference have abandoned the mediæval tradition, and in one way or other have widened the scope of logic.

The first extension was the introduc-

* From Bertrand Russell, *Our Knowledge of the External World* (London: Allen & Unwin, Ltd., 1914), pp. 42–69. Reprinted by permission of the publisher.

tion of the inductive method by Bacon and Galileo—by the former in a theoretical and largely mistaken form, by the latter in actual use in establishing the foundations of modern physics and astronomy. This is probably the only extension of the old logic which has become familiar to the general educated public. But induction, important as it is when regarded as a method of investigation, does not seem to remain when its work is done: in the final form of a perfected science, it would seem that everything ought to be deductive. If induction remains at all, which is a difficult question, it will remain merely as one of the principles according to which deductions are effected. Thus the ultimate result of the introduction of the inductive method seems not the creation of a new kind of non-deductive reasoning, but rather the widening of the scope of deduction by pointing out a way of deducing which is certainly not syllogistic, and does not fit into the mediæval scheme.

The question of the scope and validity of induction is of great difficulty, and of great importance to our knowledge. Take such a question as, "Will the sun rise to-morrow?" Our first instinctive feeling is that we have abundant reason for saying that it will, because it has risen on so many previous mornings. Now, I do not myself know whether this does afford a ground or not, but I am willing to suppose that it does. The question which then arises is: What is the principle of inference by which we pass from past sunrises to future ones? The answer given by Mill is that the inference depends upon the law of causation. Let us suppose this to be true; then what is the reason for believing in the law of causation? There are broadly three possible answers: (1) that it is itself known *a priori;* (2) that it is a postulate; (3) that it is an empirical generalisation from past instances in which it has been found to hold. The theory that

causation is known *a priori* cannot be definitely refuted, but it can be rendered very unplausible by the mere process of formulating the law exactly, and thereby showing that it is immensely more complicated and less obvious than is generally supposed. The theory that causation is a postulate, *i.e.* that it is something which we choose to assert although we know that it is very likely false, is also incapable of refutation; but it is plainly also incapable of justifying any use of the law in inference. We are thus brought to the theory that the law is an empirical generalisation, which is the view held by Mill.

But if so, how are empirical generalisations to be justified? The evidence in their favour cannot be empirical, since we wish to argue from what has been observed to what has not been observed, which can only be done by means of some known relation of the observed and the unobserved; but the unobserved, by definition, is not known empirically, and therefore its relation to the observed, if known at all, must be known independently of empirical evidence. Let us see what Mill says on this subject.

According to Mill, the law of causation is proved by an admittedly fallible process called "induction by simple enumeration." This process, he says, "consists in ascribing the nature of general truths to all propositions which are true in every instance that we happen to know of."[1] As regards its fallibility, he asserts that "the precariousness of the method of simple enumeration is in an inverse ratio to the largeness of the generalisation. The process is delusive and insufficient, exactly in proportion as the subject-matter of the observation is special and limited in extent. As the sphere widens, this unscientific method becomes less and less liable to mislead; and the most universal class

[1] *Logic,* book iii., chapter iii., § 2.

of truths, the law of causation for instance, and the principles of number and of geometry, are duly and satisfactorily proved by that method alone, nor are they susceptible of any other proof."[2]

In the above statement, there are two obvious lacunæ: (1) How is the method of simple enumeration itself justified? (2) What logical principle, if any, covers the same ground as this method, without being liable to its failures? Let us take the second question first.

A method of proof which, when used as directed, gives sometimes truth and sometimes falsehood—as the method of simple enumeration does—is obviously not a valid method, for validity demands invariable truth. Thus, if simple enumeration is to be rendered valid, it must not be stated as Mill states it. We shall have to say, at most, that the data render the result *probable*. Causation holds, we shall say, in every instance we have been able to test; therefore it *probably* holds in untested instances. There are terrible difficulties in the notion of probability, but we may ignore them at present. We thus have what at least *may* be a logical principle, since it is without exception. If a proposition is true in every instance that we happen to know of, and if the instances are very numerous, then, we shall say, it becomes very probable, on the data, that it will be true in any further instance. This is not refuted by the fact that what we declare to be probable does not always happen, for an event may be probable on the data and yet not occur. It is, however, obviously capable of further analysis, and of more exact statement. We shall have to say something like this: that every instance of a proposition[3] being true increases the probability of its being true in a fresh instance, and that a sufficient number of favourable in-

stances will, in the absence of instances to the contrary, make the probability of the truth of a fresh instance approach indefinitely near to certainty. Some such principle as this is required if the method of simple enumeration is to be valid.

But this brings us to our other question, namely, how is our principle known to be true. Obviously, since it is required to justify induction, it cannot be proved by induction; since it goes beyond the empirical data, it cannot be proved by them alone; since it is required to justify all inferences from empirical data to what goes beyond them, it cannot itself be even rendered in any degree probable by such data. Hence, *if* it is known, it is not known by experience, but independently of experience. I do not say that any such principle is known: I only say that it is required to justify the inferences from experience which empiricists allow, and that it cannot itself be justified empirically.

A similar conclusion can be proved by similar arguments concerning any other logical principle. Thus logical knowledge is not derivable from experience alone, and the empiricist's philosophy can therefore not be accepted in its entirety, in spite of its excellence in many matters which lie outside logic.

Hegel and his followers widened the scope of logic in quite a different way—a way which I believe to be fallacious, but which requires discussion if only to show how their conception of logic differs from the conception which I wish to advocate. In their writings, logic is practically identical with metaphysics. In broad outline, the way this came about is as follows. Hegel believed that, by means of *a priori* reasoning, it could be shown that the world *must* have various important and interesting characteristics, since any world without these characteristics would be impossible and self-contradictory. Thus what he calls "logic" is an investigation of the nature of the universe, in so

---

[2] Book iii., chapter xxi., § 3.

[3] Or rather a propositional function.

far as this can be inferred merely from the principle that the universe must be logically self-consistent. I do not myself believe that from this principle alone anything of importance can be inferred as regards the existing universe. But, however that may be, I should not regard Hegel's reasoning, even if it were valid, as properly belonging to logic: it would rather be an application of logic to the actual world. Logic itself would be concerned rather with such questions as what self-consistency is, which Hegel, so far as I know, does not discuss. And though he criticises the traditional logic, and professes to replace it by an improved logic of his own, there is some sense in which the traditional logic, with all its faults, is uncritically and unconsciously assumed throughout his reasoning. It is not in the direction advocated by him, it seems to me, that the reform of logic is to be sought, but by a more fundamental, more patient, and less ambitious investigation into the presuppositions which his system shares with those of most other philosophers.

The way in which, as it seems to me, Hegel's system assumes the ordinary logic which it subsequently criticises, is exemplified by the general conception of "categories" with which he operates throughout. This conception is, I think, essentially a product of logical confusion, but it seems in some way to stand for the conception of "qualities of Reality as a whole." Mr Bradley has worked out a theory according to which, in all judgment, we are ascribing a predicate to Reality as a whole; and this theory is derived from Hegel. Now the traditional logic holds that every proposition ascribes a predicate to a subject, and from this it easily follows that there can be only one subject, the Absolute, for if there were two, the proposition that there were two would not ascribe a predicate to either. Thus, Hegel's doctrine, that philosophi-

cal propositions must be of the form, "the Absolute is such-and-such," depends upon the traditional belief in the universality of the subject-predicate form. This belief, being traditional, scarcely self-conscious, and not supposed to be important, operates underground, and is assumed in arguments which, like the refutation of relations, appear at first sight such as to establish its truth. This is the most important respect in which Hegel uncritically assumes the traditional logic. Other less important respects—though important enough to be the source of such essentially Hegelian conceptions as the "concrete universal" and the "union of identity in difference"—will be found where he explicitly deals with formal logic.[4]

There is quite another direction in which a large technical development of logic has taken place: I mean the direction of what is called logistic or mathematical logic. This kind of logic is mathematical in two different senses: it is itself a branch of mathematics, and it is the

[4] . . . Hegel's argument in this portion of his "Logic" depends throughout upon confusing the "is" of predication, as in "Socrates is mortal," with the "is" of identity, as in "Socrates is the philosopher who drank the hemlock." Owing to this confusion, he thinks that "Socrates" and "mortal" must be identical. Seeing that they are different, he does not infer, as others would, that there is a mistake somewhere, but that they exhibit "identity in difference." Again, Socrates is particular, "mortal" is universal. Therefore, he says, since Socrates is mortal, it follows that the particular is the universal—taking the "is" to be throughout expressive of identity. But to say "the particular is the universal" is self-contradictory. Again Hegel does not suspect a mistake, but proceeds to synthesise particular and universal in the individual, or concrete universal. This is an example of how, for want of care at the start, vast and imposing systems of philosophy are built upon stupid and trivial confusions, which, but for the almost incredible fact that they are unintentional, one would be tempted to characterise as puns.

logic which is specially applicable to other more traditional branches of mathematics. Historically, it began as *merely* a branch of mathematics: its special applicability to other branches is a more recent development. In both respects, it is the fulfilment of a hope which Leibniz cherished throughout his life, and pursued with all the ardour of his amazing intellectual energy. Much of his work on this subject has been published recently, after his discoveries had been remade by others; but none was published by him, because his results persisted in contradicting certain points in the traditional doctrine of the syllogism. We now know that on these points the traditional doctrine is wrong, but respect for Aristotle prevented Leibniz from realising that this was possible.[5]

The modern development of mathematical logic dates from Boole's *Laws of Thought* (1854). But in him and his successors, before Peano and Frege, the only thing really achieved, apart from certain details, was the invention of a mathematical symbolism for deducing consequences from the premisses which the newer methods shared with those of Aristotle. This subject has considerable interest as an independent branch of mathematics, but it has very little to do with real logic. The first serious advance in real logic since the time of the Greeks was made independently by Peano and Frege—both mathematicians. They both arrived at their logical results by an analysis of mathematics. Traditional logic regarded the two propositions, "Socrates is mortal" and "All men are mortal," as being of the same form;[6] Peano and Frege showed that they are utterly different in

form. The philosophical importance of logic may be illustrated by the fact that this confusion—which is still committed by most writers—obscured not only the whole study of the forms of judgment and inference, but also the relations of things to their qualities, of concrete existence to abstract concepts, and of the world of sense to the world of Platonic ideas. Peano and Frege, who pointed out the error, did so for technical reasons, and applied their logic mainly to technical developments; but the philosophical importance of the advance which they made is impossible to exaggerate.

Mathematical logic, even in its most modern form, is not *directly* of philosophical importance except in its beginnings. After the beginnings, it belongs rather to mathematics than to philosophy. Of its beginnings, which are the only part of it that can properly be called *philosophical* logic, I shall speak shortly. But even the later developments, though not directly philosophical, will be found of great indirect use in philosophising. They enable us to deal easily with more abstract conceptions than merely verbal reasoning can enumerate; they suggest fruitful hypotheses which otherwise could hardly be thought of; and they enable us to see quickly what is the smallest store of materials with which a given logical or scientific edifice can be constructed. Not only Frege's theory of number, . . . but the whole theory of physical concepts . . . is inspired by mathematical logic, and could never have been imagined without it.

In both these cases, and in many others, we shall appeal to a certain principle called "the principle of abstraction." This principle, which might equally well be called "the principle which dispenses with abstraction," and is one which clears away incredible accumulations of metaphysical lumber, was directly suggested by mathematical logic, and could hardly

[5] Cf. Couturat, *La Logique de Leibniz,* pp. 361, 386.

[6] It was often recognised that there was *some* difference between them, but it was not recognised that the difference is fundamental, and of very great importance.

have been proved or practically used without its help. The principle will be explained in our fourth lecture, but its use may be briefly indicated in advance. When a group of objects have that kind of similarity which we are inclined to attribute to possession of a common quality, the principle in question shows that membership of the group will serve all the purposes of the supposed common quality, and that therefore, unless some common quality is actually known, the group or class of similar objects may be used to replace the common quality, which need not be assumed to exist. In this and other ways, the indirect uses of even the later parts of mathematical logic are very great; but it is now time to turn our attention to its philosophical foundations.

In every proposition and in every inference there is, besides the particular subject-matter concerned, a certain *form,* a way in which the constituents of the proposition or inference are put together. If I say, "Socrates is mortal," "Jones is angry," "The sun is hot," there is something in common in these three cases, something indicated by the word "is." What is in common is the *form* of the proposition, not an actual constituent. If I say a number of things about Socrates —that he was an Athenian, that he married Xantippe, that he drank the hemlock —there is a common constituent, namely Socrates, in all the propositions I enunciate, but they have diverse forms. If, on the other hand, I take any one of these propositions and replace its constituents, one at a time, by other constituents, the form remains constant, but no constituent remains. Take (say) the series of propositions, "Socrates drank the hemlock," "Coleridge drank the hemlock," "Coleridge drank opium," "Coleridge ate opium." The form remains unchanged throughout this series, but all the constituents are altered. Thus form is not an-

other constituent, but is the way the constituents are put together. It is forms, in this sense, that are the proper object of philosophical logic.

It is obvious that the knowledge of logical forms is something quite different from knowledge of existing things. The form of "Socrates drank the hemlock" is not an existing thing like Socrates or the hemlock, nor does it even have that close relation to existing things that drinking has. It is something altogether more abstract and remote. We might understand all the separate words of a sentence without understanding the sentence: if a sentence is long and complicated, this is apt to happen. In such a case we have knowledge of the constituents, but not of the form. We may also have knowledge of the form without having knowledge of the constituents. If I say, "Rorarius drank the hemlock," those among you who have never heard of Rorarius (supposing there are any) will understand the form, without having knowledge of all the constituents. In order to understand a sentence, it is necessary to have knowledge both of the constituents and of the particular instance of the form. It is in this way that a sentence conveys information, since it tells us that certain known objects are related according to a certain known form. Thus some kind of knowledge of logical forms, though with most people it is not explicit, is involved in all understanding of discourse. It is the business of philosophical logic to extract this knowledge from its concrete integuments, and to render it explicit and pure.

In all inference, form alone is essential: the particular subject-matter is irrelevant except as securing the truth of the premises. This is one reason for the great importance of logical form. When I say, "Socrates was a man, all men are mortal, therefore Socrates was mortal," the connection of premises and conclusion does not in any way depend upon its being Socrates and man and mortality that I am mentioning. The general form of the inference may be expressed in some such words as, "If a thing has a certain property, and whatever has this property has a certain other property, then the thing in question also has that other property." Here no particular things or properties are mentioned: the proposition is absolutely general. All inferences, when stated fully, are instances of propositions having this kind of generality. If they seem to depend upon the subject-matter otherwise than as regards the truth of the premises, that is because the premises have not been all explicitly stated. In logic, it is a waste of time to deal with inferences concerning particular cases: we deal throughout with completely general and purely formal implications, leaving it to other sciences to discover when the hypotheses are verified and when they are not.

But the forms of propositions giving rise to inferences are not the simplest forms: they are always hypothetical, stating that if one proposition is true, then so is another. Before considering inference, therefore, logic must consider those simpler forms which inference presupposes. Here the traditional logic failed completely: it believed that there was only one form of simple proposition (*i.e.* of proposition not stating a relation between two or more other propositions), namely, the form which ascribes a predicate to a subject. This is the appropriate form in assigning the qualities of a given thing— we may say "This thing is round, and red, and so on." Grammar favours this form, but philosophically it is so far from universal that it is not even very common. If we say "this thing is bigger than that," we are not assigning a mere quality of "this," but a relation of "this" and "that." We might express the same fact by saying "That thing is smaller than this," where grammatically the subject is changed.

Thus propositions stating that two things have a certain relation have a different form from subject-predicate propositions, and the failure to perceive this difference or to allow for it has been the source of many errors in traditional metaphysics.

The belief or unconscious conviction that all propositions are of the subject-predicate form—in other words, that every fact consists in some thing having some quality—has rendered most philosophers incapable of giving any account of the world of science and daily life. If they had been honestly anxious to give such an account, they would probably have discovered their error very quickly; but most of them were less anxious to understand the world of science and daily life, than to convict it of unreality in the interests of a super-sensible "real" world. Belief in the unreality of the world of sense arises with irresistible force in certain moods—moods which, I imagine, have some simple physiological basis, but are none the less powerfully persuasive. The conviction born of these moods is the source of most mysticism and of most metaphysics. When the emotional intensity of such a mood subsides, a man who is in the habit of reasoning will search for logical reasons in favour of the belief which he finds in himself. But since the belief already exists, he will be very hospitable to any reason that suggests itself. The paradoxes apparently proved by his logic are really the paradoxes of mysticism, and are the goal which he feels his logic must reach if it is to be in accordance with insight. It is in this way that logic has been pursued by those of the great philosophers who were mystics— notably Plato, Spinoza, and Hegel. But since they usually took for granted the supposed insight of the mystic emotion, their logical doctrines were presented with a certain dryness, and were believed by their disciples to be quite independent of the sudden illumination from which they sprang. Nevertheless their origin clung to them, and they remained—to borrow a useful word from Mr Santayana—"malicious" in regard to the world of science and common sense. It is only so that we can account for the complacency with which philosophers have accepted the inconsistency of their doctrines with all the common and scientific facts which seem best established and most worthy of belief.

The logic of mysticism shows, as is natural, the defects which are inherent in anything malicious. While the mystic mood is dominant, the need of logic is not felt; as the mood fades, the impulse to logic reasserts itself, but with a desire to retain the vanishing insight, or at least to prove that it *was* insight, and that what seems to contradict it is illusion. The logic which thus arises is not quite disinterested or candid, and is inspired by a certain hatred of the daily world to which it is to be applied. Such an attitude naturally does not tend to the best results. Everyone knows that to read an author's books simply in order to refute him is not the way to understand him; and to read the book of Nature with a conviction that it is all illusion is just as unlikely to lead to understanding. If our logic is to find the common world intelligible, it must not be hostile, but must be inspired by a genuine acceptance such as is not usually to be found among metaphysicians.

Traditional logic, since it holds that all propositions have the subject-predicate form, is unable to admit the reality of relations: all relations, it maintains, must be reduced to properties of the apparently related terms. There are many ways of refuting this opinion; one of the easiest is derived from the consideration of what are called "asymmetrical" relations. In order to explain this, I will first explain two independent ways of classifying relations.

Some relations, when they hold between *A* and *B*, also hold between *B* and *A*. Such, for example, is the relation "brother or sister." If *A* is a brother or sister of *B*, then *B* is a brother or sister of *A*. Such again is any kind of similarity, say similarity of colour. Any kind of dissimilarity is also of this kind: if the colour of *A* is unlike the colour of *B*, then the colour of *B* is unlike the colour of *A*. Relations of this sort are called *symmetrical*. Thus a relation is symmetrical if, whenever it holds between *A* and *B*, it also holds between *B* and *A*.

All relations that are not symmetrical are called *non-symmetrical*. Thus "brother" is non-symmetrical, because if *A* is a brother of *B*, it may happen that *B* is a *sister* of *A*.

A relation is called *asymmetrical* when, if it holds between *A* and *B*, it *never* holds between *B* and *A*. Thus husband, father, grandfather, etc., are asymmetrical relations. So are *before, after, greater, above, to the right of*, etc. All the relations that give rise to series are of this kind.

Classification into symmetrical, asymmetrical, and merely non-symmetrical relations is the first of the two classifications we had to consider. The second is into transitive, intransitive, and merely non-transitive relations, which are defined as follows.

A relation is said to be *transitive*, if, whenever it holds between *A* and *B* and also between *B* and *C*, it holds between *A* and *C*. Thus *before, after, greater, above* are transitive. All relations giving rise to series are transitive, but so are many others. The transitive relations just mentioned were asymmetrical, but many transitive relations are symmetrical—for instance, equality in any respect, exact identity of colour, being equally numerous (as applied to collections), and so on.

A relation is said to be *non-transitive* whenever it is not transitive. Thus "brother" is non-transitive, because a brother of one's brother may be oneself. All kinds of dissimilarity are non-transitive.

A relation is said to be *intransitive* when, if *A* has the relation to *B*, and *B* to *C*, *A* never has it to *C*. Thus "father" is intransitive. So is such a relation as "one inch taller" or "one year later."

Let us now, in the light of this classification, return to the question whether all relations can be reduced to predications.

In the case of symmetrical relations—*i.e.* relations which, if they hold between *A* and *B,* also hold between *B* and *A*—some kind of plausibility can be given to this doctrine. A symmetrical relation which is transitive, such as equality, can be regarded as expressing possession of some common property, while one which is not transitive, such as inequality, can be regarded as expressing possession of different properties. But when we come to asymmetrical relations, such as before and after, greater and less, etc., the attempt to reduce them to properties becomes obviously impossible. When for example, two things are merely known to be unequal, without our knowing which is greater, we may say that the inequality results from their having different magnitudes, because inequality is a symmetrical relation; but to say that when one thing is *greater* than another, and not merely unequal to it, that means that they have different magnitudes, is formally incapable of explaining the facts. For if the other thing had been greater than the one, the magnitudes would also have been different, though the fact to be explained would not have been the same. Thus mere *difference* of magnitude is not *all* that is involved, since, if it were, there would be no difference between one thing being greater than another, and the other being greater than the one. We shall have to say that the one magnitude is *greater* than the other, and thus we shall have

failed to get rid of the relation "greater." In short, both possession of the same property and possession of different properties are *symmetrical* relations, and therefore cannot account for the existence of *asymmetrical* relations.

Asymmetrical relations are involved in all series—in space and time, greater and less, whole and part, and many others of the most important characteristics of the actual world. All these aspects, therefore, the logic which reduces everything to subjects and predicates is compelled to condemn as error and mere appearance. To those whose logic is not malicious, such a wholesale condemnation appears impossible. And in fact there is no reason except prejudice, so far as I can discover, for denying the reality of relations. When once their reality is admitted, all *logical* grounds for supposing the world of sense to be illusory disappear. If this is to be supposed, it must be frankly and simply on the ground of mystic insight unsupported by argument. It is impossible to argue against what professes to be insight, so long as it does not argue in its own favour. As logicians, therefore, we may admit the possibility of the mystic's world, while yet, so long as we do not have his insight, we must continue to study the everyday world with which we are familiar. But when he contends that our world is impossible, then our logic is ready to repel his attack. And the first step in creating the logic which is to perform this service is the recognition of the reality of relations.

Relations which have two terms are only one kind of relations. A relation may have three terms, or four, or any number. Relations of two terms, being the simplest, have received more attention than the others, and have generally been alone considered by philosophers, both those who accepted and those who denied the reality of relations. But other relations have their importance, and are indispensable in the solution of certain problems. Jealousy, for example, is a relation between three people. Professor Royce mentions the relation "giving": when A gives B to C, that is a relation of three terms. When a man says to his wife: "My dear, I wish you could induce Angelina to accept Edwin," his wish constitutes a relation between four people, himself, his wife, Angelina, and Edwin. Thus such relations are by no means recondite or rare. But in order to explain exactly how they differ from relations of two terms, we must embark upon a classification of the logical forms of facts, which is the first business of logic, and the business in which the traditional logic has been most deficient.

The existing world consists of many things with many qualities and relations. A complete description of the existing world would require not only a catalogue of the things, but also a mention of all their qualities and relations. We should have to know not only this, that, and the other thing, but also which was red, which yellow, which was earlier than which, which was between which two others, and so on. When I speak of a "fact," I do not mean one of the simple things in the world; I mean that a certain thing has a certain quality, or that certain things have a certain relation. Thus, for example, I should not call Napoleon a fact, but I should call it a fact that he was ambitious, or that he married Josephine. Now a fact, in this sense, is never simple, but always has two or more constituents. When it simply assigns a quality to a thing, it has only two constituents, the thing and the quality. When it consists of a relation between two things, it has three constituents, the things and the relation. When it consists of a relation between three things, it has four constituents, and so on. The constituents of facts, in the sense in which we are using the word "fact," are not other facts, but are

things and qualities or relations. When we say that there are relations of more than two terms, we mean that there are single facts consisting of a single relation and more than two things. I do not mean that one relation of two terms may hold between A and B, and also between A and C, as, for example, a man is the son of his father and also the son of his mother. This constitutes two distinct facts: if we choose to treat it as one fact, it is a fact which has facts for its constituents. But the facts I am speaking of have no facts among their constituents, but only things and relations. For example, when A is jealous of B on account of C, there is only one fact, involving three people; there are not two instances of jealousy, but only one. It is in such cases that I speak of a relation of three terms, where the simplest possible fact in which the relation occurs is one involving three things in addition to the relation. And the same applies to relations of four terms or five or any other number. All such relations must be admitted in our inventory of the logical forms of facts: two facts involving the same number of things have the same form, and two which involve different numbers of things have different forms.

Given any fact, there is an assertion which expresses the fact. The fact itself is objective, and independent of our thought or opinion about it; but the assertion is something which involves thought, and may be either true or false. An assertion may be positive or negative: we may assert that Charles I. was executed, or that he did not die in his bed. A negative assertion may be said to be a denial. Given a form of words which must be either true or false, such as "Charles I. died in his bed," we may either assert or deny this form of words: in the one case we have a positive assertion, in the other a negative one. A form of words which must be either true or false I shall call a *proposition*. Thus a proposition is the same as what may be significantly asserted or denied. A proposition which expresses what we have called a fact, *i.e.* which, when asserted, asserts that a certain thing has a certain quality, or that certain things have a certain relation, will be called an atomic proposition, because, as we shall see immediately, there are other propositions into which atomic propositions enter in a way analogous to that in which atoms enter into molecules. Atomic propositions, although, like facts, they may have any one of an infinite number of forms, are only one kind of propositions. All other kinds are more complicated. In order to preserve the parallelism in language as regards facts and propositions, we shall give the name "atomic facts" to the facts we have hitherto been considering. Thus atomic facts are what determine whether atomic propositions are to be asserted or denied.

Whether an atomic proposition, such as "this is red," or "this is before that," is to be asserted or denied can only be known empirically. Perhaps one atomic fact may sometimes be capable of being inferred from another, though I do not believe this to be the case; but in any case it cannot be inferred from premises no one of which is an atomic fact. It follows that, if atomic facts are to be known at all, some at least must be known without inference. The atomic facts which we come to know in this way are the facts of sense-perception; at any rate, the facts of sense-perception are those which we most obviously and certainly come to know in this way. If we knew all atomic facts, and also knew that there were none except those we knew, we should, theoretically, be able to infer all truths of whatever form.[7] Thus logic would then supply us

with the whole of the apparatus required. But in the first acquisition of knowledge concerning atomic facts, logic is useless. In pure logic, no atomic fact is ever mentioned: we confine ourselves wholly to forms, without asking ourselves what objects can fill the forms. Thus pure logic is independent of atomic facts; but conversely, they are, in a sense, independent of logic. Pure logic and atomic facts are the two poles, the wholly *a priori* and the wholly empirical. But between the two lies a vast intermediate region, which we must now briefly explore.

"Molecular" propositions are such as contain conjunctions—*if, or, and, unless,* etc.—and such words are the marks of a molecular proposition. Consider such an assertion as, "If it rains, I shall bring my umbrella." This assertion is just as capable of truth or falsehood as the assertion of an atomic proposition, but it is obvious that either the corresponding fact, or the nature of the correspondence with fact, must be quite different from what it is in the case of an atomic proposition. Whether it rains, and whether I bring my umbrella, are each severally matters of atomic fact, ascertainable by observation. But the connection of the two involved in saying that *if* the one happens, *then* the other will happen, is something radically different from either of the two separately. It does not require for its truth that it should actually rain, or that I should actually bring my umbrella; even if the weather is cloudless, it may still be true that I should have brought my umbrella if the weather had been different. Thus we have here a connection of two propositions, which does not depend upon whether they are to be asserted or denied, but only upon the second being inferable from the first. Such propositions,

[7] This perhaps requires modification in order to include such facts as beliefs and wishes, since such facts apparently contain propositions as components. Such facts,

though not strictly atomic, must be supposed included if the statement in the text is to be true.

therefore, have a form which is different from that of any atomic proposition.

Such propositions are important to logic, because all inference depends upon them. If I have told you that if it rains I shall bring my umbrella, and if you see that there is a steady downpour, you can infer that I shall bring my umbrella. There can be no inference except where propositions are connected in some such way, so that from the truth or falsehood of the one something follows as to the truth of falsehood of the other. It seems to be the case that we can sometimes know molecular propositions, as in the above instance of the umbrella, when we do not know whether the component atomic propositions are true or false. The *practical* utility of inference rests upon this fact.

The next kind of propositions we have to consider are *general* propositions, such as "all men are mortal," "all equilateral triangles are equiangular." And with these belong propositions in which the word "some" occurs, such as "some men are philosophers" or "some philosophers are not wise." These are the denials of general propositions, namely (in the above instances), of "all men are non-philosophers" and "all philosophers are wise." We will call propositions containing the word "some" *negative* general propositions, and those containing the word "all" *positive* general propositions. These propositions, it will be seen, begin to have the appearance of the propositions in logical text-books. But their peculiarity and complexity are not known to the text-books, and the problems which they raise are only discussed in the most superficial manner.

When we were discussing atomic facts, we saw that we should be able, theoretically, to infer all other truths by logic if we knew all atomic facts and also knew that there were no other atomic facts besides those we knew. The knowledge that there are no other atomic facts is positive general knowledge; it is the knowledge that "all atomic facts are known to me," or at least "all atomic facts are in this collection"—however the collection may be given. It is easy to see that general propositions, such as "all men are mortal," cannot be known by inference from atomic facts alone. If we could know each individual man, and know that he was mortal, that would not enable us to know that all men are mortal, unless we *knew* that those were all the men there are, which is a general proposition. If we knew every other existing thing throughout the universe, and knew that each separate thing was not an immortal man, that would not give us our result unless we *knew* that we had explored the whole universe, *i.e.* unless we knew "all things belong to this collection of things I have examined." Thus general truths cannot be inferred from particular truths alone, but must, if they are to be known, be either self-evident, or inferred from premisses of which at least one is a general truth. But all *empirical* evidence is of *particular* truths. Hence, if there is any knowledge of general truths at all, there must be *some* knowledge of general truths which is independent of empirical evidence, *i.e.* does not depend upon the data of sense.

The above conclusion, of which we had an instance in the case of the inductive principle, is important, since it affords a refutation of the older empiricists. They believed that all our knowledge is derived from the senses and dependent upon them. We see that, if this view is to be maintained, we must refuse to admit that we know any general propositions. It is perfectly possible logically that this should be the case, but it does not appear to be so in fact, and indeed no one would dream of maintaining such a view except a theorist at the last extremity. We must therefore admit that there is general knowledge not derived from sense, and that some of this knowledge is not obtained by inference but is primitive.

Such general knowledge is to be found in logic. Whether there is any such knowledge not derived from logic, I do not know; but in logic, at any rate, we have such knowledge. It will be remembered that we excluded from pure logic such propositions as, "Socrates is a man, all men are mortal, therefore Socrates is mortal," because *Socrates* and *man* and *mortal* are empirical terms, only to be understood through particular experience. The corresponding proposition in pure logic is: "If anything has a certain property, and whatever has this property has a certain other property, then the thing in question has the other property." This proposition is absolutely general: it applies to all things and all properties. And it is quite self-evident. Thus in such propositions of pure logic we have the self-evident general propositions of which we were in search.

A proposition such as "If Socrates is a man, and all men are mortal, then Socrates is mortal," is true in virtue of its *form* alone. Its truth, in this hypothetical form, does not depend upon whether Socrates actually is a man, nor upon whether in fact all men are mortal; thus it is equally true when we substitute other terms for *Socrates* and *man* and *mortal*. The general truth of which it is an instance is purely formal, and belongs to logic. Since it does not mention any particular thing, or even any particular quality or relation, it is wholly independent of the accidental facts of the existent world, and can be known, theoretically, without any experience of particular things or their qualities and relations.

Logic, we may say, consists of two parts. The first part investigates what propositions are and what forms they may have; this part enumerates the different kinds of atomic propositions, of molecular propositions, of general proposi-

tions, and so on. The second part consists of certain supremely general propositions, which assert the truth of all propositions of certain forms. This second part merges into pure mathematics, whose propositions all turn out, on analysis, to be such general formal truths. The first part, which merely enumerates forms, is the more difficult, and philosophically the more important; and it is the recent progress in this first part, more than anything else, that has rendered a truly scientific discussion of many philosophical problems possible.

The problem of the nature of judgment or belief may be taken as an example of a problem whose solution depends upon an adequate inventory of logical forms. We have already seen how the supposed universality of the subject-predicate form made it impossible to give a right analysis of serial order, and therefore made space and time unintelligible. But in this case it was only necessary to admit relations of two terms. The case of judgment demands the admission of more complicated forms. If all judgments were true, we might suppose that a judgment consisted in apprehension of a *fact,* and that the apprehension was a relation of a mind to the fact. From poverty in the logical inventory, this view has often been held. But it leads to absolutely insoluble difficulties in the case of error. Suppose I believe that Charles I. died in his bed. There is no objective fact "Charles I.'s death in his bed" to which I can have a relation of apprehension. Charles I. and death and his bed are objective, but they are not, except in my thought, put together as my false belief supposes. It is therefore necessary, in analysing a belief, to look for some other logical form than a two-term relation. Failure to realise this necessity has, in my opinion, vitiated almost everything that has hitherto been written on the theory of knowledge, making the problem of error insoluble and the difference between belief and perception inexplicable.

Modern logic, as I hope is now evident, has the effect of enlarging our abstract imagination, and providing an infinite number of possible hypotheses to be applied in the analysis of any complex fact. In this respect it is the exact opposite of the logic practised by the classical tradition. In that logic, hypotheses which seem *prima facie* possible are professedly proved impossible, and it is decreed in advance that reality must have a certain special character. In modern logic, on the contrary, while the *prima facie* hypotheses as a rule remain admissible, others, which only logic would have suggested, are added to our stock, and are very often found to be indispensable if a right analysis of the facts is to be obtained. The old logic put thought in fetters, while the new logic gives it wings. It has, in my opinion, introduced the same kind of advance into philosophy as Galileo introduced into physics, making it possible at last to see what kinds of problems may be capable of solution, and what kinds must be abandoned as beyond human powers. And where a solution appears possible, the new logic provides a method which enables us to obtain results that do not merely embody personal idiosyncrasies, but must comand the assent of all who are competent to form an opinion.

P A R T   T W O

The Syllogism

INTRODUCTION Historically, the most famous form of inference has been the syllogism. Explicitly discussed first by Aristotle, it has been employed and studied by logicians ever since. In the modern period the syllogism has been criticized on various different grounds: its validity, its value, and its presuppositions have all been challenged.

The first selection included in this Part comes from Aristotle's *Prior Analytics;* it explains the constituent parts of a syllogism, such as "premiss" and "term," and defines "syllogism" itself. The final paragraph of Chapter 1:

> That one term should be included in another as in a whole is the same as for the other to be predicated of all of the first. And we say that one term is predicated of all of another, whenever no instance of the subject can be found of which the other term cannot be asserted: "to be predicated of none" must be understood in the same way.

is the passage from which the *Dictum de Omni et Nullo* was primarily derived. That *Dictum* was long regarded as the basic principle underlying all syllogistic reasoning and as such is subjected to severe attack in the succeeding selection, which is taken from Mill's *Logic.*

Mill also raises the question whether the syllogism commits the fallacy of *Petitio principii* (begging the question, or reasoning in a circle). Mill defends the syllogism from this charge, but only at the cost of regarding every syllogism as an incompletely formulated inductive argument. This recalls what F. H. Bradley wrote in another connection:

> But if the friends of the syllogism resolve on this policy, I think they are friends it might pray to be saved from. It is better to bury a delusion and forget it than to insult its memory by retaining the name when the thing has perished.

Bradley attacks the syllogism by displaying asyllogistic inferences, though he does not call them that. Some of Bradley's criticisms here seem to be directed more against extravagant claims made for the syllogism than against the syllogism itself. Bradley too provides a critical discussion of the *Dictum de Omni et Nullo* and denies the very possibility of providing an exhaustive set of rules, models, or schemata for valid reasoning.

The humor and charm of Lewis Carroll's "What the Tortoise Said to Achilles" should not be allowed to distract the reader from the serious point of the essay. That point concerns not just the difference between premisses and rules of inference, but deftly exhibits the danger of infinite regression in attempts to justify syllogistic reasoning.

Russell discusses role of the syllogism in the history of logic, applauding it as a beginning but insisting that it is *only* a beginning. He criticizes some parts of syllogistic reasoning that are treated differently today, and argues both that the syllogism has been overestimated as a form of deduction and that deduction itself has been overestimated as a form of reasoning.

These selections show changing attitudes toward the syllogism as inductive science develops, as Idealist logic develops along with Idealist metaphysics, and as Symbolic Logic develops its asyllogistic patterns of inference. Each of these writers makes an important contribution to our understanding of the syllogism, its strengths and also its limits as a technique of reasoning.

DEFINITION OF THE

SYLLOGISM*

ARISTOTLE (384–322 B.C.). See page 8.

1

We must first state the subject of our inquiry and the faculty to which it belongs: its subject is demonstration and the faculty that carries it out demonstrative science. We must next define a premiss, a term, and a syllogism and the nature of a perfect and of an imperfect syllogism; and after that, the inclusion or non-inclusion of one term in another as in a whole, and what we mean by predicating one term of all, or none, of another.

A premiss then is a sentence affirming or denying one thing of another. This is either universal or particular or indefinite. By universal I mean the statement that something belongs to all or none of something else; by particular that it belongs to some or not to some or not to all; by indefinite that it does or does not belong, without any mark to show whether it is universal or particular, e.g. 'contraries are subjects of the same science', or 'pleasure is not good'. The demonstrative premiss differs from the dialectical, because the demonstrative premiss is the assertion of one of two contradictory statements (the demonstrator does not ask for his premiss, but lays it down), whereas the dialectical premiss depends on the adversary's choice between two contradictories. But this will make no difference to the production of a syllogism in either case; for both the demonstrator and the dialectician argue syllogistically after stating that something does or does not belong to something else. Therefore a syllogistic premiss without qualification will be an affirmation or denial of something concerning something else in the way we have described; it will be demonstrative, if it is true and obtained through the first principles of its science; while a dialectical premiss is the giving of a choice between two contradictories, when a man is proceeding by question, but when he is syllogizing it is the assertion of that which is apparent and generally admitted, as has been said in the *Topics*. The nature then of a premiss and the difference between syllogistic, demonstrative, and dialectical premisses, may be taken as sufficiently defined by us in relation to our present need, but will be stated accurately in the sequel.

I call that a term into which the premiss is resolved, i. e. both the predicate and that of which it is predicated, 'being' being added and 'not being' removed, or vice versa.

A syllogism is discourse in which, cer-

* From *Prior Analytics* in *The Works of Aristotle* (1928), Volume I, translated under the editorship of W. D. Ross. Reprinted by permission of The Clarendon Press, Oxford.

tain things being stated, something other than what is stated follows of necessity from their being so. I mean by the last phrase that they produce the consequence, and by this, that no further term is required from without in order to make the consequence necessary.

I call that a perfect syllogism which needs nothing other than what has been stated to make plain what necessarily follows; a syllogism is imperfect, if it needs either one or more propositions, which are indeed the necessary consequences of the terms set down, but have not been expressly stated as premisses.

That one term should be included in another as in a whole is the same as for the other to be predicated of all of the first. And we say that one term is predicated of all of another, whenever no instance of the subject can be found of which the other term cannot be asserted: 'to be predicated of none' must be understood in the same way.

2

Every premiss states that something either is or must be or may be the attribute of something else; of premisses of these three kinds some are affirmative, others negative, in respect of each of the three modes of attribution; again some affirmative and negative premisses are universal, others particular, others indefinite. It is necessary then that in universal attribution the terms of the negative premiss should be convertible, e.g. if no pleasure is good, then no good will be pleasure; the terms of the affirmative must be convertible, not however universally, but in part, e.g. if every pleasure is good, some good must be pleasure; the particular affirmative must convert in part (for if some pleasure is good, then some good will be pleasure); but the particular negative need not convert, for if some animal is not man, it does not follow that some man is not animal.

First then take a universal negative with the terms A and B. If no B is A, neither can any A be B. For if some A (say C) were B, it would not be true that no B is A; for C is a B. But if every B is A, then some A is B. For if no A were B, then no B could be A. But we assumed that every B is A. Similarly too, if the premiss is particular. For if some B is A, then some of the As must be B. For if none were, then no B would be A. But if some B is not A, there is no necessity that some of the As should not be B; e.g. let B stand for animal and A for man. Not every animal is a man; but every man is an animal.

3

The same manner of conversion will hold good also in respect of necessary premisses. The universal negative converts universally; each of the affirmatives converts into a particular. If it is necessary that no B is A, it is necessary also that no A is B. For if it is possible that some A is B, it would be possible also that some B is A. If all or some B is A of necessity, it is necessary also that some A is B: for if there were no necessity, neither would some of the Bs be A necessarily. But the particular negative does not convert, for the same reason which we have already stated.

In respect of possible premisses, since possibility is used in several senses (for we say that what is necessary and what is not necessary and what is potential is possible), affirmative statements will all convert in a manner similar to those described. For if it is possible that all or some B is A, it will be possible that some A is B. For if that were not possible, then no B could possibly be A. This has been already proved. But in negative statements the case is different. Whatever is said to be possible, either because *B* necessarily is *A*, or because *B* is not necessarily *A*, admits of conversion like other negative statements, e.g. if one should say, it is possible that man is not horse, or that no garment is white. For in the former case the one term necessarily does not belong to the other; in the latter there is no necessity that it should: and the premiss converts like other negative statements. For if it is possible for no man to be a horse, it is also admissible for no horse to be a man; and if it is admissible for no garment to be white, it is also admissible for nothing white to be a garment. For if any white thing must be a garment, then some garment will necessarily be white. This has been already proved. The particular negative also must be treated like those dealt with above. But if anything is said to be possible because it is the general rule and natural (and it is in this way we define the possible), the negative premisses can no longer be converted like the simple negatives; the universal negative premiss does not convert, and the particular does. This will be plain when we speak about the possible. At present we may take this much as clear in addition to what has been said: the statement that it is possible that no *B* is A or some *B* is not *A* is affirmative in form: for the expression 'is possible' ranks along with 'is', and 'is' makes an affirmation always and in every case, whatever the terms to which it is added in predication, e.g. 'it is not-good' or 'it is not-white' or in a word 'it is not-this'. But this also will be proved in the sequel. In conversion these premisses will behave like the other affirmative propositions.

4

After these distinctions we now state by what means, when, and how every syllogism is produced; subsequently we must speak of demonstration. Syllogism should be discussed before demonstration, because syllogism is the more general: the demonstration is a sort of syllogism, but not every syllogism is a demonstration.

Whenever three terms are so related to one another that the last is contained in the middle as in a whole, and the middle is either contained in, or excluded from, the first as in or from a whole, the extremes must be related by a perfect syllogism. I call that term middle which is itself contained in another and contains another in itself: in position also this comes in the middle. By extremes I mean both that term which is itself contained in another and that in which another is contained. If *A* is predicated of all *B*, and *B* of all *C*, *A* must be predicated of all *C*: we have already explained what we mean by 'predicated of all'. Similarly also, if *A* is predicated of no *B*, and *B* of all *C*, it is necessary that no C will be *A*.

But if the first term belongs to all the middle, but the middle to none of the last term, there will be no syllogism in respect of the extremes; for nothing necessary follows from the terms being so related; for it is possible that the first should belong either to all or to none of the last, so that neither a particular nor a universal conclusion is necessary. But if there is no necessary consequence, there cannot be a syllogism by means of these premisses. As an example of a universal affirmative relation between the extremes we may take the terms animal, man, horse; of a universal negative relation, the terms animal, man, stone. Nor again can a syllogism be formed when neither the first term belongs to any of the middle, nor the middle to any of the last. As an example of a positive relation between the extremes take the terms science, line, medicine: of a negative relation science, line, unit.

If then the terms are universally related, it is clear in this figure when a syllogism will be possible and when not, and that if a syllogism is possible the terms must be related as described, and if they are so related there will be a syllogism.

But if one term is related universally, the other in part only, to its subject, there must be a perfect syllogism whenever universality is posited with reference to the major term either affirmatively or negatively, and particularity with reference to the minor term affirmatively: but whenever the universality is posited in relation to the minor term, or the terms are related in any other way, a syllogism is impossible. I call that term the major in which the middle is contained and that term the minor which comes under the middle. Let all *B* be *A* and some *C* be *B*. Then if 'predicated of all' means what was said above, it is necessary that some *C* is *A*. And if no *B* is *A*, but some *C* is *B*, it is necessary that some *C* is not *A*. (The meaning of 'predicated of none' has also been defined.) So there will be a perfect syllogism. This holds good also if the premiss *BC*[1] should be indefinite, provided that it is affirmative: for we shall have the same syllogism whether the premiss is indefinite or particular.

But if the universality is posited with respect to the minor term either affirmatively or negatively, a syllogism will not be possible, whether the major premiss is positive or negative, indefinite or particular: e.g. if some *B* is or is not *A*, and all *C* is *B*. As an example of a positive relation between the extremes take the terms good, state, wisdom: of a negative

relation, good, state, ignorance. Again if no *C* is *B* but some *B* is or is not *A*, or not every *B* is *A*, there cannot be a syllogism. Take the terms white, horse, swan: white, horse, raven. The same terms may be taken also if the premiss *BA* is indefinite.

Nor when the major premiss is universal, whether affirmative or negative, and the minor premiss is negative and particular, can there be a syllogism, whether the minor premiss be indefinite or particular: e.g. if all *B* is *A*, and some *C* is not *B*, or if not all *C* is *B*. For the major term may be predicable both of all and of none of the minor, to some of which the middle term cannot be attributed. Suppose the terms are animal, man, white: next take some of the white things of which man is not predicated—swan and snow: animal is predicated of all of the one, but of none of the other. Consequently there cannot be a syllogism. Again let no *B* be *A*, but let some *C* not be *B*. Take the terms inanimate, man, white: then take some white things of which man is not predicated—swan and snow: the term inanimate is predicated of all of the one, of none of the other.

Further since it is indefinite to say some *C* is not *B*, and it is true that some *C* is not *B*, whether no *C* is *B*, or not all *C* is *B*, and since if terms are assumed such that no *C* is *B*, no syllogism follows (this has already been stated), it is clear that this arrangement of terms will not afford a syllogism: otherwise one would have been possible with a *universal* negative minor premiss. A similar proof may also be given if the universal premiss is negative.

Nor can there in any way be a syllogism if both the relations of subject and predicate are particular, either positively or negatively, or the one negative and the other affirmative, or one indefinite and the other definite, or both indefinite.

---

[1] The Aristotelian formula for the proposition, *AB*, in which *B* represents the subject and *A* the predicate (*A* belongs to *B*), has been retained throughout, because in most places this suits the context better than the modern formula in which *A* represents the subject and *B* the predicate.

Terms common to all the above are animal, white, horse: animal, white, stone.

It is clear then from what has been said that if there is a syllogism in this figure with a particular conclusion, the terms must be related as we have stated: if they are related otherwise, no syllogism is possible anyhow. It is evident also that all the syllogisms in this figure are perfect (for they are all completed by means of the premisses originally taken) and that all conclusions are proved by this figure, viz. universal and particular, affirmative and negative. Such a figure I call the first.

IS THE SYLLOGISM A

PETITIO PRINCIPII?*

JOHN STUART MILL (1806–1873).   See page 53.

CHAPTER II.

1

The analysis of the syllogism has been so accurately and fully performed in the common manuals of logic, that in the present work, which is not designed as a manual, it is sufficient to recapitulate, *memoriae causa,* the leading results of that analysis, as a foundation for the remarks to be afterward made on the functions of the syllogism, and the place which it holds in science.

· · ·

All valid ratiocination, all reasoning by which, from general propositions previously admitted, other propositions equally or less general are inferred, may be exhibited in some of the above forms. The whole of Euclid, for example, might be thrown without difficulty into a series of syllogisms, regular in mood and figure.

Though a syllogism framed according to any of these formulae is a valid argument, all correct ratiocination admits of being stated in syllogisms of the first figure alone. . . . In other words, every conclusion which can be proved in any of

the last three figures, may be proved in the first figure from the same premises, with a slight alteration in the mere manner of expressing them. Every valid ratiocination, therefore, may be stated in the first figure, that is, in one of the following forms:

Every B is C		No B is C	
All A	$\}$ is $B,$	All A	$\}$ is $B,$
Some A		Some A	
therefore		therefore	
All A	$\}$ is $C.$	No A is	$\}$ $C.$
Some A		Some A is not	

· · ·

We are therefore at liberty, in conformity with the general opinion of logicians, to consider the two elementary forms of the first figure as the universal types of all correct ratiocination, the one, when the conclusion to be proved is affirmative, the other, when it is negative; even though certain arguments may have a tendency to clothe themselves in the forms of the second, third, and fourth figures, which, however, cannot possibly happen with the only class of arguments which are of first-rate scientific impor-

* From John Stuart Mill, *A System of Logic* (New York: Harper & Bros., 1874), pp. 126–157.

tance, those in which the conclusion is a universal affirmative, such conclusions being susceptible of proof in the first figure alone.

2

On examining, then, these two general formulae, we find that in both of them one premise, the major, is a universal proposition, and according as this is affirmative or negative, the conclusion is so too. All ratiocination, therefore, starts from a *general* proposition, principle, or assumption, a proposition in which a predicate is affirmed or denied of an entire class, that is, in which some attribute, or the negation of some attribute, is asserted of an indefinite number of objects distinguished by a common characteristic and designated, in consequence, by a common name.

The other premise is always affirmative and asserts that something (which may be either an individual, a class, or part of a class) belongs to, or is included in, the class respecting which something was affirmed or denied in the major premise. It follows that the attribute affirmed or denied of the entire class may (if that affirmation or denial was correct) be affirmed or denied of the object or objects alleged to be included in the class; and this is precisely the assertion made in the conclusion.

Whether or not the foregoing is an adequate account of the constituent parts of the syllogism will be presently considered; but as far as it goes it is a true account. It has accordingly been generalized and erected into a logical maxim on which all ratiocination is said to be founded, insomuch that to reason and to apply the maxim are supposed to be one and the same thing. The maxim is, "That whatever can be affirmed (or denied) of a class, may be affirmed (or denied) of everything included in the class." This axiom, supposed to be the basis of the syllogistic theory, is termed by logicians the *dictum de omni et nullo.*

This maxim, however, when considered as a principle of reasoning, appears suited to a system of metaphysics once, indeed, generally received, but which for the last two centuries has been considered as finally abandoned, though there have not been wanting in our own day attempts at its revival. So long as what are termed "universals" were regarded as a peculiar kind of substances having an objective existence distinct from the individual objects classed under them, the *dictum de omni* conveyed an important meaning, because it expressed the intercommunity of nature which it was necessary on that theory that we should suppose to exist between those general substances and the particular substances which were subordinated to them. That every thing predicable of the universal was predicable of the various individuals contained under it was then no identical proposition, but a statement of what was conceived as a fundamental law of the universe. The assertion that the entire nature and properties of the *substantia secunda* formed part of the nature and properties of each of the individual substances called by the same name, that the properties of Man, for example, were properties of all men, was a proposition of real significance when man did not *mean* all men, but something inherent in men, and vastly superior to them in dignity. Now, however, when it is known that a class, a universal, a genus or species, is not an entity *per se,* but neither more nor less than the individual substances themselves which are placed in the class, and that there is nothing real in the matter except those objects, a common name given to them, and common attributes indicated by the name, what, I should be glad to know, do we learn by being told that whatever can be affirmed of a class may be affirmed of every object contained in the class. The class *is* nothing but the objects contained in it; and the *dictum de omni* merely amounts to the identical proposition that whatever is true of certain objects is true of each of those objects. If all ratiocination were no more than the application of this maxim to particular cases, the syllogism would indeed be, what it has so often been declared to be, solemn trifling. The *dictum de omni* is on a par with another truth, which in its time was also reckoned of great importance, "Whatever is, is." To give any real meaning to the *dictum de omni,* we must consider it not as an axiom, but as a definition; we must look upon it as intended to explain, in a circuitous and paraphrastic manner, the meaning of the word *class.*

An error which seemed finally refuted and dislodged from thought often needs only put on a new suit of phrases to be welcomed back to its old quarters and allowed to repose unquestioned for another cycle of ages. Modern philosophers have not been sparing in their contempt for the scholastic dogma that genera and species are a peculiar kind of substances, which general substances being the only permanent things, while the individual substances comprehended under them are in a perpetual flux, knowledge, which necessarily imports stability, can only have relation to those general substances or universals and not to the facts or particulars included under them. Yet, though nominally rejected, this very doctrine, whether disguised under the "abstract ideas" of Locke (whose speculations, however, it has less vitiated than those of perhaps any other writer who has been infected with it), under the ultra nominalism of Hobbes and Condillac, or the ontology of the later German schools, has never ceased to poison philosophy. Once accustomed to consider scientific investigation as essentially consisting in the study of universals, men did not drop

this habit of thought when they ceased to regard universals as possessing an independent existence; and even those who went the length of considering them as mere names could not free themselves from the notion that the investigation of truth consisted entirely or partly in some kind of conjuration or juggle with those names. When a philosopher adopted fully the Nominalist view of the signification of general language, retaining along with it the *dictum de omni* as the foundation of all reasoning, two such premises fairly put together were likely, if he was a consistent thinker, to land him in rather startling conclusions. Accordingly it has been seriously held, by writers of deserved celebrity, that the process of arriving at new truths by reasoning consists in the mere substitution of one set of arbitrary signs for another, a doctrine which they suppose to derive irresistible confirmation from the example of algebra. If there were any process in sorcery or necromancy more preternatural than this, I should be much surprised. The culminating point of this philosophy is the noted aphorism of Condillac that a science is nothing, or scarcely anything, but *une langue bien faite;* in other words, that the one sufficient rule for discovering the nature and properties of objects is to name them properly, as if the reverse were not the truth, that it is impossible to name them properly except in proportion as we are already acquainted with their nature and properties. Can it be necessary to say that none, not even the most trivial knowledge with respect to things, ever was or could be originally got at by any conceivable manipulation of mere names, as such, and that what can be learned from names is only what somebody who used the names knew before? Philosophical analysis confirms the indication of common sense that the function of names is but that of enabling us to *remember* and to *communicate* our thoughts. That they also strengthen, even to an incalculable extent, the power of thought itself, is most true; but they do this by no intrinsic and peculiar virtue; they do it by the power inherent in an artificial memory, an instrument of which few have adequately considered the immense potency. As an artificial memory, language truly is, what it has so often been called, an instrument of thought; but it is one thing to be the instrument, and another to be the exclusive subject upon which the instrument is exercised. We think, indeed, to a considerable extent, by means of names, but what we think of are the things called by those names, and there cannot be a greater error than to imagine that thought can be carried on with nothing in our mind but names, or that we can make the names think for us.

3

Those who considered the *dictum de omni* as the foundation of the syllogism looked upon arguments in a manner corresponding to the erroneous view which Hobbes took of propositions. Because there are some propositions which are merely verbal, Hobbes, in order apparently that his definition might be rigorously universal, defined a proposition as if no propositions declared anything except the meaning of words. If Hobbes was right, if no further account than this could be given of the import of propositions, no theory could be given but the commonly received one of the combination of propositions in a syllogism. If the minor premise asserted nothing more than that something belongs to a class, and if the major premise asserted nothing of that class except that it is included in another class, the conclusion would only be that what was included in the lower class is included in the higher, and the result, therefore, nothing

except that the classification is consistent with itself. But we have seen that it is no sufficient account of the meaning of a proposition to say that it refers something to, or excludes something from, a class. Every proposition which conveys real information asserts a matter of fact, dependent on the laws of nature, and not on classification. It asserts that a given object does or does not possess a given attribute, or it asserts that two attributes, or sets of attributes, do or do not (constantly or occasionally) co-exist. Since such is the purport of all propositions which convey any real knowledge, and since ratiocination is a mode of acquiring real knowledge, any theory of ratiocination which does not recognize this import of propositions cannot, we may be sure, be the true one.

Applying this view of propositions to the two premises of a syllogism, we obtain the following results. The major premise, which, as already remarked, is always universal, asserts that all things which have a certain attribute (or attributes) have or have not along with it a certain other attribute (or attributes). The minor premise asserts that the thing or set of things which are the subject of that premise have the first-mentioned attribute; and the conclusion is that they have (or that they have not), the second. Thus in our former example,

> All men are mortal,
> Socrates is a man,
> therefore
> Socrates is mortal,

the subject and predicate of the major premise are connotative terms, denoting objects and connoting attributes. The assertion in the major premise is that, along with one of the two sets of attributes, we always find the other; that the attributes connoted by "man" never exist unless conjoined with the attribute called mortality. The assertion in the minor premise is that the individual named Socrates possesses the former attributes; and it is concluded that he possesses also the attribute mortality. Or, if both the premises are general propositions, as

All men are mortal,
All kings are men,
therefore
All kings are mortal,

the minor premise asserts that the attributes denoted by kingship only exist in conjunction with those signified by the word man. The major asserts, as before, that the last-mentioned attributes are never found without the attribute of mortality. The conclusion is that wherever the attributes of kingship are found, that of mortality is found also.

If the major premise were negative, as, "No men are omnipotent," it would assert, not that the attributes connoted by "man" never exist without, but that they never exist with, those connoted by "omnipotent;" from which, together with the minor premise, it is concluded, that the same incompatibility exists between the attribute omnipotence and those constituting a king. In a similar manner we might analyze any other example of the syllogism.

If we generalize this process and look out for the principle or law involved in every such inference and presupposed in every syllogism the propositions of which are anything more than merely verbal, we find, not the unmeaning *dictum de omni et nullo,* but a fundamental principle, or rather two principles, strikingly resembling the axioms of mathematics. The first, which is the principle of affirmative syllogisms, is that things which co-exist with the same thing, co-exist with one another; or (still more precisely) a thing which co-exists with another thing, which other co-exists with a third thing, also co-exists with that third thing. The second is the principle of negative syllogisms and is to this effect: that a thing which co-exists with another thing, with which other a third thing does not co-exist, is not co-existent with that third thing. These axioms manifestly relate to facts and not to conventions, and one or other of them is the ground of the legitimacy of every argument in which facts and not conventions are the matter treated of.

4

It remains to translate this exposition of the syllogism from the one into the other of the two languages in which we formerly remarked that all propositions, and of course therefore all combinations of propositions, might be expressed. We observed that a proposition might be considered in two different lights, as a portion of our knowledge of nature or as a memorandum for our guidance. Under the former or speculative aspect an affirmative general proposition is an assertion of a speculative truth, *viz.,* that whatever has a certain attribute has a certain other attribute. Under the other aspect it is to be regarded not as a part of our knowledge, but as an aid for our practical exigencies, by enabling us when we see or learn that an object possesses one of the two attributes to infer that it possesses the other, thus employing the first attribute as a mark or evidence of the second. Thus regarded, every syllogism comes within the following general formula:

Attribute A is a mark of attribute B,
The given object has the mark A,
therefore
The given object has the attribute B.

Referred to this type, the arguments which we have lately cited as specimens of the syllogism will express themselves in the following manner:

> The attributes of man are a mark of the attribute mortality,
> Socrates has the attributes of man, therefore
> Socrates has the attribute mortality.

And again,

> The attributes of man are a mark of the attribute mortality,
> The attributes of a king are a mark of the attributes of man, therefore
> The attributes of a king are a mark of the attribute mortality.

And lastly,

> The attributes of man are a mark of the absence of the attribute omnipotence,
> The attributes of a king are a mark of the attributes of man, therefore
> The attributes of a king are a mark of the absence of the attribute signified by the word omnipotent (or are evidence of the absence of that attribute).

To correspond with this alteration in the form of the syllogisms, the axioms on which the syllogistic process is founded must undergo a corresponding transformation. In this altered phraseology, both these axioms may be brought under one general expression, namely, that whatever has any mark has that which it is a mark of. Or, when the minor premise as well as the major is universal, we may state it thus, Whatever is a mark of any mark is a mark of that which this last is a mark of. . . .

CHAPTER III.

1

We have shown what is the real nature of the truths with which the syllogism is conversant, in contradistinction to the more superficial manner in which their import is conceived in the common theory, and what are the fundamental axioms on which its probative force or conclusiveness depends. We have now to inquire whether the syllogistic process, that of reasoning from generals to particulars, is or is not a process of inference, a progress from the known to the unknown, a means of coming to a knowledge of something which we did not know before.

Logicians have been remarkably unanimous in their mode of answering this question. It is universally allowed that a syllogism is vicious if there be anything more in the conclusion than was assumed in the premises. But this is, in fact, to say that nothing ever was or can be proved by syllogism which was not known or assumed to be known before. Is ratiocination, then, not a process of inference? And is the syllogism, to which the word reasoning has so often been represented to be exclusively appropriate, not really entitled to be called reasoning at all? This seems an inevitable consequence of the doctrine, admitted by all writers on the subject, that a syllogism can prove no more than is involved in the premises. Yet the acknowledgment so explicitly made has not prevented one set of writers from continuing to represent the syllogism as the correct analysis of what the mind actually performs in discovering and proving the larger half of the truths whether of science or of daily life which we believe, while those who have avoided this inconsistency and followed out the general theorem respecting the logical value of the syllogism to its legitimate corollary have been led to impute uselessness and frivolity to the syllogistic theory itself, on the ground of the *petitio principii* which they allege to be inherent in every syllogism. As I believe both these opinions to be fundamentally erroneous, I must request the attention of the reader to certain considerations without which any just appreciation of the true character of the syllogism and the functions it performs in philosophy appears to me impossible, but which seem to have been either overlooked or insufficiently adverted to both by the defenders of the syllogistic theory and by its assailants.

2

It must be granted that in every syllogism, considered as an argument to prove the conclusion, there is a *petitio principii.* When we say,

> All men are mortal,
> Socrates is a man,
> therefore
> Socrates is mortal;

it is unanswerably urged by the adversaries of the syllogistic theory that the proposition, "Socrates is mortal," is presupposed in the more general assumption, "All men are mortal"; that we cannot be assured of the mortality of all men unless we are already certain of the mortality of every individual man; that if it be still doubtful whether Socrates, or any other individual we choose to name, be mortal or not, the same degree of uncertainty must hang over the assertion, "All men are mortal"; that the general principle, instead of being given as evidence of the particular case, cannot itself be taken for true without exception until every shadow of doubt which could affect any case comprised with it is dispelled by evidence *aliundè;* and then what remains for the syllogism to prove? That, in short, no

reasoning from generals to particulars can, as such, prove anything, since from a general principle we cannot infer any particulars but those which the principle itself assumes as known.

This doctrine appears to me irrefragable, and if logicians, though unable to dispute it, have usually exhibited a strong disposition to explain it away, this was not because they could discover any flaw in the argument itself, but because the contrary opinion seemed to rest on arguments equally indisputable. In the syllogism last referred to, for example, or in any of those which we previously constructed, is it not evident that the conclusion may, to the person to whom the syllogism is presented, be actually and *bona fide* a new truth? Is it not matter of daily experience that truths previously unthought of, facts which have not been, and cannot be, directly observed, are arrived at by way of general reasoning? We believe that the Duke of Wellington is mortal. We do not know this by direct observation, so long as he is not yet dead. If we were asked how, this being the case, we know the duke to be mortal, we should probably answer, "Because all men are so." Here, therefore, we arrive at the knowledge of a truth not (as yet) susceptible of observation by a reasoning which admits of being exhibited in the following syllogism:

> All men are mortal,
> The Duke of Wellington is a man,
> therefore
> The Duke of Wellington is mortal.

And since a large portion of our knowledge is thus acquired, logicians have persisted in representing the syllogism as a process of inference or proof, though none of them has cleared up the difficulty which arises from the inconsistency between that assertion and the principle that, if there be anything in the conclusion which was not already asserted in the premises, the argument is vicious. For it is impossible to attach any serious scientific value to such a mere salvo as the distinction drawn between being involved *by implication* in the premises and being directly asserted in them. When Archbishop Whately says that the object of reasoning is "merely to expand and unfold the assertions wrapped up, as it were, and implied in those with which we set out, and to bring a person to perceive and acknowledge the full force of that which he has admitted," he does not, I think, meet the real difficulty requiring to be explained, namely, how it happens that a science, like geometry, *can* be all "wrapped up" in a few definitions and axioms. Nor does this defense of the syllogism differ much from what its assailants urge against it as an accusation, when they charge it with being of no use except to those who seek to press the consequences of an admission into which a person has been entrapped without having considered and understood its full force. When you admitted the major premise, you asserted the conclusion, but, says Archbishop Whately, you asserted it by implication merely; this, however, can here only mean that you asserted it unconsciously, that you did not know you were asserting it; but, if so, the difficulty revives in this shape— Ought you not to have known? Were you warranted in asserting the general proposition without having satisfied yourself of the truth of everything which it fairly includes? And if not, is not the syllogistic art *prima facie* what its assailants affirm it to be, a contrivance for catching you in a trap, and holding you fast in it?[1]

[1] It is hardly necessary to say that I am not contending for any such absurdity as that we *actually* "ought to have known" and considered the case of every individual man, past, present, and future, before affirming that all men are mortal, although this in-

3

From this difficulty there appears to be but one issue. The proposition that the Duke of Wellington is mortal is evidently an inference; it is got at as a conclusion from something else; but do we, in reality, conclude it from the proposition, "All men are mortal"? I answer, no.

The error committed is, I conceive, that of overlooking the distinction between two parts of the process of philosophizing, the inferring part, and the registering part, and ascribing to the latter the functions of the former. The mistake is that of referring a person to his own notes for the origin of his knowledge. If a person is asked a question and is at the moment unable to answer it, he may refresh his memory by turning to a memorandum which he carries about with him. But if he were asked how the fact came to his knowledge, he would scarcely answer because it was set down in his note-book, unless the book was written, like the Koran, with a quill from the wing of the angel Gabriel.

Assuming that the proposition, "The Duke of Wellington is mortal," is immediately an inference from the proposition, "All men are mortal," whence do

terpretation has been, strangely enough, put upon the preceding observations. There is no difference between me and Archbishop Whately or any other defender of the syllogism on the practical part of the matter; I am only pointing out an inconsistency in the logical theory of it, as conceived by almost all writers. I do not say that a person who affirmed, before the Duke of Wellington was born, that all men are mortal, *knew* that the Duke of Wellington was mortal; but I do say that he *asserted* it; and I ask for an explanation of the apparent logical fallacy of adducing in proof of the Duke of Wellington's mortality a general statement which presupposes it. Finding no sufficient resolution of this difficulty in any of the writers on logic, I have attempted to supply one.

we derive our knowledge of that general truth? Of course from observation. Now, all which man can observe are individual cases. From these all general truths must be drawn, and into these they may be again resolved, for a general truth is but an aggregate of particular truths, a comprehensive expression by which an indefinite number of individual facts are affirmed or denied at once. But a general proposition is not merely a compendious form for recording and preserving in the memory a number of particular facts, all of which have been observed. Generalization is not a process of mere naming; it is also a process of inference. From instances which we have observed, we feel warranted in concluding that what we found true in those instances holds in all similar ones, past, present, and future, however numerous they may be. We then, by that valuable contrivance of language which enables us to speak of many as if they were one, record all that we have observed together with all that we infer from our observations in one concise expression, and have thus only one proposition, instead of an endless number, to remember or to communicate. The results of many observations and inferences and instructions for making innumerable inferences in unforeseen cases are compressed into one short sentence.

When, therefore, we conclude from the death of John and Thomas, and every other person we ever heard of in whose case the experiment had been fairly tried, that the Duke of Wellington is mortal like the rest, we may, indeed, pass through the generalization, "All men are mortal," as an intermediate stage, but it is not in the latter half of the process, the descent from all men to the Duke of Wellington, that the *inference* resides. The inference is finished when we have asserted that all men are mortal. What remains to be performed after-

ward is merely deciphering our own notes.

Archbishop Whately has contended that syllogizing, or reasoning from generals to particulars, is not, agreeably to the vulgar idea, a peculiar *mode* of reasoning, but the philosophical analysis of *the* mode in which all men reason and must do so if they reason at all. With the deference due to so high an authority, I cannot help thinking that the vulgar notion is, in this case, the more correct. If, from our experience of John, Thomas, etc., who once were living, but are now dead, we are entitled to conclude that all human beings are mortal, we might surely without any logical inconsequence have concluded at once from those instances that the Duke of Wellington is mortal. The mortality of John, Thomas, and others is, after all, the whole evidence we have for the mortality of the Duke of Wellington. Not one iota is added to the proof by interpolating a general proposition. Since the individual cases are all the evidence we can possess, evidence which no logical form into which we choose to throw it can make greater than it is, and since that evidence is either sufficient in itself, or, if insufficient for the one purpose, cannot be sufficient for the other, I am unable to see why we should be forbidden to take the shortest cut from these sufficient premises to the conclusion and constrained to travel the "high priori road" by the arbitrary fiat of logicians. I cannot perceive why it should be impossible to journey from one place to another unless we "march up a hill, and then march down again." It may be the safest road, and there may be a resting-place at the top of the hill, affording a commanding view of the surrounding country, but, for the mere purpose of arriving at our journey's end, our taking that road is perfectly optional; it is a question of time, trouble, and danger.

Not only *may* we reason from particulars to particulars without passing through generals, but we perpetually do so reason. All our earliest inferences are of this nature. From the first dawn of intelligence we draw inferences, but years elapse before we learn the use of general language. The child, who, having burned his fingers, avoids to thrust them again into the fire, has reasoned or inferred, though he has never thought of the general maxim, "Fire burns." He knows from memory that he has been burned, and on this evidence believes, when he sees a candle, that if he puts his finger into the flame of it, he will be burned again. He believes this in every case which happens to arise, but without looking, in each instance, beyond the present case. He is not generalizing; he is inferring a particular from particulars. In the same way, also, brutes reason. There is no ground for attributing to any of the lower animals the use of signs of such a nature as to render general propositions possible. But those animals profit by experience and avoid what they have found to cause them pain in the same manner, though not always with the same skill, as a human creature. Not only the burned child, but the burned dog, dreads the fire.

I believe that, in point of fact, when drawing inferences from our personal experience and not from maxims handed down to us by books or tradition, we much oftener conclude from particulars to particulars directly than through the intermediate agency of any general proposition. We are constantly reasoning from ourselves to other people, or from one person to another, without giving ourselves the trouble to erect our observations into general maxims of human or external nature. When we conclude that some person will, on some given occasion, feel or act so and so, we sometimes judge from an enlarged consideration of the manner in which human beings in general, or persons of some particular character, are accustomed to feel and act, but much oftener from merely recollecting the feelings and conduct of the same person in some previous instance, or from considering how we should feel or act ourselves. It is not only the village matron who, when called to a consultation upon the case of a neighbor's child, pronounces on the evil and its remedy simply on the recollection and authority of what she accounts the similar case of her Lucy. We all, where we have no definite maxims to steer by, guide ourselves in the same way; and if we have an extensive experience and retain its impressions strongly, we may acquire in this manner a very considerable power of accurate judgment, which we may be utterly incapable of justifying or of communicating to others. Among the higher order of practical intellects there have been many of whom it was remarked how admirably they suited their means to their ends, without being able to give any sufficient reasons for what they did, and applied, or seemed to apply, recondite principles which they were wholly unable to state. This is a natural consequence of having a mind stored with appropriate particulars and having been long accustomed to reason at once from these to fresh particulars, without practicing the habit of stating to one's self or to others the corresponding general propositions. An old warrior, on a rapid glance at the outlines of the ground, is able at once to give the necessary orders for a skillful arrangement of his troops, though, if he has received little theoretical instruction and has seldom been called upon to answer to other people for his conduct, he may never have had in his mind a single general theorem respecting the relation between ground and array. But his experience of encampments, in circumstances more or less similar, has left a number of vivid, unexpressed, ungeneralized analogies in his mind, the most appropriate of which, instantly suggesting itself, determines him to a judicious arrangement.

. . .

4

From the considerations now adduced, the following conclusions seem to be established: All inference is from particulars to particulars; general propositions are merely registers of such inferences already made, and short formulae for making more; the major premise of a syllogism, consequently, is a formula of this description, and the conclusion is not an inference drawn *from* the formula, but an inference drawn *according* to the formula, the real logical antecedent, or premise, being the particular facts from which the general proposition was collected by induction. Those facts, and the individual instances which supplied them, may have been forgotten; but a record remains, not indeed descriptive of the facts themselves, but showing how those cases may be distinguished, respecting which, the facts, when known, were considered to warrant a given inference. According to the indications of this record we draw our conclusion, which is, to all intents and purposes, a conclusion from the forgotten facts. For this it is essential that we should read the record correctly, and the rules of the syllogism are a set of precautions to insure our doing so.

This view of the functions of the syllogism is confirmed by the consideration of precisely those cases which might be expected to be least favorable to it, namely, those in which ratiocination is independent of any previous induction. We have already observed that the syllogism, in the ordinary course of our reasoning, is only the latter half of the process of traveling from premises to a conclusion. There are, however, some peculiar cases in which it is the whole process. Particulars alone are capable of being subjected to observation; and all knowledge which is derived from observation begins, therefore, of necessity, in particulars; but our knowledge may, in cases of certain descriptions, be conceived as coming to us from other sources than observation. It may present itself as coming from testimony which, on the occasion and for the purpose in hand, is accepted as of an authoritative character; and the information thus communicated may be conceived to comprise not only particular facts but general propositions, as when a scientific doctrine is accepted without examination on the authority of writers or a theological doctrine on that of Scripture. Or the generalization may not be, in the ordinary sense, an assertion at all but a command, a law, not in the philosophical, but in the moral and political sense of the term, an expression of the desire of a superior that we, or any number of other persons, shall conform our conduct to certain general instructions. So far as this asserts a fact, namely, a volition of the legislator, that fact is an individual fact, and the proposition, therefore, is not a general proposition. But the description therein contained of the conduct which it is the will of the legislator that his subjects should observe is general. The proposition asserts, not that all men *are* anything, but that all men *shall* do something.

In both these cases the generalities are the original data, and the particulars are elicited from them by a process which correctly resolves itself into a series of syllogisms. The real nature, however, of the supposed deductive process is evident enough. The only point to be determined is whether the authority which declared the general proposition intended to include this case in it, and whether the legislator intended his command to apply to the present case among others or not. This is ascertained by examining whether the case possesses the marks by which, as those authorities have signified, the cases which they meant to certify or to influence may be known. The object of the inquiry is to make out the witness's or the legislator's intention, through the indication given by their words. This is a question, as the Germans express it, of hermeneutics. The operation is not a process of inference, but a process of interpretation.

In this last phrase we have obtained an expression which appears to me to characterize, more aptly than any other, the functions of the syllogism in all cases. When the premises are given by authority, the function of reasoning is to ascertain the testimony of a witness or the will of a legislator by interpreting the signs in which the one has intimated his assertion and the other his command. In like manner, when the premises are derived from observation, the function of reasoning is to ascertain what we (or our predecessors) formerly thought might be inferred from the observed facts, and to do this by interpreting a memorandum of ours or of theirs. The memorandum reminds us that from evidence, more or less carefully weighed, it formerly appeared that a certain attribute might be inferred wherever we perceive a certain mark. The proposition, "All men are mortal" (for instance) shows that we have had experience from which we thought it followed that the attributes connoted by the term man are a mark of mortality. But when we conclude that the Duke of Wellington is mortal, we do not infer this from the memorandum but from the former experience. All that we infer from the memorandum is our own previous belief (or that of those who transmitted to us the proposition) concerning the inferences which that former experience would warrant.

This view of the nature of the syllogism renders consistent and intelligible what otherwise remains obscure and confused in the theory of Archbishop Whately and other enlightened defenders of the syllogistic doctrine respecting the limits to which its functions are confined. They affirm, in as explicit terms as can be used, that the sole office of general reasoning is to prevent inconsistency in our opinions, to prevent us from assenting to anything the truth of which would contradict something to which we had previously on good grounds given our assent. And they tell us that the sole ground which a syllogism affords for assenting to the conclusion is that the supposition of its being false, combined with the supposition that the premises are true, would lead to a contradiction in terms. Now this would be but a lame account of the real grounds which we have for believing the facts which we learn from reasoning, in contradistinction to observation. The true reason why we believe that the Duke of Wellington will die is that his fathers, and our fathers, and all other persons who were contemporary with them, have died. Those facts are the real premises of the reasoning. But we are not led to infer the conclusion from those premises by the necessity of avoiding any verbal inconsistency. There is no contradiction in supposing that all those persons have died and that the Duke of Wellington may, notwithstanding, live forever. But there would be a contradiction if we first, on the ground of those same premises, made a general assertion including and covering the case of the Duke of Wellington, and then refused to stand to it in the individual case. There is an inconsistency to be avoided between the memorandum we make of the inferences which may be justly drawn in future cases and the inferences we actually draw in those cases when they arise. With this view we interpret our own formula, precisely as a judge interprets a law, in order that we may avoid drawing any inferences not conformable to our former intention, as a judge avoids giving any decision not conformable to the legislator's intention. The rules for this interpretation are the rules of the syllogism, and its sole purpose is to maintain consistency between the conclusions we draw in every particular case and the previous general directions for drawing them, whether those general directions were framed by ourselves as the result of induction or were received by us from an authority competent to give them.

5

In the above observations it has, I think, been shown that, though there is always a process of reasoning or inference where a syllogism is used, the syllogism is not a correct analysis of that process of reasoning or inference; which is, on the contrary (when not a mere inference from testimony), an inference from particulars to particulars, authorized by a previous inference from particulars to generals, and substantially the same with it, of the nature, therefore, of induction. But while these conclusions appear to me undeniable, I must yet enter a protest, as strong as that of Archbishop Whately himself, against the doctrine that the syllogistic art is useless for the purposes of reasoning. The reasoning lies in the act of generalization, not in interpreting the record of that act; but the syllogistic form is an indispensable collateral security for the correctness of the generalization itself.

It has already been seen that if we have a collection of particulars sufficient for grounding an induction we need not frame a general proposition; we may reason at once from those particulars to other particulars. But it is to be remarked withal that whenever, from a set of par-

ticular cases, we can legitimately draw any inference, we may legitimately make our inference a general one. If, from observation and experiment, we can conclude to one new case, so may we to an indefinite number. If that which has held true in our past experience will, therefore, hold in time to come, it will hold not merely in some individual case, but in all cases of some given description. Every induction, therefore, which suffices to prove one fact proves an indefinite multitude of facts; the experience which justifies a single prediction must be such as will suffice to bear out a general theorem. This theorem it is extremely important to ascertain and declare, in its broadest form of generality, and thus to place before our minds, in its full extent, the whole of what our evidence must prove if it proves anything.

This throwing of the whole body of possible inferences from a given set of particulars into one general expression operates as a security for their being just inferences, in more ways than one. First, the general principle presents a larger object to the imagination than any of the singular propositions which it contains. A process of thought which leads to a comprehensive generality is felt as of greater importance than one which terminates in an insulated fact; and the mind is, even unconsciously, led to bestow greater attention upon the process, and to weigh more carefully the sufficiency of the experience appealed to for supporting the inference grounded upon it. There is another, and a more important, advantage. In reasoning from a course of individual observations to some new and unobserved case which we are but imperfectly acquainted with (or we should not be inquiring into it) and in which, since we are inquiring into it, we probably feel a peculiar interest, there is very little to prevent us from giving way to negligence, or to any bias which may affect our wishes or our imagination and, under that influence, accepting insufficient evidence as sufficient. But if, instead of concluding straight to the particular case, we place before ourselves an entire class of facts —the whole contents of a general proposition, every tittle of which is legitimately inferable from our premises, if that one particular conclusion is so—there is then a considerable likelihood that if the premises are insufficient, and the general inference, therefore, groundless, it will comprise within it some fact or facts the reverse of which we already know to be true, and we shall thus discover the error in our generalization by a *reductio ad impossible*.

. . .

The value, therefore, of the syllogistic form and of the rules for using it correctly does not consist in their being the form and the rules according to which our reasonings are necessarily, or even usually, made, but in their furnishing us with a mode in which those reasonings may always be represented and which is admirably calculated, if they are inconclusive, to bring their inconclusiveness to light. An induction from particulars to generals, followed by a syllogistic process from those generals to other particulars, is a form in which we may always state our reasonings if we please. It is not a form in which we *must* reason, but it is a form in which we *may* reason and into which it is indispensable to throw our reasoning when there is any doubt of its validity; though when the case is familiar and little complicated, and there is no suspicion of error, we may and do reason at once from the known particular cases to unknown ones.[2]

[2] The language of ratiocination would, I think, be brought into closer agreement with the real nature of the process if the general propositions employed in reasoning, instead

These are the uses of syllogism as a mode of verifying any given argument. Its ulterior uses, as respects the general course of our intellectual operations, hardly require illustration, being in fact the acknowledged uses of general language. They amount substantially to this, that the inductions may be made once for all; a single careful interrogation of experience may suffice, and the result may be registered in the form of a general proposition which is committed to memory or to writing and from which afterward we have only to syllogize. The particulars of our experiments may then be dismissed from the memory, in which it would be impossible to retain so great a multitude of details, while the knowledge which those details afforded for future use, and which would otherwise be lost as soon as the observations were forgotten or as their record became too bulky for reference, is retained in a commodious and immediately available shape by means of general language.

. . .

6

To complete the series of considerations connected with the philosophical character of the syllogism, it is requisite to consider, since the syllogism is not the universal type of the reasoning process, what is the real type. This resolves itself into the question, what is the nature of the minor premise, and in what man-

of being in the form "All men are mortal," or "Every man is mortal," were expressed in the form "Any man is mortal." This mode of expression, exhibiting as the type of all reasoning from experience, "The men A, B, C, etc., are so and so, therefore *any* man is so and so," would much better manifest the true idea—that inductive reasoning is always, at bottom, inference from particulars to particulars, and that the whole function of general propositions in reasoning is to vouch for the legitimacy of such inferences.

ner it contributes to establish the conclusion; for, as to the major, we now fully understand that the place which it nominally occupies in our reasonings properly belongs to the individual facts or observations of which it expresses the general result, the major itself being no real part of the argument, but an intermediate halting-place for the mind, interposed by an artifice of language between the real premises and the conclusion, by way of a security, which it is in a most material degree, for the correctness of the process. The minor, however, being an indispensable part of the syllogistic expression of an argument, without doubt either is, or corresponds to, an equally indispensable part of the argument itself, and we have only to inquire what part.

. . .

In the argument, then, which proves that Socrates is mortal, one indispensable part of the premises will be as follows: "My father, and my father's father, *A, B, C,* and an indefinite number of other persons, were mortal," which is only an expression in different words of the observed fact that they have died. This is the major premise divested of the *petitio principii,* and cut down to as much as is really known by direct evidence.

In order to connect this proposition with the conclusion Socrates is mortal, the additional link necessary is such a proposition as the following: "Socrates resembles my father, and my father's father, and the other individuals specified." This proposition we assert when we say that Socrates is a man. By saying so, we likewise assert in what respect he resembles them, namely, in the attributes connoted by the word man. And we conclude that he further resembles them in the attribute mortality.

7

We have thus obtained what we were seeking, a universal type of the reasoning process. We find it resolvable in all cases into the following elements: Certain individuals have a given attribute; an individual or individuals resemble the former in certain other attributes; therefore they resemble them also in the given attribute. This type of ratiocination does not claim, like the syllogism, to be conclusive from the mere form of the expression, nor can it possibly be so. That one proposition does or does not assert the very fact which was already asserted in another may appear from the form of the expression, that is, from a comparison of the language; but when the two propositions assert facts which are *bona fide* different, whether the one fact proves the other or not can never appear from the language, but must depend on other considerations. Whether, from the attributes in which Socrates resembles those men who have heretofore died, it is allowable to infer that he resembles them also in being mortal, is a question of induction, and is to be decided by the principles or canons which we shall hereafter recognize as tests of the correct performance of that great mental operation.

Meanwhile, however, it is certain, as before remarked, that if this inference can be drawn as to Socrates, it can be drawn as to all others who resemble the observed individuals in the same attributes in which he resembles them, that is (to express the thing concisely), of all mankind. If, therefore, the argument be admissible in the case of Socrates, we are at liberty, once for all, to treat the possession of the attributes of man as a mark, or satisfactory evidence, of the attribute of mortality. This we do by laying down the universal proposition, "All men are mortal," and interpreting this, as occasion arises, in its application to Socrates and others. By this means we establish a very convenient division of the entire logical operation into two steps: first, that of ascertaining what attributes are marks of mortality; and, secondly, whether any given individuals possess those marks. And it will generally be advisable, in our speculations on the reasoning process, to consider this double operation as in fact taking place, and all reasoning as carried on in the form into which it must necessarily be thrown to enable us to apply to it any test of its correct performance.

Although, therefore, all processes of thought in which the ultimate premises are particulars, whether we conclude from particulars to a general formula, or from particulars to other particulars according to that formula, are equally induction, we shall yet, conformably to usage, consider the name induction as more peculiarly belonging to the process of establishing the general proposition, and the remaining operation, which is substantially that of interpreting the general proposition, we shall call by its usual name, deduction. And we shall consider every process by which anything is inferred respecting an unobserved case as consisting of an induction followed by a deduction; because, although the process needs not necessarily be carried on in this form, it is always susceptible of the form and must be thrown into it when assurance of scientific accuracy is needed and desired.

A MERE SUPERSTITION*

FRANCIS HERBERT BRADLEY (1846–1924) was the most distinguished of the British Absolute Idealists who dominated Anglo-American philosophy in the late nineteenth century. Although strongly influenced by Hegel, Bradley developed his own variety of Idealism and cannot be properly called a Hegelian. In the preface to the first edition of his *Principles of Logic* (1883) Bradley wrote: "Logic is not where it was, and cannot remain where it is." One of the wittiest of all writers on logic, Bradley's attack on the syllogism is entertaining as well as damaging.

BOOK II, PART I, CHAPTER I

Some Characteristics of Reasoning

1. When we first consider the subject of reasoning we seem to have nothing but a conflict of opinion. But a second glance reveals some agreement. There are three characteristic features of inference as to which in our hearts we are really at one. I do not mean that we should not deny them if our theories required it, but we should do so unwillingly and with a sense of compulsion. The first of these is a negative mark. There is a difference between reasoning and mere observation; if a truth is inferred it is not simply seen, and a conclusion is never a mere perception. The latter may seem to be given to us bodily, but the former involves some other element. It may indeed be thrust upon us, we may be compelled and constrained to make it, but we can not passively take it in. The fancies we cherish in respect of perception desert us as soon as we come to inference. The external fact or the reflection it throws off can violently break into and enter our minds, or the reality can stamp our yielding substance with its image and superscription. But we can hardly apply these ideas to a conclusion, for we feel that in this there is something that repels them. An inference can not wholly come in from without or be passively received. It is not mere vision, it is more than observation.

2. There is another mark which a conclusion possesses. It is not a mere fragment or isolated unit; it does not exist in and by itself, but is the result of a process. It rests upon a basis, and that basis is something we already know. In inference we advance from truth possessed to a further truth; and the conclu-

* From F. H. Bradley, *The Principles of Logic* (1928), pp. 245–252, 266–269. Reprinted by permission of The Clarendon Press, Oxford.

sion would never be reached at all if it were not for knowledge already attained. It is therefore dependent and in a sense adjectival.

3. But there is another attribute which a conclusion has got. It must convey some piece of information, and must tell us something else than the truths it depends upon. We have no inference at all, we have simply a frivolous show and pretence, if taking something we already know we assert the whole or part of this once more, and then say, "I have reasoned and got to a conclusion." An inference must be more than a vain repetition, and its result is no echo of senseless iteration. It is not mere observation yet it gives us something new. Though not self-existent it is more than a shadow. To those who delight in discrepant metaphors we may bring conviction when we so express ourselves: The truth which is seen in the mirror of inference has not wandered in through the window-pane of sense, nor yet is it merely a reflection cast by an article of furniture already in the mind.

4. Except in the interest of a preconceived theory, I think that these statements, at least so far, will not be denied. But I can hardly hope that the examples of reasoning I am about to produce will all escape unchallenged. Yet I shall not defend them, for I do not know how. They are palpable inferences, and the fact that they are so is much stronger than any theory of logic.

(i) A is to the right of B, B is to the right of C, therefore A is to the right of C. (ii) A is due north of B, B due west of C, therefore A is north-west of C. (iii) A is equal to (greater or less than) B, B is equal to (greater or less than) C, therefore &c. (iv) A is in tune with B, and B with C, therefore A with C. (v) A is prior to (after, simultaneous with) B, B to C, therefore A to C. (vi) Heat lengthens the pendulum, what lengthens the pendulum, makes it go slower, therefore heat makes it go slower. (vii) Charles I. was a king; he was beheaded, and so a king may be beheaded. (viii) Man is mortal, John is man, therefore John is mortal. We shall go from these facts to ask how far certain theories square with them.

CHAPTER II

Some Erroneous Views

1. The task before us in the present chapter is the removal of certain mistaken ideas. And the first to go must be the major premise. . . . there need not be always a major; and the examples we have given put this beyond doubt.

In (viii) our old friend is still to be found, but in (vi) and in (vii) you will hardly be able to distinguish him from the minor, and in all the rest he has totally vanished. You may say that in (iii) we really argue from "Things equal to the same are equal to each other," and I do not doubt you will find believers. But if such reasoning is reasoning *from* an axiom, how did people reason before axioms were invented? And if without axioms it is impossible to infer, I wonder where all the axioms can have come from. But if we take an example like number (i), will any one show me the major there? "A body is to the right of that which that, which it is to the right of, is to the right of." I know this major, because I have just manufactured it; but you who believe in major premises and who scores of times must have made the inference, confess that you never saw this premise before.

We must either admit that a major is not necessary, or else we must say that my examples are not inferences because they have no major. In either case an effete superstition will be doomed.

Begotten by an old metaphysical blunder, nourished by a senseless choice of

examples, fostered by the stupid con-
servatism of logicians, and protected by
the impotence of younger rivals, this
chimæra has had a good deal more than
its day. Really dead long since I can
hardly believe that it stands out for more
than decent burial. And decent burial has
not yet been offered it. Its ghost may lie
quiet when it sees that the truth, which
lent it life, can flourish alone.

2. The major premise, we have seen, is
a delusion, and this augers ill we may
think for the syllogism. Our suspicion is
well founded, for the syllogism itself,
like the major premise, is a mere superstition. It is possible, no doubt, as in our
seventh example, to have a syllogism
which has either no major premise, or
at all events no minor. And it is unquestionably true that in many arguments a
major premise is actually used. Nor will
I deny that some three fourths of our
valid arguments can be got within the
forms of *Barbara Celarent*. But yet after
all the syllogism is a chimæra, for it
professes to be the model of reasoning,
and there are reasonings which can not
by any fair means be conformed to its
pattern. In whatever sense you interpret
it, it turns out insufficient; and in certain
cases it will turn out worse. Let us examine the principles of reasoning it lays
down.

3. If we take first the axiom of inclusion in extension as it finds expression in
the maxim *De omni* &c., we are forced
to say that this principle is unsound. It
sins against the third characteristic of
inference, for it does not really give us
any new information. And, as has been
long ago remarked, it embodies a *petitio;*
for if, asserting the premise "All men are
mortal," I understand by the subject each
single man, then I either am aware that
John is mortal, or if not my major must
be withdrawn. The major premise has
asserted something of each member of a
collection, and the minor and conclusion

do but feebly re-echo one part of this
statement. But that is no inference.

We might try to understand the assertion differently. We might say that what
"All men" really means is the collection
or class and not each one member. But,
if so, we fall blindly into a second pitfall.
John's personality perhaps has no unity,
but he can hardly be called a collection
of *men,* and our syllogism now fails
through *quaternio terminorum.* It perhaps fails too through falsity of the
major.

The *dictum de omni* thus turns out
vicious. But if it were sound it would not
be sufficient, for it does not cover all
valid reasonings.

4. There is another mode of interpreting the major. "All men are mortal" may
be said to assert the identity of the subjects in "men" and "some mortals;" and
"John is man and therefore mortal"
assures us that the subject, which we
distinguish as John, is identical with a
member of the class of men and also of
mortals. But we know already how this
is to be read. The identity of the subject
is another way of affirming the conjunction of diverse attributes. The fact we
have got is either the co-existence in one
single subject of the attribute mortal with
the rest of John's attributes, or else the
possession by a single thing of the several
names "John," "man," and "mortal". And
interpreted in this way, though the inference is valid, it will not fall under the
dictum de omni.

5. We may illustrate the above from
complete induction. I may show that all
planets move in an ellipse by counting
and observing each single planet. But
in what sense am I then said to perform
an inference? I say *"therefore all planets
move in an ellipse,"* but I know already
that every single planet does so move. If
there were any planet which I could not
so qualify I could not go on to *therefore*
all planets. Does the "therefore" simply

reiterate the "because"? Then there is clearly no inference. Does the conclusion assert that the collection, or class, itself moves through space in an elliptical manner? If this were true the premises would not prove it. But perhaps it means that, if anything is a known planet, it must have a course which will be found elliptical. We are free to forget that the individuals we know do move in ellipses. We have firmly established a connection of attributes, so that hereafter, given any single individual which we barely perceive to be a known planet, we can go at once from the base of that attribute to elliptical movement. But the conclusion here does not rest on enumeration complete or otherwise; it proceeds from and rests upon a distinguished connection of attributes.

We may sum up the matter thus. If you say "Each individual has a certain attribute and *therefore* each has it," that is absurd. If you say "therefore the collection has it," that is invalid. If you say "Anything belonging to the collection has it and therefore this has it," then that is valid, but the "anything belonging" stands for an attribute. Complete induction shares the fortunes of the syllogism.

6. The principle of inclusion within class extension is not merely insufficient, but unless we interpret it as a connection of attributes it is intrinsically vicious. Let us see if we can find any other view which will come to the rescue and will save the syllogism. "What stands," says Kant, "under the condition of a rule stands under the rule." It is thus he interprets *"nota notæ est nota rei ipsius."* If you have an universal connection of two attributes, then, given one in a subject, you must also have the other.

It is evident that this principle of reasoning is valid, but it will not cover the whole of the ground; for, confined to the category of subject and attribute, it fails wherever you pass beyond. The subject

no doubt is in some way qualified by whatever can be asserted about any of its attributes, but it is idle to expect a result from this where we are not concerned with subject and attributes. "*A* is prior to *B* and *B* to *C*, and therefore *A* is prior to *C*," but what here am I to call the "condition of the rule" or the "*nota*" or "attribute"? I can not take *B* as the attribute of *A,* and if I look for that attribute in "prior to *B*," I fall at once into *quaternio terminorum,* since the second premise has got *B* simply.

And even when we keep to subjects and qualities, there are inferences which the principle will not justify. The syllogistic third figure can hardly be supposed to exemplify the axiom which Kant has adopted. Not only is the category of subject and attribute (as commonly applied) unable to cover the whole field of reasoning, but within that category it is a further mistake to insist on the necessity of a major premise.

7. It is evident that the syllogism can not be saved or can only be saved in such a way as to be syllogism no longer. The one chance there is of preserving the syllogism is for us to take our stand upon the third figure. "The attributes of one subject are interrelated" will then become the axiom of inference. We have seen (§4) that all syllogisms in extension can be interpreted according to this axiom, since the identity of the subject was the other side of that relation of attributes which we wished to assert. And it is evident again that all relations of attributes can be regarded as based in a subject. We shall see hereafter that Substitution of Similars can be taken as syllogism within the third figure; and I will go yet further. There is and there can be no inference whatever which may not be reduced under the head of the axiom, since everything which in any way is conjoined can be taken as related within some subject.

We may see hereafter how this reduction is effected. For our present purpose it is enough to remark that in many cases it can not be performed without processes which would horrify the conservative logician, and which gain no end worth the violence they use. Unless "subject and attribute" are used in a way which is quite unknown to the traditional logic, the axiom fails of universal validity, for it does not apply to any of those relations which two or more subjects bear to each other. "Two pianos are in tune with one fork and therefore the one is in tune with the other." But in this instance, unless the terms are manipulated freely, you will not show one subject with its attributes.

8. It is obvious, if we fairly consider the examples which have been adduced at the end of Chapter I., that the syllogism, if it keep its traditional form, is in great part impotent. And I confess I do not know what policy will seem good to the friends of the syllogism. They may boldly accept the violent alternative of excluding all examples which they can not deal with. But I think we may say that such a course as this would be nothing short of a confession of bankruptcy. If a savage may know the road that will take him from A to B, and the road that will take him from B to C, and yet may not know, and may be unable to find out, the way he should go from A to C, I do not see how it can be denied that he is ignorant because he is incapable of an operation. And if that operation is *not* an inference, I can not see why anything else should *be* inference. The plain and palpable facts of the case will, I think, be too hard for the friends of the syllogism. And if they embrace another alternative, and find their amusement in the manufacture of majors, which would never have been seen if the arguments had not come first, then I think once more that the end must be near. So barren a shift will be the dying effort of a hard-run and well-nigh spent chimæra.

But there is, as we saw, another alternative; it may perhaps be thought possible to save the syllogism by first reforming it. Throw the major premise overboard, and call anything a syllogism which can be brought into the form of elements related within one whole. But if the friends of the syllogism resolve on this policy, I think they are friends it might pray to be saved from. It is better to bury a delusion and forget it than to insult its memory by retaining the name when the thing has perished. And it is better to profess that delusion openly than ostensibly to abandon all but the name, and then covertly to re-instate the errors it once stood for. When a mistake has lasted some two thousand years I am ready to believe that it must contain truth, but I must believe too that the time is come when that truth should be able to stand by itself. We can not for ever with eyes fast closed swallow down the mass of orthodox rubbish in which that truth has wrapped itself up. And if the time has not come for extracting the kernel, the time has come for rejecting the shell.

. . .

CHAPTER IV

The Principles of Reasoning

. . .

We know what the syllogism tried to accomplish, for it professed to control from a central office every possible event in all parts of its kingdom. It issued some two dozen forms of reasoning, to which all inference was expected to conform. Thus you had always some model with relations ready drawn between all the terms both in premises and conclusion, and no liberty was left you save to fill up the blanks with terms of your own. The moods and figures were a bed of Procrustes into which all arguments had somehow to be forced, and they were therefore not merely principles of reasoning, but actual canons and tests of inference. Within this pale you were secure of salvation, and on the outside it was heresy to doubt you were lost. Such was the claim which the syllogism put forth, and enforced as long as it had any strength.

Like some other chimæras that have had their day, the syllogism is effete and its realm is masterless; and the question for us who aspire to the inheritance is to know in what character we mean to succeed. Do we wish to substitute one despotism for another? Are our principles of inference to be tests and canons? Most assuredly not; for if the thing were desirable, and I am much too staunch a Protestant to desire it, it is at all events thoroughly impossible.

. . .

6. It is impossible that there should be fixed models for reasoning; you can not draw out exhaustive *schemata* of valid inference. There are principles which are tests of the general possibility of making a construction: but of the actual construction there can be no canons. The attempt to manufacture them would lead to the search for a completed infinity; for the number of special relations has no end, and the possible connections in time, space, and degree are indefinite and inexhaustible. To find the canons of valid inference you must first make a list of valid inferences. You will manufacture a major premise for each, and that major premise derived from each operation will appear as its canon. Your success, if you succeeded, would be the capture of a phantasm, but in the endlessness of the field you would be for ever eluded. No canon will fix for us the pale of orthodoxy, until that day comes when the nature of things will change itself to gratify our stubborn illusions.

7. The popular belief in logic endows it with ability to test all reasonings offered it. In a given case of given premises the logician is thought to be a spiritual Director who, if he can not supply, at least tests right and wrong. Thus, if logic is no art which provides us with arguments, yet, once give it the premises, and it is both the art of extracting conclusions and of assaying all those which amateurs have extracted without its authority. But, understood in this sense, logic has no existence, for there is and there can be no art of reasoning. Logic has to lay down a general theory of reasoning, which is true in general and in the abstract. But when it goes beyond that, it ceases to be a science, it ceases to be logic, and it becomes, what too much of it has already become, an effete chimæra which cries out for burial.

WHAT THE TORTOISE

SAID TO ACHILLES*

LEWIS CARROLL (1832–1898) was the pseudonym under which Charles
Lutwidge Dodgson wrote several contributions to logic as well as his
perennially delightful *Alice in Wonderland, Through the Looking-
Glass,* and other logical nonsense. Under his own name Dodgson
taught mathematics at Oxford University for a quarter of a century,
and published several books on mathematics.

Achilles had overtaken the Tortoise,
and had seated himself comfortably on
its back.

"So you've got to the end of our race-
course?" said the Tortoise. "Even though
it *does* consist of an infinite series of distances? I thought some wiseacre or other
had proved that the thing couldn't be
done?"

"It *can* be done," said Achilles. "It
has been done! *Solvitur ambulando.* You
see the distances were constantly *diminishing;* and so—"

"But if they had been constantly *increasing?*" the Tortoise interrupted. "How
then?"

"Then I shouldn't be *here,*" Achilles
modestly replied; "and *you* would have
got several times round the world, by
this time!"

"You flatter me—*flatten, I mean,*"
said the Tortoise; "for you *are* a heavy
weight, and *no* mistake! Well now, would

you like to hear of a race-course, that
most people fancy they can get to the
end of in two or three steps, while it
really consists of an infinite number of
distances, each one longer than the previous one?"

"Very much indeed!" said the Grecian
warrior, as he drew from his helmet
(few Grecian warriors possessed *pockets*
in those days) an enormous note-book
and a pencil. "Proceed! And speak
slowly, please! *Shorthand* isn't invented
yet!"

"That beautiful First Proposition of
Euclid!" the Tortoise murmured dream-
ily. "You admire Euclid?"

"Passionately! So far, at least, as one
can admire a treatise that won't be
published for some centuries to come!"

"Well, now, let's take a little bit of the
argument in that First Proposition—just
two steps, and the conclusion drawn from
them. Kindly enter them in your note-

* Reprinted from Lewis Carroll, "What the Tortoise Said to Achilles," *Mind,* N.S.IV,
No. 14 (April 1895), pp. 278–280.

book. And in order to refer to them conveniently, let's call them *A, B,* and *Z*:—

(*A*) Things that are equal to the same are equal to each other.

(*B*) The two sides of this Triangle are things that are equal to the same.

(*Z*) The two sides of this Triangle are equal to each other.

Readers of Euclid will grant, I suppose, that *Z* follows logically from *A* and *B,* so that any one who accepts *A* and *B* as true, *must* accept *Z* as true?"

"Undoubtedly! The youngest child in a High School—as soon as High Schools are invented, which will not be till some two thousand years later—will grant *that.*"

"And if some reader had *not* yet accepted *A* and *B* as true, he might still accept the *sequence* as a *valid* one, I suppose?"

"No doubt such a reader might exist. He might say 'I accept as true the Hypothetical Proposition that, *if A* and *B* be true, *Z* must be true; but, I *don't* accept *A* and *B* as true.' Such a reader would do wisely in abandoning Euclid, and taking to football."

"And might there not *also* be some reader who would say 'I accept *A* and *B* as true, but I *don't* accept the Hypothetical'?"

"Certainly there might. *He,* also, had better take to football."

"And *neither* of these readers," the Tortoise continued, "is *as yet* under any logical necessity to accept *Z* as true?"

"Quite so," Achilles assented.

"Well, now, I want you to consider *me* as a reader of the *second* kind, and to force me, logically, to accept *Z* as true."

"A tortoise playing football would be —" Achilles was beginning

"—an anomaly, of course," the Tortoise hastily interrupted. "Don't wander from the point. Let's have *Z* first, and football afterwards!"

"I'm to force you to accept *Z,* am I?" Achilles said musingly. "And your present position is that you accept *A* and *B,* but you *don't* accept the Hypothetical—"

"Let's call it *C,*" said the Tortoise.

"—but you *don't* accept

(*C*) If *A* and *B* are true, *Z* must be true."

"That is my present position," said the Tortoise.

"Then I must ask you to accept *C.*"

"I'll do so," said the Tortoise, "as soon as you've entered it in that note-book of yours. What else have you got in it?"

"Only a few memoranda," said Achilles, nervously fluttering the leaves: "a few memoranda of—of the battles in which I have distinguished myself!"

"Plenty of blank leaves, I see!" the Tortoise cheerily remarked. "We shall need them *all!*" (Achilles shuddered.) "Now write as I dictate:—

(*A*) Things that are equal to the same are equal to each other.

(*B*) The two sides of this Triangle are things that are equal to the same.

(*C*) If *A* and *B* are true, *Z* must be true.

(*Z*) The two sides of this Triangle are equal to each other."

"You should call it *D,* not *Z,*" said Achilles. "It comes *next* to the other three. If you accept *A* and *B* and *C,* you *must* accept *Z.*"

"And why *must* I?"

"Because it follows *logically* from them. If *A* and *B* and *C* are true, *Z must* be true. You don't dispute *that,* I imagine?"

"If *A* and *B* and *C* are true, *Z must* be true," the Tortoise thoughtfully repeated. "That's *another* Hypothetical, isn't it? And, if I failed to see its truth, I might accept *A* and *B* and *C,* and *still* not accept *Z,* mightn't I?"

"You might," the candid hero admitted; "though such obtuseness would certainly be phenomenal. Still, the event is *possible*. So I must ask you to grant *one* more Hypothetical."

"Very good. I'm quite willing to grant it, as soon as you've written it down. We will call it

(D) If A and B and C are true, Z must be true.

Have you entered that in your note-book?"

"I *have!*" Achilles joyfully exclaimed, as he ran the pencil into its sheath. "And at last we've got to the end of this ideal race-course! Now that you accept A and B and C and D, *of course* you accept Z."

"Do I?" said the Tortoise innocently. "Let's make that quite clear. I accept A and B and C and D. Suppose I *still* refused to accept Z?"

"Then Logic would take you by the throat, and *force* you to do it!" Achilles triumphantly replied. "Logic would tell you 'You can't help yourself. Now that you've accepted A and B and C and D, you *must* accept Z!' So you've no choice, you see."

"Whatever Logic is good enough to tell me is worth *writing down*," said the Tortoise. "So enter it in your book, please. We will call it

(E) If A and B and C and D are true, Z must be true. Until I've granted *that*, of course I needn't grant Z. So it's quite a *necessary* step, you see?"

"I see," said Achilles; and there was a touch of sadness in his tone.

Here the narrator, having pressing business at the Bank, was obliged to leave the happy pair, and did not again pass the spot until some months afterwards. When he did so, Achilles was still seated on the back of the much-enduring Tortoise, and was writing in his note-book, which appeared to be nearly full. The Tortoise was saying, "Have you got that last step written down? Unless I've lost count, that makes a thousand and one. There are several millions more to come. And *would* you mind, as a personal favour, considering what a lot of instruction this colloquy of ours will provide for the Logicians of the Nineteenth Century—*would* you mind adopting a pun that my cousin the Mock-Turtle will then make, and allowing yourself to be re-named *Taught-Us?*"

"As you please!" replied the weary warrior, in the hollow tones of despair, as he buried his face in his hands. "Provided that *you*, for *your* part, will adopt a pun the Mock-Turtle never made, and allow yourself to be re-named *A Kill-Ease!*"

ARISTOTLE'S LOGIC*

BERTRAND RUSSELL (1872–   ). See page 78.

Aristotle's influence, which was very great in many different fields, was greatest of all in logic. In late antiquity, when Plato was still supreme in metaphysics, Aristotle was the recognized authority in logic, and he retained this position throughout the Middle Ages. It was not till the thirteenth century that Christian philosophers accorded him supremacy in the field of metaphysics. This supremacy was largely lost after the Renaissance, but his supremacy in logic survived. Even at the present day, all Catholic teachers of philosophy and many others still obstinately reject the discoveries of modern logic, and adhere with a strange tenacity to a system which is as definitely antiquated as Ptolemaic astronomy. This makes it difficult to do historical justice to Aristotle. His present-day influence is so inimical to clear thinking that it is hard to remember how great an advance he made upon all his predecessors (including Plato), or how admirable his logical work would still seem if it had been a stage in a continual progress, instead of being (as in fact it was) a dead end, followed by over two thousand years of stagnation. In dealing with the predecessors of Aristotle, it is not necessary to remind the reader that they are not verbally inspired; one can therefore praise them for their ability without being supposed to subscribe to all their doctrines. Aristotle, on the contrary, is still, especially in logic, a battle-ground, and cannot be treated in a purely historical spirit.

Aristotle's most important work in logic is the doctrine of the syllogism. A syllogism is an argument consisting of three parts, a major premiss, a minor premiss, and a conclusion. Syllogisms are of a number of different kinds, each of which has a name, given by the scholastics. The most familiar is the kind called "Barbara":

All men are mortal (Major premiss).
Socrates is a man (Minor premiss).
Therefore: Socrates is mortal (Conclusion).
Or: All men are mortal.
All Greeks are men.
Therefore: All Greeks are mortal.

(Aristotle does not distinguish between these two forms; this, as we shall see later, is a mistake.)
Other forms are: No fishes are rational,

* From Bertrand Russell, *A History of Western Philosophy,* pp. 195–202. Copyright, 1945, by Bertrand Russell and reprinted by permission of Simon and Schuster, Inc., New York and Allen & Unwin, Ltd., London.

all sharks are fishes, therefore no sharks are rational. (This is called "Celarent.")

All men are rational, some animals are men, therefore some animals are rational. (This is called "Darii.")

No Greeks are black, some men are Greeks, therefore some men are not black. (This is called "Ferio.")

These four make up the "first figure"; Aristotle adds a second and third figure, and the schoolmen added a fourth. It is shown that the three later figures can be reduced to the first by various devices.

There are some inferences that can be made from a single premiss. From "some men are mortal" we can infer that "some mortals are men." According to Aristotle, this can also be inferred from "all men are mortal." From "no gods are mortal" we can infer "no mortals are gods," but from "some men are not Greeks" it does not follow that "some Greeks are not men."

Apart from such inferences as the above, Aristotle and his followers thought that all deductive inference, when strictly stated, is syllogistic. By setting forth all the valid kinds of syllogism, and setting out any suggested argument in syllogistic form, it should therefore be possible to avoid all fallacies.

This system was the beginning of formal logic, and, as such, was both important and admirable. But considered as the end, not the beginning, of formal logic, it is open to three kinds of criticism:

(1) Formal defects within the system itself.

(2) Over-estimation of the syllogism, as compared to other forms of deductive argument.

(3) Over-estimation of deduction as a form of argument.

On each of these three, something must be said.

(1) *Formal defects.* Let us begin with the two statements "Socrates is a man"

and "all Greeks are men." It is necessary to make a sharp distinction between these two, which is not done in Aristotelian logic. The statement "all Greeks are men" is commonly interpreted as implying that there are Greeks; without this implication, some of Aristotle's syllogisms are not valid. Take for instance:

"All Greeks are men, all Greeks are white, therefore some men are white." This is valid if there are Greeks, but not otherwise. If I were to say:

"All golden mountains are mountains, all golden mountains are golden, therefore some mountains are golden," my conclusion would be false, though in some sense my premises would be true. If we are to be explicit, we must therefore divide the one statement "all Greeks are men" into two, one saying "there are Greeks," and the other saying "if anything is a Greek, it is a man." The latter statement is purely hypothetical, and does not imply that there are Greeks.

The statement "all Greeks are men" is thus much more complex in form than the statement "Socrates is a man." "Socrates is a man" has "Socrates" for its subject, but "all Greeks are men" does not have "all Greeks" for its subject, for there is nothing about "all Greeks" either in the statement "there are Greeks" or in the statement "if anything is a Greek it is a man."

This purely formal error was a source of errors in metaphysics and theory of knowledge. Consider the state of our knowledge in regard to the two propositions "Socrates is mortal" and "all men are mortal." In order to know the truth of "Socrates is mortal," most of us are content to rely upon testimony; but if testimony is to be reliable, it must lead us back to some one who knew Socrates and saw him dead. The one perceived fact—the dead body of Socrates—together with the knowledge that this was called "Socrates," was enough to assure us of the mortality of Socrates. But when it comes to "all men are mortal," the matter is different. The question of our knowledge of such general propositions is a very difficult one. Sometimes they are merely verbal: "all Greeks are men" is known because nothing is called "a Greek" unless it is a man. Such general statements can be ascertained from the dictionary; they tell us nothing about the world except how words are used. But "all men are mortal" is not of this sort; there is nothing logically self-contradictory about an immortal man. We believe the proposition on the basis of induction, because there is no well-authenticated case of a man living more than (say) 150 years; but this only makes the proposition probable, not certain. It cannot be certain so long as living men exist.

Metaphysical errors arose through supposing that "all men" is the subject of "all men are mortal" in the same sense as that in which "Socrates" is the subject of "Socrates is mortal." It made it possible to hold that, in some sense, "all men" denotes an entity of the same sort as that denoted by "Socrates." This led Aristotle to say that in a sense a species is a substance. He is careful to qualify this statement, but his followers, especially Porphyry, showed less caution.

Another error into which Aristotle falls through this mistake is to think that a predicate of a predicate can be a predicate of the original subject. If I say "Socrates is Greek, all Greeks are human," Aristotle thinks that "human" is a predicate of "Greek," while "Greek" is a predicate of "Socrates," and obviously "human" is a predicate of "Socrates." But in fact "human" is not a predicate of "Greek." The distinction between names and predicates, or, in metaphysical language, between particulars and universals, is thus blurred, with disastrous consequences to philosophy. One of the resulting confusions was to suppose that

a class with only one member is identical with that one member. This made it impossible to have a correct theory of the number *one*, and led to endless bad metaphysics about unity.

(2) *Over-estimation of the syllogism.* The syllogism is only one kind of deductive argument. In mathematics, which is wholly deductive, syllogisms hardly ever occur. Of course it would be possible to re-write mathematical arguments in syllogistic form, but this would be very artificial and would not make them any more cogent. Take arithmetic, for example. If I buy goods worth $4.63, and tender a $5 bill in payment, how much change is due to me? To put this simple sum in the form of a syllogism would be absurd, and would tend to conceal the real nature of the argument. Again, within logic there are non-syllogistic inferences, such as: "A horse is an animal, therefore a horse's head is an animal's head." Valid syllogisms, in fact, are only some among valid deductions, and have no logical priority over others. The attempt to give preeminence to the syllogism in deduction misled philosophers as to the nature of mathematical reasoning. Kant, who perceived that mathematics is not syllogistic, inferred that it uses extra-logical principles, which, however, he supposed to be as certain as those of logic. He, like his predecessors, though in a different way, was misled by respect for Aristotle.

(3) *Over-estimation of deduction.* The Greeks in general attached more importance to deduction as a source of knowledge than modern philosophers do. In this respect, Aristotle was less at fault than Plato; he repeatedly admitted the importance of induction, and he devoted considerable attention to the question: how do we know the first premisses from which deduction must start? Nevertheless, he, like other Greeks, gave undue prominence to deduction in his theory of knowledge. We shall agree that Mr.

Smith (say) is mortal, and we may, loosely, say that we know this because we know that all men are mortal. But what we really know is not "all men are mortal"; we know rather something like "all men born more than one hundred and fifty years ago are mortal, and so are almost all men born more than one hundred years ago." This is our reason for thinking that Mr. Smith will die. But this argument is an induction, not a deduction. It has less cogency than a deduction, and yields only a probability, not a certainty; but on the other hand it gives *new* knowledge, which deduction does not. All the important inferences outside logic and pure mathematics are inductive, not deductive; the only exceptions are law and theology, each of which derives its first principles from an unquestionable text, viz. the statute books or the scriptures.

Apart from *The Prior Analytics,* which deals with the syllogism, there are other writings of Aristotle which have considerable importance in the history of philosophy. One of these is the short work on *The Categories.* Porphyry the Neoplatonist wrote a commentary on this book, which had a very notable influence on medieval philosophy; but for the present let us ignore Porphyry and confine ourselves to Aristotle.

What, exactly, is meant by the word "category," whether in Aristotle or in Kant and Hegel, I must confess that I have never been able to understand. I do not myself believe that the term "category" is in any way useful in philosophy, as representing any clear idea. There are, in Aristotle, ten categories: substance, quantity, quality, relation, place, time, position, state, action, and affection. The only definition offered of the term "category" is: "expressions which are in no way composite signify" —and then follows the above list. This seems to mean that every word of which the meaning is not compounded of the meanings of other words signifies a substance or a quantity or etc. There is no suggestion of any principle on which the list of ten categories has been compiled.

"Substance" is primarily what is not predicable of a subject nor present in a subject. A thing is said to be "present in a subject" when, though not a part of the subject, it cannot exist without the subject. The instances given are a piece of grammatical knowledge which is present in a mind, and a certain whiteness which may be present in a body. A substance in the above primary sense is an individual thing or person or animal. But in a secondary sense a species or a genus— e.g., "man" or "animal"—may be called a substance. This secondary sense seems indefensible, and opened the door, in later writers, to much bad metaphysics.

The Posterior Analytics is a work largely concerned with a question which must trouble any deductive theory, namely: How are first premisses obtained? Since deduction must start from somewhere, we must begin with something unproved, which must be known otherwise than by demonstration. I shall not give Aristotle's theory in detail since it depends upon the notion of *essence.* A definition, he says, is a statement of a thing's essential nature. The notion of essence is an intimate part of every philosophy subsequent to Aristotle, until we come to modern times. It is, in my opinion, a hopelessly muddle-headed notion, but its historical importance requires us to say something about it.

The "essence" of a thing appears to have meant "those of its properties which it cannot change without losing its identity." Socrates may be sometimes happy, sometimes sad; sometimes well, sometimes ill. Since he can change these properties without ceasing to be Socrates, they are no part of his essence. But it is supposed to be of the essence of

Socrates that he is a man, though a Pythagorean, who believes in transmigration, will not admit this. In fact, the question of "essence" is one as to the use of words. We apply the same name, on different occasions, to somewhat different occurrences, which we regard as manifestations of a single "thing" or "person." In fact, however, this is only a verbal convenience. The "essence" of Socrates thus consists of those properties in the absence of which we should not use the name "Socrates." The question is purely linguistic: a *word* may have an essence, but a *thing* cannot.

The conception of "substance," like that of "essence," is a transference to metaphysics of what is only a linguistic convenience. We find it convenient, in describing the world, to describe a certain number of occurrences as events in the life of "Socrates," and a certain number of others as events in the life of "Mr. Smith." This leads us to think of "Socrates" or "Mr. Smith" as denoting something that persists through a certain number of years, and as in some way more "solid" and "real" than the events that happen to him. If Socrates is ill, we think that Socrates, at other times, is well, and therefore the being of Socrates is independent of his illness; illness, on the other hand, requires somebody to be ill. But although Socrates need not be ill, *something* must be occurring to him if he is to be considered to exist. He is not, therefore, really any more "solid" than the things that happen to him.

"Substance," when taken seriously, is a concept impossible to free from difficulties. A substance is supposed to be the subject of properties, and to be something distinct from all its properties. But when we take away the properties, and try to imagine the substance by itself, we find that there is nothing left. To put the matter in another way: What distinguishes one substance from another? Not

difference of properties, for, according to the logic of substance, difference of properties presupposes numerical diversity between the substances concerned. Two substances, therefore, must be *just* two, without being, in themselves, in any way distinguishable. How, then, are we ever to find out that they *are* two?

"Substance," in fact, is merely a convenient way of collecting events into bundles. What can we know about Mr. Smith? When we look at him, we see a pattern of colours; when we listen to him talking, we hear a series of sounds. We believe that, like us, he has thoughts and feelings. But what is Mr. Smith apart from all these occurrences? A mere imaginary hook, from which the occurrences are supposed to hang. They have in fact no need of a hook, any more than the earth needs an elephant to rest upon. Any one can see, in the analogous case of a geographical region, that such a word as "France" (say) is only a linguistic convenience, and that there is not a *thing* called "France" over and above its various parts. The same holds of "Mr. Smith"; it is a collective name for a number of occurrences. If we take it as anything more, it denotes something completely unknowable, and therefore not needed for the expression of what we know.

"Substance," in a word, is a metaphysical mistake, due to transference to the world-structure of the structure of sentences composed of a subject and a predicate.

I conclude that the Aristotelian doctrines with which we have been concerned in this chapter are wholly false, with the exception of the formal theory of the syllogism, which is unimportant. Any person in the present day who wishes to learn logic will be wasting his time if he reads Aristotle or any of his disciples. None the less, Aristotle's logical writings show great ability, and would have been useful to mankind if they had appeared at a time when intellectual originality was still active. Unfortunately, they appeared at the very end of the creative period of Greek thought, and therefore came to be accepted as authoritative. By the time that logical orginality revived, a reign of two thousand years had made Aristotle very difficult to dethrone. Throughout modern times, practically every advance in science, in logic, or in philosophy has had to be made in the teeth of the opposition from Aristotle's disciples.

The Laws of Thought

INTRODUCTION   Part of the logical tradition are the so-called "Laws of Thought." The first, the *Law of Identity,* asserts that *"A is A"* or "If a proposition is true then it is true." The second, the *Law of Contradiction,* asserts that *"A cannot be both B and not-B"* or *"A* proposition cannot be both true and false." The third, the *Law of Excluded Middle,* asserts that *"A* is either *B* or not-*B"* or *"A* proposition is either true or false." These three laws have been proclaimed to be the fundamental presuppositions of all (correct) reasoning.

The first selection included in this part is from Book IV of Aristotle's *Metaphysics.* In it Aristotle admits that not all propositions can be demonstrated, but maintains that it is possible to give a "negative proof" of the Law of Contradiction to someone who is willing to "say something which is *significant."* In his Chapter 7 of Book IV Aristotle attempts to provide a proof of the Law of Excluded Middle also.

In the selection from *On Interpretation,* Aristotle nevertheless argues that the Law of Excluded Middle does not apply to propositions about the future. For if propositions about the future are either true or false, then "there are no real alternatives; everything takes place of necessity and is fixed."

Hegel rejects all three laws, arguing that both common sense and the philosophy of reason have discredited the first, and that the second "most expressly controverts" it. The third is condemned also, as inane, though some doubt as to Hegel's exact meaning is raised by his remark that "In the notion of a circle, . . . centre and circumference are opposite and contradictory to each other."

Engels directs his polemical zeal against the Law of Contradiction, holding that all motion, change, and life involve actual contradictions, in which things or qualities and their negations coexist. Of course as Engels uses the term, "negation" covers mathematical, biological, and social operations rather than simply the logical operation of denial.

Mill asserts the Laws of Thought—when sufficiently qualified to be true—are known not by any logical intuition but by experience. They are as much the result of empirical inductive generalization as Laws of Chemistry, of Physics, or of Mathematics.

Bradley agrees with Hegel in rejecting the principle of Identity as both pernicious and useless. But he goes on at length to disagree with Hegel in detail about the principle of Contradiction. Finally, Bradley records still another difference with Mill, this time over the Excluded Middle.

Russell defends the Law of Excluded Middle from the point of view of logic, in which "truth" has nothing to do with *knowledge*. He concedes, however, that from the point of view of epistemology (the theory of knowledge) and an empiricist[1] definition of "truth" in terms of verification, "the law of excluded middle, in its usual form, cannot be true."

[1] See footnote on page 3.

PROVING THE LAWS

OF THOUGHT*

ARISTOTLE (384–322 B.C.).   See page 8.

Evidently then it belongs to the philosopher, i.e. to him who is studying the nature of all substance, to inquire also into the principles of syllogism. But he who knows best about each genus must be able to state the most certain principles of his subject, so that ne whose subject is existing things *qua* existing must be able to state the most certain principles of all things. This is the philosopher, and the most certain principle of all is that regarding which it is impossible to be mistaken; for such a principle must be both the best known (for all men may be mistaken about things which they do not know), and non-hypothetical. For a principle which every one must have who understands anything that is, is not a hypothesis; and that which every one must know who knows anything, he must already have when he comes to a special study. Evidently then such a principle is the most certain of all; which principle this is, let us proceed to say. It is, that the same attribute cannot at the same time belong and not belong to the same subject and in the same respect; we must presuppose, to guard against dialectical objections, any further qualifications which might be added. This, then, is the most

certain of all principles, since it answers to the definition given above. For it is impossible for any one to believe the same thing to be and not to be, as some think Heraclitus says. For what a man says, he does not necessarily believe; and if it is impossible that contrary attributes should belong at the same time to the same subject (the usual qualifications must be presupposed in this premiss too), and if an opinion which contradicts another is contrary to it, obviously it is impossible for the same man at the same time to believe the same thing to be and not to be; for if a man were mistaken on this point he would have contrary opinions at the same time. It is for this reason that all who are carrying out a demonstration reduce it to this as an ultimate belief; for this is naturally the starting-point even for all the other axioms.

4

There are some who, as we said, both themselves assert that it is possible for the same thing to be and not to be, and say that people can judge this to be the case. And among others many writers about nature use this language. But we

* From Book IV of *Metaphysics* in *The Works of Aristotle* (1928), Volume VIII, translated under the editorship of W. D. Ross. Reprinted by permission of The Clarendon Press, Oxford.

have now posited that it is impossible for anything at the same time to be and not to be, and by this means have shown that this is the most indisputable of all principles.—Some indeed demand that even this shall be demonstrated, but this they do through want of education, for not to know of what things one should demand demonstration, and of what one should not, argues want of education. For it is impossible that there should be demonstration of absolutely everything (there would be an infinite regress, so that there would still be no demonstration); but if there are things of which one should not demand demonstration, these persons could not say what principle they maintain to be more self-evident than the present one.

We can, however, demonstrate negatively even that this view is impossible, if our opponent will only say something; and if he says nothing, it is absurd to seek to give an account of our views to one who cannot give an account of anything, in so far as he cannot do so. For such a man, as such, is from the start no better than a vegetable. Now negative demonstration I distinguish from demonstration proper, because in a demonstration one might be thought to be begging the question, but if another person is responsible for the assumption we shall have negative proof, not demonstration. The starting-point for all such arguments is not the demand that our opponent shall say that something either is or is not (for this one might perhaps take to be a begging of the question), but that he shall say something which is *significant* both for himself and for another; for this is necessary, if he really is to say anything. For, if he means nothing, such a man will not be capable of reasoning, either with himself or with another. But if any one grants this, demonstration will be possible; for we shall already have something definite. The person responsible for the proof, however, is not

he who demonstrates but he who listens; for while disowning reason he listens to reason. And again he who admits this has admitted that something is true apart from demonstration [so that not every thing will be 'so and not so'].

First then this at least is obviously true, that the word 'be' or 'not be' has a definite meaning, so that not everything will be 'so and not so'.—Again if 'man' has one meaning, let this be 'two-footed animal'; by having one meaning I understand this:—if 'man' means 'X', then if A is a man 'X' will be what 'being a man' means for him. (It makes no difference even if one were to say a word has several meanings, if only they are limited in number; for to each definition there might be assigned a different word. For instance, we might say that 'man' has not one meaning but several, one of which would have one definition, viz. 'two-footed animal', while there might be also several other definitions if only they were limited in number; for a peculiar name might be assigned to each of the definitions. If, however, they were not limited but one were to say that the word has an infinite number of meanings, obviously reasoning would be impossible; for not to have one meaning is to have no meaning, and if words have no meaning our reasoning with one another, and indeed with ourselves, has been annihilated; for it is impossible to think of anything if we do not think of one thing; but if this *is* possible, one name might be assigned to this thing.)

Let it be assumed then, as was said at the beginning, that the name has a meaning and has one meaning; it is impossible, then, that 'being a man' should mean precisely 'not being a man', if 'man' not only signifies something about one subject but also has one significance (for we do not identify 'having one significance' with 'signifying something about one subject', since on *that* assumption even 'musical' and 'white' and 'man' would have had one significance, so that all things would have been one; for they would all have had the same significance).

And it will not be possible to be and not to be the same thing, except in virtue of an ambiguity, just as if one whom we call 'man', others were to call 'not-man'; but the point in question is not this, whether the same thing can at the same time be and not be a man in name, but whether it can in fact.—Now if 'man' and 'not-man' mean nothing different, obviously 'not being a man' will mean nothing different from 'being a man'; so that 'being a man' will be 'not being a man'; for they will be one. For being one means this—being related as 'raiment' and 'dress' are, if their definition is one. And if 'being a man' and 'being a not-man' are to be one, they must mean one thing. But it was shown earlier that they mean different things.—Therefore, if it is true to say of anything that it is a man, it must be a two-footed animal (for this was what 'man' meant); and if this is necessary, it is impossible that the same thing should not at that time be a two-footed animal; for this is what 'being necessary' means—that it is impossible for the thing not to be. It is, then, impossible that it should be at the same time true to say the same thing is a man and is not a man.

The same account holds good with regard to 'not being a man', for 'being a man' and 'being a not-man' mean different things, since even 'being white' and 'being a man' are different; for the former terms are much more opposed, so that they must a fortiori mean different things. And if any one says that 'white' means one and the same thing as 'man', again we shall say the same as what was said before, that it would follow that all things are one, and not only opposites. But if this is impossible, then what we have maintained will follow,

if our opponent will only answer our question.

And if, when one asks the question simply, he adds the contradictories, he is not answering the question. For there is nothing to prevent the same thing from being both a man and white and countless other things: but still, if one asks whether it is or is not true to say that this is a man, our opponent must give an answer which means one thing, and not add that 'it is also white and large'. For, besides other reasons, it is impossible to enumerate its accidental attributes, which are infinite in number; let him, then, enumerate either all or none. Similarly, therefore, even if the same thing is a thousand times a man and a not-man, he must not, in answering the question whether this is a man, add that it is also at the same time a not-man, unless he is bound to add also all the other accidents, all that the subject is or is not; and if he does this, he is not observing the rules of argument.

And in general those who say this do away with substance and essence. For they must say that all attributes are accidents, and that there is no such thing as 'being essentially a man' or 'an animal'. For if there is to be any such thing as 'being essentially a man' this will not be 'being a not-man' or 'not being a man' (yet these are negations of it[1]); for there was one thing which it meant, and this was the substance of something. And denoting the substance of a thing means that the essence of the thing is nothing else. But if its being essentially a man is to be the same as either being essentially a not-man or essentially not being a man, then its essence will be something else. Therefore our opponents must say that there cannot be such a definition of anything, but that all attributes are acci-

[1] sc. and hence (on the view attacked) should be compatible with it.

dental; for this is the distinction between substance and accident—'white' is accidental to man, because though he is white, whiteness is not his essence. But if *all* statements are accidental, there will be nothing primary about which they are made, if the accidental always implies predication about a subject. The predication, then, must go on *ad infinitum*. But this is impossible; for not even more than two terms can be combined in accidental predication. For (1) an accident is not an accident of an accident, unless it be because both are accidents of the same subject. I mean, for instance, that the white is musical and the latter is white, only because both are accidental to man. But (2) Socrates is musical, not in this sense, that both terms are accidental to something else. Since then some predicates are accidental in this and some in that sense, (*a*) those which are accidental in the latter sense, in which white is accidental to Socrates, cannot form an infinite series in the upward direction;[2] e. g. Socrates the white has not yet another accident; for no unity can be got out of such a sum. Nor again (*b*) will 'white' have another term accidental to it, e. g. 'musical'. For this is no more accidental to that than that is to this; and at the same time we have drawn the distinction, that while some predicates are accidental in this sense, others are so in the sense in which 'musical' is accidental to Socrates; and the accident is an accident of an accident not in cases of the latter kind, but only in cases of the other kind, so that not *all* terms will be accidental.[3] There must, then, even so be something which denotes substance. And if this is

so, it has been shown that contradictories cannot be predicated at the same time.

Again, if all contradictory statements are true of the same subject at the same time, evidently all things will be one. For the same thing will be a trireme, a wall, and a man, if of everything it is possible either to affirm or to deny anything (and this premiss must be accepted by those who share the views of Protagoras). For if any one thinks that the man is not a trireme, evidently he is not a trireme; so that he also *is* a trireme, if, as they say, contradictory statements are both true. And we thus get the doctrine of Anaxagoras, that all things are mixed together; so that nothing really exists. They seem, then, to be speaking of the indeterminate, and, while fancying themselves to be speaking of being, they are speaking about non-being; for it is that which exists potentially and not in complete reality that is indeterminate. But they *must* predicate of every subject the affirmation or the negation of every attribute. For it is absurd if of each subject its own negation is to be predicable, while the negation of something else which cannot be predicated of it is not to be predicable of it; for instance, if it is true to say of a man that he is not a man, evidently it is also true to say that he is either a trireme or not a trireme. If, then, the affirmative[4] can be predicated, the negative must be predicable too; and if the affirmative is not predicable, the negative, at least, will be more predicable than the negative of the subject itself. If, then, even the latter negative is predicable, the negative of 'trireme' will be also predicable; and, if this is predicable, the affirmative will be so too.

Those, then, who maintain this view are driven to this conclusion, and to the further conclusion that it is not necessary either to assert or to deny. For if it is

[2] i.e. in the direction of predicates, which are naturally wider or higher than the subject.

[3] Sense (1) reduces to sense (2), and in this an infinite number of accidents combined together is impossible; there must be substance somewhere.

[4] sc. 'trireme'.

true that a thing is a man and a not-man, evidently also it will be neither a man nor a not-man. For to the two assertions there answer two negations, and if the former[5] is treated as a single proposition compounded out of two, the latter also is a single proposition opposite to the former.

Again, either the theory is true in all cases, and a thing is both white and not-white, and existent and non-existent, and all other assertions and negations are similarly compatible, or the theory is true of some statements and not of others. And if not of all, the exceptions will be contradictories of which admittedly only one is true; but if of all, again either the negation will be true wherever the assertion is, and the assertion true wherever the negation is, or the negation will be true where the assertion is, but the assertion not always true where the negation is. And (a) in the latter case there will be something which fixedly *is not,* and this will be an indisputable belief; and if non-being is something indisputable and knowable, the opposite assertion will be more knowable. But (b) if it is equally possible also to assert all that it is possible to deny, one must either be saying what its true when one separates the predicates (and says, for instance, that a thing is white, and again that it is not-white), or not. And if (i) it is not true to apply the predicates separately, our opponent is not saying what he professes to say, and also nothing at all exists, but how could non-existent things speak or walk, as he does? Also all things would on this view be one, as has been already said, and man and God and trireme and their contradictories will be the same. For if ccntradictories can be predicated alike of each subject, one thing will in no wise differ from another; for if it differ, this difference will be some-

thing true and peculiar to it. And (ii) if one may with truth apply the predicates separately, the above-mentioned result follows none the less, and, further, it follows that all would then be right and all would be in error, and our opponent himself confesses himself to be in error. —And at the same time our discussion with him is evidently about nothing at all; for he says nothing. For he says neither 'yes' nor 'no', but 'yes and no'; and again he denies both of these and says 'neither yes nor no'; for otherwise there would already be something definite.

Again, if when the assertion is true, the negation is false, and when this is true, the affirmation is false, it will not be possible to assert and deny the same thing truly at the same time. But perhaps they might say this was the very question at issue.

Again, is he in error who judges either that the thing is so or that it is not so, and is he right who judges both? If he is right, what can they mean by saying that the nature of existing things is of this kind? And if he is not right, but more right than he who judges in the other way, being will already be of a definite nature, and this will be true, and not at the same time also not true. But if all are alike both wrong and right, one who is in this condition will not be able either to speak or to say anything intelligible; for he says at the same time both 'yes' and 'no'. And if he makes no judgement but 'thinks' and 'does not think', indifferently, what difference will there be between him and a vegetable?—Thus, then, it is in the highest degree evident that neither any one of those who maintain this view nor any one else is really in this position. For why does a man walk to Megara and not stay at home, when he thinks he ought to be walking there? Why does he not walk early some morning into a well or over a precipice, if one happens to be in his way? Why do we observe him

---

[5] *sc.* that the thing is a man and a not-man.

guarding against this, evidently because he does not think that falling in is alike good and not good? Evidently, then, he judges one thing to be better and another worse. And if this is so, he must also judge one thing to be a man and another to be not-a-man, one thing to be sweet and another to be not-sweet. For he does not aim at and judge all things alike, when, thinking it desirable to drink water or to see a man, he proceeds to aim at these things; yet he *ought,* if the same thing were alike a man and not-a-man. But, as was said, there is no one who does not obviously avoid some things and not others. Therefore, as it seems, all men make unqualified judgements, if not about all things, still about what is better and worse. And if this is not knowledge but opinion, they should be all the more anxious about the truth, as a sick man should be more anxious about his health than one who is healthy; for he who has opinions is, in comparison with the man who knows, not in a healthy state as far as the truth is concerned.

Again, however much all things may be 'so and not so', still there is a more and a less in the nature of things; for we should not say that two and three are equally even, nor is he who thinks four things are five equally wrong with him who thinks they are a thousand. If then they are not equally wrong, obviously one is less wrong and therefore more right. If then that which has more of any quality is nearer the norm, there must be some truth to which the more true is nearer. And even if there is not, still there is already something better founded and liker the truth, and we shall have got rid of the unqualified doctrine which would prevent us from determining anything in our thought.

5

From the same opinion proceeds the doctrine of Protagoras, and both doc-trines must be alike true or alike untrue. For on the one hand, if all opinions and appearances are true, all statements must be at the same time true and false. For many men hold beliefs in which they conflict with one another, and think those mistaken who have not the same opinions as themselves; so that the same thing must both be and not be. And on the other hand, if this is so, all opinions must be true; for those who are mistaken and those who are right are opposed to one another in their opinions; if, then, reality is such as the view in question supposes, all will be right in their beliefs.

Evidently, then, both doctrines proceed from the same way of thinking. But the same method of discussion must not be used with all opponents; for some need persuasion, and others compulsion. Those who have been driven to this position by difficulties in their thinking can easily be cured of their ignorance; for it is not their expressed argument but their thought that one has to meet. But those who argue for the sake of argument can be cured only by refuting the argument as expressed in speech and in words.

Those who really feel the difficulties have been led to this opinion by observation of the sensible world. (1) They think that contradictories or contraries are true at the same time, because they see contraries coming into existence out of the same thing. If, then, that which is not cannot come to be, the thing must have existed before as both contraries alike, as Anaxagoras says all is mixed in all, and Democritus too; for *he* says the void and the full exist alike in every part, and yet one of these is being, and the other non-being. To those, then, whose belief rests on these grounds, we shall say that in a sense they speak rightly and in a sense they err. For 'that which is' has two meanings, so that in some sense a thing can come to be out of that which is not, while in some sense it cannot, and the same thing can at the same time be in being and not in being—but not in the same respect. For the same thing can be potentially at the same time two contraries, but it cannot actually. And again we shall ask them to believe that among existing things there is also another kind of substance to which neither movement nor destruction nor generation at all belongs.

And (2) similarly some have inferred from observation of the sensible world the truth of appearances. For they think that the truth should not be determined by the large or small number of those who hold a belief, and that the same thing is thought sweet by some when they taste it, and bitter by others, so that if all were ill or all were mad, and only two or three were well or sane, these would be thought ill and mad, and not the others.

And again, they say that many of the other animals receive impressions contrary to ours; and that even to the senses of each individual, things do not always seem the same. Which, then, of these impressions are true and which are false is not obvious; for the one set is no more true than the other, but both are alike. And this is why Democritus, at any rate, says that either there is no truth or to us at least it is not evident.

And in general it is because these thinkers suppose knowledge to be sensation, and this to be a physical alteration, that they say that what appears to our senses must be true; for it is for these reasons that both Empedocles and Democritus and, one may almost say, all the others have fallen victims to opinions of this sort. For Empedocles says that when men change their condition they change their knowledge.

For wisdom increases in men according to what is before them. And elsewhere he says that

So far as their nature changed, so far to them always
Came changed thoughts into mind.

And Parmenides also expresses himself in the same way:

For as at each time the much-bent limbs are composed,
So is the mind of men; for in each and all men
'Tis one thing thinks—the substance of their limbs:
For that of which there is more is thought.

A saying of Anaxagoras to some of his friends is also related—that things would be for them such as they supposed them to be. And they say that Homer also evidently had this opinion, because he made Hector, when he was unconscious from the blow, lie 'thinking other thoughts' —which implies that even those who are bereft of thought have thoughts, though not the same thoughts. Evidently, then, if both are forms of knowledge, the real things also are at the same time 'both so and not so'. And it is in this direction that the consequences are most difficult. For if those who have seen most of such truth as is possible for us (and these are those who seek and love it most)—if these have such opinions and express these views about the truth, is it not natural that beginners in philosophy should lose heart? For to seek the truth would be to follow flying game.

But the reason why these thinkers held this opinion is that while they were inquiring into the truth of that which is, they thought 'that which is' was identical with the sensible world; in this, however, there is largely present the nature of the indeterminate—of that which exists in the peculiar sense which we have explained; and therefore, while they speak plausibly, they do not say what is true (for it is fitting to put the matter so rather than as Epicharmus put it against Xenophanes[6]). And again, because they saw that all this

[6] Epicharmus may have said that Xenophanes' views were 'neither plausible nor true', or that they were 'true but not plausible'.

world of nature is in movement, and that about that which changes no true statement can be made, they said that of course, regarding that which everywhere in every respect is changing, nothing could truly be affirmed. It was this belief that blossomed into the most extreme of the views above mentioned, that of the professed Heracliteans, such as was held by Cratylus, who finally did not think it right to say anything but only moved his finger, and criticized Heraclitus for saying that it is impossible to step twice into the same river; for *he* thought one could not do it even once.

But we shall say in answer to this argument also, that while there is some justification for their thinking that the changing, when it is changing, does not exist, yet it is after all disputable; for that which is losing a quality has something of that which is being lost, and of that which is coming to be, something must already be. And in general if a thing is perishing, there will be present something that exists; and if a thing is coming to be, there must be something from which it comes to be and something by which it is generated, and this process cannot go on *ad infinitum*.—But, leaving these arguments, let us insist on this, that it is not the same thing to change in quantity and in quality. Grant that in quantity a thing is not constant; still it is in respect of its form that we know each thing.—And again, it would be fair to criticize those who hold this view for asserting about the whole material universe what they saw only in a minority even of sensible things. For only that region of the sensible world which immediately surrounds us is always in process of destruction and generation; but this is—so to speak—not even a fraction of the whole, so that it would have been juster to acquit this part of the world because of the other part, than to condemn the other because of this.—And

again, obviously we shall make to them also the same reply that we made long ago; we must show them and persuade them that there is something whose nature is changeless. Indeed, those who say that things at the same time are and are not, should in consequence say that all things are at rest rather than that they are in movement; for there is nothing into which they can change, since all attributes belong already to all subjects.

Regarding the nature of truth, we must maintain that not everything which appears is true; firstly, because even if sensation—at least of the object peculiar to the sense in question—is not false, still appearance is not the same as sensation. —Again, it is fair to express surprise at our opponents' raising the question whether magnitudes are as great, and colours are of such a nature, as they appear to people at a distance, or as they appear to those close at hand, and whether they are such as they appear to the healthy or to the sick, and whether those things are heavy which appear so to the weak or those which appear so to the strong, and those things true which appear to the sleeping or to the waking. For obviously they do not think these to be open questions; no one, at least, if when he is in Libya he has fancied one night that he is in Athens, starts for the concert hall.—And again with regard to the future, as Plato says,[7] surely the opinion of the physician and that of the ignorant man are not equally weighty, for instance, on the question whether a man will get well or not.—And again, among sensations themselves the sensation of a foreign object and that of the appropriate object, or that of a kindred object and that of the object of the sense in question,[8] are not equally authoritative,

[7] Cf. *Theaetetus* 178 B–179 A.
[8] e. g. the awareness which smell gives us of savour and of odour respectively.

but in the case of colour sight, not taste, has the authority, and in the case of flavour taste, not sight; each of which senses never says at the same time of the same object that it simultaneously is 'so and not so'.—But not even at different times does one sense disagree about the quality, but only about that to which the quality belongs. I mean, for instance, that the same wine might seem, if either it or one's body changed, at one time sweet and at another time not sweet; but at least the sweet, such as it is when it exists, has never yet changed, but one is always right about it, and that which is to be sweet is of necessity of such and such a nature. Yet all these views destroy this necessity, leaving nothing to be of necessity, as they leave no essence of anything; for the necessary cannot be in this way and also in that, so that if anything is of necessity, it will not be 'both so and not so'.

And, in general, if only the sensible exists, there would be nothing if animate things were not; for there would be no faculty of sense. Now the view that neither the sensible qualities nor the sensations would exist is doubtless true (for they are affections of the perceiver), but that the substrata which cause the sensation should not exist even apart from sensation is impossible. For sensation is surely not the sensation of itself, but there is something beyond the sensation, which must be prior to the sensation; for that which moves is prior in nature to that which is moved, and if they are correlative terms, this is no less the case.

6

There are, both among those who have these convictions and among those who merely profess these views, some who raise a difficulty by asking, who is to be the judge of the healthy man, and in general who is likely to judge rightly on each class of questions. But such inquiries are like puzzling over the question whether we are now asleep or awake. And all such questions have the same meaning. These people demand that a reason shall be given for everything;[9] for they seek a starting-point, and they seek to get this by demonstration, while it is obvious from their actions that they have no conviction. But their mistake is what we have stated it to be; they seek a reason for things for which no reason can be given; for the starting-point of demonstration is not demonstration.

These, then, might be easily persuaded of this truth, for it is not difficult to grasp; but those who seek merely compulsion in argument seek what is impossible; for they demand to be allowed to contradict themselves—a claim which contradicts itself from the very first.—But if not all things are relative, but some are self-existent, not everything that appears will be true; for that which appears is apparent to some one; so that he who says all things that appear are true, makes all things relative. And, therefore, those who ask for an irresistible argument, and at the same time demand to be called to account for their views, must guard themselves by saying that the truth is not that what appears exists, but that what appears exists *for him to whom* it appears, and *when,* and *to the sense to which,* and *under the conditions under which* it appears. And if they give an account of their view, but do not give it in this way, they will soon find themselves contradicting themselves. For it is possible that the same thing may appear to be honey to the sight, but not to the taste, and that, since we have two eyes, things may not appear the same to each, if their sight is unlike. For to those who for the reasons named some time ago

[9] The reference may be to Antisthenes.

say that what appears is true, and therefore that all things are alike false and true, for things do not appear either the same to all men or always the same to the same man, but often have contrary appearances at the same time (for touch says there are two objects when we cross our fingers, while sight says there is one), —to these we shall say 'yes, but not to the same sense and in the same part of it and under the same conditions and at the same time', so that what appears will be with these qualifications true. But perhaps for this reason those who argue thus not because they feel a difficulty but for the sake of argument, should say that this is not true, but true for this man. And as has been said before, they must make everything relative—relative to opinion and perception, so that nothing either has come to be or will be without some one's first thinking so. But if things *have* come to be or will be,[10] evidently not all things will be relative to opinion.—Again, if a thing is one, it is in relation to one thing or to a definite number of things; and if the same thing is both half and equal, it is not to the double that the equal is correlative.[11] If, then, in relation to that which thinks, man and that which is thought are the same, man will not be that which thinks, but only that which is thought. And if each thing is to be relative to that which thinks, that which thinks will be relative to an infinity of specifically different things.

Let this, then, suffice to show (1) that the most indisputable of all beliefs is that contradictory statements are not at the same time true, and (2) what consequences follow from the assertion that they are, and (3) why people do assert this. Now since it is impossible that contradictories should be at the same time

true of the same thing, obviously contraries also cannot belong at the same time to the same thing. For of contraries, one is a privation no less than it is a contrary —and a privation of the essential nature; and privation is the denial of a predicate to a determinate genus. If, then, it is impossible to affirm and deny truly at the same time, it is also impossible that contraries should belong to a subject at the same time, unless both belong to it in particular relations, or one in a particular relation and one without qualification.

7

But on the other hand there cannot be an intermediate between contradictories, but of one subject we must either affirm or deny any one predicate. This is clear, in the first place, if we define what the true and the false are. To say of what is that it is not, or of what is not that it is, is false, while to say of what is that it is, and of what is not that it is not, is true; so that he who says of anything that it is, or that it is not, will say either what is true or what is false; but neither what is nor what is not is said to be or not to be.[12]—Again, the intermediate between the contradictories will be so either in the way in which grey is between black and white,[13] or as that which is neither man nor horse is between man and horse. (a) If it were of the latter kind, it could not change into the extremes (for change is from not-good to good, or from good to not-good), but as a matter of fact when there is an intermediate it is always observed to

---

[10] *sc.* without some one's first thinking so.
[11] *sc.* but the equal to the equal, the half to the double.

[12] *sc.* by those who say there is an intermediate between contradictories. Hence such a statement is neither true nor false, which is absurd.
[13] Though of course it differs from this case in being between contradictories, not contraries.

change into the extremes. For there is no change except to opposites[14] and to their intermediates. (*b*) But if it is really intermediate,[15] in this way too there would have to be a change to white, which was not from not-white; but as it is, this is never seen.—Again, every object of understanding or reason the understanding either affirms or denies—this is obvious from the definition—whenever it says what is true or false. When it connects in one way by assertion or negation, it says what is true, and when it does so in another way, what is false.—Again, there must be an intermediate between *all* contradictories, if one is not arguing merely for the sake of argument; so that it will be possible for a man to say what is neither true nor untrue, and there will be a middle between that which is and that which is not, so that there will also be a kind of change intermediate between generation and destruction. —Again, in all classes in which the negation of an attribute involves the assertion of its contrary, even in these there will be an intermediate; for instance, in the sphere of numbers there will be number which is neither odd nor not-odd. But this is impossible, as is obvious from the definition.—Again, the process will go on *ad infinitum,* and the number of realities will be not only half as great again, but even greater. For again it will be possible to deny this intermediate with reference both to its assertion and to its negation,[16] and this new term will be some definite thing; for its essence is something different.—Again, when a man, on being asked whether a thing is white, says 'no', he has denied nothing except that it is; and its not being is a negation.

[14] *sc.* contrary, not contradictory opposites.
[15] *sc.* as grey is between black and white.
[16] i. e. if there is a term *B* which is neither *A* nor not-*A*, there will be a new term *C* which is neither *B* nor not-*B*.

Some people have acquired this opinion as other paradoxical opinions have been acquired; when men cannot refute eristical arguments, they give in to the argument and agree that the conclusion is true. This, then, is why some express this view; others do so because they demand a reason for everything.[17] And the starting-point in dealing with all such people is definition. Now the definition rests on the necessity of their meaning something; for the form of words of which the word is a sign will be its definition.—While the doctrine of Heraclitus, that all things are and are not, seems to make everything true, that of Anaxagoras, that there is an intermediate between the terms of a contradiction, seems to make everything false; for when things are mixed, the mixture is neither good nor not-good, so that one cannot say anything that is true.

8

In view of these distinctions it is obvious that the one-sided theories which some people express about all things cannot be valid—on the one hand the theory that nothing is true (for, say they, there is nothing to prevent every statement from being like the statement 'the diagonal of a square is commensurate with the side'), on the other hand the theory that everything is true. These views are practically the same as that of Heraclitus; for he who says that 'all things are true and all are false' also makes each of these statements separately, so that since they are impossible, the double statement must be impossible too.—Again, there are obviously contradictories which cannot be at the same time true—nor on the other hand can all statements be false; yet this would *seem* more possible in the light of what has

[17] The reference may be to Antisthenes.

been said.—But against all such views we must postulate, as we said above, not that something is or is not, but that something has a meaning, so that we must argue from a definition, viz. by assuming what falsity or truth means. If that which it is true to affirm is nothing other than that which it is false to deny, it is impossible that all statements should be false; for one side of the contradiction must be true. Again, if it is necessary with regard to everything either to assert or to deny it, it is impossible that both should be false; for it is *one* side of the contradiction that is false.—Therefore all such views are also exposed to the often expressed objection, that they destroy themselves. For he who says that everything is true makes even the statement contrary to his own true, and therefore his own not true (for the contrary statement denies that it is true), while he who says everything is false makes himself also false.—And if the former person excepts the contrary statement, saying it alone is not true, while the latter excepts his own as being not false, none the less they are driven to postulate the truth or falsity of an infinite number of statements; for that which says the true statement is true is true, and this process will go on to infinity.

Evidently, again, those who say all things are at rest are not right, nor are those who say all things are in movement. For if all things are at rest, the same statements will always be true and the same always false—but this obviously changes; for he who makes a statement, himself at one time was not and again will not be. And if all things are in motion, nothing will be true; everything therefore will be false. But it has been shown that this is impossible. Again, it must be that which is that changes; for change is from something to something. But again it is not the case that all things are at rest or in motion *sometimes,* and nothing *for ever;* for there is something which always moves the things that are in motion, and the first mover is itself unmoved.

THE SEA FIGHT

TOMORROW*

ARISTOTLE (384–322 B.C.). See page 8.

An affirmation is opposed to a denial in the sense which I denote by the term 'contradictory', when, while the subject remains the same, the affirmation is of universal character and the denial is not. The affirmation 'every man is white' is the *contradictory* of the denial 'not every man is white', or again, the proposition 'no man is white' is the *contradictory* of the proposition 'some men are white'. But propositions are opposed as *contraries* when both the affirmation and the denial are universal, as in the sentences 'every man is white', 'no man is white', 'every man is just', 'no man is just'.

We see that in a pair of this sort both propositions cannot be true, but the contradictories of a pair of contraries can sometimes both be true with reference to the same subject; for instance 'not every man is white' and 'some men are white' are both true. Of such corresponding positive and negative propositions as refer to universals and have a universal character, one must be true and the other false. This is the case also when the reference is to individuals, as in the propositions 'Socrates is white', 'Socrates is not white'.

When, on the other hand, the reference is to universals, but the propositions are not universal, it is not always the case that one is true and the other false, for it is possible to state truly that man is white and that man is not white and that man is beautiful and that man is not beautiful; for if a man is deformed he is the reverse of beautiful, also if he is progressing towards beauty he is not yet beautiful.

This statement might seem at first sight to carry with it a contradiction, owing to the fact that the proposition 'man is not white' appears to be equivalent to the proposition 'no man is white'. This, however, is not the case, nor are they necessarily at the same time true or false.

It is evident also that the denial corresponding to a single affirmation is itself single; for the denial must deny just that which the affirmation affirms concerning the same subject, and must correspond with the affirmation both in the universal or particular character of the subject and in the distributed or undistributed sense in which it is understood.

For instance, the affirmation 'Socrates is white' has its proper denial in the proposition 'Socrates is not white'. If

* From *On Interpretation* in *The Works of Aristotle* (1928), Volume I, translated under the editorship of W. D. Ross. Reprinted by permission of The Clarendon Press, Oxford.

anything else be negatively predicated of the subject or if anything else be the subject though the predicate remain the same, the denial will not be the denial proper to that affirmation, but one that is distinct.

The denial proper to the affirmation 'every man is white' is 'not every man is white'; that proper to the affirmation 'some men are white' is 'no man is white', while that proper to the affirmation 'man is white' is 'man is not white'.

We have shown further that a single denial is contradictorily opposite to a single affirmation and we have explained which these are; we have also stated that contrary are distinct from contradictory propositions and which the contrary are; also that with regard to a pair of opposite propositions it is not always the case that one is true and the other false. We have pointed out, moreover, what the reason of this is and under what circumstances the truth of the one involves the falsity of the other.

An affirmation or denial is single, if it indicates some one fact about some one subject; it matters not whether the subject is universal and whether the statement has a universal character, or whether this is not so. Such single propositions are: 'every man is white', 'not every man is white'; 'man is white', 'man is not white'; 'no man is white', 'some men are white'; provided the word 'white' has one meaning. If, on the other hand, one word has two meanings which do not combine to form one, the affirmation is not single. For instance, if a man should establish the symbol 'garment' as significant both of a horse and of a man, the proposition 'garment is white' would not be a single affirmation, nor its opposite a single denial. For it is equivalent to the proposition 'horse and man are white', which, again, is equivalent to the two propositions 'horse is white', 'man is white'. If, then, these two propositions have more

than a single significance, and do not form a single proposition, it is plain that the first proposition either has more than one significance or else has none; for a particular man is not a horse.

This, then, is another instance of those propositions of which both the positive and the negative forms may be true or false simultaneously.

In the case of that which is or which has taken place, propositions, whether positive or negative, must be true or false. Again, in the case of a pair of contradictories, either when the subject is universal and the propositions are of a universal character, or when it is individual, as has been said, one of the two must be true and the other false; whereas when the subject is universal, but the propositions are not of a universal character, there is no such necessity. We have discussed this type also in a previous chapter.

When the subject, however, is individual, and that which is predicated of it relates to the future, the case is altered. For if all propositions whether positive or negative are either true or false, then any given predicate must either belong to the subject or not, so that if one man affirms that an event of a given character will take place and another denies it, it is plain that the statement of the one will correspond with reality and that of the other will not. For the predicate cannot both belong and not belong to the subject at one and the same time with regard to the future.

Thus, if it is true to say that a thing is white, it must necessarily be white; if the reverse proposition is true, it will of necessity not be white. Again, if it is white, the proposition stating that it is white was true; if it is not white, the proposition to the opposite effect was true. And if it is not white, the man who states that it is is making a false statement; and if the man who states that it is white is making a false statement, it follows that it is not white. It may therefore be argued that it is necessary that affirmations or denials must be either true or false.

Now if this be so, nothing is or takes place fortuitously, either in the present or in the future and there are no real alternatives; everything takes place of necessity and is fixed. For either he that affirms that it will take place or hc that denies this is in correspondence with fact, whereas if things did not take place of necessity, an event might just as easily not happen as happen; for the meaning of the word 'fortuitous' with regard to present or future events is that reality is so constituted that it may issue in either of two opposite directions.

Again, if a thing is white now, it was true before to say that it would be white, so that of anything that has taken place it was always true to say 'it is' or 'it will be'. But if it was always true to say that a thing is or will be, it is not possible that it should not be or not be about to be, and when a thing cannot not come to be, it is impossible that it should not come to be, and when it is impossible that it should not come to be, it must come to be. All, then, that is about to be must of necessity take place. It results from this that nothing is uncertain or fortuitous, for if it were fortuitous it would not be necessary.

Again, to say that neither the affirmation nor the denial is true, maintaining, let us say, that an event neither will take place nor will not take place, is to take up a position impossible to defend. In the first place, though facts should prove the one proposition false, the opposite would still be untrue. Secondly, if it was true to say that a thing was both white and large, both these qualities must necessarily belong to it; and if they will belong to it the next day, they must necessarily belong to it the next day. But if an event is neither to take place nor not to take place the next day, the element of chance will be eliminated. For example, it would be necessary that a sea-fight should neither take place nor fail to take place on the next day.

These awkward results and others of the same kind follow, if it is an irrefragable law that of every pair of contradictory propositions, whether they have regard to universals and are stated as universally applicable, or whether they have regard to individuals, one must be true and the other false, and that there are no real alternatives, but that all that is or takes place is the outcome of necessity. There would be no need to deliberate or to take trouble, on the supposition that if we should adopt a certain course, a certain result would follow, while, if we did not, the result would not follow. For a man may predict an event ten thousand years beforehand, and another may predict the reverse; that which was truly predicted at the moment in the past will of necessity take place in the fullness of time.

Further, it makes no difference whether people have or have not actually made the contradictory statements. For it is manifest that the circumstances are not influenced by the fact of an affirmation or denial on the part of anyone. For events will not take place or fail to take place because it was stated that they would or would not take place, nor is this any more the case if the prediction dates back ten thousand years or any other space of time. Wherefore, if through all time the nature of things was so constituted that a prediction about an event was true, then through all time it was necessary that that prediction should find fulfilment; and with regard to all events, circumstances have always been such that their occurrence is a matter of necessity. For that of which someone has said truly that it will be, cannot fail to take place; and of that which takes place, it was always true to say that it would be.

Yet this view leads to an impossible conclusion; for we see that both deliberation and action are causative with regard to the future, and that, to speak more generally, in those things which are not continuously actual there is a potentiality in either direction. Such things may either be or not be; events also therefore may either take place or not take place. There are many obvious instances of this. It is possible that this coat may be cut in half, and yet it may not be cut in half, but wear out first. In the same way, it is possible that it should not be cut in half; unless this were so, it would not be possible that it should wear out first. So it is therefore with all other events which possess this kind of potentiality. It is therefore plain that it is not of necessity that everything is or takes place; but in some instances there are real alternatives, in which case the affirmation is no more true and no more false than the denial; while some exhibit a predisposition and general tendency in one direction or the other, and yet can issue in the opposite direction by exception.

Now that which is must needs be when it is, and that which is not must needs not be when it is not. Yet it cannot be said without qualification that all existence and non-existence is the outcome of necessity. For there is a difference between saying that that which is, when it is, must needs be, and simply saying that all that is must needs be, and similarly in the case of that which is not. In the case, also, of two contradictory propositions this holds good. Everything must either be or not be, whether in the present or in the future, but it is not always possible to distinguish and state determinately which of these alternatives must necessarily come about.

Let me illustrate. A sea-fight must either take place to-morrow or not, but it is not necessary that it should take place to-morrow, neither is it necessary that it should not take place, yet it is necessary that it either should or should not take place to-morrow. Since propositions correspond with facts, it is evident that when in future events there is a real alternative, and a potentiality in contrary directions, the corresponding affirmation and denial have the same character.

This is the case with regard to that which is not always existent or not always non-existent. One of the two propositions in such instances must be true and the other false, but we cannot say determinately that this or that is false, but must leave the alternative undecided. One may indeed be more likely to be true than the other, but it cannot be either actually true or actually false. It is therefore plain that it is not necessary that of an affirmation and a denial one should be true and the other false. For in the case of that which exists potentially, but not actually, the rule which applies to that which exists actually does not hold good. The case is rather as we have indicated.

REFUTING THE LAWS

OF THOUGHT*

G. W. F. HEGEL (1770–1831). See page 43.

The propositions thus arising have been stated as universal Laws of Thought. Thus the first of them, the maxim of Identity, reads: Everything is identical with itself, A = A: and, negatively, A cannot at the same time be A and not A.—This maxim, instead of being a true law of thought, is nothing but the law of abstract understanding. The propositional form itself contradicts it: for a proposition always promises a distinction between subject and predicate; while the present one does not fulfil what its form requires. But the Law is particularly set aside by the following so-called Laws of Thought, which make laws out of its opposite.— It is asserted that the maxim of Identity, though it cannot be proved, regulates the procedure of every consciousness, and that experience shows it to be accepted as soon as its terms are apprehended. To this alleged experience of the logic-books may be opposed the universal experience that no mind thinks or forms conceptions or speaks, in accordance with this law, and that no existence of any kind whatever conforms to it. Utterances after the fashion of this pretended law (A planet is —a planet; Magnetism is—magnetism; Mind is—mind) are, as they deserve to

be, reputed silly. That is certainly matter of general experience. The logic which seriously propounds such laws and the scholastic world in which alone they are valid have long been discredited with practical common sense as well as with the philosophy of reason.

Identity is, in the first place, the repetition of what we had earlier as Being, but as *become*, through supersession of its character of immediateness. It is therefore Being as Ideality.—It is important to come to a proper understanding on the true meaning of Identity: and, for that purpose, we must especially guard against taking it as abstract Identity, to the exclusion of all Difference. That is the touch-stone for distinguishing all bad philosophy from what alone deserves the name of philosophy. Identity in its truth, as an Ideality of what immediately is, is a high category for our religious modes of mind as well as all other forms of thought and mental activity. The true knowledge of God, it may be said, begins when we know Him as identity,—as absolute identity. To know so much is to see that all the power and glory of the world sinks into nothing in God's presence, and subsists only as the reflection of His power and His glory. In the same way, Identity, as self-consciousness, is what distinguishes man from nature, particularly from the brutes which never reach the point of comprehending themselves as 'I,' that is, pure self-contained unity. So again,

* From *The Logic of Hegel*, pp. 184–192, translated from *The Encyclopaedia of the Philosophical Sciences* by William Wallace (Oxford, Eng.: The Clarendon Press, 1874).

in connexion with thought, the main thing is not to confuse the true Identity, which contains Being and its characteristics ideally transfigured in it, with an abstract Identity, identity of bare form. All the charges of narrowness, hardness, meaninglessness, which are so often directed against thought from the quarter of feeling and immediate perception, rest on the perverse assumption that thought acts only as a faculty of abstract Identification. The Formal Logic itself confirms this assumption by laying down the supreme law of thought (so-called) which has been discussed above. If thinking were no more than an abstract Identity, we could not but own it to be a most futile and tedious business. No doubt the notion, and the idea too, are identical with themselves: but identical only in so far as they at the same time involve distinction.

(β) Difference

116

Essence is mere Identity and reflection in itself only as it is self-relating negativity, and in that way self-repulsion. It contains therefore essentially the characteristic of Difference.

Other-being is here no longer qualitative, taking the shape of the character or limit. It is now in Essence, in self-relating essence, and therefore the negation is at the same time a relation,—is, in short, Distinction, Relativity, Mediation.

To ask, 'How Identity comes to Difference,' assumes that Identity as mere abstract Identity is something of itself, and Difference also something else equally independent. This supposition renders an answer to the question impossible. If Identity is viewed as diverse from Difference, all that we have in this way is but Difference; and hence we cannot demonstrate the advance to difference, because the person who asks for the How of the progress thereby implies that for him the starting-point is non-existent. The question then when put to the test has obviously no meaning, and its proposer may be met with the question what he means by Identity; whereupon we should soon see that he attaches no idea to it at all, and that Identity is for him an empty name. As we have seen, besides, Identity is undoubtedly a negative,—not however an abstract empty Nought, but the negation of Being and its characteristics. Being so, Identity is at the same time self-relation, and, what is more, negative self-relation; in other words, it draws a distinction between it and itself.

117

Difference is, first of all, (1) immediate difference, i. e. Diversity or Variety. In Diversity the different things are each individually what they are, and unaffected by the relation in which they stand to each other. This relation is therefore external to them. In consequence of the various things being thus indifferent to the difference between them, it falls outside them into a third thing, the agent of Comparison. This external difference, as an identity of the objects related, is Likeness; as a non-identity of them, is Unlikeness.

The gap which understanding allows to divide these characteristics, is so great, that although comparison has one and the same substratum for likeness and unlikeness, which are explained to be different aspects and points of view in it, still likeness by itself is the first of the elements alone, viz. identity, and unlikeness by itself is difference.

Diversity has, like Identity, been transformed into a maxim: 'Everything is various or different': or, 'There are no two things completely like each other.' Here Everything is put under a predicate, which is the reverse of the identity attributed to it in the first maxim; and therefore under a law contradicting the first. However there is an explanation. As the diversity is supposed due only to external comparison, anything taken *per se* is expected and understood always to be identical with itself, so that the second law need not interfere with the first. But, in that case, variety does not belong to the something or everything in question: it constitutes no intrinsic characteristic of the subject: and the second maxim on this showing does not admit of being stated at all. If, on the other hand, the something *itself* is as the maxim says diverse, it must be in virtue of its own proper character: but in this case the specific difference, and not variety as such, is what is intended. And this is the meaning of the maxim of Leibnitz.

When understanding sets itself to study Identity, it has already passed beyond it, and is looking at Difference in the shape of bare Variety. If we follow the so-called law of Identity, and say,—The sea is the sea, The air is the air, The moon is the moon, these objects pass for having no bearing on one another. What we have before us therefore is not Identity, but Difference. We do not stop at this point however, or regard things merely as different. We compare them one with another, and thus discover the features of likeness and unlikeness. The work of the finite sciences lies to a great extent in the application of these categories, and the phrase 'scientific treatment' generally means no more than the method which has for its aim comparison of the objects under examination. This method has undoubtedly led to some important results;—we may particularly mention the great advance of modern times in the provinces of comparative anatomy and comparative linguistic. But it is going too far to suppose that the comparative method can be employed with equal success in all branches of knowledge. Nor—and this must be emphasized—can mere comparison ever ultimately satisfy the requirements of science. Its results are indeed indispensable, but they are still labours only preliminary to truly intelligent cognition.

If it be the office of comparison to reduce existing differences to Identity, the science, which most perfectly fulfils that end, is mathematics. The reason of that is, that quantitative difference is only the difference which is quite external. Thus, in geometry, a triangle and a quadrangle, figures qualitatively different, have this qualitative difference discounted by abstraction, and are equalised to one another in magnitude. It follows from what has been formerly said about the mere Identity of understanding

that, as has also been pointed out, neither philosophy nor the empirical sciences need envy this superiority of Mathematics.

The story is told that, when Leibnitz propounded the maxim of Variety, the cavaliers and ladies of the court, as they walked round the garden, made efforts to discover two leaves indistinguishable from each other, in order to confute the law stated by the philosopher. Their device was unquestionably a convenient method of dealing with metaphysics,—one which has not ceased to be fashionable. All the same, as regards the principle of Leibnitz, difference must be understood to mean not an external and indifferent diversity merely, but difference essential. Hence the very nature of things implies that they must be different.

118

Likeness is an Identity only of those things which are not the same, not identical with each other: and Unlikeness is a relation of things unlike. The two therefore do not fall on different aspects or points of view in the thing, without any mutual affinity: but one throws light into the other. Variety thus comes to be reflexive difference, or difference (distinction) implicit and essential, determinate or specific difference.

While things merely various show themselves unaffected by each other, likeness and unlikeness on the contrary are a pair of characteristics which are in completely reciprocal relation. The one of them cannot be thought without the other. This advance from simple variety to opposition appears in our common acts of thought, when we allow that comparison has a meaning only upon the hypothesis of an existing difference, and that on the other hand we can distinguish only on the hypothesis of existing similarity. Hence, if the problem be the discovery of a difference, we attribute no great cleverness to the man who only distinguishes those objects, of which the difference is palpable, *e.g.* a pen and a camel: and similarly, it implies no very advanced faculty of comparison, when the objects compared, *e.g.* a beech and an oak, a temple and a church, are near akin. In the case of difference, in short, we like to see identity, and in the case of identity we like to see difference. Within the range of the empirical sciences however, the one of these two categories is often allowed to put the other out of sight and mind. Thus the scientific problem at one time is to reduce existing differences to identity; on another occasion, with equal one-sidedness, to discover new differences. We see this especially in physical science. There the problem consists, in the first place, in the continual search for new 'elements,' new forces, new genera, and species. Or, in another direction,, it seeks to show that all bodies hitherto believed to be simple are compound: and modern physicists and chemists smile at the ancients, who were satisfied with four elements, and these not simple. Secondly, and on the other hand, mere identity is made the chief question. Thus electricity and chemical affinity are regarded as the same, and even the organic processes of digestion and assimilation are looked upon as a mere chemical operation. Modern philosophy has often been nicknamed the Philosophy of Identity. But, as was already remarked, it is precisely philosophy, and in particular speculative logic, which lays bare the nothingness of the abstract, undifferentiated identity, known to understanding; though it also undoubtedly urges its disciples not to rest at mere diversity, but to ascertain the inner unity of all existence.

119

Difference implicit is essential difference, the Positive and the Negative: and that is this way. The Positive is the identical self-relation in such a way as not to be the Negative, and the Negative is the different by itself so as not to be the Positive. Thus either has an existence of its own in proportion as it is not the other. The one is made visible in the other, and is only in so far as that other is. Essential difference is therefore Opposition; according to which the different is not confronted by *any* other but by *its* other. That is, either of these two (Positive and Negative) is stamped with a characteristic of its own only in its relation to the other: the one is only reflected into itself as it is reflected into

the other. And so with the other. Either in this way is the other's *own* other.

Difference implicit or essential gives the maxim, Everything is essentially distinct; or, as it has also been expressed, Of two opposite predicates the one only can be assigned to anything, and there is no third possible. This maxim of contrast or Opposition most expressly controverts the maxim of Identity: the one says a thing should be only self-relation, the other says that it must be an opposite, a relation to its other. The native unintelligence of abstraction betrays itself by setting in juxtaposition two contrary maxims, like these, as laws, without even so much as comparing them.— The Maxim of Excluded Middle is the maxim of the definite understanding, which would fain avoid contradiction, but in so doing falls into it. A must be either $+A$ or $-A$, it says. It virtually declares in these words a third A which is neither $+$ nor $-$, and which at the same time is yet invested with $+$ and $-$ characters. If $+W$ mean 6 miles to the West, and $-W$ mean 6 miles to the East, and if the $+$ and $-$ cancel each other, the 6 miles of way or space remain what they were with and without the contrast. Even the mere *plus* and *minus* of number or abstract direction have, if we like, zero, for their third: but it need not be denied that the empty contrast, which understanding institutes between *plus* and *minus,* is not without its value in such abstractions as number, direction, &c.

In the doctrine of contradictory concepts, the one notion is, say, blue (for in this doctrine even the sensuous generalised image of a colour is called a notion) and the other not-blue. This other then would not be an affirmative, say, yellow, but would merely be kept at the abstract negative.—That the Negative in its own nature is quite as much Positive, is implied in saying that what is opposite to another is *its* other. The inanity of the opposition between what are called contradictory notions is fully exhibited in what we may call the grandiose formula of a general law, that Everything has the one and not the other of *all* predicates which are in such opposition. In this way, mind is either white or not-white, yellow or not-yellow, &c., *ad infinitum*.

It was forgotten that Identity and Opposition are themselves c pposed, and the maxim of Opposition was taken even for that of Identity, in the shape of the principle of Contradiction. A notion, which possesses neither or both of two mutually contradictory marks, *e.g.* a quadrangular circle, is held to be logically false. Now though a multangular circle and a rectilineal arc no less contradict this maxim, geometers never hesitate to treat the circle as a polygon with rectilineal sides. But anything like a circle (that is to say its mere character or nominal definition) is still no notion. In the notion of a circle, centre and circumference are equally essential; both marks belong to it: and yet centre and circumference are opposite and contradictory to each other.

The conception of Polarity, which is so dominant in physics, contains by implication the more correct definition of Opposition. But physics for its theory of the laws of thought adheres to the ordinary logic; it might therefore well be horrified in case it should ever work out the conception of Polarity, and get at the thoughts which are implied in it.

(1) With the positive we return to identity, but in its higher truth as identical self-relation, and at the same time with the note that it is not the negative. The negative *per se* is the same as difference itself. The identical as such is primarily the yet uncharacterised: the positive on the other hand is what is self-identical, but with the mark of antithesis to an other. And the negative is difference as such, characterised as not identity. This is the difference of difference within its own self.

Positive and negative are supposed to express an absolute difference. The two however are at bottom the same: the name of either might be transferred to the other. Thus, for example, debts and assets are not two particular, self-subsisting species of property. What is negative to the debtor, is positive to the creditor. A way to the east is also a way to the west. Positive and negative are therefore intrinsically conditioned by one another, and are only in relation to each other. The north pole of the magnet cannot be without the south pole, and *vice versa*. If we cut a magnet in two, we have not a north pole in one piece, and a south pole in the other. Similarly, in electricity, the positive and the negative are not two diverse and independent fluids. In opposition, the different is not confronted by any other, but by *its* other. Usually we regard different things as unaffected by each other. Thus we say: I am a human being, and around me are air, water, animals, and all sorts of things. Everything is thus put outside of every other. But the aim of philosophy is to banish indifference, and to ascertain the necessity of things. By that means the other is seen to stand over against *its* other. Thus, for example, inorganic nature is not to be considered merely something else than organic nature, but the necessary antithesis of it. Both are in essential relation to one another; and the one of the two is, only in so far as it excludes the other from it, and thus relates itself thereto. Nature in like manner is not without mind, nor mind without nature. An important step has been taken, when we cease in thinking to use phrases like: Of course something else is also possible. While we so speak, we are still tainted with contingency: and all true thinking, we have already said, is a thinking of necessity.

In modern physical science the opposition, first observed to exist in magnetism as polarity, has come to be regarded as a universal law pervading the whole of nature. This would be a real scientific advance, if care were at the same time taken not to let mere variety revert without explanation, as a valid category, side by side with opposition. Thus at one time the colours are regarded as in polar opposition to one another, and called complementary colours: at another time they are looked at in their indifferent and merely quantitative difference of red, yellow, green, &c.

(2) Instead of speaking by the maxim of

Excluded Middle (which is the maxim of abstract understanding) we should rather say: Everything is opposite. Neither in heaven nor in earth, neither in the world of mind nor of nature, is there anywhere such an abstract 'Either—or' as the understanding maintains. Whatever exists is concrete, with difference and opposition in itself. The finitude of things will then lie in the want of correspondence between their immediate being, and what they essentially are: Thus, in inorganic nature, the acid is implicitly at the same time the base: in other words, its only being consists in its relation to its other. Hence also the acid is not something that persists quietly in the contrast: it is always in effort to realise what it potentially is. Contradiction is the very moving principle of the world: and it is ridiculous to say that contradiction is unthinkable. The only thing correct in that statement is that contradiction is not the end of the matter, but cancels itself. But contradiction, when cancelled, does not leave abstract identity; for that is itself only one side of the contrariety. The proximate result of opposition (when realised as contradiction) is the Ground, which contains identity as well as difference superseded and deposed to elements in the completer notion.

THE NEGATION OF

THE NEGATION*

FRIEDRICH ENGELS (1820–1895) was a German social philosopher who collaborated with Karl Marx in writing the *Communist Manifesto*. Engels wrote on a wide variety of economic, political, and historical topics from the socialist point of view. In two of his books, *Dialectics of Nature* and *Anti-Dühring,* Engels argued that a materialist version of Hegel's logic is implicit in both human history and in the theory and practice of modern science.

"The first and most important principle of the basic logical characteristics of being is the *exclusion of contradiction.* Contradiction is a category which can only appertain to a combination of thoughts, but not to reality. There are no contradictions in things, or, to put it another way, contradiction applied to reality is itself the apex of absurdity. . . . The antagonism of contrary forces measured against each other is in fact the basic form of all actions in the life of the world and of the creatures on it. But this opposition of forces, which is found both in the elements and in individuals, is not even in the most distant way identical with the absurd idea of contradictions. . . . We can be content here with having cleared the fogs which generally rise from the supposed mysteries of logic by presenting a clear picture of the actual absurdity of contradictions in reality, and with having

shown the uselessness of the incense which is burnt in some quarters in honour of the dialectics of contradiction—the very clumsily carved wooden doll which is substituted for the antagonistic world schematism."—This is practically all we are told about dialectics in the *Course of Philosophy.* In his *Critical History,* on the other hand, the dialectics of contradiction, and with it Hegel, is treated quite differently. "Contradiction, indeed, according to the Hegelian logic (or rather Logos doctrine), is not present in thought, which by its nature can only be conceived as subjective and conscious, but is objectively present themselves in things and processes and so to speak appears in corporeal form, so that absurdity does not remain an impossible combination of thoughts but becomes an actual force. The reality of the absurd is the first article of faith in the Hegelian unity of the logical and the illogical. . . . The

* From Friedrich Engels, *Anti-Dühring (Herr Eugen Dühring's Revolution in Science),* translated by Emile Burns, edited by C. P. Dutt. Reprinted by permission of Lawrence & Wishart, Ltd., London, and International Publishers, New York.

more contradictory a thing the truer it is, or in other words the more absurd the more credible it is. This maxim, which is not even newly invented but is borrowed from the theology of the Revelation and from mysticism, is the undisguised expression of the so-called dialectical principle."

The thought-content of the two passages cited is contained in the statement that contradiction = absurdity, and therefore cannot be found in the real world. People who in other respects show a fair degree of common sense may regard this statement as having the same self-evident validity as the statement that a straight line cannot be a curve and a curve cannot be straight. But, regardless of all protests made by common sense, the differential calculus assumes that under certain circumstances straight lines and curves are nevertheless identical, and with this assumption reaches results which common sense, insisting on the absurdity of straight lines being identical with curves, can never attain. And in view of the important role which the so-called dialectics of contradiction has played in philosophy from the time of the earliest Greeks up to the present, even a stronger opponent than Herr Dühring should have felt obliged to attack it with other arguments besides one assertion and a good many abusive epithets.

So long as we consider things as static and lifeless, each one by itself, alongside of and after each other, it is true that we do not run up against any contradictions in them. We find certain qualities which are partly common to, partly diverse from, and even contradictory to each other, but which in this case are distributed among different objects and therefore contain no contradiction. Within the limits of this sphere of thought we can get along on the basis of the usual metaphysical mode of thought. But the position is quite different as soon as we consider things in their motion, their change, their life, their reciprocal influence on one another. Then we immediately become involved in contradictions. Motion itself is a contradiction: even simple mechanical change of place can only come about through a body at one and the same moment of time being both in one place and in another place, being in one and the same place and also not in it. And the continuous assertion and simultaneous solution of this contradiction is precisely what motion is.

Here, therefore, we have a contradiction which "is objectively present in things and processes themselves and so to speak appears in corporeal form." And what has Herr Dühring to say about it? He asserts that up to the present there is absolutely "no bridge, in rational mechanics, from the strictly static to the dynamic." The reader can now at last see what is hiding behind this favourite phrase of Herr Dühring's—it is nothing but this: the mind which thinks metaphysically is absolutely unable to pass from the idea of rest to the idea of motion, because the contradiction pointed out above blocks its path. To it, motion is simply incomprehensible because it is a contradiction. And in asserting the incomprehensibility of motion, it thereby against its will admits the existence of this contradiction, and in so doing admits the objective presence of a contradiction in things and processes themselves, a contradiction which is moreover an actual force.

And if simple mechanical change of place contains a contradiction, this is even more true of the higher forms of motion of matter, and especially of organic life and its development. We saw above that life consists just precisely in this—that a living thing is at each moment itself and yet something else. Life is therefore also a contradiction which is present in things and processes themselves, and which constantly asserts and solves itself; and as soon as the contradiction ceases, life too comes to an end, and death steps in. We likewise saw that in the sphere of thought also we could not avoid contradictions, and that for example the contradiction between man's inherently unlimited faculty of knowledge and its actual realisation in men who are limited by their external conditions and limited also in their intellectual faculties finds its solution in what is, for us at least, and from a practical standpoint, an endless succession of generations, in infinite progress.

We have already noted that one of the basic principles of higher mathematics is the contradiction that in certain circumstances straight lines and curves are identical. It establishes also this other contradiction: that lines which intersect each other before our eyes nevertheless, only five or six centimetres from their point of intersection, can be shown to be parallel, that is, that they will never meet even if extended to infinity. And yet, working with these and with even far greater contradictions, it can attain results which are not only correct but are also quite unattainable for lower mathematics.

But even lower mathematics teems with contradictions. It is for example a contradiction that a root of a should be a power of a, and yet $a^{1/2} = \sqrt{a}$. It is a contradiction that a negative magnitude should be the square of anything, for every negative magnitude multiplied by itself gives a positive square. The square root of minus one is therefore not only a contradiction, but even an absurd contradiction, a real absurdity. And yet $\sqrt{-1}$ is in many cases a necessary result of correct mathematical operations; in fact, we might go further and ask: where would mathematics— either lower or higher—be, if it were prohibited from operating with $\sqrt{-1}$?

In its operations with variable magni-tudes mathematics itself enters the field of dialectics, and it is significant that it was a dialectical philosopher, Descartes, who first introduced this advance in mathematics. The relation between the mathematics of variable and the mathematics of constant magnitudes is in general the same as the relation of dialectical to metaphysical thought. But this does not prevent the great mass of mathematicians from recognising dialectics only in the sphere of mathematics, and a good many of them from continuing to work in the old, limited metaphysical way with methods that have been obtained dialectically.

. . .

And now I ask the reader: where are the dialectical frills and mazes and intellectual arabesques; where the mixed and misconceived ideas as a result of which everything is all one in the end; where the dialectical miracles for his faithful followers; where the mysterious dialectical rubbish and the contortions based on the Hegelian Logos doctrine, without which Marx, according to Herr Dühring, is quite unable to accomplish his development? Marx merely show from history, and in this passage states in a summarised form, that just as the former petty industry necessarily, through its own development, created the conditions of its annihilation, *i.e.,* of the expropriation of the small proprietors, so now the capitalist mode of production has likewise itself created the material conditions which will annihilate it. The process is a historical one, and if it is at the same time a dialectical process, this is not Marx's fault, however annoying it may be for Herr Dühring.

It is only at this point, after Marx has completed his proof on the basis of historical and economic facts, that he proceeds: "The capitalist mode of production and appropriation, and hence capitalist private property, is the first negation of individual private property founded on the labours of the proprietor. But capitalist production begets, with the inexorability of a law of Nature, its own negation. It is the negation of the negation"—and so on (as quoted above).

In characterising the process as the negation of the negation, therefore, Marx does not dream of attempting to prove by this that the process was historically necessary. On the contrary: after he has proved from history that in fact the process has partially already occurred, and partially must occur in the future, he then also characterises it as a process which develops in accordance with a definite dialectical law. That is all. It is therefore once again a pure distortion of the facts by Herr Dühring, when he declares that the negation of the negation has to serve as the midwife to deliver the future from the womb of the past, or that Marx wants anyone to allow himself to be convinced of the necessity of the common ownership of land and capital (which is itself a Dühringian corporeal contradiction) on the basis of the negation of the negation.

Herr Dühring's total lack of understanding as to the nature of dialectics is shown by the very fact that he regards it as a mere instrument through which things can be proved, as in a more limited way formal logic or elementary mathematics can be regarded. Even formal logic is primarily a method of arriving at new results, of advancing from the known to the unknown—and dialectics is the same, only in a much more important sense, because in forcing its way beyond the narrow horizon of formal logic it contains the germ of a more comprehensive view of the world. It is the same with mathematics. Elementary mathematics, the mathematics of constant magnitudes, moves within the confines of formal logic, at any rate taken as a whole; the mathematics of variable magnitudes, whose most important part is the infinitesimal calculus, is in essence nothing other than the application of dialectics to mathematical relations. In it, the simple question of proof is definitely pushed into the background, as compared with the manifold application of the method to new spheres of research. But almost all the proofs of higher mathematics, from the first—that of the differential calculus—on, are false, from the standpoint of elementary mathematics taken rigidly. And it is necessarily so, when, as happens in this case, an attempt is made to prove by formal logic results obtained in the field of dialectics. To attempt to prove anything by means of dialectics alone to a crass metaphysician like Herr Dühring would be as much a waste of time as the attempt made by Leibnitz and his pupils to prove the principles of the infinitesimal calculus to the mathematicians of his time. The differential calculus produced in them the same convulsions as Herr Dühring gets from the negation of the negation, in which, moreover, as we shall see, the differential calculus also plays a certain role. Ultimately these gentlemen—or those of them who had not died in the interval—grudgingly gave way, not because they were convinced, but because it always produced correct results. Herr Dühring, as he himself tells us, has only just entered the forties, and if he attains old age, as we hope he may, perhaps his experience will be the same.

But what then is this fearful negation of the negation, which makes life so bitter for Herr Dühring and fulfils the same role with him of the unpardonable crime as the sin against the Holy Ghost does in Christianity?—A very simple process which is taking place everywhere and every day, which any child can understand, as soon as it is stripped of the veil of mystery in which it was wrapped by the old idealist philosophy and in which it is to the advantage of helpless metaphysicians of Herr Dühring's calibre to keep it enveloped. Let us take a grain of barley. Millions of such grains of barley are milled, boiled and brewed and then consumed. But if such a grain of barley meets with conditions which for it are normal, if it falls on suitable soil, then under the influence of heat and moisture a specific change takes place, it germinates; the grain as such ceases to exist, it is negated, and in its place appears the plant which has arisen from it, the negation of the grain. But what is the normal life-process of this plant? It grows, flowers, is fertilised and finally once more produces grains of barley, and as soon as these have ripened the stalk dies, is in its turn negated. As a result of this negation of the negation we have once again the original grain of barley, but not as a single unit, but ten, twenty or thirty fold. Species of grain change extremely slowly, and so the barley of today is almost the same as it was a century ago.

But if we take an ornamental plant which can be modified in cultivation, for example a dahlia or an orchid: if we treat the seed and the plant which grows from it as a gardener does, we get as the result of this negation of the negation not only more seeds, but also qualitatively better seeds, which produce more beautiful flowers, and each fresh repetition of this process, each repeated negation of the negation increases this improvement. With most insects, this process follows the same lines as in the case of the grain of barley. Butterflies, for example, spring from the egg through a negation of the egg, they pass through certain transformations until they reach sexual maturity, they pair and are in turn negated, dying as soon as the pairing process has been completed and the female has laid its numerous eggs. We

are not concerned at the moment with the fact that with other plants and animals the process does not take such a simple form, that before they die they produce seeds, eggs or offspring not once but many times; our purpose here is only to show that the negation of the negation *takes place in reality* in both divisions of the organic world. Furthermore, the whole of geology is a series of negated negations, a series arising from the successive shattering of old and the depositing of new rock formations. First the original earth-crust brought into existence by the cooling of the liquid mass was broken up by oceanic, meteorological and atmospherico-chemical action, and these disintegrated masses were deposited on the ocean floor. Local elevations of the ocean floor above the surface of the sea subject portions of these first strata once more to the action of rain, the changing temperature of the seasons and the oxygen and carbonic acid of the atmosphere. These same influences acted on the molten masses of rock which issued from the interior of the earth, broke through the strata and subsequently solidified. In this way, in the course of millions of centuries, ever new strata are formed and in turn are for the most part destroyed, ever anew serving as material for the formation of new strata. But the result of this process has been a very positive one: the creation, out of the most varied chemical elements, of a mixed and mechanically pulverised soil which makes possible the most abundant and diverse vegetation.

It is the same in mathematics. Let us take any algebraical magnitude whatever: for example a. If this is negated, we get $-a$ (minus a). If we negate that negation, by multiplying $-a$ by $-a$, we get $+a^2$, i.e., the original positive magnitude, but at a higher degree, raised to its second power. In this case also it makes no difference that we can reach the same

a^2 by multiplying the positive a by itself, thus also getting a^2. For the negated negation is so securely entrenched in a^2 that the latter always has two square roots, namely a and $-a$. And the fact that it is impossible to get rid of the negated negation, the negative root of the square, acquires very obvious significance as soon as we get as far as quadratic equations. The negation of the negation is even more strikingly obvious in the higher analyses, in those "summations of indefinitely small magnitudes" which Herr Dühring himself declares are the highest operations of mathematics, and in ordinary language are known as the differential and integral calculus. How are these forms of calculus used? In a given problem, for example, I have two variable magnitudes x and y, neither of which can vary without the other also varying in a relation determined by the conditions of the case. I differentiate x and y, i.e., I take x and y as so infinitely small that in comparison with any real magnitude, however small, they disappear, so that nothing is left of x and y but their reciprocal relation without any, so to speak, material basis, a quantitative relation in which there is no quantity. Therefore, dy/dx, the relation between the differentials of x and y, is equal to $0/0$, but $0/0$ as the expression of y/x. I only mention in passing that this relation between two magnitudes which have disappeared, caught at the moment of their disappearance, is a contradiction; it cannot disturb us any more than it has disturbed the whole of mathematics for almost two hundred years. And yet what have I done but negate x and y, though not in such a way that I need not bother about them any more, not in the way that metaphysics negates, but in the way that corresponds with the facts of the case? In place of x and y, therefore, I have their negation, dx and dy in the formulae of equations before me. I con-

tinue then to operate with these formulae, treating dx and dy as magnitudes which are real, though subject to certain exceptional laws, and at a certain *point I negate the negation, i.e.,* I integrate the differential formula, and in place of dx and dy again get the real magnitudes x and y, and am not then where I was at the beginning, but by using this method I have solved the problem on which ordinary geometry and algebra might perhaps have broken their teeth in vain.

It is the same, too, in history. All civilised peoples begin with the common ownership of the land. With all peoples who have passed a certain primitive stage, in the course of the development of agriculture this common ownership becomes a fetter on production. It is abolished, negated, and after a long or shorter series of intermediate stages is transformed into private property. But at a higher stage of agricultural development, brought about by private property in land itself, private property in turn becomes a fetter on production as is the case today, both with small and large landownership. The demand that it also should be negated, that it should once again be transformed into common property, necessarily arises. But this demand does not mean the restoration of the old original common ownership, but the institution of a far higher and more developed form of possession in common which, far from being a hindrance to production, on the contrary for the first time frees production from all fetters and gives it the possibility of making full use of modern chemical discoveries and mechanical inventions.

Or let us take another example: the philosophy of antiquity was primitive, natural materialism. As such, it was incapable of clearing up the relation between thought and matter. But the need to get clarity on this question led to the doctrine of a soul separable from the body, then to assertion of the immortality of this soul, and finally to monotheism. The old materialism was therefore negated by idealism. But in the course of the further development of philosophy, idealism too became untenable and was negated by modern materialism. This modern materialism, the negation of the negation, is not the mere reestablishment of the old, but adds to the permanent foundations of this old materialism the whole thought content of two thousand years of development of philosophy and natural science, as well as of the historical development of these two thousand years. It is in fact no longer a philosophy, but a simple world outlook which has to establish its validity and be applied not in a science of sciences standing apart, but within the positive sciences. In this development philosophy is therefore "sublated," that is, "both overcome and preserved"; overcome as regards its form, and preserved as regards its real content. Where Herr Dühring sees only "verbal jugglery," closer inspection therefore reveals a positive content.

. . .

What therefore is the negation of the negation? An extremely general—and for this reason extremely comprehensive and important—law of development of Nature, history and thought; a law which, as we have seen, holds good in the animal and plant kingdoms, in geology, in mathematics, in history and in philosophy—a law which even Herr Dühring, in spite of all his struggles and resistance, has unwittingly and in his own way to follow. It is obvious that in describing any evolutionary process as the negation of the negation I do not say anything concerning the *particular* process of development, for example, of the grain of barley from germination to the death of the fruit-bearing plant. For, as the integral calculus also is a negation of the negation, if I said anything of the sort I should only be making the nonsensical statement that the life-process of a barley plant was the integral calculus or for that matter that it was socialism. That, however, is what the metaphysicians are constantly trying to impute to dialectics. When I say that all these processes are the negation of the negation, I bring them all together under this one law of motion, and for this very reason I leave out of account the peculiarities of each separate individual process. Dialectics is nothing more than the science of the general laws of motion and development of Nature, human society and thought.

But someone may object: the negation that has taken place in this case is not a real negation: I negate a grain of barley also when I grind it down, an insect when I crush it underfoot, or the positive magnitude *a* when I cancel it, and so on. Or I negate the sentence; the rose is a rose, when I say: the rose is not a rose; and what do I get if I then negate the negation and say: but after all the rose is a rose?—These objections are in fact the chief arguments put forward by the metaphysicians against dialectics, and they are eminently worthy of the narrow-mindedness of this mode of thought. Negation in dialectics does not mean simply saying no, or declaring that something does not exist, or destroying it in any way one likes. Long ago Spinoza said: *Omnis determinatio est negatio*—every limitation or determination is at the same time a negation. And further: the kind of negation is here determined in the first place by the general, and secondly by the particular, nature of the process. I must not only negate, but also in turn sublate the negation. I must therefore so construct the first negation that the second remains or becomes possible. In what way? This depends on the particular nature of each individual case. If I grind a grain of barley, or crush an insect, it is true I have carried out the first part of the action, but I have made the second part impossible. Each class of things therefore has its appropriate form of being negated in such a way that it gives rise to a development, and it is just the same with each class of conceptions and ideas. The infinitesimal calculus involves a form of negation which is different from that used in the formation of positive powers from negative roots. This has to be learnt, like everything else. The mere knowledge that the barley plant and the infinitesimal calculus are both governed by the negation of the negation does not enable me either to grow barley successfully or to use the calculus; just as little as the mere knowledge of the laws of the determination of sound by the thickness of strings enables me to play the violin.

But it is clear that in a negation of the negations which consists of the childish pastime of alternately writing and cancelling *a* or of alternately declaring that a rose is a rose and that it is not a rose, nothing comes out of it but the stupidity of the person who adopts such a tedious procedure. And yet the metaphysicians try to tell us that this is the right way to carry out the negation of the negation, if we ever want to do such a thing.

Once again, therefore, it is no one but Herr Dühring who is mystifying us when he asserts that the negation of the negation is a stupid analogy invented by Hegel, borrowed from the sphere of religion and based on the story of the fall of man and redemption. Men thought dialectically long before they knew what dialectics was, just as they spoke prose long before the term prose existed. The law of the negation of the negation, which is unconsciously operative in Nature and history, and until it has been recognised, also in our heads, was only clearly formulated for the first time by Hegel. And if Herr Dühring wants to use it himself on the quiet and it is only the name which he cannot stand, let him find a better name. But if his aim is to expel the process itself from thought, we must ask him to be so good as first to banish it from Nature and history and to invent a mathematical system in which $-a \times -a$ is not $+a^2$ and in which the differential and integral calculus are prohibited under severe penalties.

GENERALIZATIONS

FROM EXPERIENCE*

JOHN STUART MILL (1806–1873).   See page 53.

Sir William Hamilton holds as I do, that inconceivability is no criterion of impossiblity. "There is no ground for inferring a certain fact to be impossible, merely from our inability to conceive its possibility." "Things there are which *may*, nay *must*, be true, of which the understanding is wholly unable to construe to itself the possibility." Sir William Hamilton is, however, a firm believer in the *a priori* character of many axioms, and of the sciences deduced from them; and is so far from considering those axioms to rest on the evidence of experience, that he declares certain of them to be true even of Noumena—of the Unconditioned—of which it is one of the principal aims of his philosophy to prove that the nature of our faculties debars us from having any knowledge. The axioms to which he attributes this exceptional emancipation from the limits which confine all our other possibilities of knowledge; the chinks through which, as he represents, one ray of light finds its way to us from behind the curtain which veils from us the mysterious world of Things in themselves—are the two principles, which he terms, after the school-men, the Principle of Contradiction, and the

Principle of Excluded Middle: the first, that two contradictory propositions can not both be true; the second, that they can not both be false. Armed with these logical weapons, we may boldly face Things in themselves, and tender to them the double alternative, sure that they must absolutely elect one or the other side, though we may be forever precluded from discovering which. To take his favorite example, we can not conceive the infinite divisibility of matter, and we can not conceive a minimum, or end to divisibility: yet one or the other must be true.

As I have hitherto said nothing of the two axioms in question, those of Contradiction and of Excluded Middle, it is not unseasonable to consider them here. The former asserts that an affirmative proposition and the corresponding negative proposition can not both be true; which has generally been held to be intuitively evident. Sir William Hamilton and the Germans consider it to be the statement in words of a form or law of our thinking faculty. Other philosophers, not less deserving of consideration, deem it to be an identical proposition; an assertion involved in the meaning of terms;

* From John Stuart Mill, *A System of Logic* (New York: Harper & Bros., 1874), pp. 204–206.

a mode of defining Negation, and the word Not.

I am able to go one step with these last. An affirmative assertion and its negative are not two independent assertions, connected with each other only as mutually incompatible. That if the negative be true, the affirmative must be false, really is a mere identical proposition; for the negative proposition asserts nothing but the falsity of the affirmative, and has no other sense or meaning whatever. The Principium Contradictionis should therefore put off the ambitious phraseology which gives it the air of a fundamental antithesis pervading nature, and should be enunciated in the simpler form, that the same proposition can not at the same time be false and true. But I can go no further with the Nominalists; for I can not look upon this last as a merely verbal proposition. I consider it to be, like other axioms, one of our first and most familiar generalizations from experience. The original foundation of it I take to be, that Belief and Disbelief are two different mental states, excluding one another. This we know by the simplest observation of our own minds. And if we carry our observation outward, we also find that light and darkness, sound and silence, motion and quiescence, equality and inequality, preceding and following, succession and simultaneousness, any positive phenomenon whatever and its negative, are distinct phenomena, pointedly contrasted, and the one always absent where the other is present. I consider the maxim in question to be a generalization from all these facts.

In like manner as the Principle of Contradiction (that one of two contradictories must be false) means that an assertion can not be *both* true and false, so the Principle of Excluded Middle, or that one of two contradictories must be true, means that an assertion must be *either* true or false: either the affirmative is true, or otherwise the negative is true, which means that the affirmative is false. I can not help thinking this principle a surprising specimen of a so-called necessity of Thought, since it is not even true, unless with a large qualification. A proposition must be either true or false, *provided* that the predicate be one which can in any intelligible sense by attributed to the subject; (and as this is always assumed to be the case in treatises on logic, the axiom is always laid down there as of absolute truth). "Abracadabra is a second intention" is neither true nor false. Between the true and the false there is a third possibility, the Unmeaning: and this alternative is fatal to Sir William Hamilton's extension of the maxim to Noumena. That Matter must either have a minimum of divisibility or be infinitely divisible, is more than we can ever know. For in the first place, Matter, in any other than the phenomenal sense of the term, may not exist: and it will scarcely be said that a nonentity must be either infinitely or finitely divisible. In the second place, though matter, considered as the occult cause of our sensations, do really exist, yet what we call divisibility may be an attribute only of our sensations of sight and touch, and not of their uncognizable cause. Divisibility may not be predicable at all, in any intelligible sense, of Things in themselves, nor therefore of Matter in itself; and the assumed necessity of being either infinitely or finitely divisible, may be an inapplicable alternative.

On this question I am happy to have the full concurrence of Mr. Herbert Spencer, from whose paper in the *Fortnightly Review* I extract the following passage. The germ of an idea identical with that of Mr. Spencer may be found in the present chapter, on a preceding page; but in Mr. Spencer it is not an undeveloped thought, but a philosophical theory.

"When remembering a certain thing as in a certain place, the place and the thing are mentally represented together; while to think of the non-existence of the thing in that place implies a consciousness in which the place is represented, but not the thing. Similarly, if instead of thinking of an object as colorless, we think of its having color, the change consists in the addition to the concept of an element that was before absent from it—the object can not be thought of first as red and then as not red, without one component of the thought being totally expelled from the mind by another. The law of the Excluded Middle, then, is simply a generalization of the universal experience that some mental states are directly destructive of other states. It formulates a certain absolutely constant law, that the appearance of any positive mode of consciousness can not occur without excluding a correlative negative mode; and that the negative mode can not occur without excluding the correlative positive mode: the antithesis of positive and negative being, indeed, merely an expression of this experience. Hence it follows that if consciousness is not in one of the two modes it must be in the other."

A DEFENSE OF THE PRINCIPLE OF CONTRADICTION*

FRANCIS HERBERT BRADLEY (1846–1924). See page 116.

The principle of Identity is often stated in the form of a tautology, *"A is A."* If this really means that no difference exists on the two sides of the judgment, we may dismiss it at once. It is no judgment at all. As Hegel tells us, it sins against the very form of judgment; for, while professing to say something, it really says nothing. It does not even assert identity. For identity without difference is nothing at all. It takes two to make the same, and the least we can have is some change of event in a self-same thing, or the return to that thing from some suggested difference. For, otherwise, to say "It is the same as itself" would be quite unmeaning. We could not even have the appearance of judgment in *"A is A,"* if we had not at least the difference of position in the different *A*'s; and we can not have the reality of judgment, unless some difference actually enters into the content of what we assert.

2

We never at any time wish to use tautologies. No one is so foolish in ordinary life as to try to assert without some difference. We say indeed "I am myself," and "Man is man and master of his fate." But such sayings as these are no tautologies. They emphasize an attribute of the subject which some consideration, or passing change, may have threatened to obscure; and to understand them rightly we must always supply "for all that," "notwithstanding," or again, "once more." It is a mere mistake to confuse what Kant calls "analytical judgments" with tautologous statements. In the former the predicate is part of the content of the conception *A*, which stands in the place of, and appears as, the subject. But in every judgment of every kind a synthesis is asserted. The synthesis in Kant's analytical judgment holds good within the sphere of the conception; and

* From Francis H. Bradley, *The Principles of Logic* (1928). Reprinted by permission of The Clarendon Press, Oxford, pp. 141–156.

the real subject is not the whole of *A,* but is certain other attributes of *A* which are *not* the attribute asserted in the predicate. In "All bodies are extended" what we mean to assert is the connection, within the subject "bodies," of extension with some other property of bodies. And even if "extended" and "body" were synonymous, we still might be very far from tautology. As against some incompatible suggestion, we might mean to assert that, after all misapprehension and improper treatment, the extended is none the less the extended. And, again, we might be making a real assertion of a verbal nature. We might mean that, despite their difference as words, the meaning of "body" and "extended" was the same. But mere tautology with deliberate purpose we never commit. Every judgment is essentially synthetical.

3

The axiom of Identity, if we take it in the sense of a principle of tautology, is no more than the explicit statement of an error. And the question is, would it not be better to banish irrevocably from the field of logic such a source of mistake? If the axiom of Identity is not just as much an axiom of Difference, then, whatever shape we like to give it, it is not a principle of analytical judgments or of any other judgments at all. On the other hand, perhaps something may be gained if a traditional form can get a meaning which conveys vital truth. Let us try to interpret the principle of Identity in such a way that it may really be an axiom.

4

We might take it to mean that in every judgment we assert the identity of subject and predicate. Every connection of elements we affirm, in short all relations and every difference, holds good only within a whole of fact. All attributes imply the identity of a subject. And taken in this sense the principle of Identity would certainly be true. But this perhaps is not the meaning which, for logical purposes, it is best to mark specially.

5

There remains a most important principle which, whether it be true or open to criticism, is at least the *sine qua non* of inference. And we can not do better than give this the name of principle of Identity, since its essence is to emphasize sameness in despite of difference. What is this principle? It runs thus: "Truth is at all times true," or, "Once true always true, once false always false. Truth is not only independent of me, but it does not depend upon change and chance. No alteration in space or time, no possible difference of any event or context, can make truth falsehood. If that which I say is really true, then it stands for ever."

So stated the principle is not very clear, but perhaps it will find acceptance with most readers. What it means, however, is much more definite, and will be much less welcome. The real axiom of Identity is this: *What is true in one context is true in another.* Or, If any truth is stated so that a change in events will make it false, then it is not a genuine truth at all.

6

To most readers this axiom, I have little doubt, will seem a false statement. For the present it may stand to serve as a test if our previous discussions have been understood. If every judgment in the end is hypothetical, except those not directly concerned with phenomena—if each merely asserts a connection of adjectives, in this sense that *given* A then B must follow—we see at once that under any conditions it will always be true. And we shall see hereafter that in every inference this result is assumed as a principle of reasoning, and that we can not argue one step without it.

7

We saw that such judgments as "I have a toothache," in their sensuous form, are not really true. They fail and come short of categorical truth, and they hardly have attained to hypothetical. To make them true we should have to give the conditions of the toothache, in such a way that the connection would hold beyond the present case. When the judgment gave the toothache as the consequent coming according to law from the ground, when the judgment had thus become universal, and, becoming this, had become hypothetical, then at last it would be really true, and its truth would be unconditional and eternal.

I know how absurd such a statement sounds. It is impossible, I admit, however much we believe it, not to find it in a certain respect ridiculous. That I do not complain of, for it is not our fault. But it is our fault if the common view does not seem *more* ridiculous. I say that "I have a toothache" to-day. It is gone to-morrow. Has my former judgment become therefore false? The popular view would loudly protest that it still is true, for I *had* a toothache, and the judgment now holds good of the past. But what that comes to is simply this. The judgment is true because answering to fact. The fact alters so that it does not answer; and yet the judgment is still called true, because of something that does not exist. Can anything be more inconsistent and absurd? If the change of circumstance and change of day is not a fresh context which falsifies *this* truth, why should any change of context falsify *any* truth? And if changed conditions

make any truth false, why should not all truth be in perpetual flux, and be true or false with the fashion of the moment?

8

We shall discuss this question more fully hereafter, but may here anticipate a misunderstanding. To ask "Does space or time make no difference" is wholly to ignore the meaning of our principle. We ask in reply, "Does this difference enter into the content of *A?* If it does, then *A* becomes *perceptibly* diverse, and we confessedly have left the sphere of our principle. But, if it does not so enter, then the truth of *A* is considered in abstraction from spaces and times, and their differences are confessedly irrelevant to its truth. We thus meet the objection by offering a dilemma. You have abstracted from the differences of space and time, or you have not done so. In the latter case your subject itself is different; in the former case it is you yourself who have excluded the difference.

We may indeed on the other side be assailed with an objection. We may be asked, "What now has become of the identity? Has it not disappeared together with the differences? For if the different contexts are not allowed to enter into the subject, how then can we say what is true in one context is true in another? It will not be true in any context at all." But we answer, The identity is not contained *in* the judgment "$S - P$," since that takes no kind of account of the differences. The identity lies in the judgment, "$S - P$ is true everywhere and always." It is this "everywhere" and "always" that supply the difference against which $S - P$ becomes an identity. The predicate attributed to the real belongs to it despite the difference of its diverse appearances. We do not say the appearances are always the same, but the quality keeps its nature throughout the appearances. And with this reply we must here content ourselves.

9

When we come to discuss the nature of inference we shall see more fully the bearing of the principle. It stands here on the result of our former enquiries, that every judgment, if it really is true, asserts some quality of that ultimate real which is not altered by the flux of events. This is not the place for metaphysical discussion, or we might be tempted to ask if identity was not implied in our view of the real. For if anything is individual it is self-same throughout, and in all diversity must maintain its character.

The Principle of Contradiction

10

Like the principle of Identity, the principle of Contradiction has been often misunderstood. And in the end it must always touch on a field of metaphysical debate. But, for logical purposes, I think it is easy to formulate it in a satisfactory way.

It is necessary before all things to bear in mind that the axiom does not in any way explain, that it can not and must not attempt to account for the existence of opposites. That discrepants or incompatibles or contraries exist, is the fact it is based on. It takes for granted the nature of things in which certain elements are exclusive of others, and it gives not the smallest reason for the world being such in nature and not quite otherwise. If we ever forget this, the Law of Contradiction will become a copious source of illusion.

11

If the principle of Contradiction states a fact, it says no more than that the discrepant is discrepant, that the exclusive, despite all attempts to persuade it, remains incompatible. Again, if we take it as laying down a rule, all it says is, "Do not try to combine in thought what is really contrary. When you add any quality to any subject, do not treat the subject as if it were not altered. When you add a quality, which not only removes the subject as it was, but removes it altogether, then do not treat it as if it remained." This is all the meaning it is safe to give to the axiom of Contradiction; and this meaning, I think, will at once be clear, if we bear in mind our former discussions. The contrary is always the base of the contradictory, and the latter is the general idea of the contrary. Not-*A* for example is any and every possible contrary of *A*.

12

We have to avoid, in dealing with Contradiction, the same mistake that we we found had obscured the nature of Identity. We there were told to produce tautologies, and here we are by certain persons forbidden to produce anything else. "*A* is not not-*A*" may be taken to mean that *A* can be nothing but what is simply *A*. This is, once again, the erroneous assertion of mere abstract identity without any difference. It is ordering us to deny as a quality of *A* everything that is *different* from *A*, and in this sense not-*A*. But differents and discrepants should never be confused. The former do not exclude one another; they only exclude the denial of their difference. The discrepant with *A* can never be found together with *A* in any possible subject, or be joined to it in the relation of subject and attribute. The different from *A* does not exclude, unless you attempt to identify it with *A*. It is not *A* generally, but one single relation to *A*, which it repels.

As we saw before, there is no logical principle which will tell us what qualities are really discrepant. Metaphysics, indeed, must ask itself the question if any further account can be given of incompatibility. It must recognize the problem, if it can not solve it. We might remark that no thing excludes any other so long as they are able to remain side by side, that incompatibility begins when you occupy the same area; and we might be tempted to conclude that in space would be found the key of our puzzle. But such other experiences as that assertion and denial, or pain and pleasure, are incompatible, would soon force us to see that our explanation is insufficient. But in logic we are not called upon to discuss the principle, but rest upon the fact. Certain elements we find *are* incompatible; and, where they are so, we must treat them as such.

13

There is no real question of principle involved in such different ways of stating the axiom as *"A* is not not-*A,"* *"A* is not both *b* and not-*b"* *"A* can not at once both be and not be."* For if *A* were not-*A*, it would be so because it had some quality contrary to *A*. So also, if *A* has a quality *b,* it could only be not-*b* by virtue of a quality discrepant with *b.* And again, if *A* both were and were not, that would be because the ultimate reality had contrary qualities. The character in which it accepted *A,* would be opposite to the quality which excluded *A* from existence. Under varieties of detail we find the same basis, repulsion of discrepants.

A simple method of stating the principle is to say, "Denial and affirmation of the self-same judgment is wholly inadmissible." And this does not mean that if a miracle in psychology were brought about, and the mind did judge both affirmatively and negatively, both judgments might be true. It means that, if at once you affirm and deny, you must be speaking falsely. For denial asserts the positive contrary of affirmation. In the nature of things (this is what it all comes to) there are certain elements which either can not be conjoined at all, or can not be conjoined in some special way; and the nature of things must be respected by logic.

14

If we wish to show that our axiom is only the other side of the Law of Identity, we may state it thus, "Truth is unchangeable, and, as discrepant assertions alter one another, they can not be true." And again, if we desire to glance in passing at the metaphysical side of the matter, we may remind ourselves that the real is individual, and the individual is harmonious and self-consistent. It does not fly apart, as it would if its qualities were internally discrepant.

15

Having now said all that I desire to say, I would gladly pass on. For, notwithstanding the metaphysics into which we have dipped, I am anxious to keep logic, so far as is possible, clear of first principles. But in the present instance the law of Contradiction has had the misfortune to be flatly denied from a certain theory of the nature of things. So far is that law (it has been contended) from being the truth, that in the nature of things contradiction exists. It is the fact that opposites are conjoined, and they are to be found as discrepant moments of a single identity.

I need hardly say that it is not my intention compendiously to dispose in a single paragraph of a system which, with all its shortcomings, has been worked over as wide an area of experience as any system offered in its place. My one idea here is to disarm opposition to the axiom of contradiction, as it stands above. But I clearly recognize that, if not-*A* were taken as a pure negation, no compromise would be possible. You would then have to choose between the axiom of contradiction and the dialectical method.

I will say, in the first place, that whatever is conjoined is therefore *ipso facto* shown not to be discrepant. If the elements co-exist, *cadit quæstio;* there is no contradiction, for there can be no contraries. And, saying so much, I feel tempted to retire. But yet with so much I shall hardly escape. "Have not we got," I hear the words called after me, "have we not got elements which any one can see negate one another, so that, while one is, the other can not be; and yet have we not got very many conceptions in which these discrepants somehow co-exist? It is all very well to say, 'then not contrary;' but try them, and see if they are not exclusive."

It is plain that I must stand and say something in reply. But I think I shall hardly be so foolish as to answer, "These conceptions of yours are merely phenomenal. Come to us and learn that knowledge is relative, and with us give up the Thing-in-itself." For without knowing all that would be poured on my head, I can guess some part of what I should provoke. *"You* say 'give up the Thing-in-itself'? Why that is all that you have not given up. You profess that your knowledge is only phenomenal, and then you make the law of Contradiction valid of the Absolute, so that what it excludes you are able to know is *not* the Absolute. That is surely inconsistent. And then, for the sake of saving from contradiction this wretched ghost of a Thing-in-itself, you are ready to plunge the whole world of phenomena, everything you know or

can know, into utter confusion. You are willing to turn every fact into nonsense, so long as this Thing-in-itself is saved. It is plain, then, for which you really care most. And as for 'relativity,' it is you yourselves who violate that principle. Your turning of the relative into hard and fast contraries is just what has brought you to your miserable pass." I confess I should hardly care to subject myself to all these insults; and I had rather Mr. Spencer, or some other great authority—whoever may feel himself able to bear them, or unable to understand them—should take them on himself.

If I chose to turn and provoke a contest, I know of another weapon I might use. I might say, "Your conceptions are partial illusions. They are crude popular modes of representing a reality whose nature can not be so portrayed. And the business of philosophy is to purify these ideas, and never to leave them until, by removal of their contradictions, they are made quite adequate to the actual fact." But, after all, perhaps I could only say this for the sake of controversy, and controversy is what I am anxious to avoid. And for this end I think that some compromise may perhaps be come to. Without calling in question the reality of negation, and the identity of opposites, are we sure that we can not understand that doctrine in a sense which will bear with the axiom of Contradiction? This axiom is not like the principle of Identity. It is a very old and most harmless veteran; and for myself I should never have the heart to attack it, unless with a view to astonish common-sense and petrify my enemies. And in metaphysics we can always do that in many other ways.

What I mean is this. Supposing that, in such a case as continuity, we seem to find contradictions united, and *A* to be *b* and not-*b* at once, this may yet be reconciled with the axiom of Contradiction. *A* we say is composed of *b* and not-*b;* for, dissecting *A,* we arrive at these elements, and, uniting these, we get *A* once more. But the question is, while these elements are *in A,* can they be said, while there, to exist in their fully discrepant character of *b* and not-*b?* I do not mean to suggest that the union of contraries may be that misunderstanding of the fact which is our only way to understand it. For, if I felt sure myself that this were true, I know it is a heresy too painful to be borne. But, in the object and within the whole, the truth may be that we never really do have these discrepants. We only have moments which *would be* incompatible if they really were separate, but, conjoined together, have been subdued into something within the character of the whole. If we so can understand the identity of opposites—and I am not sure that we may not do so— then the law of Contradiction flourishes untouched. If, in coming into one, the contraries as such no longer exist, then where is the contradiction?

But, I fear, I shall be told that the struggle of negatives is the soul of the world, and that it is precisely *because* of their identity that we have their contradiction. It is true that the opposition which for ever breaks out leads to higher unity in which it is resolved; but still the process of negation is there. It is one side of the world which can not be got rid of, and it is irreconcileable with the non-existence of discrepants in a single subject. Each element of the whole, without the other, is incompatible with itself; but it is none the less incompatible with the other, which for ever it produces or rather becomes.

I am after all not quite convinced. If the law of Contradiction is objected against because, in isolating and fixing the discrepant, it becomes one-sided, is it not quite possible that, in denying the law, we have become one-sided in another way? If the negation itself, while

negative on one side, is on the other side the return from itself to a higher harmony—if, that is to say, the elements are not discrepant without each at once, by virtue of its discrepancy and so far as it is discrepant, thereby *ipso facto* ceasing to be discrepant, then surely, in denying the law of Contradiction, we ourselves have fixed one side of the process, and have treated the contrary as simply contrary. The contrary which the law has got in its head, is the contrary that entirely kills its opposite, and remains triumphant on the field of battle. It is not the contrary whose blows are suicidal, and whose defeat must always be the doom of its adversary. It is incompatibles fixed as such, it is dicrepants which wholly exclude one another and have no other side, that the axiom speaks of. But dialectical contraries are only partially contrary and it is *our* mistake if we keep back the other side. And if an opponent of the law reminds me that the existence of these two sides within one element is just the contradiction, that in the *b* which is contrary to not-*b* the implication of not-*b* makes it self-contradictory, then I must be allowed to say in reply that I think my objector has not learnt his lesson. The not-*b* in *b* is itself self-discrepant, and is just as much *b:* and so on for ever. We never have a mere one-sided contrary.

But it is one-sided and stationary contraries that the axiom contemplates. It says that they are found, and no sober man could contend that they are not found. No one ever did maintain that the dialectical implication of opposites could be set going in the case of every conjunction that we deny. It can hardly be maintained that there *are* no discrepants, except these contraries which at the same time imply each other. And the law of Contradiction does not say any more than that, when such sheer incompatibles are found, we must not conjoin them. Its claims, if we consider them, are so absurdly feeble, it is itself so weak and perfectly inoffensive, that it can not quarrel, for it has not a tooth with which to bite any one. The controversy, first as to our actual ability to think in the way recommended by Hegel, and secondly as to the extent to which his dialetic is found in fact, can not only *not* be settled by an appeal to the axiom, but falls entirely outside its sphere. Starting from the fact of the absolute refusal of certain elements to come together, and wholly dependent upon that fact, so soon as these elements do come together the axiom ceases forthwith to be applicable. It is based upon the self-consistency of the real, but it has no right to represent that consistency except as against one kind of discrepancy. So that, if we conclude that the dialectic of the real would in the end destroy its unity, that has nothing to do with the axiom of Contradiction. Like every other question of the kind, the validity of dialectic is a question of fact, to be discussed and settled upon its own merits, and not by an appeal to so-called "principles." And I think I may venture to hazard the remark, that one must not first take up from uncritical views certain elements in the form of incompatible discrepants, and then, because we find they are conjoined, fling out against the laws of Contradiction and Excluded Middle. They, such as they are, can be no one's enemy; and since no one in the end can perhaps disbelieve in them, it is better on all accounts to let them alone.

Principle of Excluded Middle

16

The axiom that every possible judgment must be true or false, we shall see is based on what may be called a principle. It is however doubtful if the axiom itself should receive that title, since it comes under the head of disjunctive judgment. We must not imagine that our axiom supplies the principle of disjunction. It is merely one instance and application of that principle.

17

If we recall the character of the disjunctive judgment, we shall remember that there we had a real, known to be further determined. Its quality fell (i) within a certain area; and (ii) since that area was a region of discrepants, the real was determined as one single member. On this basis we erected our hypotheticals, and so the "either—or" was completed.

Excluded Middle shows all these characteristics. In it we affirm (i) that any subject *A,* when the relation to any quality is suggested, is determined at once with respect to that predicate within the area of position and negation, and by no relation which is incompatible with both. And (ii) we assert that, within this area, the subject is qualified as one single member. And then we proceed to our "either —or."

18.

Excluded Middle is one case of disjunction: it can not be considered co-extensive with it. Its dual and contradictory alternative rests on the existence of contrary opposites. The existence of exclusives without reference to their number is the ground of disjunction, and the special case of assertion and denial is developed from that basis in the way in which contradiction is developed from exclusion. Common discrepant disjunction is the base, and the dual alternative of *b* and not-*b* rests entirely upon this.

19

Excluded Middle is one kind of disjunction: and we must proceed to investigate the nature of that kind. (i) Disjunction asserts a common quality. In "*b* or not-*b*" the common quality asserted of *A* is that of general relation to *b*. (ii) Disjunction asserts an area of incompatibles. Affirmation or denial of *b* is here the area within which *A* falls. The evidence that it does not fall outside and that all the discrepants are completely given, may be called my impotence to find any other. (iii) Disjunction attributes to the subject *A* one single element of the area. And this part of the process does not call here for any special remark.

20

We find however, when we investigate further, a point in which the axiom of Excluded Middle goes beyond the limits of disjunctive judgment. It contains a further principle, since it asserts a common quality of all possible existence. It says, Every real has got a character which determines it in judgment with reference to every possible predicate. That character furnishes the ground of some judgment in respect of every suggested relation to every object. Or, to put the same more generally still, Every element of the Cosmos possesses a quality, which can determine it logically in relation to every other element.

21

This principle is prior to the actual disjunction. It says beforehand that there is a ground of relation, though it does not know what the relation is. The disjunction proceeds from the further result that the relation falls within a discrepant sphere. We thus see that, on the one hand, Excluded Middle transcends disjunction, since it possesses a self-determining principle which disjunction has not got. On the other hand, in its further development, it is nothing whatever but a case of disjunction, and must wait for

the sphere of discrepant predicates to be *given it as a fact.*

22

The disjunction is completed by the fact that, when any predicate is suggested, the quality of every element is a ground of either the affirmation or the denial of the predicate. It compels us to one and to one alone; for no other alternative can possibly be found.

And here the opposition, directed before against the axiom of Contradiction, must again be confronted. It is false, we are told, the *A* must either be *c* or not-*c*. We have often to say "both," and sometimes "neither." But I think perhaps the discussion at the end of the foregoing chapter will have strengthened us to persist. I fully admit that often, when challenged to reply Yes or No, it is necessary to answer "Yes *and* No" or "Neither." But, I venture to think, that is always because the question is ambiguous, and is asked from the standpoint of a false alternative. "Is motion continuous? Yes or no." I decline to answer until you tell me if, by saying Yes, I am taken to deny that it is *also* discrete. In that case perhaps, instead of saying Yes, I should go so far as to answer No. There may be a middle between continuity and discretion; there can be none between continuous and not-continuous.

The ground of the objection to the Excluded Middle is, I am bold enough to think, fallacious. Given not fixed discrepants but dialectical opposites, the existence of these together in one single subject does not give us the right to a negative judgment. One can not be made use of as the positive ground on which to build the denial of the other. One does not wholly remove the other, and, failing to do so, it is not qualified as a logical contrary. For it is only the discrepant which destroys its opposite that can serve as the base of a negative judgment. And, failing the denial of one quality through the other, the answer must be that both are present, and the denial of either is wholly excluded. But I fear it is hard altogether on this point to effect a compromise. If the negative of *b* is ever simply not-*b*, and if this is the other which is implicated with *b* in one subject *A*, then I grant the Excluded Middle disappears. But, I think, in this case it will carry along with it enough to ruin what is left behind. And I must leave the matter so.

23

The Excluded Middle, as we saw before, is a peculiar case of the disjunctive judgment; and I think this insight may serve us further to dispel some illusions which have gathered round it.

In the first place we must not think it is a formula, by applying which we can magically conjure elements of knowledge from the unknown deep. It is nonsense to say that it gives us a revelation that any subject must have one of two predicates. For, even if we do not make a logical mistake and really have got contradictory qualities, that is still not the right way to put the matter. Denial is not the predication of a contradictory; and all that Excluded Middle tells us is that, given any possible element of knowledge, you must be right in either affirming or denying any suggestion that is made about that.

We learnt, in our chapter on the Disjunctive Judgment, that this judgment must assume the existence of its subject, though that subject may not be the grammatical subject. And when, in the case of Excluded Middle, we are told it will guarantee us the truth of either *b* or not-*b* as a predicate of *A*, we naturally ask, "But what guarantees to us the existence of *A?*" And we get no answer.

Things in themselves either are *b* or are not *b*. Undoubtedly so, but *what is the real subject of this statement?* It perhaps after all is not "Things-in-themselves," but is ultimate reality, which may totally reject the whole offered synthesis. In this case we shall at once be able to say that Things-in-themselves are not anything at all in the real world, though, considered as illusions, they no doubt have qualifies. On the other hand, if Things-in-themselves *are* taken as such to have existence, then that is not proved by our Excluded Middle, but is a sheer assumption on which we base it and which it presupposes.

24

But when we are told, "Between the true and the false there is a third possibility, the Unmeaning" (Mill, *Logic,* II. vii. §5), we must answer, "Yes, an unmeaning possibility, and therefore none at all." The doctrine that propositions need neither be true nor yet be false because they may be senseless, would introduce, I agree, "a large qualification" into the doctrine of the Excluded Middle. But I am inclined to think that this "qualification" might be larger than it seems to be, and might be operative perhaps beyond the limits so sparingly assigned to it. But surely, on the one hand, it is clear that a proposition which has no meaning is no proposition; and surely again, on the other hand, it is clear that, if it does mean anything, it is either true or else false. And when a predicate is really known *not* to be "one which can in any intelligible sense be attributed to the subject"—is not that itself ground enough for denial? But logicians who actually (Mill, *loc. cit.*) are ready to take divisible finitely and divisible infinitely as *contradictories,* are justified in expecting extraordinary events. Suppose these terms to be absolutely incompatible, that would hardly bring them under Excluded Middle, unless we are prepared to formulate the axiom thus: Whenever predicates are incompatible, then, although there be *three or more* possibilities, it is certain that one of *these two* possibilities must always be true. But perhaps this "qualification" might tend to create more difficulties than it solves.

25

If we turn from these somewhat elementary mistakes, and consider the amount of actual knowledge vouchsafed to us by the Excluded Middle, I hardly think we shall be much puffed up. We must remember that, even if we are able to assert about such a subject as Things-in-themselves, we must always be on our guard against an error. We may be affirming about the meaning of a word, or about a mere idea in our heads, and may confuse these facts with another kind of fact. But, even supposing we keep quite clear of this mistake, yet when we come to negative judgments there is ambiguity, unavoidable and ceaseless, about the positive ground of the denial. We may penetrate so far into hidden mysteries as perhaps to be privileged solemnly to avouch that Things-in-them-

selves are not three-cornered, nor coloured rose-red, nor pock-marked nor dyspeptic. But what does this tell us? What more should we know, if we spent our breath and wasted our days in endless denials of senseless suggestions? If the ground of negation remains the same, each particular denial asserts nothing in particular.

26

Confined to its limits the Excluded Middle is rigidly true. But you may easily assert it in a shape which would exhibit a parallel falsehood to those we considered in examining the Principles of Identity and Contradiction. "Everything," we might say, "is either simply the same as any other, or else has nothing whatever to do with it."

Once again, in conclusion, I must call attention to the positive principle which underlies the Excluded Middle. We assume that every element of knowledge can stand in some relation with every other element. And we may give this, if we please, a metaphysical turn, though in doing so we go beyond the equivalent of the Excluded Middle. We may say, If the real is harmonious and individual, it must exist in its members and must inter-relate them.

A DEFENSE OF THE LAW
OF EXCLUDED MIDDLE*

BERTRAND RUSSELL (1872–   ). See page 78.

In general, in this book, I am avoiding logical questions, but in this chapter, as in the last, I shall be concerned with a logical topic, namely the law of excluded middle. As every one knows, Brouwer has challenged the law, and has done so on epistemological grounds. He, in common with many others, holds that "truth" can only be defined in terms of "verifiability", which is obviously a concept belonging to theory of knowledge. If he is right, it follows that the law of excluded middle, and the law of contradiction also, belong to epistemology, and must be reconsidered in the light of whatever definition of truth and falsehood epistemology permits. . . . It is fairly obvious that, if an epistemological definition is adhered to, the law of excluded middle, in its usual form, cannot be true, though the law of contradiction may be. We have to consider . . . whether to sacrifice the law of excluded middle or to attempt a definition of truth which is independent of knowledge.

The difficulties of either view are appalling. If we define truth in relation to knowledge, logic collapses, and much hitherto accepted reasoning, including large parts of mathematics, must be re-

jected as invalid. But if we adhere to the law of excluded middle, we shall find ourselves committed to a realist metaphysic which may seem, in the spirit if not in the letter, incompatible with empiricism. The question is fundamental, and of the greatest importance.

Before attempting to decide it, let us develop the alternatives.

Brouwer is not concerned with phrases that are syntactically nonsensical, such as "quadruplicity drinks procrastination". He is concerned with sentences that are grammatically and logically correct, but epistemologically incapable of being proved or disproved. We must be clear as to the point at issue before we begin to discuss it.

Brouwer argues that "true" is a useless conception unless we have ways of discovering whether a proposition is true or not. He therefore substitutes "verifiable" for "true", and he does not call a proposition "false" unless its contradictory is verifiable. There thus remains an intermediate class of propositions, which are syntactically correct, but neither verifiable nor the contradictories of verifiable propositions. This intermediate class Brouwer refuses to call

* From Bertrand Russell, *An Inquiry into Meaning and Truth* (1940). Reprinted by permission of Allen & Unwin, Ltd., London.

either true or false, and in regard to them he regards the law of excluded middle as mistaken.

No one has yet gone so far as to define "truth" as "what *is* known"; the epistemological definition of "truth" is "what *can* be known". The word "verifiable" is commonly used, and a proposition is verifiable if it *can* be verified. possibility is an awkward concept. If This at once introduces difficulties, since the definition is to be definite, the particular kind of possibility that is intended will have to be elucidated. In mathematics, Brouwer and his school have done this, with a considerable measure of success; but so far as I know, they have given little thought to more ordinary propositions, such as historical hypotheses concerning which there is no evidence either way. Much is to be learnt from Carnap's *Logical Syntax of Language,* but mainly by way of suggestion. He holds that a general proposition, such as "all men are mortal", which is inherently incapable of being completely proved, is to be taken (provisionally) as true if many instances of its truth are known, and none of its falsehood.

A definition of "truth" as "what can be known" will have to advance step by step from basic propositions. I shall assume . . . that my present factual premisses consist of: (1) a very small number asserting present percepts; (2) a considerably larger number of negative propositions derived from present percepts as we arrive at "this is not red" when we see a buttercup; (3) memories, in so far as no argument exists to throw doubt on them; (4) the law of contradiction, but not the law of excluded middle. The law of excluded middle will be true, to begin with, of a certain class of propositions, namely those that can be confronted with percepts. If you are letting off fireworks on the fifth of November, and you say "look out, there's going to

be a bang", either there is a bang, or the fireworks are damp and there isn't. In such a case, your statement is true or false. There are other cases, derived from this kind, to which the law of excluded middle applies; the definition of the class of cases is much the same problem as the epistemological definition of "truth".

It is to be observed that, when the law of excluded middle fails, the law of double negation also fails. If p is neither true nor false, it is false that p is false; if the principle of double negation held, this would imply that p is true, whereas, by hypothesis, p is neither true nor false. Consequently, in this logic, "it is false that p is false" is not equivalent to "p is true".

To give ourselves a chance, we will, at least to begin with, allow inductive generalizations from basic propositions. These may turn out to be false if a negative instance occurs; until that happens, we shall, following Carnap, provisionally accept them as true. In either case, we shall regard them as subject to the law of excluded middle. We will allow also the testimony of others, subject to common sense provisos. We can now build up science; and having accepted inductive generalizations, we will admit as true such of their consequences as cannot be disproved. For example, we will say that eclipses occurred in prehistoric times as astronomy leads us to suppose; but we say this with the degree of hesitation appropriate to the inductive generalizations that constitute the laws of astronomy.

We can thus assert and deny all propositions that, as empiricists, we see reason to assert or deny. The difficulties come (*a*) in logic and mathematics (*b*) as to extra-logical propositions in regard to which there is no evidence either way.

Let us consider a definite extra-logical proposition as to which there is no evidence. Take "it snowed on Manhattan Island on the first of January in the year 1 A.D". Let us call this proposition "P". What do we know about P? Having accepted inductive generalizations, history tells us that there was a year 1 A.D., and geology assures us that Manhattan Island existed then. We know that snow often falls there in winter. We therefore *understand* P just as well as if it related to a snowfall of which there is historical record. In theory, a Laplacean calculator could infer the weather of former times, just as the astronomer infers the eclipses. In practice, however, this is impossible, not only because the calculations would be too difficult, but because more data would be required than could ever be obtained. We must therefore admit that we have not any evidence as to whether P is true or false, and that, so far as we can see, we are never likely to have any. We must conclude, if "truth" is to be defined epistemologically, the P is neither true nor false.

Our reluctance to accept this conclusion comes from our obstinate belief in a "real" world independent of our observation. We feel that we *might* have been there, and we should then have seen whether it was snowing, and the fact of our looking on would have made no difference to the snow. We are ready enough to concede that the whiteness of the snow's appearance has to do with our eyes, just as the cold feeling has to do with our temperature nerves; but we suppose these sensations to have an outside cause, which is the snow as dealt with in physics. And this, we believe, except where certain very delicate quantum observations are concerned, is just the same whether we know of it or not.

But all this was already conceded when we accepted inductive generalizations, and allowed ourselves to believe that Manhattan Island probably existed at the date in question. If we are going to allow inductions of this sort, there seems no reason for refusing to extend the law of excluded middle to every proposition for or against which there is any evidence, however slender. Now there might easily be evidence that the climate of Manhattan Island has not changed much in the last two thousand years, and in that case weather records give the probability of snow on any given day of the year. We shall therefore conclude that P is either true or false, for, though we cannot *decide* the question, we know something of the likelihood of each alternative.

There will still be propositions as to which there is no evidence whatever, for instance: "there is a cosmos which has no spatio-temporal relation to the one in which we live". Such a cosmos can be imagined by a writer of scientific romances, but by the very nature of the hypothesis there can be no inductive argument either for or against it. When we feel that there must be or not be such a cosmos, I think that we imagine a Deity contemplating all the worlds that He has made, and thereby we surreptitiously restore the link with our own world which, in words, we have denied.[1] If we rigidly exclude both this conception and that of a miraculous heightening of our own perceptive faculties, it is perhaps possible to suppose that our hypothesis has no meaning. In that case, it is neither true nor false, but it is not a proposition, and therefore fails to show that there are propositions which do not obey the law of excluded middle.

We must face the question: in what circumstances, if any, does a sentence which is syntactically correct fail to have a meaning? We suggested, a moment ago, that perhaps the sentence: "something has no spatio-temporal relation to my present percept", is devoid of meaning;

[1] Cf. *The Star Maker,* by Olaf Stapledon.

for that is what the rejection of the imagined cosmos amounts to. It seems to follow that the contradictory of the above sentence, namely: "everything has some spatio-temporal relation to my present percept", is also devoid of meaning; but this seems far less plausible. If this is to be meaningless, it must be because of the word "everything". The word "everything", it may be said, implies that the whole universe can be laid out for inspection, whereas, in fact, new percepts perpetually occur, and all totality is illusory except that of an enumerated set of objects.

This question of totality is very important. Can we define a total conceptually, as we define the class of men or the class of natural numbers? Some think that we can do so if the class is finite, but not otherwise. I cannot see, however, that this is a relevant consideration, except when a general word is a mere abbreviation for "these objects in this given collection". In that case, the general word is unnecessary. Whenever, as in the case of men, actual enumeration is impossible, the question whether the collection is finite or infinite seems irrelevant. "All men are mortal" raises the same problems, in this connection, as "all integers are odd or even".

When we say "all men are mortal", are we saying anything, or are we making meaningless noises? I am not asking whether the sentence is true, but whether it is significant. Let us first exclude some untenable views. (1) We cannot try to reduce the proposition to a prescription, to wit: "if I see a man, I shall judge him to be mortal". For the occasions on which I shall see a man are just as impossible to enumerate as men are. I might, with my dying breath, say "all the men I have met were mortal", because then they could be enumerated; but until then the collection is only defined conceptually. (2) We cannot say:

"a statement about a collection is legitimate when there is a *possible* set of experiences which would cover the whole collection, but not otherwise". For we shall find, if we attempt to define "possible experiences", that we are taken into just the hypothetical conceptual realm from which we wished to escape. How are we to know whether an experience is "possible"? Obviously this will require knowledge that transcends *actual* experience. (3) We cannot confine "all men are mortal" to past experience, for in that case it would have to mean "all the men who have died hitherto were mortal", which is a tautology. (4) It is sometimes thought possible to interpret general statements—especially inductive generalizations—as practical advice. Thus "all men are mortal" will mean: "next time you meet a man, I should advise you to behave as if he were mortal, for if you chop his head in two in the hope that he is immortal, you will be hanged". But this advice is only sound because the man *is* mortal. If you seriously doubt whether all men are mortal, you may do well to go about making experiments on the subject. The pragmatic interpretation, in fact, is only an evasion.

If we exclude such sentences as "all men are mortal", which deal with collections defined conceptually, general propositions will be confined to history, or rather to collections composed of objects which now exist or have existed. We can say "all the men in this room will die", but not "all the children of the men in this room will die". This is surely absurd.

It seems to me that, when we understand the words "man" and "mortal", we can understand "all men are mortal", without having to be acquainted with each individual man. And in like manner, I should say, we can understand "all integers are odd or even". But if this view is to be maintained, there must be such a thing as understanding "all-ness", independently of enumeration. This is really a question of understanding what is hypothetical. The analysis of general propositions is very difficult, since it seems quite clear that we can know propositions about all of a collection without knowing its several members. We say that "I hear nothing" may be a basic proposition; yet it is for logic a statement about everything in the universe. . . .

When we were discussing snow in 1 A.D., we allowed ourselves to accept inductive generalizations. It is questionable whether, when we are doubting the law of excluded middle, we have any right to do this, except at most in the way of inferring percepts. Inductions in the physical sciences are always phrased in realist terms, i.e., they suppose that what you observe can happen without your observation, and does happen in suitable circumstances. If we arrive at an uninhabited island and find luxuriant vegetation, we shall infer that it has rained there, although no one has seen the rain. Now it is obvious that, from the standpoint of inductive verification, two hypotheses which only differ as to unobserved occurrences are precisely on a level. From the epistemological point of view, therefore, we may suppose that there are no unobserved occurrences, or that there are a few, or that there are many; we can, as physicists do, insert whatever number and kind of unobserved occurrences will make it easiest to formulate the laws of observed occurrences. They serve the same sort of purpose as may be served by complex numbers in a calculation which begins and ends with real numbers.

Is there any sense in asking whether these unobserved occurrences really occur? According to Carnap, there is only a linguistic question: "reality" is a metaphysical term for which there is no legitimate use. Well and good, but let us be consistent. I have not myself observed what I have learnt from testimony or from history; I have observed only what has come within my own experience. Therefore, on the view in question, the hypotheses that testimony is not merely noises or shapes, and that the world existed before the earliest moment that I can remember, are mere linguistic conveniences.

This view is one which, in fact, no one accepts. If a doctor says to you "your wife has cancer", you feel no doubt that what you hear expresses a thought; you also have no doubt that, if the doctor is right, your wife is having and will have painful experiences which will not be yours. Your emotions would be quite different if you thought the whole thing merely a linguistic abbreviation for describing certain experiences of your own. This, of course, is no argument. But I notice that those who take the sort of view that I am combating always avoid applying it as against other human beings, and are content to apply it to such matters as the glacial epoch, which have very little emotional content. This is illogical. If the glacial epoch is only a linguistic convenience, so are your parents and your children, your friends and your colleagues. It is, of course, still possible to accept testimony. You may say: "Mr. A, so far as I know, is a series of noises and shapes; but I have found, odd as it may seem, that if I interpret the noises as those which I should make to express certain thoughts or percepts, they frequently turn out to be true. I have therefore decided to behave as if Mr. A were an intelligent being". But your emotions will not be what they would be if you believed that he "really" had intelligence.

When we ask: "do any occurrences not observed by me really occur?" we are asking a question which, at least as regards other human beings, has a very great emotional content, and can hardly, it would seem, be totally devoid of significance. We are interested in other people's loves and hates, pleasures and pains, because we are firmly persuaded that they are as "real" as our own. We mean *something* when we say this. A person in a novel manifests himself, but deceptively: the emotions which he expresses have not been actually felt. "Real" people are different; but how?

I am not concerned, at the moment, to argue that unobserved events occur; I am only concerned to argue that the question whether they occur or not is more than a linguistic question. I take the question, to begin with, in connection with the percepts, thoughts, and feelings of other people, because in that case what we are inferring is closely analogous to what we know from our own experience. In the case of unobserved matter, there is not only the fact that it is unobserved, but that it must be very different from anything of which we have experience, since it cannot have any sensible qualities. This additional problem is avoided by considering the experiences of other people. If we see a man apparently suffering, the hypothesis that he *is* suffering adds something, and is not merely the adoption of a different linguistic convention from that of the solipsist.

It is no use to say: "but this does not take you outside experience; it only takes you outside *your* experience". You do not know that this is true unless you know that the other man has experiences, and is not merely what you perceive; but this is the very piece of knowledge that was to be justified. Epistemology cannot *begin* by accepting testimony, for the correctness of testimony is certainly not among basic propositions.

I conclude, then, that there is a substantial meaning in the hypothesis that something occurs which I do not experience, at least when this is something analogous to my experiences, e.g. the experiences which I attribute to other people.

This, however, does not settle the question whether there is any meaning in the hypothesis of physical phenomena which are observed by no one, which we must now consider.

There are here certain distinctions to be made. On empirical grounds we believe that there cannot be visual objects except where there are eyes and nerves and a brain, but there is no *logical* difficulty in the hypothesis of such objects existing elsewhere. In fact, every person who is philosophically and scientifically naïve believes that what we see when we look at something is still there when we are no longer looking. This what is called naïve realism—a doctrine which must be held to be false in fact, but not logically impossible. The problem in connection with physics is: having admitted that where there is no sentient percipient there cannot be anything having the sensible qualities that we know from experience, is there any meaning in the hypothesis that there is *something* there? There are in fact two questions: First, is there significance in the hypothesis that something not experienced exists? Second, is there significance in the hypothesis that something exists which is unlike objects of perception as we should have to suppose occurrences to be where there are no percipients?

As to the first, I see no difficulty. The fact that we experience a phenomenon is not an essential part of our understanding of the phenomenon, but only a cause of our knowledge that it occurs, and there is no logical obstacle to the hypothesis that the phenomenon could exist unperceived. In fact, we all hold that we have many sensations which we do not notice, and these are, strictly speaking, not experienced.

There is more difficulty as to the

second question, namely: is there any significance in the hypothesis of physical phenomena as different from our percepts as they would have to be if they were neither visual nor auditory nor of any of the familiar kinds? The question is not quite that of the Kantian *Ding-an-Sich*, which is outside time; the kind of occurrences concerning which we are inquiring are certainly in time, and they are in space of a sort, though not quite of the sort to which we are accustomed in percepts. Physical space—i.e. the space of physics—is not directly sensible, but is definable by relation to sensible spaces. It would seem, therefore, that a proposition concerning a purely physical phenomenon can be enunciated in terms which are known through experience; if so, the proposition is certainly, in one sense, significant, even if we do not know how to discover whether it is true or false. If it is significant to say "everything that exists is sensible", the contradictory of this, namely "something non-sensible exists", must also be significant. If it be maintained that "sensible" has no meaning, we can substitute "visual or auditory, or etc." It seems, therefore, that we cannot deny significance to the hypothesis of occurrences having none of the qualities which we believe to be causally dependent upon a sensorium.

It remains to inquire in what sense, if any, such a hypothesis can be regarded as either true or false.

This brings us to the question of "fact" as what makes propositions true. According to the correspondence theory of truth, as Tarski points out, the proposition "it is snowing" is true if it is snowing. This has, *prima facie*, nothing to do with knowledge. If you do not realize that it is snowing, that does not make the proposition "it is snowing" any less true. You may find several inches of snow on the ground when at last you do look out, and say "it must have been

snowing for hours". Surely it would have been snowing just the same if you had not been going to look out afterwards? All the time that you were not looking out, the proposition "it is snowing" was true, although you did not know that it was. This is the view of realism and of common sense. And it is this view which has made the law of excluded middle seem self-evident.

Let us set to work to state this view in such a way as to avoid all avoidable difficulties. First, as to "facts": they are not to be conceived as "that grass is green" or "that all men are mortal"; they are to be conceived as occurrences. We shall say that all percepts are facts, but according to the realist view they are only some among facts. They may be defined as facts that some one knows without inference; but on the realist hypothesis there are other facts which can only be known by inference, and perhaps yet others which cannot be known at all.

Percepts, in this view, may be defined as events having a certain kind of spatio-temporal relation to a living body with suitable organs. Suppose, for example, you are measuring the velocity of sound, and for this purpose you occasionally fire a gun, while a man a mile away waves a flag as soon as he hears the report. Throughout the intervening space—if we are to believe the physicists—there are events, namely air-waves. When this train of events reaches an ear, it undergoes various modifications, much as sunlight undergoes modifications when it sets up the manufacture of chlorophyll in plants. One of the events resulting from the impact of sound-waves on an ear, provided the ear is attached to a normal brain, is what is called "hearing" the sound. After this event, the chain of causation runs out of the brain into the arm, and leads to the waving of the flag. What is odd about the brain and the sensation is the character of the causal laws that operate at this point in the chain: they involve habit, and "mnemic" causation. To say that we "know" a percept is to say that it has set up a certain habit in the brain. Only events in the brain can set up habits in the brain; therefore only events in the brain can be known in the kind of way in which we know percepts.

Some such view as the above is assumed technically in physics and physiology. I do not mean that physicists and physiologists are necessarily prepared to defend it theoretically, or that their results are not compatible with other views. I mean only that the language they naturally use is one which implies some such outlook.

I do not know whether there is any argument which shows that this view is false. Various idealistic philosophies have attempted to prove it untenable, but in so far as they appealed to logic I shall take it for granted that they failed. The argument from epistemology, which unlike that from logic, is as powerful as it ever was, does not attempt to show that the view in question is false, but only that it is gratuitous, in the sense that it sins against Occam's razor by assuming the existence of unnecessary entities. What we know, says the epistemological argument, is percepts; the sound-waves, the brain, etc., are mere convenient hypotheses in the interconnecting of percepts. They enable me, when I have fired my shot, to calculate how long (according to the visual perceptions which I call "seeing a stopwatch") it will be before I have the percept which I call the waving of the flag. But there is no more need to suppose that these hypotheses have any "reality" than there is to suppose that parallel lines "really" meet in a point at infinity, which also is for some purposes a convenient way of speaking.

This epistemological scepticism has a logical foundation, namely the principle that it is never possible to deduce the existence of something from the existence of something else. This principle must be stated more clearly, and without the use of the word "existence". Let us take an illustration. You look out of the window, and observe that you can see three houses. You turn back into the room and say "three houses are visible from the window". The kind of sceptic that I have in mind would say "you mean three houses *were* visible". You would reply "but they can't have vanished in this little moment". You might look again and say "yes, there they are still". The sceptic would retort: "I grant that when you looked again they were there again, but what makes you think they had been there in the interval?" You would only be able to say "because I see them whenever I look". The sceptic would say "then you ought to infer that they are caused by your looking". You will never succeed in getting any evidence against this view, because you can't find out what the houses look like when no one is looking at them.

Our logical principle may be stated as follows: "no proposition about what occurs in one part of space-time logically implies any proposition about what occurs in another part of space-time". If the reference to space-time is thought unduly suggestive of physicalism, it can easily be eliminated. We may say: "the perceptive propositions derivable from one perceived event never logically imply any proposition about any other event". I do not think this can be questioned by anyone who understands the logic of truth-functions.

But outside pure mathematics the important kinds of inference are not logical; they are analogical and inductive. Now the kind of partial sceptic whom we have been having in mind allows such inferences, for he accepts physicalism whenever it enables us to prophesy our own future percepts. He will allow the man measuring the velocity of sound to say "in five seconds I shall see the flag wave"; he will only not allow him to say "in five seconds the flag will wave". These two inferences, however, are exactly on a level as regards induction and analogy, without which science, however interpreted, becomes impossible. Our logical foundation thus becomes irrelevant, and we have to consider whether induction and analogy can ever make it probable that there are unperceived events.

At this point there is danger of a fallacy, so simple that it ought to be easy to avoid, but nevertheless not always avoided. A man may say: "everything that I have ever perceived was perceived; therefore there is inductive evidence that everything is perceived". The argument would be the same if I said: "everything I know is known; therefore probably everything is known".

We are left, then, with a substantial question: assuming the legitimacy of induction and analogy, do they afford evidence for unperceived events? This is a difficult but by no means insoluble question. I shall, however, not discuss it now, since it assumes as conceded, what is for us at present the essential point, that the difference between a theory which allows unperceived events and one which does not is a difference which need not be merely linguistic.

Although the above discussion has been so far very inconclusive, I find myself believing, at the end of it, that truth and knowledge are different, and that a proposition may be true although no method exists of discovering that it is so. In that case, we may accept the law of excluded middle. We shall define "truth" by reference to "events" (I am speaking of non-logical truth), and "knowledge" by relation to "percepts". Thus "truth" will be a wider conception than "knowledge". It would be a practically useless conception, but for the fact that knowledge has very vague boundaries. When we embark upon an investigation, we assume that the propositions concerning which we are inquiring are either true or false; we may find evidence, or we may not. Before the spectroscope, it would have seemed impossible ever to ascertain the chemical constitution of the stars; but it would have been a mistake to maintain that they neither do nor do not contain the elements we know. At present, we do not know whether there is life elsewhere in the universe, but we are right to feel sure that there either is or is not. Thus we need "truth" as well as "knowledge", because the boundaries of knowledge are uncertain, and because, without the law of excluded middle, we could not ask the questions that give rise to discoveries.

P A R T   F O U R

Symbolic Logic

INTRODUCTION The history of mathematics is a continuing lesson that improved notations and symbolic innovations help in solving problems. Mathematics has thus served as both an inspiration and a model in the development of symbolic logic—also called, appropriately, mathematical logic.

The selections in this Part do not develop the techniques of symbolic logic, but talk about it. The two short essays by Leibniz reveal his dream of replacing ratiocination by calculation, which would make fallacies in reasoning as rare and as easily discovered as mistakes in bookkeeping. All that is needed is the invention of appropriate symbols: ". . . it is manifest that if we could find characters or signs appropriate for expressing all our thoughts as definitely and as exactly as arithmetic expresses numbers or geometric analysis expresses lines, we could in all subjects *in so far as they are amenable to reasoning* accomplish what is done in Arithmetic and Geometry."

Boole accomplished this aim for a modest class of inferences. His purpose was "to give expression . . . to the fundamental laws of reasoning in the symbolical language of a Calculus." In the course of his investigations he decided that "syllogism, conversion, etc., are not the ultimate processes of Logic . . . they are founded upon, and are resolvable into, ulterior and more simple processes which constitute the real elements of method in Logic."

Frege developed the notion of a *formal system of logic* in which a passage from premises to conclusion is made only according to antecedently specified rules of procedure, thus eliminating (or at least diminishing) the possibility of error. Frege also stated and attempted to establish the *logistic thesis,*[1] which was formulated later independently by Russell and which Whitehead and Russell's *Principia Mathematica* purports to demonstrate.

---

[1] The *logistic thesis,* propounded independently by Frege and Russell asserts that
1. All concepts of mathematics are definable in terms of purely logical concepts; and
2. All truths of mathematics are deducible from purely logical truths.

Whitehead explains in a few words some of the great advantages to be achieved by good notation. Although his remarks concern mathematics proper, they are equally applicable to mathematical or symbolic logic.

In the first of the two selections from Russell included in this Part it is stated that the employment of special symbols in symbolic logic is "merely a theoretically irrelevant convenience." In the second Russell insists that "logical symbolism is absolutely necessary to any exact or thorough treatment of our subject." Both essays are entertaining as well as instructive, and their differences are easily accounted for by their dates. The first was published in 1903, the second in 1919. Between them lay the enormous labor of writing *Principia Mathematica* (1910–1913) with A. N. Whitehead.

Poincaré criticizes symbolic logic from the point of view of a mathematician. He attacks the logistic thesis on a number of different counts, poking considerable fun at some of the definitions of numbers proposed by logicians. More seriously, Poincaré points out that for the logistic thesis to be even remotely plausible, a new logic is required. And in truth, no proponent of the reduction of mathematics to logic ever maintained that it was reducible to the logic of Aristotle.

Croce rejects both the traditional formal logic and the newer symbolic logic. From his point of view as an Idealist, "the nature of mathematical Logic in no respect differs from that of formalist Logic." Both of them are concerned with "verbal propositions," linguistic or symbolic entities of which thinking is wholly independent. Some of Croce's grounds for condemning symbolic logic are akin to, though not identical with, Bradley's grounds for condemning the syllogism.

THE METHOD OF

MATHEMATICS*

GOTTFRIED WILHELM LEIBNIZ (1646–1716) was a German jurist, mathematician, historian, philosopher, theologian, scientist, and diplomat. He shared with Newton the honor of having discovered the Infinitesimal Calculus, and met and corresponded with the greatest scientists and philosophers of his day. Leibniz's philosophical system is set forth in *Theodicy* (1710) and *Monadology* (1714). Leibniz made extremely important contributions to symbolic logic, but his manuscripts did not come to light until recently, after his discoveries in symbolic logic had been rediscovered independently by others.

Preface to the General Science

Since happiness consists in peace of mind, and since durable peace of mind depends on the confidence we have in the future, and since that confidence is based on the science we should have of the nature of God and the soul, it follows that science is necessary for true happiness.

But science depends on demonstration, and the discovery of demonstrations *by a certain Method* is not known to everybody. For while every man is able to judge a demonstration (it would not deserve this name if all those who consider it attentively were not convinced and persuaded by it), nevertheless not every man is able to discover demonstrations on his own initiative, nor to present them distinctly once they are discovered, if he lacks leisure or method.

The *true Method* taken in all of its scope is to my mind a thing hitherto quite unknown, and has not been practised except in mathematics. It is even very imperfect in regard to mathematics itself, as I have had the good fortune to reveal by means of surprising proofs to some of those considered to be among the best mathematicians of the century. And I expect to offer some samples of it, which perhaps will not be considered unworthy of posterity.

However, if the Method of Mathematicians has not sufficed to discover everything that might be expected from them, it has remained at least able to save them from mistakes, and if they have not said everything they were supposed to say, they have also not said anything they were not expected to say.

If those who have cultivated the other sciences had imitated the mathematicians at least on this point, we should be quite content, and we should have long since had a secure Metaphysics, as well as an ethics depending on Metaphysics since the latter includes the sort of knowledge of God and the soul which should rule our life.

In addition, we should have the science of motion which is the key to physics, and consequently, to medicine. True, I believe we are ready now to aspire to it, and some of my first thoughts have been received with such applause by the most learned men of our time on account of the wonderful simplicity introduced, that I believe that all we have to do now is perform certain experiments on a deliberate plan and scale (rather than by the haphazard fumbling which is so common) in order to build thereupon the stronghold of a sure and demonstrative physics.

Now the reason why the art of demonstrating has been until now found only in mathematics has not been well fathomed by the average person, for if the cause of the trouble had been known, the remedy would have long since been found out. The reason is this: Mathematics carries its own test with it. For when I am presented with a false theorem, I do not need to examine or even to know the demonstration, since I shall discover its falsity a posteriori by means of an easy experiment, that is, by a calculation, costing no more than paper and ink, which will show the error no matter how small it is. If it were as easy in other matters to verify reasonings by experiments, there would not be such differing opinions. But the trouble is that experiments in physics are difficult and cost a great deal; and in metaphysics they are impossible, unless God out of love for us perform a miracle in order to acquaint us with remote immaterial things.

This difficulty is not insurmountable

though at first it may seem so. But those who will take the trouble to consider what I am going to say about it will soon change their mind. We must then notice that the tests or experiments made in mathematics to guard against mistakes in reasoning (as, for example, the test of casting out nines, the calculation of Ludolph of Cologne concerning the magnitude of circles, tables of sines, etc.), these tests are not made on a thing itself, but on the characters which we have substituted in place of the thing. Take for example a numerical calculation: if 1677 times 365 are 612,105, we should hardly ever have reached this result were it necessary to make 365 piles of 1677 pebbles each and then to count them all finally in order to know whether the aforementioned number is found. That is why we are satisfied to do it with characters on paper, by means of the test of nines, etc. Similarly, when we propose an approximately exact value of π in the quadrature of a circle, we do not need to make a big material circle and tie a string around it in order to see whether the ratio of the length of this string or the circumference to the diameter has the value proposed; that would be troublesome, for if the error is one-thousandth or less part of the diameter, we should need a large circle constructed with a great deal of accuracy. Yet we still refute the false value of π by the experiment and use of the calculus or numerical test. But this test is performed only on paper, and consequently, on the characters which represent the thing, and not on the thing itself.

This consideration is fundamental in this matter, and although many persons of great ability, especially in our century, may have claimed to offer us demonstrations in questions of physics, metaphysics, ethics, and even in politics, jurisprudence, and medicine, nevertheless they have either been mistaken (because every step is on slippery ground and it is difficult not to fall unless guided by some tangible directions), or even when they succeed, they have been unable to convince everyone with their reasoning (because there has not yet been a way to examine arguments by means of some easy tests available to everyone).

Whence it is manifest that if we could find characters or signs appropriate for expressing all our thoughts as definitely and as exactly as arithmetic expresses numbers or geometric analysis expresses lines, we could in all subjects *in so far as they are amenable to reasoning* accomplish what is done in Arithmetic and Geometry.

For all inquiries which depend on reasoning would be performed by the transposition of characters and by a kind of calculus, which would immediately facilitate the discovery of beautiful results. For we should not have to break our heads as much as is necessary today, and yet we should be sure of accomplishing everything the given facts allow.

Moreover, we should be able to convince the world what we should have found or concluded, since it would be easy to verify the calculation either by doing it over or by trying tests similar to that of casting out nines in arithmetic. And if someone would doubt my results, I should say to him: "Let us calculate, Sir," and thus by taking to pen and ink, we should soon settle the question.

I still add: *in so far as the reasoning allows on the given facts.* For although certain experiments are always necessary to serve as a basis for reasoning, nevertheless, once these experiments are given, we should derive from them everything which anyone at all could possibly derive; and we should even discover what experiments remain to be done for the clarification of all further doubts. That would be an admirable help, even in political science and medicine, to steady and perfect reasoning concerning given symptoms and circumstances. For even while there will not be enough given circumstances to form an infallible judgment, we shall always be able to determine what is most probable on the data given. And that is all that reason can do.

Now the characters which express all our thoughts will constitute a new language which can be written and spoken; this language will be very difficult to construct, but very easy to learn. It will be quickly accepted by everybody on account of its great utility and its surprising facility, and it will serve wonderfully in communication among various peoples, which will help get it accepted. Those who will write in this language will not make mistakes provided they avoid the errors of calculation, barbarisms, solecisms, and other errors of grammar and construction. In addition, this language will possess the wonderful property of silencing ignorant people. For people will be unable to speak or write about anything except what they understand, or if they try to do so, one of two things will happen: either the vanity of what they advance will be apparent to everybody, or they will learn by writing or speaking. As indeed those who calculate learn by writing and those who speak sometimes meet with a success they did not imagine, the tongue running ahead of the mind. This will happen especially with our language on account of its exactness. So much so, that there will be no equivocations or amphibolies, and everything which will be said intelligibly in that language will be said with propriety. This language will be the greatest instrument of reason.

I dare say that this is the highest effort of the human mind, and when the project will be accomplished it will simply be up to men to be happy since they will have an instrument which will exalt reason no less than what the Telescope does to perfect our vision.

It is one of my ambitions to accomplish this project if God gives me enough time. I owe it to nobody but myself, and I had the first thought about it when I was 18 years old, as I have a little later evidenced in a published treatise (*De Arte Combinatoria*, 1666). And as I am confident that there is no discovery which approaches this one, I believe there is nothing so capable of immortalizing the name of the inventor. But I have much stronger reasons for thinking so, since the religion I follow closely assures me that the love of God consists in an ardent desire to procure the general welfare, and reason teaches me that there is nothing which contributes more to the general welfare of mankind than the perfection of reason.

Towards a Universal Characteristic

An ancient saying has it that God created everything according to weight, measure, and number. However, there are many things which cannot be weighed, namely, whatever is not affected by force or power; and anything which is not divisible into parts escapes measurement. On the other hand, there is nothing which is not subsumable under number. Number is therefore, so to speak, a fundamental metaphysical form, and arithmetic a sort of statics of the universe, in which the powers of things are revealed.

That the profoundest secrets are hidden in numbers has been a conviction of men ever since the time of Pythagoras himself who, according to a reliable source, transmitted this and many another intuition to Greece from the Orient. However, since the right key to the secret was not possessed, man's curiosity was led to nilities and superstitions of all sorts from which arose a kind of vulgar Cabal, far removed from the true one, and also—under the false name of magic —an abundance of phantasies with which books teem. Meanwhile there are still men who persist in the old belief that wonderful discoveries are imminent with the help of numbers, characters or signs of a new language, which the "adamite" Jacob Böhme calls a nature-language.

Nevertheless, no one perhaps has penetrated to the true principle, namely, that we can assign to every object its determined characteristic number. For the most learned men, whenever I divulged something of the sort to them, led me to believe that they understood nothing of what I meant by it. Indeed, for a long time excellent men have brought to light a kind of "universal language" or "characteristic" in which diverse concepts and things were to be brought together in an appropriate order; with its help, it was to become possible for people of different nations to communicate their thoughts to one another and to translate into their own language the written signs of a foreign language. However, nobody, so far, has gotten hold of a language which would embrace both the technique of discovering new propositions and their critical examination—a language whose signs or characters would play the same rôle as the signs of arithmetic for numbers and those of algebra for quantities in general. And yet it is as if God, when he bestowed these two sciences on mankind, wanted us to realize that our understanding conceals a far deeper secret, foreshadowed by these two sciences.

Now through some sort of destiny, I had as a boy already been led into these reflections, and they have since, as is often the case with first inclinations, remained most deeply impressed on my mind. This was wonderfully advantageous to me in two ways—though often both dubious and injurious to many—: first, I was thoroughly self-taught; as soon as I entered into the study of any science, I immediately sought out something new, frequently before I even completely understood its known, familiar contents. Thus I gained in two ways: I did not fill my head with empty assertions (resting on learned authority rather than on actual evidence) which are forgotten sooner or later; furthermore, I did not rest until I had penetrated to the root and fiber of each and every theory and reached the principles themselves from which I might with my own power find out everything I could that was relevant.

I had early in my youth shown a preference for historical books and rhetorical exercises, and shown such facility in prose and poetry that my teachers feared I might remain suspended in these delights. Consequently, I was led to logic and philosophy. Scarcely before I had understood anything at all of these subjects, I set down on paper an abundance of fanciful thoughts which had risen to the surface of my brain, and when I presented them to my teachers they were amazed. One of the things I explored was the problem of the categories. What I intended especially to show was that just as we have categories predicating classes of simple concepts, so there must be a new sort of category which embraces propositions themselves or complex terms in their natural order. I had no inkling at the time of methods of proof, and did not know that what I was advancing was already being done by geometers when they arrange their propositions in a consecutive order so that in a proof one proposition proceeds from others in an orderly way. Thus my reflection was absolutely superfluous, but since my teachers did not satisfy my doubts, I had to take on the task all by myself to establish the aforementioned categories of complex terms or theorems.

As a result of my assiduous concern with this problem I arrived by a kind of internal necessity at a reflection of astounding import: there must be invented, I reflected, a kind of alphabet of human thoughts, and through the connection of its letters and the analysis of words which are composed out of them, everything else can be discovered and judged. This inspiration gave me then a very rare joy which was, of course, quite premature, for I did not yet then grasp the true significance of the matter. Later, however, the conclusion forced itself on me, with every step in the growth of my knowledge, that an object of such significance had to be pursued further. Chance had it then that as a young man of twenty I had to compose an academic dissertation. So I wrote the dissertation on "ars combinatoria" (art of combination) which in 1666 was published in book form, and thus my astounding discovery was made public. Of course, people observe that this treatise is the work of a youngster who has just gotten out of school and has not yet become familiar with the sciences; for I lived in a place where mathematics was not cultivated, and had I like Pascal lived my early life in Paris, I should have succeeded earlier in advancing the sciences. Still I do not regret having written this dissertation, for two reasons: first, because it met with the approbation of many men of the highest intellect; secondly, because it already gave the world an intimation of my discovery so that the suspicion that it was discovered only recently cannot be supported.

I have often wondered why nobody until now, so far as any written evidence indicates, had ever put his hands on such an important subject. For if one had only followed step by step a strict method of procedure from the start there should have immediately been forced on one's mind considerations of this sort—

which I still as a boy missed in the study of Logic, without any acquaintance with mathematics, natural and moral sciences —considerations which came home to me simply because I always sought first, original principles. The main reason, however, why people fail to go so far lies in the fact that abstract principles are usually dry and not very exciting, and after a momentary brush with them people let them alone. But there were three men, especially, who left me wondering why they had not entered into a problem of this significance: Aristotle, Joachim Jungius, and René Descartes. For Aristotle in the Organon and Metaphysics investigated with the greatest acuteness of mind the innermost nature of concepts. Joachim Jungius of Lübeck, however— who, of course, was himself scarcely known in Germany—is a man of such penetrating judgment and of so comprehensive a mind that one should have expected from him as from no other person—not excepting even Descartes— a fundamental renovation of the sciences, had he only been known and supported. He was already an old man when Descartes' work took effect, and it is regrettable that they both did not get to know each other. This is not the place to indicate what is to be extolled in Descartes whose mind stands far above any praise. He surely set foot on the true and right path in the country of ideas, the path which might have led to our goal—but for the fact that later, as it appears, in the course of his essay [Discourse on Method] he dropped the burden of the problem of method, and contented himself with metaphysical meditations and applications of his analytic geometry with which he attracted so much attention. In addition, he decided to investigate the nature of bodies for the purposes of medicine, which he was surely right in doing, had he only first solved the other problem, namely, the ordering of judgments and ideas. For from the latter there might have emerged a greater intellectual illumination than one was to believe possible, which would have shed light on experimental subjects also. That he did not direct his efforts to this end can be explained only by the fact that he did not grasp the deeper significance of the problem. Had he seen a method for establishing a rational philosophy with the same incomparable clarity as that of arithmetic, he would have chosen no other path than this one in order to establish a school which he so ambitiously strove to do. For a school which followed such a method in philosophy would naturally attract from among its tyros the same leadership in the kingdom of reason as geometry has, and would not totter or collapse if as a result of invasion, in a new barbaric era, the sciences themselves went under with mankind.

I, on the contrary, no matter how busy or diverted I might be, have steadfastly persisted in this line of reflection; I was alone in this matter, because I had intuited its whole significance and had perceived a marvelous and easy way to reach the goal. It took strenuous reflection on my part, but I finally discovered the way. In order to establish the Characteristic which I was after—at least in what pertains to the grammar of this wonderful universal language and to a dictionary which would be adequate for the most numerous and most recurrent cases—in order to establish, in other words, the characteristic numbers for all ideas, nothing less is required than the founding of a mathematical-philosophical course of study according to a new method, which I can offer, and which involves no greater difficulties than any other procedure not too far removed from familiar concepts and the usual method of writing. Also it would not require more work than is now already expended on lectures or encyclopedias.

I believe that a few selected persons might be able to do the whole thing in five years, and that they will in any case after only two years arrive at a mastery of the doctrines most needed in practical life, namely, the propositions of morals and metaphysics, according to an infallible method of calculation.

Once the characteristic numbers are established for most concepts, mankind will then possess a new instrument which will enhance the capabilities of the mind to a far greater extent than optical instruments strengthen the eyes, and will supersede the microscope and telescope to the same extent that reason is superior to eyesight. Great as is the benefit which the magnetic needle has brought to sailors, far greater will be the benefits which this constellation will bring to all those who ply the seas of investigation and experiment. What further will come out of it, lies within the lap of destiny, but it can only be results of significance and excellence. For all other gifts may corrupt man, but genuine reason alone is unconditionally wholesome for him. Its authority, however, will not be open any longer to doubt when it becomes possible to reveal the reason in all things with the clarity and certainty which was hitherto possible only in arithmetic. It will put an end to that sort of tedious objecting with which people plague each other, and which takes away for many the pleasure of reasoning and arguing in general. For instead of testing an argument, an adversary usually makes the following objection: "How do you know that your reason is better than mine? What criterion of truth do you have?" If the first party then again refers to his reasons, his interlocutor lacks the patience to test them; since for the most part there must still be a great many other questions to settle, which would take a week's labor if he observed the traditionally valid procedures and rules

of reasoning. Instead, after long pro and con discussions, most of the time it is emotion rather than reason that claims the victory, and the struggle ends there with the Gordian knot cut rather than untied. This is especially pertinent to the deliberations of practical life in which some decision must be finally made. Here it is only rarely the case that advantages and disadvantages which are so often distributed in many different ways on both sides, are weighed as on a balance. The stronger the representation or rather misrepresentation one party makes of this or that point according to his variable disposition, persuading others against his adversary by rhetorical effects of sharp relief and contrasting colors, the more dogmatically does he make up his own mind or indoctrinate others especially when he skillfully appeals to their prejudices. On the other hand, there is hardly anyone who is ever able to weigh and figure out the whole table of pros and cons on both sides, i.e., not only to count the advantages and disadvantages, but also to weigh them accurately against one another. Hence, I regard the two disputants as though they were two merchants who owe each other various moneys and have never drawn up a financial statement of their balance, but instead, always cross out the various postings of their outstanding debts and insist on inserting their own claims with respect to the legitimacy and magnitude of their debts. In this way, of course, conflicts could never end. We need not be surprised then that most disputes arise from the lack of clarity in things, that is, from the failure to reduce them to numbers.

Our Characteristic, however, will reduce all questions to numbers, and thus present a sort of statics by virtue of which rational evidence may be weighed. Besides, since probabilities lie at the basis of estimation and proof, we can consequently always estimate which event under given circumstances can be expected with the highest probability. Whoever is firmly convinced of the truth of religion and its implications and at the same time in his love of mankind longs for its conversion, will surely have to understand, as soon as he grasps our method, that (besides the miracles and acts of the saints or the conquests of a great ruler) there can be no more effective means conceived for the spread of the faith than the discovery under discussion here. For once missionaries are able to introduce this universal language, then also will the true religion, which stands in intimate harmony with reason, be established, and there will be as little reason to fear any apostasy in the future as to fear a renunciation of arithmetic and geometry once they have been learnt. I repeat, therefore, what I have frequently said, that nobody, whether a prophet or prince, can set himself a task of greater significance for human welfare as well as for the glory of God. We should nevertheless not remain content with words. Since, however, the wonderful interrelatedness of all things makes it extremely difficult to formulate explicitly the characteristic numbers of individual things, I have invented an elegant artifice by virtue of which certain relations may be represented and fixed numerically and which may thus then be further determined in numerical calculation. I make the arbitrary assumption, namely, that some special characteristic numbers are already given, and that some peculiar general property is observable in them. Thus, in the meantime, I take numbers which are correlated with the peculiar property, and then am able with their help immediately to demonstrate with astonishing facility all the rules of logic numerically, and can offer a criterion to ascertain whether a given argument is formally conclusive. Whether, however, a demonstration is materially conclusive may for the first time be judged without any trouble and without the danger of error, once we are put in possession of the true characteristic numbers of things themselves.

A LOGICAL CALCULUS*

GEORGE BOOLE (1815–1864)   was an English mathematician who is generally
credited with founding the modern algebra of logic and thus symbolic
logic. He introduced methods for operating on variables representing
terms or classes analogous to the familiar algebraic methods for operating
on variables representing numbers. His contributions to symbolic logic
are contained in *The Mathematical Analysis of Logic* (1847) and *An
Investigation of The Laws of Thought* (1853).

1

The design of the following treatise is
to investigate the fundamental laws of
those operations of the mind by which
reasoning is performed; to give expression to them in the symbolical language of a Calculus, and upon this foundation to establish the science of Logic
and construct its method; to make that
method itself the basis of a general
method for the application of the mathematical doctrine of Probabilities; and,
finally, to collect from the various elements of truth brought to view in the
course of these inquiries some probable
intimations concerning the nature and
constitution of the human mind.

2

That this design is not altogether a
novel one it is almost needless to remark, and it is well known that to its

two main practical divisions of Logic and
Probabilities a very considerable share
of the attention of philosophers has been
directed. In its ancient and scholastic
form, indeed, the subject of Logic stands
almost exclusively associated with the
great name of Aristotle. As it was presented to ancient Greece in the partly
technical, partly metaphysical disquisi-
tions of the Organon, such, with scarcely
any essential change, it has continued to
the present day. The stream of original
inquiry has rather been directed towards
questions of general philosophy, which,
though they have arisen among the disputes of the logicians, have outgrown
their origin, and given to successive ages
of speculation their peculiar bent and
character. The eras of Porphyry and
Proclus, of Anselm and Abelard, of
Ramus, and of Descartes, together with
the final protests of Bacon and Locke,
rise up before the mind as examples of
the remoter influences of the study upon

* From George Boole, *An Investigation of The Laws of Thought* (London: Walton and
Maberley, 1854).

197

the course of human thought, partly in suggesting topics fertile of discussion, partly in provoking remonstrance against its own undue pretensions. The history of the theory of Probabilities, on the other hand, has presented far more of that character of steady growth which belongs to science. In its origin the early genius of Pascal,—in its maturer stages of development the most recondite of all the mathematical speculations of Laplace, —were directed to its improvement; to omit here the mention of other names scarcely less distinguished than these. As the study of Logic has been remarkable for the kindred questions of Metaphysics to which it has given occasion, so that of Probabilities also has been remarkable for the impulse which it has bestowed upon the higher departments of mathematical science. Each of these subjects has, moreover, been justly regarded as having relation to a speculative as well as to a practical end. To enable us to deduce correct inferences from given premises is not the only object of Logic; nor is it the sole claim of the theory of Probabilities that it teaches us how to establish the business of life assurance on a secure basis; and how to condense whatever is valuable in the records of innumerable observations in astronomy, in physics, or in that field of social inquiry which is fast assuming a character of great importance. Both these studies have also an interest of another kind, derived from the light which they shed upon the intellectual powers. They instruct us concerning the mode in which language and number serve as instrumental aids to the processes of reasoning; they reveal to us in some degree the connexion between different powers of our common intellect; they set before us what, in the two domains of demonstrative and of probable knowledge, are the essential standards of truth and correctness,—standards not derived from without, but deeply founded in the constitution of the human faculties. These ends of speculation yield neither in interest nor in dignity, nor yet, it may be added, in importance, to the practical objects, with the pursuit of which they have been historically associated. To unfold the secret laws and relations of those high faculties of thought by which all beyond the merely perceptive knowledge of the world and of ourselves is attained or matured, is an object which does not stand in need of commendation to a rational mind.

3

But although certain parts of the design of this work have been entertained by others, its general conception, its method, and, to a considerable extent, its results, are believed to be original. For this reason I shall offer, in the present chapter, some preparatory statements and explanations, in order that the real aim of this treatise may be understood, and the treatment of its subject facilitated.

It is designed, in the first place, to investigate the fundamental laws of those operations of the mind by which reasoning is performed. It is unnecessary to enter here into any argument to prove that the operations of the mind are in a certain real sense subject to laws, and that a science of the mind is therefore *possible*. If these are questions which admit of doubt, that doubt is not to be met by an endeavour to settle the point of dispute *a priori*, but by directing the attention of the objector to the evidence of actual laws, by referring him to an actual science. And thus the solution of that doubt would belong not to the introduction to this treatise, but to the treatise itself. Let the assumption be granted, that a science of the intellectual powers is possible, and let us for a moment consider how the knowledge of it is to be obtained.

4

Like all other sciences, that of the intellectual operations must primarily rest upon observations,—the subject of such observation being the very operations and processes of which we desire to determine the laws. But while the necessity of a foundation in experience is thus a condition common to all sciences, there are some special differences between the modes in which this principle becomes available for the determination of general truths when the subject of inquiry is the mind, and when the subject is external nature. To these it is necessary to direct attention.

The general laws of Nature are not, for the most part, immediate objects of perception. They are either inductive inferences from a large body of facts, the common truth in which they express, or, in their origin at least, physical hypotheses of a causal nature serving to explain phaenomena with undeviating precision, and to enable us to predict new combinations of them. They are in all cases, and in the strictest sense of the term, *probable* conclusions, approaching, indeed, ever and ever nearer to certainty, as they receive more and more of the confirmation of experience. But of the character of probability, in the strict and proper sense of that term, they are never wholly divested. On the other hand, the knowledge of the laws of the mind does not require as its basis any extensive collection of observations. The general truth is seen in the particular instance, and it is not confirmed by the repetition of instances. We may illustrate this position by an obvious example. It may be a question whether that formula of reasoning, which is called the *dictum* of Aristotle, *de omni et nullo*, expresses

a primary law of human reasoning or not; but it is no question that it expresses a general truth in Logic. Now that truth is made manifest in all its generality by reflection upon a single instance of its application. And this is both an evidence that the particular principle or formula in question is founded upon some general law or laws of the mind, and an illustration of the doctrine that the perception of such general truths is not derived from an induction from many instances, but is involved in the clear apprehension of a single instance. In connexion with this truth is seen the not less important one that our knowledge of the laws upon which the science of the intellectual powers rests, whatever may be its extent or its deficiency, is not probable knowledge. For we not only see in the particular example the general truth, but we see it also as a certain truth,—a truth, our confidence in which will not continue to increase with increasing experience of its practical verifications.

5

But if the general truths of Logic are of such a nature that when presented to the mind they at once command assent, wherein consists the difficulty of constructing the Science of Logic? Not, it may be answered, in collecting the materials of knowledge, but in discriminating their nature, and determining their mutual place and relation. All sciences consist of general truths, but of those truths some only are primary and fundamental, others are secondary and derived. The laws of elliptic motion, discovered by Kepler, are general truths in astronomy, but they are not its fundamental truths. And it is so also in the purely mathematical sciences. An almost boundless diversity of theorems, which are known, and an infinite possibility of others, as yet unknown, rest together upon the foundation of a few simple axioms; and yet these are all *general* truths. It may be added, that they are truths which to an intelligence sufficiently refined would shine forth in their own unborrowed light, without the need of those connecting links of thought, those steps of wearisome and often painful deduction, by which the knowledge of them is actually acquired. Let us define as fundamental those laws and principles from which all other general truths of science may be deduced, and into which they may all be again resolved. Shall we then err in regarding that as the true science of Logic which, laying down certain elementary laws, confirmed by the very testimony of the mind, permits us thence to deduce, by uniform processes, the entire chain of its secondary consequences, and furnishes, for its practical applications, methods of perfect generality? Let it be considered whether in any science, viewed either as a system of truth or as the foundation of a practical art, there can properly be any other test of the completeness and the fundamental characters of its laws, than the completeness of its system of derived truths, and the generality of the methods which it serves to establish. Other questions may indeed present themselves. Convenience, prescription, individual preference, may urge their claims and deserve attention. But as respects the question of what constitutes science in its abstract integrity, I apprehend that no other considerations than the above are properly of any value.

6

It is designed, in the next place, to give expression in this treatise to the fundamental laws of reasoning in the symbolical language of a Calculus. Upon this head it will suffice to say, that those laws are such as to suggest this mode of expression, and to give to it a peculiar and exclusive fitness for the ends in view. There is not only a close analogy between the operations of the mind in general reasoning and its operations in the particular science of Algebra, but there is to a considerable extent an exact agreement in the laws by which the two classes of operations are conducted. Of course the laws must in both cases be determined independently; any formal agreement between them can only be establish *a posteriori* by actual comparison. To borrow the notation of the science of Number, and then assume that in its new application the laws by which its use is governed will remain unchanged, would be mere hypothesis. There exist, indeed, certain general principles founded in the very nature of language, by which the use of symbols, which are but the elements of scientific language, is determined. To a certain extent these elements are arbitrary. Their interpretation is purely conventional: we are permitted to employ them in whatever sense we please. But this permission is limited by two indispensable conditions, —first, that from the sense once conventionally established we never, in the same process of reasoning, depart; secondly, that the laws by which the process is conducted be founded exclusively upon the above fixed sense or meaning of the symbols employed. In accordance with these principles, any agreement which may be established between the laws of the symbols of Logic and those of Algebra can but issue in an agreement of processes. The two provinces of interpretation remain apart and independent, each subject to its own laws and conditions.

Now the actual investigations of the following pages exhibit Logic, in its practical aspect, as a system of processes carried on by the aid of symbols having a definite interpretation, and subject to laws founded upon that interpretation alone. But at the same time they exhibit those laws as identical in form with the laws of the general symbols of Algebra, with this single addition, viz., that the symbols of Logic are further subject to a special law, to which the symbols of quantity, as such, are not subject. Upon the nature and the evidence of this law it is not purposed here to dwell. These questions will be fully discussed in a future page. But as constituting the essential ground of difference between those forms of inference with which Logic is conversant, and those which present themselves in the particular science of Number, the law in question is deserving of more than a passing notice. It may be said that it lies at the very foundation of general reasoning,— that it governs those intellectual acts of conception or of imagination which are preliminary to the processes of logical deduction, and that it gives to the processes themselves much of their actual form and expression. It may hence be affirmed that this law constitutes the germ or seminal principle, of which every approximation to a general method in Logic is the more or less perfect development.

7

The principle has already been laid down that the sufficiency and truly fundamental character of any assumed system of laws in the science of Logic must partly be seen in the perfection of the methods to which they conduct us. It remains, then, to consider what the requirements of a general method in Logic are, and how far they are fulfilled in the system of the present work.

Logic is conversant with two kinds of relations,—relations among things, and relations among facts. But as facts are expressed by propositions, the latter species of relation may, at least for the purposes of Logic, be resolved into a relation among propositions. The asser-

tion that the fact or event A is an invariable consequent of the fact or event B may, to this extent at least, be regarded as equivalent to the assertion, that the truth of the proposition affirming the occurrence of the event B always implies the truth of the proposition affirming the occurrence of the event A. Instead, then, of saying that Logic is conversant with relations among things and relations among facts, we are permitted to say that it is concerned with relations among things and relations among propositions. Of the former kind of relations we have an example in the proposition—"All men are mortal"; of the latter kind in the proposition—"If the sun is totally eclipsed, the stars will become visible." The one expresses a relation between "men" and "mortal beings," the other between the elementary propositions—"The sun is totally eclipsed"; "The stars will become visible." Among such relations I suppose to be included those which affirm or deny existence with respect to things, and those which affirm or deny truth with respect to propositions. Now let those things or those propositions among which relation is expressed be termed the elements of the propositions by which such relation is expressed. Proceeding from this definition, we may then say that the *premises* of any logical argument express *given* relations among certain elements, and that the *conclusion* must express an *implied* relation among those elements, or among a part of them, *i.e.* a relation implied by or inferentially involved in the premises.

8

Now this being premised, the requirements of a general method in Logic seem to be the following:—

1st. As the conclusion must express a relation among the whole or among a part of the elements involved in the premises, it is requisite that we should possess the means of eliminating those elements which we desire not to appear in the conclusion, and of determining the whole amount of relation implied by the premises among the elements which we wish to retain. Those elements which do not present themselves in the conclusion are, in the language of the common Logic, called middle terms; and the species of elimination exemplified in treatises on Logic consists in deducing from two propositions, containing a common element or middle term, a conclusion connecting the two remaining terms. But the problem of elimination, as contemplated in this work, possesses a much wider scope. It proposes not merely the elimination of one middle term from two propositions, but the elimination generally of middle terms from propositions, without regard to the number of either of them, or to the nature of their connexion. To this object neither the processes of Logic nor those of Algebra, in their actual state, present any strict parallel. In the latter science the problem of elimination is known to be limited in the following manner:—From two equations we can eliminate one symbol of quantity; from three equations two symbols; and, generally, from n equations $n - 1$ symbols. But though this condition, necessary in Algebra, seems to prevail in the existing Logic also, it has no essential place in Logic as a science. There, no relation whatever can be proved to prevail between the number of terms to be eliminated and the number of propositions from which the elimination is to be effected. From the equation representing a single proposition, any number of symbols representing terms or elements in Logic may be eliminated; and from any number of equations representing propositions, one or any other number of symbols of this kind may be eliminated in a similar

manner. For such elimination there exists one general process applicable to all cases. This is one of the many remarkable consequences of that distinguishing law of the symbols of Logic, to which attention has been already directed.

2ndly. It should be within the province of a general method in Logic to express the final relation among the elements of the conclusion by any admissible *kind* of proposition, or in any selected *order* of terms. Among varieties of kind we may reckon those which logicians have designated by the terms categorical, hypothetical, disjunctive, &c. To a choice or selection in the order of the terms, we may refer whatsoever is dependent upon the appearance of particular elements in the subject or in the predicate, in the antecedent or in the consequent, of that proposition which forms the "conclusion." But waiving the language of the schools, let us consider what really distinct species of problems may present themselves to our notice. We have seen that the elements of the final or inferred relation may either be *things* or *propositions*. Suppose the former case; then it might be required to deduce from the premises a definition or description of some one thing, or class of things, constituting an element of the conclusion in terms of the other things involved in it. Or we might form the conception of some thing or class of things, involving more than one of the elements of the conclusion, and require its expression in terms of the other elements. Again, suppose the elements retained in the conclusion to be propositions, we might desire to ascertain such points as the following, viz., Whether, in virtue of the premises, any of those propositions, taken singly, are true or false?—Whether particular combinations of them are true or false? —Whether, assuming a particular proposition to be true, any consequences will follow, and if so, what consequences, with respect to the other propositions?—Whether any particular condition being assumed with reference to certain of the propositions, any consequences, and what consequences, will follow with respect to the others? and so on. I say that these are general questions, which it should fall within the scope or province of a general method in Logic to solve. Perhaps we might include them all under this one statement of the final problem of practical Logic. Given a set of premises expressing relations among certain elements, whether things or propositions: required explicitly the whole relation consequent among *any* of those elements under any proposed conditions, and in any proposed form. That this problem, under all its aspects, is resolvable, will hereafter appear. But it is not for the sake of noticing this fact, that the above inquiry into the nature and the functions of a general method in Logic has been introduced. It is necessary that the reader should apprehend what are the specific ends of the investigation upon which we are entering, as well as the principles which are to guide us to the attainment of them.

9

Possibly it may here be said that the Logic of Aristotle, in its rules of syllogism and conversion, sets forth the elementary processes of which all reasoning consists, and that beyond these there is neither scope nor occasion for a general method. I have no desire to point out the defects of the common Logic, nor do I wish to refer to it any further than is necessary, in order to place in its true light the nature of the present treatise. With this end alone in view, I would remark:—1st. That syllogism, conversion, &c., are not the ultimate processes of Logic. It will be shown in this treatise that they are founded upon, and are

resolvable into, ulterior and more simple processes which constitute the real elements of method in Logic. Nor is it true in fact that all inference is reducible to the particular forms of syllogism and conversion. 2ndly. If all inference were reducible to these two processes (and it has been maintained that it is reducible to syllogism alone), there would still exist the same necessity for a general method. For it would still be requisite to determine in what order the processes should succeed each other, as well as their particular nature, in order that the desired relation should be obtained. By the desired relation I mean that full relation which, in virtue of the premises, connects any elements selected out of the premises at will, and which, moreover, expresses that relation in any desired form and order. If we may judge from the mathematical sciences, which are the most perfect examples of method known, this *directive* function of Method constitutes its chief office and distinction. The fundamental processes of arithmetic, for instance, are in themselves but the elements of a possible science. To assign their nature is the first business of its method, but to arrange their succession is its subsequent and higher function. In the more complex examples of logical deduction, and especially in those which form a basis for the solution of difficult questions in the theory of Probabilities, the aid of a directive method, such as a Calculus alone can supply, is indispensable.

10

Whence it is that the ultimate laws of Logic are mathematical in their form; why they are, except in a single point, identical with the general laws of Number; and why in that particular point they differ;—are questions upon which it might not be very remote from presumption to endeavor to pronounce a positive judgment. Probably they lie beyond the reach of our limited faculties. It may, perhaps, be permitted to the mind to attain a knowledge of the laws to which it is itself subject, without its being also given to it to understand their ground and origin, or even, except in a very limited degree, to comprehend their fitness for their end, as compared with other and conceivable systems of law. Such knowledge is, indeed, unnecessary for the ends of science, which properly concerns itself with what is, and seeks not for grounds of preference or reasons of appointment. These considerations furnish a sufficient answer to all protests against the exhibition of Logic in the form of a Calculus. It is not because we choose to assign to it such a mode of manifestation, but because the ultimate laws of thought render that mode possible, and prescribe its character, and forbid, as it would seem, the perfect manifestation of the science in any other form, that such a mode demands adoption. It is to be remembered that it is the business of science not to create laws, but to discover them. We do not originate the constitution of our own minds, greatly as it may be in our power to modify their character. And as the laws of the human intellect do not depend upon our will, so the forms of the science, of which they constitute the basis, are in all essential regards independent of individual choice.

11

Beside the general statement of the principles of the above method, this treatise will exhibit its application to the analysis of a considerable variety of propositions, and of trains of propositions constituting the premises of demonstrative arguments. These examples have been selected from various writers, they differ greatly in complexity, and they embrace a wide range of subjects. Though in this particular respect it may appear to some that too great a latitude of choice has been exercised, I do not deem it necessary to offer any apology upon this account. That Logic, as a science, is susceptible of very wide applications is admitted; but it is equally certain that its ultimate forms and processes are mathematical. Any objection *a priori* which may therefore be supposed to lie against the adoption of such forms and processes in the discussion of a problem of morals or of general philosophy must be founded upon misapprehension or false analogy. It is not of the essence of mathematics to be conversant with the ideas of number and quantity. Whether as a general habit of mind it would be desirable to apply symbolical processes to moral argument, is another question. Possibly, as I have elsewhere observed, the perfection of the method of Logic may be chiefly valuable as an evidence of the speculative truth of its principles. To supersede the employment of common reasoning, or to subject it to the rigour of technical forms, would be the last desire of one who knows the value of that intellectual toil and warfare which imparts to the mind an athletic vigour, and teaches it to contend with difficulties, and to rely upon itself in emergencies. Nevertheless, cases may arise in which the value of a scientific procedure, even in those things which fall confessedly under the ordinary dominion of the reason, may be felt and acknowledged. Some examples of this kind will be found in the present work.

A FORMAL SYSTEM OF

LOGIC AND MATHEMATICS*

GOTTLOB FREGE (1848–1925) was a German mathematician and philosopher who is regarded as the second founder (after Boole) of modern symbolic logic. Although his symbolic notation was clumsy and forbidding, it was enormously powerful. In it he was able to establish a good part of the logistic thesis† as well as to develop many strictly logical results. Frege's *Begriffsschrift* (1879) was the first strictly formal system of logic and his *Grundlagen der Arithmetik* (1884) and *Grundgestze der Arithmetik* Volume I (1893) and Volume II (1903) contain his derivation of arithmetic from logic.

The ideal of a strictly scientific method in mathematics, which I have tried to realize here, and which perhaps might be named after Euclid, I should like to describe in the following way.

It cannot be required that we should prove everything, because that is impossible; but we can demand that all propositions used without proof should be expressly mentioned as such, so that we can see distinctly what the whole construction rests upon. We should, accordingly, strive to diminish the number of these fundamental laws as much as possible, by proving everything that can be proved. Furthermore I demand—and in this I go beyond Euclid—that all the methods of inference used must be specified in advance. Otherwise it is impossible to ensure satisfying the first demand.

This ideal I believe I have attained in essentials; only in a few points could one possibly be more exacting. In order to secure more flexibility and not fall into excessive prolixity, I have taken the liberty of making tacit use of the interchangeability of the sub-clauses (conditions) and of the possibility of amalgamating identical sub-clauses;[1] and I have not reduced the modes of inference to the smallest possible number. Those who have read my *Begriffsschrift* will be able to gather from it that even in this respect it would be possible to satisfy the severest demands, but likewise that this would involve a considerable increase in volume.

* From Gottlob Frege, "The Fundamental Laws of Arithmetic," translated by Johann Stachelroth and Philip E. B. Jourdain from Frege's *Grundgesetze der Arithmetik, The Monist,* **XXV** (October 1915), pp. 481–494; and **XXVI** (April 1916), pp. 182–199.

† See footnote on page 187.

[1] Frege means the possibility of passing from 'if A, then, if B, then Γ' to 'if B, then if A, then Γ,' and again from 'if A then, if A, then B' to 'if A, then B.'

I believe that, apart from this, the only objections that could justly be raised against this book do not concern rigour but only the choice of the course of proofs and of the intermediate steps in them. Often there are several modes of proof possible; I have not tried to follow all of them out, and thus it is possible—even probable—that I have not always chosen the shortest. But if anybody has any fault to find in this regard, let him do better himself. Other matters will be disputable. Some might have preferred to increase the number of permissible modes of inference and thereby to attain greater flexibility and brevity. But we have to stop somewhere, if my ideal is approved of at all; and wherever we stop, people will always be able to say: 'It would have been better to allow still more modes of inference.'

Since there are no gaps in the chains of inference, each axiom, assumption, hypothesis, or whatever you like to call it, upon which a proof is founded, is brought to light; and so we gain a basis for deciding the epistemological nature of the law that is proved. It has often been said that arithmetic is only a more highly developed logic; but that remains disputable as long as the proofs contain steps that are not performed according to acknowledged logical laws, but seem to rest on intuitive knowledge. Only when these are resolved into simple logical steps can we be sure that arithmetic is founded solely upon logic. I have gathered together everything that can make it easier to decide whether the chains of inference are convincing and the buttresses firm. If any one perchance finds anything faulty, he must be able to indicate exactly where, to his thinking, the mistake lies—whether in the fundamental laws, in the definitions, in the rules, or in their application at a definite place. If we find everything correct, we thus know the exact bases upon which each single

theorem is founded. A dispute can only arise, so far as I can see, because of my fundamental law about 'ranges of values,'[2] which perhaps has not yet been specifically expressed by logicians, though it is in their minds when, e.g., they speak of extensions of concepts. I hold that it is purely logical. In any case the place is indicated where the decision has to be made.

My purpose requires many deviations from what is usual in mathematics. The requirements with regard to the rigour of proofs inevitably entail greater length. Whoever does not bear this in mind will often be surprised at the roundabout way in which a proposition is here proved, whereas he believes he can grasp the proof directly by a single act of understanding. This will surprise us especially if we compare the work of Dedekind, *Was sind und was sollen die Zahlen?*[3] which is the most thorough work on the foundation of arithmetic that I have lately seen. In a much smaller compass it follows the laws of arithmetic much farther than I do here. This brevity is only arrived at, to be sure, because much is not really proved at all. Dedekind often says only that the proof follows from such-and-such theorems; he uses little dots, as in the symbol M $(A, B, C, \ldots)$; nowhere is there a statement of the logical or other laws on which he builds, and, even if there were, we could not possibly find out whether really no others were used—for to make that possible the proof

[2] This axiom is numbered V on pp. 36 and 240 of Vol. I (1893) of the *Grundgesetze;* and expresses that an equality of ranges both implies and is implied by the statement that an equation between functions holds generally. It first appeared on page 10 of Frege's lecture, *Funktion und Begriff* (Jena. 1891). Cf. p. 253 of Vol. II of the *Grundgesetze* (1903).

[3] English translation on pp. 29–115 of Dedekind's *Essays on the Theory of Numbers* (Chicago and London, 1901).

must be not merely indicated but completely carried out. Dedekind also is of opinion that the theory of number is a part of logic; but his work hardly goes to strengthen this opinion, because the expressions 'system' and 'a thing belongs to a thing' used by him are not usual in logic and are not reduced to accepted logical notions. I do not say this as a reproach, for his method may have been the most serviceable to him for his purpose; I only say it in order to make my intentions clear by the contrast. The length of a proof is not to be measured by the yard. It is easy to make a proof appear short on paper by omitting many connecting links in the chain of inference and just indicating many points. Generally we are satisfied if every step in the proof is obviously correct; and we may well be so if we just want to convince someone as to the truth of the theorem to be proved. If we wish to bring about an insight into the nature of this obviousness this method does not suffice, but we must put down all the intermediate stages of reasoning, in order that the full light of consciousness may fall upon them. As a rule mathematicians are only interested in the content of a theorem and in the fact that it is to be proved. The novelty of this book does not lie in the content of the theorems, but in the development of the proofs and the foundations on which they are based. That this altogether different point of view needs a quite different treatment ought not to appear strange. If one of our theorems is deduced in the usual way, it will be easy to overlook a proposition which does not appear necessary for the proof. If my proof is carefully followed in thought, the indispensability of this proposition will, I believe, be seen, unless an altogether different mode of procedure is adopted. Thus perhaps you find here and there in our theorems conditions that appear at first to be unnecessary;

but these nevertheless turn out to be necessary, or at least to admit of removal only by means of a proposition that must be specially proved.

. . .

. . . the years have not passed in vain since the appearance of my *Begriffsschrift* and *Grundlagen;* they have brought my work to maturity. But just that which I recognize as an important advance forms, as I cannot help seeing, a great obstacle in the way of the circulation and effectiveness of my book. And the strict avoidance of gaps in the chain of conclusions, which to my way of thinking is not its least value, will win me, I am afraid, little gratitude. I have got farther away from the traditional ideas and by so doing have given an appearance of paradox to my views. An expression encountered here and there on rapidly turning over these pages may easily appear strange and produce a prejudice against me. I myself can judge in a way what opposition my innovations will be met with because I have had to overcome something similar in myself. For it was not at random or because of the desire for innovation that I arrived at them; I was forced into them by the nature of the case.

With this I arrive at the second reason for my delay: the discouragement which at times came over me because of the cool reception, or rather the lack of reception, accorded by mathematicians,[4] to my works mentioned above and the opposing currents of scientific thought against which my book would have to fight. Even the first impression must

[4] In vain do we seek a notice of my *Grundlagen der Arithmetik* in the *Jahrbuch über die Fortschritte der Mathematik.* Investigators in the same domain, Dedekind, Otto Stolz, and von Helmholtz, do not seem to know my works. Nor does Kronecker mention them in his essay on the concept of number.

frighten people away: unfamiliar signs, pages of nothing but strange-looking formulas. It is for that reason that I turned at times toward other subjects. But I could not keep the results of my thinking, which seemed valuable to me myself, locked up in my desk for any length of time; and the labour I had spent always required renewed labour that it might not be in vain. So the subject did not let go its hold upon me. In a case like the present one, when the value of a book cannot be recognized by a hasty perusal, criticism ought to be a help. But criticism is generally too badly repaid. A critic can never hope to get paid in cash for the pains which the thorough study of this book will cost him. The only remaining hope is that somebody may have beforehand sufficient confidence in the matter to expect that the mental profit will be sufficient recompense, and that he will then publish the results of his searching examination. It is not as if only a laudatory review would satisfy me; quite the contrary. I would far rather have an attack based on a thorough acquaintance with the subject than be praised in general terms which do not touch the root of the matter. . . .

I must give up hope of securing as readers all those mathematicians who, when they come across logical expressions like 'concept,' 'relation,' 'judgment,' think: *Metaphysica sunt, non leguntur;* and those philosophers who at the sight of a formula call out: *Mathematica sunt, non leguntur.* The number of these people cannot be very small. Perhaps also the number of mathematicians who trouble themselves about the foundation of their science is not great, and even those who do often seem in a great hurry to get past the foundations. And I hardly dare hope that my reasons for laborious rigour and consequent lengthiness will convince many of them. As we know, what is long established has great power

over the minds of men. If I compare arithmetic with a tree which develops at the top into a multitude of methods and theorems while the root pushes downward, it seems to me that the growth of the root is, at least in Germany, rather weak. Even in a work which might be classed among those dealing with foundations, the *Algebra der Logik* of E. Schröder, the top-growth soon predominates and, even before a great depth has been reached, causes a bending upward and a development into methods and theorems.

The widespread inclination to recognize only what can be perceived by the senses as existing is also unfavourable for my book. It is sought to deny, or at least to overlook, what cannot be thus perceived. Now the objects of arithmetic, that is to say numbers, are of a kind which cannot be thus perceived. How are we to deal with them? Very simply; the signs used for the numbers are explained to be the numbers themselves. Then in the signs we have something visible, and that is the chief thing. No doubt the signs have altogether different properties from the numbers themselves, but what does that matter? We simply ascribe to them the desired properties by means of what we call definitions. How on earth there can be a definition where there is no question about connexions between sign and thing signified by it is a puzzle. We merge the sign and what it signifies as far as possible, without making any distinction between them; and according to our present requirement, we can either assert the existence of the result by referring to its tangibility,[5] or bring into prominence the real properties of numbers. Some-

[5] Cf. E. Heine, 'Die Elemente der Funktionslehre,' Crelle's *Journal für Math.,* Vol. LXXIV, p. 173: 'As regards definition I adopt a purely formalistic point of view: I give the name *numbers* to certain tangible signs, so that the existence of these numbers is thus unquestionable.'

times these number signs are, it seems, regarded as chessmen and the so-called definitions as rules of the game. The sign then does not signify anything, but is itself the subject-matter. It is true that in this one little thing is overlooked; viz. that we express a thought by $3^2 + 4^2 = 5^2$, while a position of chessmen does not express anything. Where people are satisfied with such superficialities, there is, of course, no basis for a deeper understanding.

Here it is of importance to make clear what definition is and what we can reach by means of it. It is, it seems, often credited with a creative power; but really all there is to definition is that something is brought out, precisely limited and given a name. The geographer does not create a sea when he draws border lines and says: The part of the surface of the ocean, delimited by these lines, I am going to call the Yellow Sea; and no more can the mathematician really create anything by his act of definition. Nor can we by a mere definition magically give to a thing a property which it has not got, apart from the property of now being called by whatever name one has given it. But that an oval drawn on paper with pen and ink should acquire by definition the property that, when it is added to one, one is the result, I can only regard as a scientific superstition.

One might just as well make a lazy pupil diligent by a mere definition. Confusion easily arises here through our not making a sufficient distinction between concept and object. If we say: 'A square is a rectangle in which the adjacent sides are equal,' we define the concept *square* by specifying what properties something must have in order to fall under this concept. I call these properties 'marks' of the concept. But it must be carefully noted that these marks of the concept are not properties of the concept. The concept *square* is not a rectangle; only the objects which fall under this concept are rectangles; similarly the concept

black cloth is neither black nor a cloth. Whether such objects exist is not immediately known by means of their definitions. Now, for instance, suppose we try to define the number zero by saying: 'It is something which when added to one gives the result one.' With that we have defined a concept by stating what property an object must have to fall under the concept. But this property is not a property of the concept defined. It seems that people often imagine that we have created by our definition something which when added to one gives one. This is a delusion. Neither has the concept defined got this property, nor is the definition a guarantee that the concept is realized. That must first of all be a matter for investigation. Only when we have proved that there exists one object and one only with the required property are we in a position to give this object the proper name 'zero.' To create zero is consequently impossible. I have already repeatedly explained this but, as it seems, without result.

From the prevailing logic I cannot hope for approval of the distinction that I make between the mark of a concept and the property of an object, for it seems to be thoroughly infected by psychology. If people consider, instead of things themselves, only subjective representations of them, only their own mental images—then all the more delicate distinctions in the things themselves are naturally lost, and others appear instead which are logically quite worthless. . . .

Let us now see how the finer distinctions in the subject-matter become obliterated in psychological logic. This has already been referred to above when we spoke of mark and property. With this is connected the distinction between object and concept emphasized by myself, and that between first-level and second-level concepts. These distinctions are, of course, indiscernible to the psychological logician; with such logicians everything is just idea. They have no right conception of those judgments which we express by 'there is.' This existence is confused by Erdmann with actuality, which, as we have seen, is not clearly distinguished from objectivity. Of what thing do we assert that it is actual when we say that there are square roots of 4? Is it 2 or −2? But neither the one nor the other is named here in any way. And if I were to say that the number 2 acts or is active or actual, it would be false and quite different from what I mean by the sentence 'there are square roots of 4.' The confusion here under consideration is nearly the grossest possible; for it is not one between concepts of the same level, but a concept of the first level is confused with one of the second level. This is characteristic of the obtuseness of psychological logic. When we have arrived at a somewhat broader standpoint we may be surprised that such a mistake could be made by a professional logician; but we must have grasped the distinction between concepts of the first and second level before we can estimate the magnitude of this mistake, and psychological logic cannot do that. Here what most stands in the way of psychological logic is that its exponents have such a high opinion of psychological profundity, which is, after all, nothing but a psychological falsification of logic. And that is how our thick books of logic came to be; they are puffed out with unhealthy psychological fat which conceals all finer forms. Thus a fruitful collaboration of mathematicians and logicians is made impossible. While the mathematician defines objects, concepts, and relations, the psychological logician watches the becoming and and changing of ideas, and at bottom the mathematicians' way of defining must appear to him just silly, because it does not reproduce the essence of ideation. He looks into his psychological peepshow

and says to the mathematician: 'I cannot see anything at all of what you are defining.' And the mathematician can only reply: 'No wonder, for it is not where you are looking for it.'

This may be enough to throw a clearer light on my logical standpoint, by means of a contrast. This seems to me poles apart from psychological logic so that there is no prospect of my having at present any influence through my book upon psychological logic. It seems to me that the tree planted by me would have to lift an enormous weight of stone in order to gain room and light for itself. Nevertheless I should not like to give up all hope that my book may later on help to overthrow psychological logic. The notice that mathematicians cannot fail to take of my book will work to this end, and thus logicians will be compelled to come to terms with it. And I believe that I may expect some help from mathematicians; for they have at bottom a common cause with me against the psychological logicians. As soon as mathematicians condescend to occupy themselves seriously with my book, if only in order to refute it, I believe I have won. For the whole of the second part is really a test of my logical convictions. It is improbable that such an edifice could be erected upon an unsound base. Those who have other convictions have only to try to erect a similar construction upon them, and they will soon be convinced that it is not possible, or at least is not easy. As a proof of the contrary, I can only admit the production by some one of an actual demonstration that upon other fundamental convictions a better and more durable edifice can be erected, or the demonstration by some one that my premises lead to manifestly false conclusions. But nobody will be able to do that. May my book then, even though it comes rather late, contribute to a revival of logic.

THE IMPORTANCE OF

GOOD NOTATION*

ALFRED NORTH WHITEHEAD (1861–1947) was a British mathematician and philosopher who taught mathematics in England and philosophy in America. His contributions to symbolic logic appeared in his *Treatise on Universal Algebra* (1903) and in the monumental *Principia Mathematica* (1910–1913) which he co-authored with Bertrand Russell. His philosophical writings include *Science and the Modern World* (1926), *Process and Reality* (1929), and *Adventures of Ideas* (1933).

Let us assume for the present that we have sufficiently clear ideas about the integral numbers, represented in the Arabic notation by 0, 1, 2, . . . , 9, 10, 11, . . . 100, 101, . . . and so on. This notation was introduced into Europe through the Arabs, but they apparently obtained it from Hindoo sources. The first known work[1] in which it is systematically explained is a work by an Indian mathematician, Bhaskara (born 1114 A.D.). But the actual numerals can be traced back to the seventh century of our era, and perhaps were originally invented in Tibet. For our present purposes, however, the history of the notation is a detail. The interesting point to notice is the admirable illustration which this numeral system affords of the enormous importance of a good notation. By relieving the brain of all unnecessary

work, a good notation sets it free to concentrate on more advanced problems, and in effect increases the mental power of the race. Before the introduction of the Arabic notation, multiplication was difficult, and the division even of integers called into play the highest mathematical faculties. Probably nothing in the modern world would have more astonished a Greek mathematician than to learn that, under the influence of compulsory education, a large proportion of the population of Western Europe could perform the operation of division for the largest numbers. This fact would have seemed to him a sheer impossibility. The consequential extension of the notation to decimal fractions was not accomplished till the seventeenth century. Our modern power of easy reckoning with decimal fractions is the almost miraculous result

* From Alfred North Whitehead, *An Introduction to Mathematics* (London: Oxford University Press, 1948). Reprinted by permission of the publisher.

[1] For the detailed historical facts relating to pure mathematics, I am chiefly indebted to *A Short History of Mathematics,* by W. W. R. Ball.

of the gradual discovery of a perfect notation.

Mathematics is often considered a difficult and mysterious science, because of the numerous symbols which it employs. Of course, nothing is more incomprehensible than a symbolism which we do not understand. Also a symbolism, which we only partially understand and are unaccustomed to use, is difficult to follow. In exactly the same way the technical terms of any profession or trade are incomprehensible to those who have never been trained to use them. But this is not because they are difficult in themselves. On the contrary they have invariably been introduced to make things easy. So in mathematics, granted that we are giving any serious attention to mathematical ideas, the symbolism is invariably an immense simplification. It is not only of practical use, but is of great interest. For it represents an analysis of the ideas of the subject and an almost pictorial representation of their relations to each other. If anyone doubts the utility of symbols, let him write out in full, without any symbol whatever, the whole meaning of the following equations which represent some of the fundamental laws of algebra:[2]—

$$x + y = y + x \tag{1}$$
$$(x + y) + z = x + (y + z) \tag{2}$$

[2] In reading these equations it must be noted that a bracket is used in mathematical symbolism to mean that the operations within it are to be performed first. Thus $(1 + 3) + 2$ directs us first to add 3 to 1, and then to add 2 to the result; and $1 + (3 + 2)$ directs us first to add 2 to 3, and then to add the result to 1. Again a numerical example of equation (5) is

$$2 \times (3 + 4) = (2 \times 3) + (2 \times 4).$$

We perform first the operations in brackets and obtain

$$2 \times 7 = 6 + 8$$

which is obviously true.

$$x \times y = y \times x \tag{3}$$
$$(x \times y) \times z = x \times (y \times z) \tag{4}$$
$$x \times (y + z) = (x \times y) + (x \times z) \tag{5}$$

Here (1) and (2) are called the commutative and associative laws for addition, (3) and (4) are the commutative and associative laws for multiplication, and (5) is the distributive law relating addition and multiplication. For example, without symbols, (1) becomes: If a second number be added to any given number the result is the same as if the first given number had been added to the second number.

This example shows that, by the aid of symbolism, we can make transitions in reasoning almost mechanically by the eye, which otherwise would call into play the higher faculties of the brain.

It is a profoundly erroneous truism, repeated by all copy-books and by eminent people when they are making speeches, that we should cultivate the habit of thinking of what we are doing. The precise opposite is the case. Civilization advances by extending the number of important operations which we can perform without thinking about them. Operations of thought are like cavalry charges in a battle—they are strictly limited in number, they require fresh horses, and must only be made at decisive moments.

One very important property for symbolism to possess is that it should be concise, so as to be visible at one glance of the eye and to be rapidly written. Now we cannot place symbols more concisely together than by placing them in immediate juxtaposition. In a good symbolism therefore, the juxtaposition of important symbols should have an important meaning. This is one of the merits of the Arabic notation for numbers; by means of ten symbols, 0, 1, 2, 3, 4, 5, 6, 7, 8, 9, and by simple juxtaposition it symbolizes any number whatever. Again in algebra, when we have two variable numbers x and y, we have to make a choice as to what shall be denoted by their juxtaposition xy. Now the two most important ideas on hand are those of addition and multiplication. Mathematicians have chosen to make their symbolism more concise by defining xy to stand for $x \times y$. Thus the laws (3), (4), and (5) above are in general written,

$$xy = yx, \quad (xy)z = x(yz),$$
$$x(y + z) = xy + xz$$

thus securing a great gain in conciseness. The same rule of symbolism is applied to the juxtaposition of a definite number and a variable: we write $3x$ for $3 \times x$, and $30x$ for $30 \times x$.

THE STUDY OF INFERENCE

IN GENERAL*

BERTRAND RUSSELL (1872–   ). See page 78.

11

Symbolic or Formal Logic—I shall use these terms as synonyms—is the study of the various general types of deduction. The word *symbolic* designates the subject by an accidental characteristic, for the employment of mathematical symbols, here as elsewhere, is merely a theoretically irrelevant convenience. The syllogism in all its figures belongs to Symbolic Logic, and would be the whole subject if all deduction were syllogistic, as the scholastic tradition supposed. It is from the recognition of asyllogistic inferences that modern Symbolic Logic, from Leibniz onward, has derived the motive to progress. Since the publication of Boole's *Laws of Thought* (1854), the subject has been pursued with a certain vigour, and has attained to a very considerable technical development. Nevertheless, the subject achieved almost nothing of utility either to philosophy or to other branches of mathematics, until it was transformed by the new methods of Professor Peano. Symbolic Logic has now become not only absolutely essential to every philosophical logician, but also necessary for the comprehension of mathematics generally, and even for the successful practice of certain branches of mathematics. How useful it is in practice can only be judged by those who have experienced the increase of power derived from acquiring it; its theoretical functions must be briefly set forth in the present chapter.

12

Symbolic Logic is essentially concerned with inference in general,[1] and is distinguished from various special branches of mathematics mainly by its generality. Neither mathematics nor symbolic logic will study such special relations as (say) temporal priority, but mathematics will deal explicitly with the class of relations possessing the formal properties of temporal priority—properties which are summed up in the notion of continuity. And the formal properties of a relation may be defined as those that can be expressed in terms

* From *Principles of Mathematics,* Second Edition, 1937, by Bertrand Russell. Reprinted by permission of W. W. Norton & Company, Inc., all rights reserved, and George Allen & Unwin Ltd., London.

[1] I may as well say at once that I do not distinguish between inference and deduction. What is called induction appears to me to be either disguised deduction or a mere method of making plausible guesses.

of logical constants, or again as those which, while they are preserved, permit our relation to be varied without invalidating any inference in which the said relation is regarded in the light of a variable. But symbolic logic, in the narrower sense which is convenient, will not investigate what inferences are possible in respect of continuous relations (*i.e.* relations generating continuous series); this investigation belongs to mathematics, but is still too special for symbolic logic. What symbolic logic does investigate is the general rules by which inferences are made, and it requires a classification of relations or propositions only in so far as these general rules introduce particular notions. The particular notions which appear in the propositions of symbolic logic, and all others definable in terms of these notions, are the logical constants. The number of indefinable logical constants is not great: it appears, in fact, to be eight or nine. These notions alone form the subject-matter of the whole of mathematics: no others, except such as are definable in terms of the original eight or nine, occur anywhere in Arithmetic, Geometry, or rational Dynamics. For the technical study of Symbolic Logic, it is convenient to take as a single indefinable the notion of a formal implication, *i.e.* of such propositions as "x is a man implies x is a mortal, for all values of x"—propositions whose general type is: "$\phi(x)$ implies $\psi(x)$ for all values of x," where $\phi(x)$, $\psi(x)$, for all values of x, are propositions. The analysis of this notion of formal implication belongs to the principles of the subject, but is not required for its formal development. In addition to this notion, we require as indefinables the following: Implication between propositions not containing variables, the relation of a term to a class of which it is a member, the notion of *such that,* the notion of relation, and truth. By means of these notions, all the propositions of symbolic logic can be stated.

MATHEMATICS AND LOGIC*

BERTRAND RUSSELL (1872–   ). See page 78.

Mathematics and logic, historically speaking, have been entirely distinct studies. Mathematics has been connected with science, logic with Greek. But both have developed in modern times: logic has become more mathematical and mathematics has become more logical. The consequence is that it has now become wholly impossible to draw a line between the two; in fact, the two are one. They differ as boy and man: logic is the youth of mathematics and mathematics is the manhood of logic. This view is resented by logicians who, having spent their time in the study of classical texts, are incapable of following a piece of symbolic reasoning, and by mathematicians who have learnt a technique without troubling to inquire into its meaning or justification. Both types are now fortunately growing rarer. So much of modern mathematical work is obviously on the border-line of logic, so much of modern logic is symbolic and formal, that the very close relationship of logic and mathematics has become obvious to every instructed student. The proof of their identity is, of course, a matter of detail: starting with premisses which would be universally admitted to belong to logic, and arriving by deduction at results which as obviously belong to mathematics, we find that there is no point at which a sharp line can be drawn, with logic to the left and mathematics to the right. If there are still those who do not admit the identity of logic and mathematics, we may challenge them to indicate at what point, in the successive definitions and deductions of *Principia Mathematica,* they consider that logic ends and mathematics begins. It will then be obvious that any answer must be quite arbitrary.

In the earlier chapters of this book, starting from the natural numbers, we have first defined "cardinal number" and shown how to generalise the conception of number, and have then analysed the conceptions involved in the definition, until we found ourselves dealing with the fundamentals of logic. In a synthetic, deductive treatment these fundamentals come first, and the natural numbers are only reached after a long journey. Such treatment, though for-

* Reprinted with permission of The Macmillan Company from *Introduction to Mathematical Philosophy* by Bertrand Russell. First published in 1919 by George Allen & Unwin, Ltd., London.

mally more correct than that which we have adopted, is more difficult for the reader, because the ultimate logical concepts and propositions with which it starts are remote and unfamiliar as compared with the natural numbers. Also they represent the present frontier of knowledge, beyond which is the still unknown; and the dominion of knowledge over them is not as yet very secure.

It used to be said that mathematics is the science of "quantity." "Quantity" is a vague word, but for the sake of argument we may replace it by the word "number." The statement that mathematics is the science of number would be untrue in two different ways. On the one hand, there are recognised branches of mathematics which have nothing to do with number—all geometry that does not use co-ordinates or measurement, for example: projective and descriptive geometry, down to the point at which coordinates are introduced, does not have to do with number, or even with quantity in the sense of *greater* and *less*. On the other hand, through the definition of cardinals, through the theory of induction and ancestral relations, through the general theory of series, and through the definitions of the arithmetical operations, it has become possible to generalise much that used to be proved only in connection with numbers. The result is that what was formerly the single study of Arithmetic has now become divided into numbers of separate studies, no one of which is specially concerned with numbers. The most elementary properties of numbers are concerned with one-one relations, and similarity between classes. Addition is concerned with the construction of mutually exclusive classes respectively similar to a set of classes which are not known to be mutually exclusive. Multiplication is merged in the theory of "selections," *i.e.* of a certain kind of one-many relations. Finitude is merged in the general study of ancestral relations, which yields the whole theory of mathematical induction. The ordinal properties of the various kinds of number-series, and the elements of the theory of continuity of functions and the limits of functions, can be generalised so as no longer to involve any essential reference to numbers. It is a principle, in all formal reasoning, to generalise to the utmost, since we thereby secure that a given process of deduction shall have more widely applicable results; we are, therefore, in thus generalising the reasoning of arithmetic, merely following a precept which is universally admitted in mathematics. And in thus generalising we have, in effect, created a set of new deductive systems, in which traditional arithmetic is at once dissolved and enlarged; but whether any one of these new deductive systems—for example, the theory of selections—is to be said to belong to logic or to arithmetic is entirely arbitrary, and incapable of being decided rationally.

We are thus brought face to face with the question: What is this subject, which may be called indifferently either mathematics or logic? Is there any way in which we can define it?

Certain characteristics of the subject are clear. To begin with, we do not, in this subject, deal with particular things or particular properties: we deal formally with what can be said about *any* thing or *any* property. We are prepared to say that one and one are two, but not that Socrates and Plato are two, because, in our capacity of logicians or pure mathematicians, we have never heard of Socrates and Plato. A world in which there were no such individuals would still be a world in which one and one are two. It is not open to us, as pure mathematicians or logicians, to mention anything at all, because, if we do so, we introduce something irrelevant and not formal. We may make this clear by applying it to the case of the syllogism. Traditional logic says: "All men are mortal, Socrates is a man, therefore Socrates is mortal." Now it is clear that what we *mean* to assert, to begin with, is only that the premisses imply the conclusion, not that premisses and conclusion are actually true; even the most traditional logic points out that the actual truth of the premisses is irrelevant to logic. Thus the first change to be made in the above traditional syllogism is to state it in the form: "If all men are mortal and Socrates is a man, then Socrates is mortal." We may now observe that it is intended to convey that this argument is valid in virtue of its *form*, not in virtue of the particular terms occurring in it. If we had omitted "Socrates is a man" from our premisses, we should have had a non-formal argument, only admissible because Socrates is in fact a man; in that case we could not have generalised the argument. But when, as above, the argument is *formal*, nothing depends upon the terms that occur in it. Thus we may substitute a for *men*, β for *mortals*, and x for Socrates, where a and β are any classes whatever, and x is any individual. We then arrive at the statement: "No matter what possible values x and a and β may have, if all a's are β's and x is an a, then x is a β"; in other words, "the propositional function 'if all a's are β and x is an a, then x is a β' is always true." Here at last we have a proposition of logic—the one which is only *suggested* by the traditional statement about Socrates and men and mortals.

It is clear that, if *formal* reasoning is what we are aiming at, we shall always arrive ultimately at statements like the above, in which no actual things or properties are mentioned; this will happen through the mere desire not to waste our time proving in a particular case what can be proved generally. It would be ridiculous to go through a long argument about Socrates, and then go through precisely the same argument again about Plato. If our argument is one (say) which holds of all men, we shall prove it concerning "x," with the hypothesis "if x is a man." With this hypothesis, the argument will retain its hypothetical validity even when x is not a man. But now we shall find that our argument would still be valid if, instead of supposing x to be a man, we were to suppose him to be a monkey or a goose or a Prime Minister. We shall therefore not waste our time taking as our premiss "x is a man" but shall take "x is an a," where a is any class of individuals, or "ϕx" where ϕ is any propositional function of some assigned type. Thus the absence of all mention of particular things or properties in logic or pure mathematics is a necessary result of the fact that this study is, as we say, "purely formal."

At this point we find ourselves faced with a problem which is easier to state than to solve. The problem is: "What are the constituents of a logical proposition?" I do not know the answer, but I propose to explain how the problem arises.

Take (say) the proposition "Socrates was before Aristotle." Here it seems obvious that we have a relation between two terms, and that the constituents of the proposition (as well as of the corresponding fact) are simply the two terms and the relation, i.e. Socrates, Aristotle, and *before*. (I ignore the fact that Socrates and Aristotle are not simple; also the fact that what appear to be their names are really truncated descriptions. Neither of these facts is relevant to the present issue.) We may represent the general form of such propositions by "$x \, R \, y$," which may be read "x has the relation R to y." This general form may occur in logical propositions, but no particular instance of it can occur. Are we to infer that the general form itself is a constituent of such logical propositions?

Given a proposition, such as "Socrates is before Aristotle," we have certain constituents and also a certain form. But the form is not itself a new constituent; if it were, we should need a new form to embrace both it and the other constituents. We can, in fact, turn *all* the constituents of a proposition into variables, while keeping the form unchanged. This is what we do when we use such a schema as "*x* R *y*," which stands for any one of a certain class of propositions, namely, those asserting relations between two terms. We can proceed to general assertions, such as "*x* R *y* is sometimes true"—*i.e.* there are cases where dual relations hold. This assertion will belong to logic (or mathematics) in the sense in which we are using the word. But in this assertion we do not mention any particular things or particular relations; no particular things or relations can ever enter into a proposition of pure logic. We are left with pure *forms* as the only possible constituents of logical propositions.

I do not wish to assert positively that pure forms—*e.g.* the form "*x* R *y*"—do actually enter into propositions of the kind we are considering. The question of the analysis of such propositions is a difficult one, with conflicting considerations on the one side and on the other. We cannot embark upon this question now, but we may accept, as a first approximation, the view that *forms* are what enter into logical propositions as their constituents. And we may explain (though not formally define) what we mean by the "form" of a proposition as follows:

The "form" of a proposition is that, in it, that remains unchanged when every constituent of the proposition is replaced by another.

Thus "Socrates is earlier than Aristotle" has the same form as "Napoleon is greater than Wellington," though every constituent of the two propositions is different.

We may thus lay down, as a necessary (though not sufficient) characteristic of logical or mathematical propositions, that they are to be such as can be obtained from a proposition containing no variables (*i.e.* no such words as *all, some, a, the,* etc.) by turning every constituent into a variable and asserting that the result is always true or sometimes true, or that it is always true in respect of some of the variables that the result is sometimes true in respect of the others, or any variant of these forms. And another way of stating the same thing is to say that logic (or mathematics) is concerned only with *forms,* and is concerned with them only in the way of stating that they are always or sometimes true—with all the permutations of "always" and "sometimes" that may occur.

There are in every language some words whose sole function is to indicate form. These words, broadly speaking, are commonest in languages having fewest inflections. Take "Socrates is human." Here "is" is not a constituent of the proposition, but merely indicates the subject-predicate form. Similarly in "Socrates is earlier than Aristotle," "is" and "than" merely indicate form; the proposition is the same as "Socrates precedes Aristotle," in which these words have disappeared and the form is otherwise indicated. Form, as a rule, *can* be indicated otherwise than by specific words: the order of the words can do most of what is wanted. But this principle must not be pressed. For example, it is difficult to see how we could conveniently express molecular forms of propositions (*i.e.* what we call "truth-functions") without any word at all. We saw in Chapter XIV. that one word or symbol is enough for this purpose, namely, a word or symbol expressing incompatibility. But without even one we should find ourselves in difficulties. This, however, is not the point that is important for our present purpose. What is important for us is to observe that form may be the one concern of a general proposition, even when no word or symbol in that proposition designates the form. If we wish to speak about the form itself, we must have a word for it; but if, as in mathematics, we wish to speak about all propositions that have the form, a word for the form will usually be found not indispensable; probably in theory it is *never* indispensable.

Assuming—as I think we may—that the forms of propositions *can* be represented by the forms of the propositions in which they are expressed without any special word for forms, we should arrive at a language in which everything formal belonged to syntax and not to vocabulary. In such a language we could express *all* the propositions of mathematics even if we did not know one single word of the language. The language of mathematical logic, if it were perfected, would be such a language. We should have symbols for variables, such as *"x"* and "R" and *"y,"* arranged in various ways; and the way of arrangement would indicate that something was being said to be true of all values or some values of the variables. We should not need to know any words, because they would only be needed for giving values to the variables, which is the business of the applied mathematician, not of the pure mathematician or logician. It is one of the marks of a proposition of logic that, given a suitable language, such a proposition can be asserted in such a language

by a person who knows the syntax without knowing a single word of the vocabulary.

But, after all, there are words that express form, such as "is" and "than." And in every symbolism hitherto invented for mathematical logic there are symbols having constant formal meanings. We may take as an example the symbol for incompatibility which is employed in building up truth-functions. Such words or symbols may occur in logic. The question is: How are we to define them?

Such words or symbols express what are called "logical constants." Logical constants may be defined exactly as we defined forms; in fact, they are in essence the same thing. A fundamental logical constant will be that which is in common among a number of propositions, any one of which can result from any other by substitution of terms one for another. For example, "Napoleon is greater than Wellington" results from "Socrates is earlier than Aristotle" by the substitution of "Napoleon" for "Socrates," "Wellington" for "Aristotle," and "greater" for "earlier." Some propositions can be obtained in this way from the prototype "Socrates is earlier than Aristotle" and some cannot; those that can are those that are of the form "*x* R *y*," *i.e.* express dual relations. We cannot obtain from the above prototype by term-for-term substitution such propositions as "Socrates is human" or "the Athenians gave the hemlock to Socrates," because the first is of the subject-predicate form and the second expresses a three-term relation. If we are to have any words in our pure logical language, they must be such as express "logical constants," and "logical constants" will always either be, or be derived from, what is in common among a group of propositions derivable from each other, in the above manner, by term-for-term substitution. And this which is in common is what we call "form."

In this sense all the "constants" that occur in pure mathematics are logical constants. The number I, for example, is derivative from propositions of the form: "There is a term c such that ϕx is true when, and only when, x is c." This is a function of ϕ, and various different propositions result from giving different values to ϕ. We may (with a little omission of intermediate steps not relevant to our present purpose) take the above function of ϕ as what is meant by "the class determined by ϕ is a unit class" or "the class determined by ϕ is a member of I" (I being a class of classes). In this way, propositions in which I occurs acquire a meaning which is derived from a certain constant logical form. And the same will be found to be the case with all mathematical constants: all are logical constants, or symbolic abbreviations whose full use in a proper context is defined by means of logical constants.

But although all logical (or mathematical) propositions can be expressed wholly in terms of logical constants together with variables, it is not the case that, conversely, all propositions that can be expressed in this way are logical. We have found so far a necessary but not a sufficient criterion of mathematical propositions. We have sufficiently defined the character of the primitive *ideas* in terms of which all the ideas of mathematics can be *defined,* but not of the primitive propositions from which all the propositions of mathematics can be *deduced.* This is a more difficult matter, as to which it is not yet known what the full answer is.

We may take the axiom of infinity as an example of a proposition which, though it can be enunciated in logical

terms, cannot be asserted by logic to be true. All the propositions of logic have a characteristic which used to be expressed by saying that they were analytic, or that their contradictories were self-contradictory. This mode of statement, however, is not satisfactory. The law of contradiction is merely one among logical propositions; it has no special preeminence; and the proof that the contradictory of some proposition is self-contradictory is likely to require other principles of deduction besides the law of contradiction. Nevertheless, the characteristic of logical propositions that we are in search of is the one which was felt, and intended to be defined, by those who said that it consisted in deducibility from the law of contradiction. This characteristic, which, for the moment, we may call *tautology,* obviously does not belong to the assertion that the number of individuals in the universe is n, whatever number n may be. But for the diversity of types, it would be possible to prove logically that there are classes of n terms, where n is any finite integer; or even that there are classes of $\aleph_0$ terms. But, owing to types, such proofs, as we saw in Chapter XIII., are fallacious. We are left to empirical observation to determine whether there are as many as n individuals in the world. Among "possible" worlds, in the Leibnizian sense, there will be worlds having one, two, three, . . . individuals. There does not even seem any logical necessity why there should be even one individual[1]—why, in fact, there should be any world at all. The ontological proof of the existence of God, if it were valid, would establish the logical neces-

[1] The primitive propositions in *Principia Mathematica* are such as to allow the inference that at least one individual exists. But I now view this as a defect in logical purity.

sity of at least one individual. But it is generally recognised as invalid, and in fact rests upon a mistaken view of existence—*i.e.* it fails to realise that existence can only be asserted of something described, not of something named, so that it is meaningless to argue from "this is the so-and-so" and "the so-and-so exists" to "this exists." If we reject the ontological argument, we seem driven to conclude that the existence of a world is an accident—*i.e.* it is not logically necessary. If that be so, no principle of logic can assert "existence" except under a hypothesis, *i.e.* none can be of the form "the propositional function so-and-so is sometimes true." Propositions of this form, when they occur in logic, will have to occur as hypotheses or consequences of hypotheses, not as complete asserted propositions. The complete asserted propositions of logic will all be such as affirm that some propositional function is *always* true. For example, it is always true that if p implies q and q implies r then p implies r, or that, if all a's are β's and x is an a then x is a β. Such propositions may occur in logic, and their truth is independent of the existence of the universe. We may lay it down that, if there were no universe, *all* general propositions would be true; for the contradictory of a general proposition (as we saw in Chapter XV.) is a proposition asserting existence, and would therefore always be false if no universe existed.

Logical propositions are such as can be known *a priori*, without study of the actual world. We only know from a study of empirical facts that Socrates is a man, but we know the correctness of the syllogism in its abstract form (*i.e.* when it is stated in terms of variables) without needing any appeal to experience. This is a characteristic, not of logical propositions in themselves, but of the way in which we know them. It has,

however, a bearing upon the question what their nature may be, since there are some kinds of propositions which it would be very difficult to suppose we could know without experience.

It is clear that the definition of "logic" or "mathematics" must be sought by trying to give a new definition of the old notion of "analytic" propositions. Although we can no longer be satisfied to define logical propositions as those that follow from the law of contradiction, we can and must still admit that they are a wholly different class of propositions from those that we come to know empirically. They all have the characteristic which, a moment ago, we agreed to call "tautology." This, combined with the fact that they can be expressed wholly in terms of variables and logical constants (a logical constant being something which remains constant in a proposition even when *all* its constituents are changed)—will give the definition of logic or pure mathematics. For the moment, I do not know how to define "tautology."[1] It would be easy to offer a definition which might seem satisfactory for a while; but I know of none that I feel to be satisfactory, in spite of feeling thoroughly familiar with the characteristic of which a definition is wanted. At this point, therefore, for the moment, we reach the frontier of knowledge on our backward journey into the logical foundations of mathematics.

We have now come to an end of our somewhat summary introduction to mathematical philosophy. It is impossible to convey adequately the ideas that are concerned in this subject so long as we abstain from the use of logical symbols.

---

[1] The importance of "tautology" for a definition of mathematics was pointed out to me by my former pupil Ludwig Wittgenstein, who was working on the problem. I do not know whether he has solved it, or even whether he is alive or dead.

Since ordinary language has no words that naturally express exactly what we wish to express, it is necessary, so long as we adhere to ordinary language, to strain words into unusual meanings; and the reader is sure, after a time if not at first, to lapse into attaching the usual meanings to words, thus arriving at wrong notions as to what is intended to be said. Moreover, ordinary grammar and syntax is extraordinarily misleading. This is the case, *e.g.*, as regards numbers; "ten men" is grammatically the same form as "white men," so that 10 might be thought to be an adjective qualifying "men." It is the case, again, wherever propositional functions are involved, and in particular as regards existence and descriptions. Because language is misleading, as well as because it is diffuse and inexact when applied to logic (for which it was never intended), logical symbolism is absolutely necessary to any exact or thorough treatment of our subject. Those readers, therefore, who wish to acquire a mastery of the principles of mathematics, will, it is to be hoped, not shrink from the labour of mastering the symbols—a labour which is, in fact, much less than might be thought. As the above hasty survey must have made evident, there are innumerable unsolved problems in the subject, and much work needs to be done. If any student is led into a serious study of mathematical logic by this little book, it will have served the chief purpose for which it has been written.

A NEGATIVE APPRAISAL

BY A MATHEMATICIAN*

HENRI POINCARÉ (1854–1912)   was a French mathematician and scientist
who made many original and important contributions to pure and applied mathematics. He also wrote in the areas of philosophy of science
and foundations of mathematics, in which his chief publications were
Science and Hypothesis (1903), *The Value of Science* (1904), and
Science and Method (1908). Poincaré was vigorously opposed to the
logistic thesis,† against which he wrote closely reasoned polemics distinguished for both their graceful style and their sardonic wit.

Can mathematics be reduced to logic
without having to appeal to principles
peculiar to mathematics? There is a
whole school, abounding in ardor and
full of faith, striving to prove it. They
have their own special language, which
is without words, using only signs. This
language is understood only by the
initiates, so that commoners are disposed
to bow to the trenchant affirmations of
the adepts. It is perhaps not unprofitable
to examine these affirmations somewhat
closely, to see if they justify the peremp-
tory tone with which they are presented.

. . .

It is time to administer justice on these
exaggerations. I do not hope to convince
them; for they have lived too long in this
atmosphere. Besides, when one of their
demonstrations has been refuted, we are
sure to see it resurrected with insignifi-

cant alterations, and some of them have
already risen several times from their
ashes. Such long ago was the Lernaean
hydra with its famous heads which always grew again. Hercules got through,
since his hydra had only nine heads, or
eleven; but here there are too many,
some in England, some in Germany, in
Italy, in France, and he would have to
give up the struggle. So I appeal only to
men of good judgment unprejudiced.

. . .

The symbolic language created by
Peano plays a very grand rôle in these
new researches. It is capable of rendering some service, but I think M. Couturat
attaches to it an exaggerated importance
which must astonish Peano himself.

The essential element of this language
is certain algebraic signs which represent
the different conjunctions: if, and, or,

* From Henri Poincaré, *The Foundations of Science,* translated by G. B. Halsted (Lan-
caster, Pa.: The Science Press, 1913).
† See footnote on page 187.

therefore. That these signs may be convenient is possible; but that they are destined to revolutionize all philosophy is a different matter. It is difficult to admit that the word *if* acquires, when written C, a virtue it had not when written if. This invention of Peano was first called *pasigraphy*, that is to say the art of writing a treatise on mathematics without using a single word of ordinary language. The name defined its range very exactly. Later, it was raised to a more eminent dignity by conferring on it the title of *logistic*. This word is, it appears, employed at the Military Academy, to designate the art of the quartermaster of cavalry, the art of marching and cantoning troops; but here no confusion need be feared, and it is at once seen that this new name implies the design of revolutionizing logic.

· · ·

First we see Burali-Forti define the number 1 as follows:

$$1 = {}_\iota T' \{Ko\widehat{n}(u,h) \, \epsilon \, (u_\epsilon \, Un)\},$$

a definition eminently fitted to give an idea of the number 1 to persons who had never heard speak of it.

I understand Peanian too ill to dare risk a critique, but still I fear this definition contains a petitio principii, considering that I see the figure 1 in the first number and Un in letters in the second.

However that may be, Burali-Forti starts from this definition and, after a short calculation, reaches the equation:

(27) $1 \, \epsilon \, No,$

which tells us that One is a number.

And since we are on these definitions of the first numbers, we recall that M. Couturat has also defined 0 and 1.

What is zero? It is the number of elements of the null class. And what is the null class? It is that containing no element.

To define zero by null, and null by no, is really to abuse the wealth of language; so M. Couturat has introduced an improvement in his definition, by writing:

$$0 = {}_\iota \Lambda : \phi x = \Lambda \cdot \mathtt{o} \cdot \Lambda = (x_\epsilon \phi x),$$

which means: zero is the number of things satisfying a condition never satisfied.

But as never means *in no case* I do not see that the progress is great.

I hasten to add that the definition M. Couturat gives of the number 1 is more satisfactory.

One, says he in substance, is the number of elements in a class in which any two elements are identical.

It is more satisfactory, I have said, in this sense that to define 1, he does not use the word one; in compensation, he uses the word two. But I fear, if asked what is two, M. Couturat would have to use the word one.

· · ·

To justify its pretensions, logic had to change. We have seen new logics arise of which the most interesting is that of Russell. It seems he has nothing new to write about formal logic, as if Aristotle there had touched bottom. But the domain Russell attributes to logic is infinitely more extended than that of the classic logic, and he has put forth on the subject views which are original and at times well warranted.

First, Russell subordinates the logic of classes to that of propositions, while the logic of Aristotle was above all the logic of classes and took as its point of departure the relation of subject to predicate. The classic syllogism, "Socrates is a man," etc., gives place to the hypothetical syllogism: "If *A* is true, *B* is true; now if *B* is true, *C* is true," etc. And this is, I think, a most happy idea, because the classic syllogism is easy to carry back to the hypothetical syllogism, while the inverse transformation is not without difficulty.

And then this is not all. Russell's logic of propositions is the study of the laws of combination of the conjunctions *if, and, or,* and the negation *not.*

In adding here two other conjunctions *and* and *or,* Russell opens to logic a new field. The symbols *and, or* follow the same laws as the two signs $\times$ and $+$, that is to say the commutative associative and distributive laws. Thus *and* represents logical multiplication, while *or* represents logical addition. This also is very interesting.

Russell reaches the conclusion that any false proposition implies all other propositions true or false. M. Couturat says this conclusion will at first seem paradoxical. It is sufficient however to have corrected a bad thesis in mathematics to recognize how right Russell is. The candidate often is at great pains to get the first false equation; but that once obtained, it is only sport then for him to accumulate the most surprising results, some of which even may be true.

We see how much richer the new logic is than the classic logic; the symbols are multiplied and allow of varied combinations *which are no longer limited in number.* Has one the right to give this extension to the meaning of the word *logic?* It would be useless to examine this question and to seek with Russell a mere quarrel about words. Grant him what he demands; but be not astonished if certain verities declared irreducible to logic in the old sense of the word find themselves now reducible to logic in the new sense—something very different.

A great number of new notions have been introduced, and these are not simply combinations of the old. Russell knows this, and not only at the beginning of the first chapter, 'The Logic of Propositions,' but at the beginning of the second and third, 'The Logic of Classes' and 'The Logic of Relations,' he introduces new words that he declares indefinable.

And this is not all; he likewise introduces principles he declares indemonstrable. But these indemonstrable principles are appeals to intuition, synthetic judgments *a priori.* We regard them as intuitive when we meet them more or less explicitly enunciated in mathematical treatises; have they changed character because the meaning of the word logic has been enlarged and we now find them in a book entitled *Treatise on Logic? They have not changed nature; they have only changed place.*

Could these principles be considered as disguised definitions? It would then be necessary to have some way of proving that they imply no contradiction. It would be necessary to establish that, however far one followed the series of deductions, he would never be exposed to contradicting himself.

We might attempt to reason as follows: We can verify that the operations of the new logic applied to premises exempt from contradiction can only give consequences equally exempt from contradiction. If therefore after n operations we have not met contradiction, we shall not encounter it after $n + 1$. Thus it is impossible that there should be a moment when contradiction *begins,* which shows we shall never meet it. Have we the right to reason in this way? No, for this would be to make use of complete induction; and *remember, we do not yet know the principle of complete induction.*

We therefore have not the right to regard these assumptions as disguised definitions and only one resource remains for us, to admit a new act of intuition for each of them. Moreover I believe this is indeed the thought of Russell and M. Couturat.

Thus each of the nine indefinable notions and of the twenty indemonstrable propositions (I believe if it were I that did the counting, I should have found some more) which are the foundation of the new logic, logic in the broad sense, presupposes a new and independent act of our intuition and (why not say it?) a veritable synthetic judgment *a priori.* On this point all seem agreed, but what Russell claims, and *what seems to me doubtful, is that after these appeals to intuition, that will be the end of it; we need make no others and can build all mathematics without the intervention of any new element.*

M. Couturat often repeats that this new logic is altogether independent of the idea of number. I shall not amuse myself by counting how many numeral adjectives his exposition contains, both cardinal and ordinal, or indefinite adjectives such as several. We may cite, however, some examples:

"The logical product of *two* or *more* propositions is . . .";

"All propositions are capable only of *two* values, true and false";

"The relative product of *two* relations is a relation";

"A relation exists between *two* terms," etc., etc.

Sometimes this inconvenience would not be unavoidable, but sometimes also it is essential. A relation is incomprehensible without two terms; it is impossible to have the intuition of the relation, without having at the same time that of its two terms, and without noticing they are two, because, if the relation is to be conceivable, it is necessary that there be two and only two.

. . .

The logicians have attempted to answer the preceding considerations. For that, a transformation of logistic was necessary, and Russell in particular has modified on certain points his original views. Without entering into the details of the debate, I should like to return to the two questions to my mind most important: Have the rules of logistic demonstrated their fruitfulness and infallibility? Is it true they afford means of proving the principle of complete induction without any appeal to intuition?

On the question of fertility, it seems M. Couturat has naïve illusions. Logistic, according to him, lends invention 'stilts and wings,' and on the next page: *"ten years ago,* Peano published the first edition of his *Formulaire."* How is that, ten years of wings and not to have flown!

I have the highest esteem for Peano, who has done very pretty things (for instance his 'space-filling curve,' a phrase now discarded); but after all he has not gone further nor higher nor quicker than the majority of wingless mathematicians, and would have done just as well with his legs.

On the contrary I see in logistic only shackles for the inventor. It is no aid to conciseness—far from it, and if twenty-seven equations were necessary to establish that 1 is a number, how many would be needed to prove a real theorem? If we distinguish, with Whitehead, the individual x, the class of which the only member is x and which shall be called ιx, then the class of which the only member is the class of which the only member is x and which shall be called $\iota\iota x$, do you think these distinctions, useful as they may be, go far to quicken our pace?

Logistic forces us to say all that is ordinarily left to be understood; it makes us advance step by step; this is perhaps surer but not quicker.

It is not wings you logisticians give us, but leading-strings. And then we have the right to require that these leading-strings prevent our falling. This will be their only excuse. When a bond does not bear much interest, it should at least be an investment for a father of a family.

Should your rules be followed blindly? Yes, else only intuition could enable us to distinguish among them; but then they must be infallible; for only in an infallible authority can one have a blind confidence. This, therefore, is for you a necessity. Infallible you shall be, or not at all.

You have no right to say to us: "It is true we make mistakes, but so do you." For us to blunder is a misfortune, a very great misfortune; for you it is death.

Nor may you ask: Does the infallibility of arithmetic prevent errors in addition? The rules of calculation are infallible, and yet we see those blunder *who do not apply these rules;* but in checking their calculation it is at once seen where they went wrong. Here it is not at all the case; the logicians *have applied* their rules, and they have fallen into contradiction; and so true is this, that they are preparing to change these rules and to "sacrifice the notion of class." Why change them if they were infallible?

"We are not obliged," you say, "to solve *hic et nunc* all possible problems." Oh, we do not ask so much of you. If, in face of a problem you would give *no* solution, we should have nothing to say; but on the contrary you give us *two* of them and those contradictory, and consequently at least one false; this it is which is failure.

Russell seeks to reconcile these contradictions, which can only be done, according to him, "by restricting or even sacrificing the notion of class." And M. Couturat, discovering the success of his attempt, adds: "If the logicians succeed where others have failed, M. Poincaré

will remember this phrase, and give the honor of the solution to logistic."

But no! Logistic exists, it has its code which has already had four editions; or rather this code is logistic itself. Is Mr. Russell preparing to show that one at least of the two contradictory reasonings has transgressed the code? Not at all; he is preparing to change these laws and to abrogate a certain number of them. If he succeeds, I shall give the honor of it to Russell's intuition and not to the Peanian logistic which he will have destroyed.

. . .

I made two principal objections to the definition of whole number adopted in logistic. What says M. Couturat to the first of these objections?

What does the word *exist* mean in mathematics? It means, I said, to be free from contradiction. This M. Couturat contests. "Logical existence," says he, "is quite another thing from the absence of contradiction. It consists in the fact that a class is not empty." To say: *a*'s exist, is, by definition, to affirm that the class *a* is not null.

And doubtless to affirm that the class *a* is not null, is, by definition, to affirm that *a*'s exist. But one of the two affirmations is as denuded of meaning as the other, if they do not both signify, either that one may see or touch *a*'s which is the meaning physicists or naturalists give them, or that one may conceive an *a* without being drawn into contradictions, which is the meaning given them by logicians and mathematicians.

For M. Couturat, "it is not non-contradiction that proves existence, but it is existence that proves non-contradiction." To establish the existence of a class, it is necessary therefore to establish, by an *example,* that there is an individual belonging to this class: "But, it will be said, how is the existence of this individual proved? Must not this existence be established, in order that the existence of the class of which it is a part may be deduced? Well, no; however paradoxical may appear the assertion, we never demonstrate the existence of an individual. Individuals, just because they are individuals, are always considered as existent. . . . We never have to express that an individual exists, absolutely speaking, but only that it exists in a class." M. Couturat finds his own assertion paradoxical, and he will certainly not be the only one. Yet it must have a meaning. It doubtless means that the existence of an individual, alone in the world, and of which nothing is affirmed, can not involve contradiction; in so far as it is all alone it evidently will not embarrass any one. Well, so let it be; we shall admit the existence of the individual, 'absolutely speaking,' but nothing more. It remains to prove the existence of the individual 'in a class,' and for that it will always be necessary to prove that the affirmation, "Such an individual belongs to such a class," is neither contradictory in itself, nor to the other postulates adopted.

"It is then," continues M. Couturat, "arbitrary and misleading to maintain that a definition is valid only if we first prove it is not contradictory." One could not claim in prouder and more energetic terms the liberty of contradiction. "In any case, the *onus probandi* rests upon those who believe that these principles are contradictory." Postulates are presumed to be compatible until the contrary is proved, just as the accused person is presumed innocent. Needless to add that I do not assent to this claim. But, you say, the demonstration you require of us is impossible, and you can not ask us to jump over the moon. Pardon me; that is impossible for you, but not for us, who admit the principle of induction as a synthetic judgment *a priori*. And that would be necessary for you, as for us.

To demonstrate that a system of postulates implies no contradiction, it is necessary to apply the principle of complete induction; this mode of reasoning not only has nothing 'bizarre' about it, but it is the only correct one. It is not 'unlikely' that it has ever been employed; and it is not hard to find 'examples and precedents' of it. I have cited two such instances borrowed from Hilbert's article. He is not the only one to have used it, and those who have not done so have been wrong. What I have blamed Hilbert for is not his having recourse to it (a born mathematician such as he could not fail to see a demonstration was necessary and this the only one possible), but his having recourse without recognizing the reasoning by recurrence.

. . .

A demonstration truly founded upon the principles of analytic logic will be composed of a series of propositions. Some, serving as premises, will be identities or definitions; the others will be deduced from the premises step by step. But though the bond between each proposition and the following is immediately evident, it will not at first sight appear how we get from the first to the last, which we may be tempted to regard as a new truth. But if we replace successively the different expressions therein by their definition and if this operation be carried as far as possible, there will finally remain only identities, so that all will reduce to an immense tautology. Logic therefore remains sterile unless made fruitful by intuition.

This I wrote long ago; logistic professes the contrary and thinks it has proved it by actually proving new truths. By what mechanism? Why in applying to their reasonings the procedure just described—namely, replacing the terms defined by their definitions—do we not see them dissolve into identities like ordinary reasonings? It is because this procedure is not applicable to them. And why? Because their definitions are not predicative and present this sort of hidden vicious circle which I have pointed out above; non-predicative definitions can not be substituted for the terms defined. Under these conditions *logistic is not sterile, it engenders antinomies.*

. . .

Russell has perceived the peril and takes counsel. He is about to change everything, and, what is easily understood, he is preparing not only to introduce new principles which shall allow of operations formerly forbidden, but he is preparing to forbid operations he formerly thought legitimate. Not content to adore what he burned, he is about to burn what he adored, which is more serious. He does not add a new wing to the building, he saps its foundation.

The old logistic is dead, so much so that already the zigzag theory and the no-classes theory are disputing over the succession. To judge of the new, we shall await its coming.

A NEGATIVE APPRAISAL

BY AN IDEALIST LOGICIAN*

BENEDETTO CROCE (1866–1952) was an Italian historian, art critic, and philosopher. Best known for his writings on aesthetics (philosophy of art), Croce also developed an elaborate Idealist metaphysics related to but independent of that of Hegel. As an Idealist he was critical of formal logic in general. Croce was especially opposed to the new symbolic logic, to which several Italian mathematicians had made important contributions around the turn of the century.

Formalist Logic has been the object of many violent attacks from the Renaissance onwards; but it cannot be said that it has been struck in its essential part, because up to the present, the principle itself, or the incoherence from which it springs, has not been attacked. Several attempts at reform have followed and still follow; they have all of them the same defect, which is the wish to reform formal Logic without issuing from its circle, and without refuting its tacit presumption —the pretension of obtaining thought in words, concepts in propositions. The most considerable attempt of the kind that has been made, which has many zealous followers in our day, is *mathematical Logic,* also called *calculatory, algebraical, algorhythmic, symbolic, a new analytic,* or a *Logical calculus or Logistic.*

It is admitted by those who profess it and is for the rest evident from the definitions of Logistic that have been given, that it has nothing in common with mathematics, for although the majority of its cultivators are mathematicians and use is made of the phraseology usual in Mathematics, and it is directed toward Mathematics, in certain of its practical intentions, there is nothing intrinsically mathematical in it. Logistic is a science which deals, not with quantity alone, but with *quantity and quality together;* it is a science of *things in general;* it is *universal mathematics,* containing also, subordinated to itself, the mathematical sciences properly so-called, but not coinciding with these. It means to be, not mathematics, but *a general science of thought.*

But the "thought" of Logistic is nothing but the "verbal proposition," which, in fact, supplies its starting-point. What the proposition is; whether it be possible truly to distinguish the proposition we call "verbal" from all the others, poetical, musical, pictorial; whether the verbal proposition does not bear indistinctly in itself, a series of very diverse spiritual formations, from poetry to mathematics, from history and philosophy to the natural sciences; what

* From Benedetto Croce, *Logic as the Science of the Pure Concept* (1917), translated by Douglas Ainslie. Reprinted by permission of Macmillan & Co., Ltd., London.

language is and what the concept is—these and all other questions concerning the forms of the spirit and the nature of thought, remain altogether extraneous to Logistic and do not disturb it in its work. The propositions (the concept of the proposition remaining an unexplained presupposition) can be indicated by p, q, etc.; the relation of implication of one proposition in another can be indicated by the sign $\mathfrak{I}$, hence an isolated proposition is "that which implies itself" $(p.\mathfrak{I}.q.)$. By following a method such as this, many distinctions of the traditional formalist Logic are eliminated, and in compensation for this, new ones are added and old and new are dressed in a new phraseology. The logical *sum* $a + b$ is the smallest concept, which contains the other two a and b and is what was previously called the "sphere of the concept"; the logical *product* $a \times b$ indicates the greater concept contained in a and in b, and answers to that which was previously called "comprehension." There are also new or renovated laws, like the law of *identity*, by force of which, in Logic (differently from Algebra), $a + a + a \cdots = a$; by which it is desired to signify this profound truth, that the repetition of one and the same concept as many times as one wishes, always gives the same concept;—the law of *commutation*, by which $ab = ba$;—or that of absorption, by which $a(a + b) = a$; or —(the convention being that the negation of a concept is indicated by placing against it a vertical line) the other beautiful laws and formulæ: $a + a \mid = a$; $(a \mid)a = a$; $aa \mid = o$. This is a charming amusement for those who have a taste for it.

Thus it is seen that if the words and the formulæ be somewhat different, the nature of mathematical Logic in no respect differs from that of formalist Logic. Where the new Logic contradicts the old, it is not possible to say which of the two is right; as of two people walking side by side over insecure ground, it is impossible to say which of the two walks securely. The very doctrine of the *quantification of the predicate* (which has been the leaven of the reform) in no wise alters the traditional manner of conceiving the judgment, with the corresponding arbitrary manner of distinguishing subject and predicate. It simply establishes a convention with the object of being able to symbolize, with the sign of equality, the subject and the predicate:—the subject being included in the predicate, is part of it: "men are mortal" equals: "men are some mortals"; and so, "men" being indicated with a and "some mortals" with b, the judgment can be symbolized: $a = b$. For us, it is indifferent whether the modes of the syllogism be the 64 and the 19 recognized as valid by traditional Logic, or the 12 affirmative and the 24 negative of Hamilton's Logic, which distinguishes four classes of affirmative and four of negative propositions. It is indifferent whether the methods of conversion be three or two or one. It is indifferent whether logical laws or principles be enumerated as two, three, five or ten. Since we do not accept the point of departure, it is impossible for us, far from admitting the development, even to discuss it; save to demonstrate that from capricious choice comes capricious choice, as we have made sufficiently clear in our treatment of formalist Logic. Mathematical Logic is a new manifestation of this formalist Logic, involving a great change in traditional formulæ, but none in the intimate substance of that pretended science of thought.

As the *science of thought*, Logistic is a laughable thing; worthy, for that matter, of the brains that conceive and advocate it, which are the same that are promulgating a new Philosophy of language, indeed a new Æsthetic, with their insipid theories of the *universal Language*. As a formula of *practical utility* it is not incumbent upon us to examine it here; all the more since we have already had occasion to give our opinion upon this subject. In the time of Leibnitz, fifty years later in the last days of Wolffianism; a century ago in Hamilton's time; forty years ago in the time of Jevons and of others; and finally now, when Peano, Boole, and Couturat are flourishing, these new arrangements are offered on the market. But every one has always found them too costly and complicated, so that they have not hitherto been generally used. Will they be so in the future? The practical work of persuasion, proper to the commercial traveller seeking purchasers of a new product, and the foresight of the merchant or manufacturer as to the fortune that may await that product, are not pertinent to Philosophy; which, being disinterested, could here, at the most, reply with words of benevolent patience: "If they be roses, they will bloom."

Induction

INTRODUCTION Induction stands in sharp contrast to deduction. The latter is usually regarded as the method of the *a priori* or mathematical sciences; the former is the method of the *a posteriori* or empirical sciences. Various definitions of induction have been offered. In the *Topics* Aristotle wrote "induction is a passage from individuals to universals," a characterization of induction that still has currency today. The selections in this Part deal with some of the problems of induction, and reflect changing conceptions of induction from Aristotle to the present.

The selection from Aristotle's *Posterior Analytics* shows the classical conception of scientific knowledge as demonstrative or necessary. Science was said to be concerned with substance, with essences or natures, that is, with essential natures. Aristotle wrestled with the question of the source of the premises from which scientific conclusions are demonstrated. And we are given his account of the way that sense perception gives rise to memory, and that to experience, from which "originate the skill of the craftsman and the knowledge of the man of science."

Roger Bacon praised experience over argumentation as a way of knowing, and urged the necessity of all things being "certified by the way of experience." A medieval advocate of experimental science, his ideas have a very modern ring to them.

Francis Bacon criticized the traditional induction by simple enumeration for being "childish," and proposed instead that nature be analyzed "by proper rejections and exclusions." He esteemed his new instrument, his *Novum Organum,* as much superior to the older *Organon* of Aristotle. Bacon believed himself to have devised a recipe that anyone could use to make scientific discoveries, writing: "For my way of discovering sciences goes far to level men's wits, and leaves but little to individual excellence; because it performs everything by the surest rules and demonstrations."

Hume raises a quite different question: what is the basis of inference from experience? He suggests that all such inferences "suppose, as their foundation, that the future will resemble the past."

But we cannot, then, without circularity, except "that any arguments from experience can prove this resemblance of the past to the future." Hume himself gives what he calls a sceptical conclusion, that: "All inferences from experience, therefore, are effects of custom, not of reasoning."

Whewell offers a very modern conception of the process of induction, which he equates with the framing of a *hypothesis* to explain the observed facts on which the induction is based. In the selection here Whewell is not concerned with Hume's problem, but (without mentioning him by name) denies Bacon's claim to have given rules for inductive reasoning. In Whewell's words, "The *Logic of Induction* has not yet been constructed."

The selection from Mill is concerned with Hume's problem. Mill states "that the course of nature is uniform" is "our warrant for all inferences from experience." This principle of the uniformity of nature is said by Mill to be "the ultimate major premise of all inductions." He also calls it "the fundamental principle, or general axiom, of Induction." But the principle is not self-evident. It is not arrived at by ratiocination. It is itself established by induction.

Bradley's criticism of Mill's methods (or Canons) of inductive inference is one of the classical polemics in the history of logic. It is clear, vigorous, witty, and devastating!

The "doctrine of necessity" examined by Peirce is "the common belief that every single fact in the universe is precisely determined by law." Peirce challenges that belief, and rejects what Mill called "the fundamental principle, or general axiom, of Induction." As a scientist, of course, Peirce accepts Induction—but an induction whose conclusions are inferred with probability, and which permits margins of "error." Much of Peirce's essay is devoted to arguing that scientific inference does not require strict uniformity of nature as an "ultimate major premise."

The selection from Russell deals with Hume's problem. Russell disagrees with Mill's position, and insists that "All arguments which, on the basis of experience, argue as to the future or the unexperienced parts of the past or present, assume the inductive principle; hence we can never use experience to prove the inductive principle without begging the question." Russell expresses his belief that the use of probabilities can help produce a solution to Hume's problem.

The same optimism is found in the selection from John Maynard Keynes. He too feels that acknowledging the merely probable nature of induction will clear the way for an answer to Hume. Keynes also provides an illuminating appreciation of the work on induction done by Bacon, Hume, and Mill.

THE CLASSICAL

CONCEPTION OF SCIENCE*

ARISTOTLE (384–322 B.C.). See page 8.

6

Demonstrative knowledge must rest on necessary basic truths; for the object of scientific knowledge[1] cannot be other than it is. Now attributes attaching essentially to their subjects attach necessarily to them: for essential attributes are either elements in the essential nature of their subjects, or contain their subjects as elements in their own essential nature. (The pairs of opposites which the latter class includes are necessary because one member or the other necessarily inheres.) It follows from this that premisses of the demonstrative syllogism must be con-nexions essential in the sense explained: for all attributes must inhere essentially or else be accidental, and accidental attributes are not necessary to their subjects.

We must either state the case thus, or else premise that the conclusion of demonstration is necessary and that a demonstrated conclusion cannot be other than it is, and then infer that the conclusion must be developed from necessary premisses. For though you may reason from true premisses without demonstrating, yet if your premisses are necessary you will as-

suredly demonstrate—in such necessity you have at once a distinctive character of demonstration. That demonstration proceeds from necessary premisses is also indicated by the fact that the objection we raise against a professed demonstration is that a premiss of it is not a necessary truth—whether we think it altogether devoid of necessity, or at any rate so far as our opponent's previous argument goes. This shows how naïve it is to suppose one's basic truths rightly chosen if one starts with a proposition which is (1) popularly accepted and (2) true, such as the sophists' assumption that to know is the same as to possess knowledge. For (1) popular acceptance or rejection is no criterion of a basic truth, which can only be the primary law of the genus constituting the subject matter of the demonstration; and (2) not *all* truth is 'appropriate'.

A further proof that the conclusion must be the development of necessary premisses is as follows. Where demonstration is possible, one who can give no account which includes the cause has no scientific knowledge. If, then, we suppose a syllogism in which, though A necessarily inheres in C, yet B, the middle term of the demonstration, is not necessarily con-

* From *Posterior Analytics* in *The Works of Aristotle* (1928), Volume I, translated under the editorship of W. D. Ross. Reprinted by permission of The Clarendon Press, Oxford.

[1] i.e. that which is known by demonstration.

nected with A and C, then the man who argues thus has no reasoned knowledge of the conclusion, since this conclusion does not owe its necessity to the middle term; for though the conclusion is necessary, the mediating link is a contingent fact. Or again, if a man is without knowledge now, though he still retains the steps of the argument, though there is no change in himself or in the fact and no lapse of memory on his part; then neither had he knowledge previously. But the mediating link, not being necessary, may have perished in the interval; and if so, though there be no change in him nor in the fact, and though he will still retain the steps of the argument, yet he has not knowledge, and therefore had not knowledge before. Even if the link has not actually perished but is liable to perish, this situation is possible and might occur. But such a condition cannot be knowledge.

When the conclusion is necessary, the middle through which it was proved may yet quite easily be non-necessary. You can in fact infer the necessary even from a non-necessary premiss, just as you can infer the true from the not true. On the other hand, when the middle is necessary the conclusion must be necessary; just as true premisses always give a true conclusion. Thus, if A is necessarily predicated of B and B of C, then A is necessarily predicated of C. But when the conclusion is non-necessary the middle cannot be necessary either. Thus: let A be predicated non-necessarily of C but necessarily of B, and let B be a necessary predicate of C; then A too will be a necessary predicate of C, which by hypothesis it is not.

To sum up, then: demonstrative knowledge must be knowledge of a necessary nexus, and therefore must clearly be obtained through a necessary middle term; otherwise its possessor will know neither the cause nor the fact that his conclusion is a necessary connexion. Either he will

mistake the non-necessary for the necessary and believe the necessity of the conclusion without knowing it, or else he will not even believe it—in which case he will be equally ignorant, whether he actually infers the mere fact through middle terms or the reasoned fact and from immediate premisses.[2]

Of accidents that are not essential according to our definition of essential there is no demonstrative knowledge; for since an accident, in the sense in which I here speak of it, may also not inhere, it is impossible to prove its inherence as a necessary conclusion. A difficulty, however, might be raised as to why in dialectic, if the conclusion is not a necessary connexion, such and such determinate premisses should be proposed in order to deal with such and such determinate problems. Would not the result be the same if one asked any questions whatever and then merely stated one's conclusion? The solution is that determinate questions have to be put, not because the replies to them affirm facts which necessitate facts affirmed by the conclusion, but because these answers are propositions which if the answerer affirm, he must affirm the conclusion—and affirm it with truth if they are true.

Since it is just those attributes within every genus which are essential and possessed by their respective subjects as such that are necessary, it is clear that both the conclusions and the premisses of demonstrations which produce scientific knowledge are essential.[3] For accidents are not

[2] . . . taking Aristotle to mean that you may construct a formally perfect syllogism, inferring the fact, or even the reasoned fact, from what are actually true and necessary premisses; yet because you do not realize their necessity, you have not knowledge. . . .

[3] The implied minor premiss required for this conclusion is the already proved fact that the conclusions and premisses of demonstration are necessary.

necessary: and, further,[4] since accidents are not necessary one does not necessarily have reasoned knowledge of a conclusion drawn from them (this is so even if the accidental premises are invariable but not essential, as in proofs through signs;[5] for though the conclusion be actually essential, one will not know it as essential nor know its reason); but to have reasoned knowledge of a conclusion is to know it through its cause. We may conclude that the middle must be consequentially connected with the minor, and the major with the middle.

. . .

Scientific knowledge is not possible through the act of perception. Even if perception as a faculty is of 'the such' and not merely of a 'this somewhat', yet one must at any rate actually perceive a 'this somewhat', and at a definite present place and time: but that which is commensurately universal and true in all cases one cannot perceive, since it is not 'this' and it it not 'now'; if it were, it would not be commensurately universal—the term we apply to what is always and everywhere. Seeing, therefore, that demonstrations are commensurately universal and universals imperceptible, we clearly cannot obtain scientific knowledge by the act of perception: nay, it is obvious that even if it were possible to perceive that a triangle has its angles equal to two right angles, we should still be looking for a demonstration —we should not (as some say) possess knowledge of it; for perception must be of a particular, whereas scientific knowledge involves the recognition of the com-

mensurate universal. So if we were on the moon, and saw the earth shutting out the sun's light, we should not know the cause of the eclipse: we should perceive the present fact of the eclipse, but not the reasoned fact at all, since the act of perception is not of the commensurate universal. I do not, of course, deny that by watching the frequent recurrence of this event we might, after tracking the commensurate universal, possess a demonstration, for the commensurate universal is elicited from the several groups of singulars.

The commensurate universal is precious because it makes clear the cause; so that in the case of facts like these which have a cause other than themselves universal knowledge is more precious than sense-perceptions and than intuition. (As regards primary truths there is of course a different account to be given.) Hence it is clear that knowledge of things demonstrable cannot be acquired by perception, unless the term perception is applied to the possession of scientific knowledge through demonstration. Nevertheless certain points do arise with regard to connexions to be proved which are referred for their explanation to a failure in sense-perception: there are cases when an act of vision would terminate our inquiry, not because in seeing we should be knowing, but because we should have elicited the universal from seeing; if, for example, we saw the pores in the glass and the light passing through, the reason of the kindling would be clear to us because we should at the same time see it in each instance and intuit that it must be so in all instances.

. . .

Scientific knowledge and its object differ from opinion and the object of opinion in that scientific knowledge is commensurately universal and proceeds by

[4] A further reason for excluding accidental premises from demonstration; they cannot give reasoned knowledge of a conclusion, i.e. knowledge of it through its cause (and this, Aristotle implies, was one of the first conditions of demonstration).

[5] Usually proofs from effect to cause.

necessary connexions, and that which is necessary cannot be otherwise. So though there are things which are true and real and yet can be otherwise, *scientific knowledge* clearly does not concern them: if it did, things which can be otherwise would be incapable of being otherwise. Nor are they any concern of *rational intuition*—by rational intuition I mean an originative source of scientific knowledge—nor of indemonstrable knowledge, which is the grasping of the immediate premiss. Since then rational intuition, science, and opinion, and what is revealed by these terms, are the only things that can be 'true', it follows that it is *opinion* that is concerned with that which may be true or false, and can be otherwise: opinion in fact is the grasp of a premiss which is immediate but not necessary. This view also fits the observed facts, for opinion is unstable, and so is the kind of being we have described as its object. Besides, when a man thinks a truth incapable of being otherwise he always thinks that he knows it, never that he opines it. He thinks that he opines when he thinks that a connexion, though actually so, may quite easily be otherwise; for he believes that such is the proper object of opinion, while the necessary is the object of knowledge.

In what sense, then, can the same thing be the object of both opinion and knowledge? And if any one chooses to maintain that all that he knows he can also opine, why should not opinion be knowledge? For he that knows and he that opines will follow the same train of thought through the same middle terms until the immediate premisses are reached; because it is possible to opine not only the fact but also the reasoned fact, and the reason is the middle term; so that, since the former knows, he that opines also has knowledge.

The truth perhaps is that if a man grasp truths that cannot be other than they are, in the way in which he grasps the definitions through which demonstra-

tions take place, he will have not opinion but knowledge: if on the other hand he apprehends these attributes as inhering in their subjects, but not in virtue of the subjects' substance and essential nature, he possesses opinion and not genuine knowledge; and his opinion, if obtained through immediate premisses, will be both of the fact and of the reasoned fact; if not so obtained, of the fact alone. The object of opinion and knowledge is not quite identical; it is only in a sense identical, just as the object of true and false opinion is in a sense identical. The sense in which some maintain that true and false opinion can have the same object leads them to embrace many strange doctrines, particularly the doctrine that what a man opines falsely he does not opine at all. There are really many senses of 'identical', and in one sense the object of true and false opinion can be the same, in another it cannot. Thus, to have a true opinion that the diagonal is commensurate with the side would be absurd: but because the diagonal with which they are both concerned is the same, the two opinions have objects so far the same: on the other hand, as regards their essential definable nature these objects differ. The identity of the objects of knowledge and opinion is similar. Knowledge is the apprehension of, e.g., the attribute 'animal' as incapable of being otherwise, opinion the apprehension of 'animal' as capable of being otherwise—e.g. the apprehension that animal is an element in the essential nature of man is knowledge; the apprehension of animal as predicable of man but not as an element in man's essential nature is opinion: man is the subject in both judgments, but the mode of inherence differs.

This also shows that one cannot opine and know the same thing simultaneously; for then one would apprehend the same thing as both capable and incapable of being otherwise—an impossibility.

Knowledge and opinion of the same thing can coexist in two different people in the sense we have explained, but not simultaneously in the same person. That would involve a man's simultaneously apprehending, e. g., (1) that man is essentially animal—i. e. cannot be other than animal—and (2) that man is not essentially animal, that is, we may assume, may be other than animal.

Further consideration of modes of thinking and their distribution under the heads of discursive thought, intuition, science, art, practical wisdom, and metaphysical thinking, belongs rather partly to natural science, partly to moral philosophy.

. . .

As regards syllogism and demonstration, the definition of, and the conditions required to produce each of them, are now clear, and with that also the definition of, and the conditions required to produce, demonstrative knowledge, since it is the same as demonstration. As to the basic premises, how they become known and what is the developed state of knowledge of them is made clear by raising some preliminary problems.

We have already said that scientific knowledge through demonstration is impossible unless a man knows the primary immediate premises. But there are questions which might be raised in respect of the apprehension of these immediate premises: one might not only ask whether it is of the same kind as the apprehension of the conclusions, but also whether there is or is not scientific knowledge of both; or scientific knowledge of the latter, and of the former a different kind of knowledge; and, further, whether the developed states of knowledge are not innate but come to be in us, or are innate but at first unnoticed. Now it is strange if we possess them from birth; for it means that we possess apprehensions more ac-

curate than demonstration and fail to notice them. If on the other hand we acquire them and do not previously possess them, how could we apprehend and learn without a basis of pre-existent knowledge? For that is impossible, as we used to find in the case of demonstration. So it emerges that neither can we possess them from birth, nor can they come to be in us if we are without knowledge of them to the extent of having no such developed state at all. Therefore we must possess a capacity of some sort, but not such as to rank higher in accuracy than these developed states. And this at least is an obvious characteristic of all animals, for they possess a congenital discriminative capacity which is called sense-perception. But though sense-perception is innate in all animals, in some the sense-impression comes to persist, in others it does not. So animals in which this persistence does not come to be have either no knowledge at all outside the act of perceiving, or no knowledge of objects of which no impression persists; animals in which it does come into being have perception and can continue to retain the sense-impression in the soul: and when such persistence is frequently repeated a further distinction at once arises between those which out of the persistence of such sense-impressions develop a power of systematizing them and those which do not. So out of sense-perception comes to be what we call memory, and out of frequently repeated memories of the same thing develops experience; for a number of memories constitute a single experience. From experience again—i.e. from the universal now stabilized in its entirety within the soul, the one beside the many which is a single identity within them all—originate the skill of the craftsman and the knowledge of the man of science, skill in the sphere of coming to be and science in the sphere of being.

We conclude that these states of knowledge are neither innate in a determinate form, nor developed from other higher states of knowledge, but from sense-perception. It is like a rout in battle stopped by first one man making a stand and then another, until the original formation has been restored. The soul is so constituted as to be capable of this process.

Let us now restate the account given already, though with insufficient clearness. When one of a number of logically indiscriminable particulars has made a stand, the earliest universal is present in the soul, for though the act of sense-perception is of the particular, its content is universal—is man, for example, not the man Callias. A fresh stand is made among these rudimentary universals, and the process does not cease until the indivisible concepts, the true universals,[6] are established: e.g. such and such a species of animal is a step towards the genus animal, which by the same process is a step towards a further generalization.

Thus it is clear that we must get to know the primary premisses by induction; for the method by which even sense-per-

ception implants the universal is inductive. Now of the thinking states by which we grasp truth, some are unfailingly true, others admit of error—opinion, for instance, and calculation, whereas scientific knowing and intuition are always true: further, no other kind of thought except intuition is more accurate than scientific knowledge, whereas primary premisses are more knowable than demonstrations, and all scientific knowledge is discursive. From these considerations it follows that there will be no scientific knowledge of the primary premisses, and since except intuition nothing can be truer than scientific knowledge, it will be intuition that apprehends the primary premisses—a result which also follows from the fact that demonstration cannot be the originative source of demonstration, nor, consequently, scientific knowledge of scientific knowledge. If, therefore, it is the only other kind of true thinking except scientific knowing, intuition will be the originative source of scientific knowledge. And the originative source of science grasps the original basic premiss, while science as a whole is similarly related as originative source to the whole body of fact.[7]

[6] i.e. the categories, which are *par excellence* universal and are indivisible because not constituted of genus and differentia.

[7] i.e. the conclusions.

A MEDIEVAL ADVOCATE OF

EXPERIMENTAL SCIENCE*

ROGER BACON (c. 1214–c. 1292)   was an English Franciscan Friar who taught
at both Oxford and Paris. He wrote knowledgeably on mathematics,
optics, geography, astronomy, alchemy, and philology. Bacon seems
not to have contributed greatly to any of these fields himself, but was a
powerful advocate of the experimental method of inquiry.

Having laid down the roots of the
wisdom of the latins so far as they are
found in languages and mathematics
and perspective, I wish now to take up
the roots of experimental science, because without experience nothing can be
known sufficiently. There are, in fact,
two ways of knowing, namely, by argumentation and experience. Argumentation concludes and makes us grant the
conclusion, but does not make certain
nor remove doubt that the mind may
be quiet in the contemplation of truth,
unless if finds truth by the way of experience; many, because they have arguments for the knowable but do not have
experience, neglect the arguments and
neither avoid the hurtful nor follow the
good. For if a man who has never seen
fire should prove by sufficient argument
that fire burns and that it injures things
and destroys them, the mind of one hearing it would never be satisfied by that nor
would a hearer avoid fire until he had
put a hand or a combustible object into

the fire that he might prove by experience what argument had taught. But
once he has had experience of combus-
tion, his mind is made sure and rests in
the brightness of truth. Therefore, argumentation does not suffice but experience
does.

This is evident too in mathematics,
where demonstration is most convincing.
But the mind of one who has a most
convincing demonstration of the equilateral triangle will never adhere to the
conclusion without experience nor will
such an one trouble about it, but will
neglect it until experience is offered him
by the intersection of two circles, from
the intersection of which are drawn two
lines to the extremities of the given line;
but then the man accepts the conclusion
with full repose. What Aristotle says
therefore to the effect that the demonstration is a syllogism that makes us
know, is to be understood if the experience of it accompanies the demonstration, and it is not to be understood of

* Extracts from *Selections from Medieval Philosophers*, Volumes I and II, edited by
Richard McKeon, are used by permission of Charles Scribner's Sons. Copyright 1929
Charles Scribner's Sons; renewal copyright © 1957.

the bare demonstration. What he says, likewise, in the first book of the Metaphysics, that those who have the reason and the cause are wiser than those who are experienced, is said of experienced men who know only the bare truth without the cause. But I speak here of the man of experience who knows the reason and cause by experience. These men are perfect in wisdom, as Aristotle holds in the sixth book of the Ethics, and their simple statements must be believed as if they offered demonstration, as he states in the same place.

He, therefore, who wishes to enjoy without doubt the truths of things, should know how to devote his time to experiment; this is evident in examples. For authors write of and the people maintain many doctrines by arguments which they fashion without experiment and which are wholly false. For it is commonly believed that the diamond can not be broken except by goat's blood, and philosophers and theologians misuse this opinion. But no certainty has been arrived at yet concerning fraction by blood of this sort although an attempt has been made at it; and without goat's blood the diamond can be broken easily. For I have seen it with my own eyes; and it is necessary, because gems can not be carved except with fragments of this stone. In the same way, it is held generally that the follicles [of beavers], which physicians use, are the testicles of the male animal. But that is not true because the beaver has them under its breast, and both the male and the female produce testicles of this sort. And besides these follicles the male has his proper testicles in their natural place; and therefore, what is added to this is a horrible lie, namely, that when hunters are tracking the beaver, he, knowing what they seek, tears off the follicles with his teeth. Moreover, it has come to be held generally that hot water congeals in vessels

more quickly than cold, and it is argued as basis for this that contrary is excited by contrary, as enemies resist each other. But it is certain that cold water congeals more quickly, to any one who makes the experiment. People read this into Aristotle in the second book of the Meteorologics but he certainly does not say that, but he does affirm something like it, by which they have been deceived, namely, that if cold and hot water be poured into a cold place, as upon ice, the hot water is congealed more quickly, and this is true. But if cold and hot water be placed in two vessels, the cold will be congealed more quickly. It is necessary, therefore, that all things be certified by the way of experience.

But experience is double: one is by means of the exterior senses, and such are those experiences which show things that are in the heavens through instruments made for these experiments and those things that we find below by visual ascertainments. We know things which are not present in the places in which we are, through other wise men who have experienced them. Just as Aristotle sent, by the authority of Alexander, two thousand men to various places of the world to learn of all things which are on the surface of the earth, as Pliny testifies in the Natural History. This experience is human and philosophical, as much as man can do in accordance with the grace given him; but this experience does not suffice man, in that it does not certify fully concerning corporeal things because of its difficulty, and it touches on nothing at all of spiritual things. Therefore, it is necessary that the understanding of man be aided otherwise, and therefore the holy patriarchs and prophets, who first gave the sciences to the world, received interior illuminations and were not dependent only on sense. In the same way in the case of many of the faithful since the time of Christ. For the grace of faith illumines greatly and divine inspirations likewise, not only in spiritual but in corporeal things and in the sciences of philosophy, according to what Ptolemy says in the Centilogium, that the way to come to a knowledge of things is twofold, one by the experience of philosophy, the other by divine inspiration, which is far the better, as he says.

There are seven grades of this interior knowledge. The first by purely scientific illuminations. The second grade consists in the virtues. For the evil man is ignorant, as Aristotle says in the second book of the Ethics. And Algazeli says in his Logic that the soul which is cast down by sins is like a rusty mirror, in which the species of things can not be seen well; but the soul adorned with virtues is like a well-polished mirror, in which the forms of things are clearly seen. For this reason true philosophers have labored the more in morals for the integrity of virtue, concluding among themselves that they can not see the causes of things unless they have souls free from sins. Saint Augustine recounts this of Socrates in the eighth book of the City of God in the third chapter. For this reason the Scripture says, *Wisdom will not enter into an ill-disposed soul*. For it is impossible that the soul repose in the light of truth while it is stained with sins, but it will recite like a parrot or a magpie the words of another which it learned by long practice. And the test of this is that beauty of a cognized truth attracts men by its refulgence to love it, but the proof of love is the exhibition of work. And, therefore, he who acts contrary to the truth, must necessarily be ignorant of it, although he may know how to put together very elegant phrases and to quote the opinions of others, like a brute animal that imitates human voices or like a monkey who attempts to perform the actions of men, although it does not understand the reason of them. Vir-

tue, therefore, clarifies the mind that man may understand more easily not only moral things, but scientific things. And I have tested this carefully in many fine youths, who because of innocence of soul advanced to greater knowledge than can be stated when they have had sound counsel on their study. Of this number is the bearer of the present writings, whose foundations very few of the latins acquire. Since, indeed, he is very young, that is, about twenty years of age, and extremely poor, he could not have masters, nor has he devoted the time of one year to learning the great things which he knows, nor is he of great genius or of great memory, so that there can be no other cause than the grace of God which gave him, because of the purity of his soul, that which it has refused to give to almost all students. For he has gone from me an uncorrupted virgin nor have I been able to find in him any kind of mortal sin although I have searched out carefully, and therefore he has a soul so clear and perspicuous that he learned with little instruction more than can be judged. And I have done what I could to bring about that these two youths should be useful vessels in the Church of God to the end that they may rectify by the grace of God all the studies of the latins.

The third step consists in the seven gifts of the Holy Spirit which Isaiah enumerates. The fourth consists in the beatitudes, which the Lord defines in the Gospels. The fifth consists in the spiritual senses. The sixth is in fruits among which is the peace of the Lord which exceeds all understanding. The seventh consists in raptures [*raptus*] and the modes of them, according to which different men are seized differently to see many things of which it is not given to man to speak. And he who is carefully disciplined in these experiences or in several of them, can assure himself and others not only as regards spiritual things but as regards all human sciences. Therefore, since all parts of speculative philosophy proceed by arguments which are based either on grounds of authority or on other grounds of argumentation, except this part which I am now investigating, that science is necessary to us which is called experimental. And I want to explain it, as it is useful not only to philosophy but to the wisdom of God and to the guidance of the whole world, as I have shown in the case of languages and sciences above in relation to their end, which is divine wisdom by which all things are disposed.

· · ·

And because this Experimental Science is wholly ignored by the general run of students, for that reason I can not convince people of its utility unless I show at the same time its excellence and its property. This science alone, then, knows how to test perfectly by experience what can be done by nature, what by the industry of art, what by imposture; what the incantations, conjurations, invocations, deprecations, sacrifices (which are magical devices) seek and dream of; and what is done in them, so that all falsity may be removed and that only the truth of art and nature be retained. This science alone teaches one to consider all the insanities of magicians, not that they may be confirmed but that they may be avoided, just as logic considers sophistical argument.

This experimental science has three great prerogatives with respect to the other sciences. The first is that it investigates by experiment the noble conclusions of all of the sciences. For the other sciences know how to discover their principles by experiments, but their conclusions are reached by arguments based on the discovered principles. But if they must have particular and complete experience of their conclusions,

then it is necessary that they have it by the aid of this noble science. It is true, indeed, that mathematics has universal experiences concerning its conclusions in figuring and numbering, which are applied likewise to all the sciences and to this experimental science, because no science can be known without mathematics. But if we turn our attention to the experiences which are particular and complete and certified wholly in their own discipline, it is necessary to go by way of the considerations of this science which is called experimental autonymically. I use the example of the rainbow and of the phenomena connected with it, of which sort are the circle around the sun and the stars, likewise the rod [*virga*] lying at the side of the sun or of a star which appears to the eye in a straight line and is called by Aristotle, in the third book of the Meteorologics, the perpendicular, but is called the rod by Seneca, and the circle is called the corona, which often has the colors of the rainbow. The natural philosopher, to be sure, holds discussions concerning these things and the perspectivist has many things to add which pertain to the mode of seeing, which is very necessary in this case. But neither Aristotle nor Avicenna, in their Natural Histories, has given us knowledge of things of this sort, nor has Seneca, who composed a special book on them. But Experimental Science makes certain of them.

The experimenter, then, should first examine visible things to discover colors ordered as in the above mentioned things and in the same figure. Let him, indeed, take the hexagonal stones of Ireland or India, which are called iris stones in Solinus on the Wonders of the World, and let him hold them in the solar ray falling through a window so that he may find in the shadow near the ray all the colors of the rainbow and ordered as in it. And further let the same experimenter betake himself to any shady place, and let him place the stone to his eye, almost closed, and he will see the colors of the rainbow clearly ordered as in the rainbow. And since many who use these stones think that it is because of a special virtue of the stones and because of their hexagonal figure, for that reason let the same experimenter proceed further and he will find this property in crystalline stones which are properly shaped and in other clear stones. Moreover not only in white stones like the irish, but in black stones, as is evident in the dark crystal and in all stones of similar transparency. He will find it, too, in another figure than the hexagonal, provided the surfaces are corrugated like the irish stone and neither altogether polished nor more rough than they are, and provided they are such property of surface as nature produces in the irish. For the diversity of wrinkles produces a diversity of colors. And after that, [the experimenter] considers rowers and he finds the same colors in the falling drops dripping from the raised oars when the solar rays penetrate drops of this sort. It is the same with waters falling from the wheels of a mill; and when a man sees the drops of dew in summer of a morning lying on the grass in the meadow or the field, he will see the colors. And in the same way when it rains, if he stands in a shady place and if the rays beyond it pass through dripping moisture, then the colors will appear in the shadow nearby; and very frequently of a night colors appear around the wax-candle. Moreover, if a man in summer, when he rises from sleep and while his eyes are yet only partly opened, looks suddenly toward an aperture through which a ray of the sun enters, he will see colors. And if, while seated beyond the sun, he extend his hat before his eyes, he will see colors; and in the same way if he closes his eye, the same thing happens under the shade of the eyebrow; and again, the same phenomenon occurs through a glass vessel filled with water, placed in the rays of the sun. Or similarly if any one holding water in his mouth sprinkles it vigorously into the rays and stands to the side of the rays; and if rays in the proper position pass through an oil lamp hanging in the air, so that the light falls on the surface of the oil, colors will be produced. And so in an infinite number of ways, as well natural as artificial, colors of this sort appear, as the careful experimenter is able to discover. . . .

AN IMPROVED METHOD OF INDUCTION*

FRANCIS BACON (1561–1626). See page 25.

FROM BOOK I

CV

In establishing axioms, another form of induction must be devised than has hitherto been employed; and it must be used for proving and discovering not first principles (as they are called) only, but also the lesser axioms, and the middle, and indeed all. For the induction which proceeds by simple enumeration is childish; its conclusions are precarious, and exposed to peril from a contradictory instance; and it generally decides on too small a number of facts, and on those only which are at hand. But the induction which is to be available for the discovery and demonstration of sciences and arts, must analyze nature by proper rejections and exclusions; and then, after a sufficient number of negatives, come to a conclusion on the affirmative instances: which has not yet been done or even attempted, save only by Plato, who does indeed employ this form of induction to a certain extent for the purpose of discussing definitions and ideas. But in order to furnish this induction or demonstration well and duly for its work, very many things are to be provided which no mortal has yet thought of; insomuch that greater labor will have to be spent in it than has hitherto been spent on the syllogism. And this induction must be used not only to discover axioms, but also in the formation of notions. And it is in this induction that our chief hope lies.

. . .

CXXII

It may be thought also a strange and a harsh thing that we should at once and with one blow set aside all sciences and all authors; and that too without calling in any of the ancients to our aid and support, but relying on our own strength.

And I know that if I had chosen to deal less sincerely, I might easily have found authority for my suggestions by referring them either to the old times before the Greeks (when natural science was perhaps more flourishing, though it made less noise, not having yet passed into the pipes and trumpets of the Greeks), or even, in part at least, to some of the Greeks themselves; and so gained for them both support and honor; as men of no family devise for them-

* From Francis Bacon, *Novum Organum* (1620).

248

selves by the good help of genealogies the nobility of a descent from some ancient stock. But for my part, relying on the evidence and truth of things, I reject all forms of fiction and imposture; nor do I think that it matters any more to the business in hand, whether the discoveries that shall now be made were long ago known to the ancients, and have their settings and their risings according to the vicissitude of things and course of ages, than it matters to mankind whether the new world be that island of Atlantis with which the ancients were acquainted, or now discovered for the first time. For new discoveries must be sought from the light of nature, not fetched back out of the darkness of antiquity.

And as for the universality of the censure, certainly if the matter be truly considered, such a censure is not only more probable but more modest too, than a partial one would be. For if the errors had not been rooted in primary notions, there must have been some true discoveries to correct the false. But the errors being fundamental, and not so much of false judgment as of inattention and oversight, it is no wonder that men have not obtained what they have not tried for, nor reached a mark which they never set up, nor finished a course which they never entered on or kept.

And as for the presumption implied in it; certainly if a man undertakes by steadiness of hand and power of eye to describe a straighter line or more perfect circle than anyone else, he challenges a comparison of abilities; but if he only says that he with the help of a rule or a pair of compasses can draw a straighter line or a more perfect circle than anyone else can by eye and hand alone, he makes no great boast. And this remark, be it observed, applies not merely to this first and inceptive attempt of mine, but to all that shall take the work

in hand hereafter. For my way of discovering sciences goes far to level men's wits, and leaves but little to individual excellence; because it performs everything by the surest rules and demonstrations. And therefore I attribute my part in all this, as I have often said, rather to good luck than to ability, and account it a birth of time rather than of wit. For certainly chance has something to do with men's thoughts, as well as with their works and deeds.

• • •

CXXIV

Again, it will be thought, no doubt, that the goal and mark of knowledge which I myself set up (the very point which I object to in others) is not the true or the best; for that the contemplation of truth is a thing worthier and loftier than all utility and magnitude of works; and that this long and anxious dwelling with experience and matter and the fluctuations of individual things, drags down the mind to earth, or rather sinks it to a very Tartarus of turmoil and confusion; removing and withdrawing it from the serene tranquillity of abstract wisdom, a condition far more heavenly. Now to this I readily assent; and indeed this which they point at as so much to be preferred, is the very thing of all others which I am about. For I am building in the human understanding a true model of the world, such as it is in fact, not such as a man's own reason would have it to be; a thing which cannot be done without a very diligent dissection and anatomy of the world. But I say that those foolish and apish images of worlds which the fancies of men have created in philosophical systems, must be utterly scattered to the winds. Be it known then how vast a difference there is (as I said above) between the idols of the human mind and the ideas of the divine. The former are nothing more than arbitrary abstractions; the latter are the creator's own stamp upon creation, impressed and defined in matter by true and exquisite lines. Truth therefore and utility are here the very same things: and works themselves are of greater value as pledges of truth than as contributing to the comforts of life.

. . .

CXXX

And now it is time for me to propound the art itself of interpreting nature; in which, although I conceive that I have given true and most useful precepts, yet I do not say either that it is absolutely necessary (as if nothing could be done without it) or that it is perfect. For I am of opinion that if men had ready at hand a just history of nature and experience, and labored diligently thereon; and if they could bind themselves to two rules,—the first, to lay aside received opinions and notions; and the second, to refrain the mind for a time from the highest generalizations, and those next to them,—they would be able by the native and genuine force of the mind, without any other art, to fall into my form of interpretation. For interpretation is the true and natural work of the mind when freed from impediments. It is true however that by my precepts everything will be in more readiness, and much more sure.

Nor again do I mean to say that no improvement can be made upon these. On the contrary, I that regard the mind not only in its own faculties but in its connection with things, must needs hold that the art of discovery may advance as discoveries advance.

. . .

FROM BOOK II

X

Having thus set up the mark of knowledge, we must go on to precepts, and that in the most direct and obvious order. Now my directions for the interpretation of nature embrace two generic divisions: the one how to educe and form axioms from experience; the other how to deduce and derive new experiments from axioms. The former again is divided into three ministrations: a ministration to the sense, a ministration to the memory, and a ministration to the mind or reason.

For first of all we must prepare a *Natural and Experimental History,* sufficient and good; and this is the foundation of all; for we are not to imagine or suppose, but to discover, what nature does or may be made to do.

But natural and experimental history is so various and diffuse, that it confounds and distracts the understanding, unless it be ranged and presented to view in a suitable order. We must therefore form *Tables and Arrangements of Instances,* in such a method and order that the understanding may be able to deal with them.

And even when this is done, still the understanding, if left to itself and its own spontaneous movements, is incompetent and unfit to form axioms, unless it be directed and guarded. Therefore in the third place we must use *Induction,* true and legitimate induction, which is the very key of interpretation. But of this, which is the last, I must speak first, and then go back to the other ministrations.

XI

The investigation of Forms proceeds thus: a nature being given, we must first of all have a muster or presentation before the understanding of all known instances which agree in the same nature, though in substances the most unlike. And such collection must be made in the manner of a history, without premature speculation, or any great amount of subtlety. For example, let the investigation be into the Form of heat.

Instances Agreeing in the Nature of Heat

1. The rays of the sun, especially in summer and at noon.

2. The rays of the sun reflected and condensed, as between mountains, or on walls, and most of all in burning-glasses and mirrors.

3. Fiery meteors.

4. Burning thunderbolts.

5. Eruptions of flame from the cavities of mountains.

6. All flame.

7. Ignited solids.

8. Natural warm-baths.

9. Liquids boiling or heated.

10. Hot vapors and fumes, and the air itself, which conceives the most powerful and glowing heat, if confined; as in reverbatory furnaces.

11. Certain seasons that are fine and cloudless by the constitution of the air itself, without regard to the time of year.

12. Air confined and underground in some caverns, especially in winter.

13. All villous substances, as wool, skins of animals, and down of birds, have heat.

14. All bodies, whether solid or liquid, whether dense or rare (as the air itself is), held for a time near the fire.

15. Sparks struck from flint and steel by strong percussion.

16. All bodies rubbed violently, as stone, wood, cloth, &c., insomuch that poles and axles of wheels sometimes catch fire; and the way they kindled fire in the West Indies was by attrition.

17. Green and moist vegetables confined and bruised together, as roses packed in baskets; insomuch that hay, if damp when stacked, often catches fire.

18. Quick lime sprinkled with water.

19. Iron, when first dissolved by strong waters in glass, and that without being put near the fire. And in like manner tin, &c., but not with equal intensity.

20. Animals, especially and at all times internally; though in insects the heat is not perceptible to the touch by reason of the smallness of their size.

21. Horse-dung and like excrements of animals when fresh.

22. Strong oil of sulphur and of vitriol has the effect of heat in burning linen.

23. Oil of marjoram and similar oils have the effect of heat in burning the bones of the teeth.

24. Strong and well rectified spirit of wine has the effect of heat; insomuch that the white of an egg being put into it hardens and whitens almost as if it were boiled; and bread thrown in becomes dry and crusted like toast.

25. Aromatic and hot herbs, as *dracunculus, nasturtium vetus,* &c., although not warm to the hand (either whole or in powder), yet to the tongue and palate, being a little masticated, they feel hot and burning.

26. Strong vinegar, and all acids, on all parts of the body where there is no epidermis, as the eye, tongue, or on any part when wounded and laid bare of the skin; produce a pain but little differing from that which is created by heat.

27. Even keen and intense cold produces a kind of sensation of burning;

Nec Borae pentrabile frigus adurit.[1]

28. Other instances.

This table I call the *Table of Essence and Presence.*

[1] Nor burns the sharp cold of the northern blast.

XII

Secondly, we must make a presentation to the understanding of instances in which the given nature is wanting; because the Form, as stated above, ought no less to be absent when the given nature is absent, than present when it is present. But to note all these would be endless.

The negatives should therefore be subjoined to the affirmatives, and the absence of the given nature inquired of in those subjects only that are most akin to the others in which it is present and forthcoming. This I call the *Table of Deviation, or of Absence in Proximity*.

Instances in Proximity Where the Nature of Heat Is Absent

1. The rays of the moon and of stars and comets are not found to be hot to the touch; indeed the severest colds are observed to be at the full moons.

The larger fixed stars however, when passed or approached by the sun, are supposed to increase and give intensity to the heat of the sun; as is the case when the sun is in the sign Leo, and in the Dog-days.

2. The rays of the sun in what is called the middle region of the air do not give heat; for which there is commonly assigned not a bad reason, viz. that that region is neither near enough to the body of the sun from which the rays emanate, nor to the earth from which they are reflected. And this appears from the fact that on the tops of mountains, unless they are very high, there is perpetual snow. On the other hand it has been observed that on the peak of Teneriffe, and among the Andes of Peru, the very tops of the mountains are free from snow; which lies only somewhat lower down. Moreover the air itself at the very top is found to be by

no means cold, but only rare and keen; insomuch that on the Andes it pricks and hurts the eyes by its excessive keenness, and also irritates the mouth of the stomach, producing vomiting.

. . .

5. Let the experiment be carefully tried, whether by means of the most powerful and best constructed burning-glasses, the rays of the moon can be so caught and collected as to produce even the least degree of warmth. But should this degree of warmth prove too subtle and weak to be perceived and apprehended by the touch, recourse must be had to those glasses which indicate the state of the atmosphere in respect of heat and cold. Thus, let the rays of the moon fall through a burning-glass on the top of a glass of this kind, and then observe whether there ensues a sinking of the water through warmth.

6. Let a burning-glass also be tried with a heat that does not emit rays or light, as that of iron or stone heated but not ignited, boiling water, and the like; and observe whether there ensue an increase of the heat, as in the case of the sun's rays.

7. Let a burning-glass also be tried with common flame.

. . .

31. There is an acridity or pungency both in cold things, as vinegar and oil of vitriol, and in hot, as oil of marjoram and the like. Both alike therefore cause pain in animate substances, and tear asunder and consume the parts in such as are inanimate. To this Instance again there is no Negative subjoined. Moreover we find no pain in animals, save with a certain sensation of heat.

32. There are many actions common both to heat and cold, though in a very different manner. For boys find that snow after a while seems to burn their

hands; and cold preserves meat from putrefaction, no less than fire; and heat contracts bodies, which cold does also. But these and similar instances may more conveniently be referred to the inquiry concerning Cold.

XIII

Thirdly, we must make a presentation to the understanding of instances in which the nature under inquiry is found in different degrees, more or less; which must be done by making a comparison either of its increase and decrease in the same subject, or of its amount in different subjects, as compared one with another. For since the Form of a thing is the very thing itself, and the thing differs from the form no otherwise than as the apparent differs from the real, or the external from the internal, or the thing in reference to man from the thing in reference to the universe; it necessarily follows that no nature can be taken as the true form, unless it always decrease when the nature in question decreases, and in like manner always increase when the nature in question increases. This Table therefore I call the *Table of Degrees* or the *Table of Comparison*.

Table of Degrees or Comparison in Heat

I will therefore first speak of those substances which contain no degree at all of heat perceptible to the touch, but seem to have a certain potential heat only, or disposition and preparation for hotness. After that I shall proceed to substances which are hot actually, and to the touch, and to their intensities and degrees.

1. In solid and tangible bodies we find nothing which is in its nature originally hot. For no stone, metal, sulphur, fossil, wood, water, or carcass of animal is found to be hot. And the hot water in baths seems to be heated by external causes; whether it be by flame or subterraneous fire, such as is thrown up from Aetna and many other mountains, or by the conflict of bodies, as heat is caused in the dissolutions of iron and tin. There is therefore no degree of heat palpable to the touch in animate substances; but they differ in degree of cold, wood not being equally cold with metal. But this belongs to the Table of Degrees in Cold.

2. As far however as potential heat and aptitude for flame is concerned, there are many inanimate substances found strongly disposed thereto, as sulphur, naphtha, rock oil.

3. Substances once hot, as horse-dung from animal heat, and lime or perhaps ashes and soot from fire, retain some latent remains of their former heat. Hence certain distillations and resolutions of bodies are made by burying them in horse-dung, and heat is excited in lime by sprinkling it with water, as already mentioned.

4. In the vegetable creation we find no plant or part of plant (as gum or pitch) which is warm to the human touch. But yet, as stated above, green herbs gain warmth by being shut up; and to the internal touch, as the palate or stomach, and even to external parts, after a little time, as in plasters and ointments, some vegetables are perceptibly warm and others cold.

. . .

40. The less the mass of a body, the sooner is it heated by the approach of a hot body; which shows that all heat of which we have experience is in some sort opposed to tangible matter.

41. Heat, as far as regards the sense and touch of man, is a thing various and relative; insomuch that tepid water

feels hot if the hand be cold, but cold if the hand be hot.

XIV

How poor we are in history anyone may see from the foregoing tables; where I not only insert sometimes mere traditions and reports (though never without a note of doubtful credit and authority) in place of history proved and instances certain, but am also frequently forced to use the words "Let trial be made," or "Let it be further inquired."

XV

The work and office of these three tables I call the Presentation of Instances to the Understanding. Which presentation having been made, Induction itself must be set at work; for the problem is, upon a review of the instances, all and each, to find such a nature as is always present or absent with the given nature, and always increases and decreases with it; and which is, as I have said, a particular case of a more general nature. Now if the mind attempt this affirmatively from the first, as when left to itself it is always wont to do, the result will be fancies and guesses and notions ill defined and axioms that must be mended every day; unless like the schoolmen we have a mind to fight for what is false; though doubtless these will be better or worse according to the faculties and strength of the understanding which is at work. To God, truly, the Giver and Architect of Forms, and it may be to the angels and higher intelligences, it belongs to have an affirmative knowledge of Forms immediately, and from the first contemplation. But this assuredly is more than man can do, to whom it is granted only to proceed at first by negatives, and at last to end in affirmatives, after exclusion has been exhausted.

XVI

We must make therefore a complete solution and separation of nature, not indeed by fire, but by the mind, which is a kind of divine fire. The first work therefore of true induction (as far as regards the discovery of Forms) is the rejection or exclusion of the several natures which are not found in some instance where the given nature is present, or are found in some instance where the given nature is absent, or are found to increase in some instance when the given nature decreases, or to decrease when the given nature increases. Then indeed after the rejection and exclusion has been duly made, there will remain at the bottom, all light opinions vanishing into smoke, a Form affirmative, solid and true and well defined. This is quickly said; but the way to come at it is winding and intricate. I will endeavor however not to overlook any of the points which may help us towards it.

XVII

But when I assign so prominent a part to Forms, I cannot too often warn and admonish men against applying what I say to those forms to which their thoughts and contemplations have hitherto been accustomed.

For in the first place I do not at present speak of Compound Forms, which are, as I have remarked, combinations of simple natures according to the common course of the universe; as of the lion, eagle, rose, gold, and the like. It will be time to treat of these when we come to the Latent Processes and Latent Configurations, and the discovery of them, as they are found in what are called substances or natures concrete.

And even in the case of simple natures I would not be understood to speak of abstract Forms and Ideas, either not defined in matter at all, or ill defined. For when I speak of Forms, I mean nothing more than those laws and determinations of absolute actuality, which govern and constitute any simple nature, as heat, light, weight, in every kind of matter and subject that is susceptible of them. Thus the Form of heat or the Form of light is the same thing as the Law of heat or the Law of light. Nor indeed do I ever allow myself to be drawn away from things themselves and the operative part. And therefore when I say (for instance) in the investigation of the Form of heat, "Reject rarity," or "Rarity does not belong to the form of heat;" it is the same as if I said, "It is possible to superinduce heat on a dense body," or "It is possible to take away or keep out heat from a rare body."

But if anyone conceive that my Forms too are of a somewhat abstract nature, because they mix and combine things heterogeneous (for the heat of heavenly bodies and the heat of fire seem to be very heterogeneous; so do the fixed red of the rose or the like, and the apparent red in the rainbow, the opal, or the diamond; so again do the different kinds of death, death by drowning, by hanging, by stabbing, by apoplexy, by atrophy; and yet they agree severally in the nature of heat, redness, death); if anyone, I say, be of this opinion, he may be assured that his mind is held in captivity by custom, by the gross appearance of things, and by men's opinions. For it is most certain that these things, however heterogeneous and alien from each other, agree in the Form or Law which governs heat, redness and death; and that the power of man cannot possibly be emancipated and freed from the common course of nature, and expanded and exalted to new efficients and new modes of operation, except by the revelation and discovery of Forms of

this kind. And yet, when I have spoken of this union of nature, which is the point of most importance, I shall proceed to the divisions and veins of nature, as well the ordinary as those that are more inward and exact, and speak of them in their place.

xviii

I must now give an example of the Exclusion or Rejection of natures which by the Tables of Presentation are found not to belong to the Form of heat; observing in the meantime that not only each table suffices for the rejection of any nature, but even any one of the particular instances contained in any of the tables. For it is manifest from what has been said that any one contradictory instance overthrows a conjecture as to the Form. But nevertheless for clearness' sake and that the use of the tables may be more plainly shown, I sometimes double or multiply an exclusion.

An Example of Exclusion, or Rejection of Natures from the Form of Heat

1. On account of the rays of the sun, reject the nature of the elements.

2. On account of common fire, and chiefly subterraneous fires (which are the most remote and most completely separate from the rays of heavenly bodies), reject the nature of heavenly bodies.

3. On account of the warmth acquired by all kinds of bodies (minerals, vegetables, skin of animals, water, oil, air, and the rest) by mere approach to a fire, or other hot body, reject the distinctive or more subtle texture of bodies.

4. On account of ignited iron and other metals, which communicate heat to other bodies and yet lose none of their weight or substance, reject the com-

munication or admixture of the substance of another hot body.

5. On account of boiling water and air, and also on account of metals and other solids that receive heat but not to ignition or red heat, reject light or brightness.

6. On account of the rays of the moon and other heavenly bodies, with the exception of the sun, also reject light and brightness.

. . .

14. On account of heat being kindled by the attrition of bodies, reject a principial nature. By principial nature I mean that which exists in the nature of things positively, and not as the effect of any antecedent nature.

There are other natures beside these; for these tables are not perfect, but meant only for examples.

All and each of the above mentioned natures do *not* belong to the Form of heat. And from all of them man is freed in his operations on heat.

xix

In the process of Exclusion are laid the foundations of true Induction, which however is not completed till it arrives at an Affirmative. Nor is the Exclusive part itself at all complete, nor indeed can it possibly be so at first. For Exclusion is evidently the rejection of simple natures; and if we do not yet possess sound and true notions of simple natures, how can the process of Exclusion be made accurate? Now some of the above-mentioned notions (as that of the nature of the elements, of the nature of heavenly bodies, of rarity) are vague and ill-defined. I therefore, well knowing and nowise forgetting how great a work I am about (viz., that of rendering the human understanding a match for things and nature), do not rest satisfied with the precepts I have laid down; but pro-

ceed further to devise and supply more powerful aids for the use of the understanding; which I shall now subjoin. And assuredly in the Interpretation of Nature the mind should by all means be so prepared and disposed, that while it rests and finds footing in due stages and degrees of certainty, it may remember withal (especially at the beginning) that what it has before it depends in great measure upon what remains behind.

xx

And yet since truth will sooner come out from error than from confusion, I think it expedient that the understanding should have permission, after the three Tables of First Presentation (such as I have exhibited) have been made and weighed, to make an essay of the Interpretation of Nature in the affirmative way; on the strength both of the instances given in the tables, and of any others it may meet with elsewhere. Which kind of essay I call the *indulgence of the understanding,* or the *commencement of interpretation,* or the *First Vintage.*

First Vintage Concerning the Form of Heat

It is to be observed that the Form of a thing is to be found (as plainly appears from what has been said) in each and all the instances, in which the thing itself is to be found; otherwise it would not be the Form. It follows therefore that there can be no contradictory instance. At the same time the Form is found much more conspicuous and evident in some instances than in others; namely in those wherein the nature of the Form is less restrained and obstructed and kept within bounds by other natures. Instances of this kind I call *Shining or Striking Instances.* Let us now therefore proceed to the First Vintage concerning the Form of Heat.

From a survey of the instances, all

and each, the nature of which Heat is a particular case appears to be Motion. This is displayed most conspicuously in flame, which is always in motion, and in boiling or simmering liquids, which also are in perpetual motion. It is also shown in the excitement or increase of heat caused by motion, as in bellows and blasts; on which see Tab. 3. Inst. 29.; and again in other kinds of motion, on which see Tab. 3. Inst. 28. and 31. Again it is shown in the extinction of fire and heat by any strong compression, which checks and stops the motion; on which see Tab. 3. Inst. 30. and 32. It is shown also by this, that all bodies are destroyed, or at any rate notably altered, by all strong and vehement fire and heat; whence it is quite clear that heat causes a tumult and confusion and violent motion in the internal parts of a body, which perceptibly tends to its dissolution.

When I say of Motion that it is as the genus of which heat is a species, I would be understood to mean, not that heat generates motion or that motion generates heat (though both are true in certain cases), but that Heat itself, its essence and quiddity, is Motion and nothing else; limited however by the specific differences which I will presently subjoin, as soon as I have added a few cautions for the sake of avoiding ambiguity.

• • •

Having thus removed all ambiguity, I come at length to the true specific differences which limit Motion and constitute it the Form of Heat.

The first difference then is this. Heat is an expansive motion, whereby a body strives to dilate and stretch itself to a larger sphere or dimension than it had previously occupied. This difference is most observable in flame, where the smoke or thick vapor manifestly dilates and expands itself into flame.

It is shown also in all boiling liquid, which manifestly swells, rises, and bubbles; and carries on the process of self-expansion, till it turns into a body far more extended and dilated than the liquid itself, namely, into vapor, smoke, or air.

It appears likewise in all wood and combustibles, from which there generally arises exudation and always evaporation.

It is shown also in the melting of metals, which, being of the compactest texture, do not readily swell and dilate; but yet their spirit being dilated in itself, and thereupon conceiving an appetite for further dilation, forces and agitates the grosser parts into a liquid state. And if the heat be greatly increased it dissolves and turns much of their substance to a volatile state.

• • •

It is shown also in the opposite nature of cold. For cold contracts all bodies and makes them shrink; insomuch that in intense frosts nails fall out from walls, brazen vessels crack, and heated glass on being suddenly placed in the cold cracks and breaks. . . . But on these points I shall speak more at length in the inquiry concerning Cold.

Nor is it surprising that heat and cold should exhibit many actions in common (for which see Inst. 32. Tab. 2.), when we find two of the following specific differences (of which I shall speak presently) suiting either nature; though in this specific difference (of which I am now speaking) their actions are diametrically opposite. For heat gives an expansive and dilating, cold a contractive and condensing motion.

The second difference is a modification of the former; namely, that heat is a motion expansive or towards the circumference, but with this condition, that the body has at the same time a motion upwards. For there is no doubt that there are many mixed motions. For instance, an arrow or dart turns as it goes forward, and goes forward as it turns. And in like manner the motion of heat is at once a motion of expansion and a motion upwards. This difference is shown by putting a pair of tongs or a poker in the fire. If you put it in perpendicularly and hold it by the top, it soon burns your hand; if at the side or from below, not nearly so soon.

It is also observable in distillations *per descensorium;* which men use for delicate flowers, that soon lose their scent. For human industry has discovered the plan of placing the fire not below but above, that it may burn the less. For not only flame tends upwards, but also all heat.

But let trial be made of this in the opposite nature of cold; viz. whether cold does not contract a body downwards, as heat dilates a body upwards. Take therefore two iron rods, or two glass tubes, exactly alike; warm them a little, and place a sponge steeped in cold water or snow at the bottom of the one, and the same at the top of the other. For I think that the extremities of the rod which has the snow at the top will cool sooner than the extremities of the other which has the snow at the bottom; just as the opposite is the case with heat.

The third specific difference is this; that heat is a motion of expansion, not uniformly of the whole body together, but in the smaller parts of it; and at the same time checked, repelled, and beaten back, so that the body acquires a motion alternative, perpetually quivering, striving and struggling, and irritated by repercussion, whence springs the fury of fire and heat.

. . .

The fourth specific difference is a modification of the last; it is, that the preceding motion of stimulation or penetration must be somewhat rapid and not sluggish, and must proceed by particles, minute indeed, yet not the finest of all, but a degree larger.

This difference is shown by a comparison of the effects of fire with the effects of time or age. Age or time dries, consumes, undermines and reduces to ashes, no less than fire; indeed with an action far more subtle; but because such motion is very sluggish, and acts on particles very small, the heat is not perceived.

It is also shown by comparing the dissolution of iron and gold. Gold is dissolved without any heat being excited, while the dissolution of iron is accompanied by a violent heat, though it takes place in about the same time. The reason is that in gold the separating acid enters gently and works with subtlety, and the parts of the gold yield easily; whereas in iron the entrance is rough and with conflict, and the parts of the iron have greater obstinacy.

It is shown also to some degree in some gangrenes and mortifications, which do not excite great heat or pain on account of the subtle nature of putrefaction.

Let this then be the First Vintage or Commencement of Interpretation concerning the Form of Heat, made by way of indulgence to the understanding.

Now from this our First Vintage it follows that the Form or true definition of heat (heat, that is, in relation to the universe, not simply in relation to man) is in few words as follows: *Heat is a motion, expansive, restrained, and acting in its strife upon the smaller particles of bodies.* But the expansion is thus modified: *while it expands all ways, it has at the same time an inclination upwards.* And the struggle in the particles is modified also: *it is not sluggish, but hurried and with violence.*

THE PROBLEM OF

INDUCTION*

DAVID HUME (1711–1776)   was a British philosopher, historian, and essayist. He made important contributions to the theory of knowledge, to metaphysics, to ethics, and to philosophy of religion. Hume's conclusions tended to be sceptical: the questions and difficulties he raised, in his graceful but closely reasoned writings, have been debated by later philosophers down to the present day.

SECTION IV

Sceptical Doubts Concerning the Operations of the Understanding

Part I

All the objects of human reason or enquiry may naturally be divided into two kinds, to wit, *Relations of Ideas,* and *Matters of Fact.* Of the first kind are the sciences of Geometry, Algebra, and Arithmetic; and in short, every affirmation which is either intuitively or demonstratively certain. *That the square of the hypothenuse is equal to the squares of the two sides,* is a proposition which expresses a relation between these figures. *That three times five is equal to the half of thirty,* expresses a relation between these numbers. Propositions of this kind are discoverable by the mere operation of thought, without dependence on what is anywhere existent in the universe. Though there never were a circle or triangle in nature, the truths demonstrated by Euclid would for ever retain their certainty and evidence.

Matters of fact, which are the second objects of human reason, are not ascertained in the same manner; nor is our evidence of their truth, however great, of a like nature with the foregoing. The contrary of every matter of fact is still possible; because it can never imply a contradiction, and is conceived by the mind with the same facility and distinctness, as if ever so conformable to reality. *That the sun will not rise tomorrow* is no less intelligible a proposition, and implies no more contradiction than the affirmation, *that it will rise.* We should in vain, therefore, attempt to demonstrate its falsehood. Were it demonstratively false, it would imply a contradiction and could never be distinctly conceived by the mind.

It may, therefore, be a subject worthy of curiosity, to enquire what is the nature of that evidence which assures us of any real existence and matter of fact, beyond the present testimony of our senses, or the records of our memory. This part of philosophy, it is observable,

* From David Hume, *An Enquiry Concerning Human Understanding* (1748), Sections IV and V.

has been little cultivated, either by the ancients or moderns; and therefore our doubts and errors, in the prosecution of so important an enquiry, may be the more excusable; while we march through such difficult paths without any guide or direction. They may even prove useful, by exciting curiosity, and destroying that implicit faith and security, which is the bane of all reasoning and free enquiry. The discovery of defects in the common philosophy, if any such there be, will not, I presume, be a discouragement, but rather an incitement, as is usual, to attempt something more full and satisfactory than has yet been proposed to the public.

All reasonings concerning matter of fact seem to be founded on the relation of *Cause and Effect*. By means of that relation alone we can go beyond the evidence of our memory and senses. If you were to ask a man, why he believes any matter of fact, which is absent; for instance, that his friend is in the country, or in France; he would give you a reason; and this reason would be some other fact; as a letter received from him, or the knowledge of his former resolutions and promises. A man finding a watch or any other machine in a desert island, would conclude that there had once been men on that island. All our reasonings concerning fact are of the same nature. And here it is constantly supposed that there is a connexion between the present fact and that which is inferred from it. Were there nothing to bind them together, the inference would be entirely precarious. The hearing of an articulate voice and rational discourse in the dark assures us of the presence of some person: Why? because these are the effects of the human make and fabric, and closely connected with it. If we anatomize all the other reasonings of this nature, we shall find that they are founded on the relation of cause and

effect, and that this relation is either near or remote, direct or collateral. Heat and light are collateral effects of fire, and the one effect may justly be inferred from the other.

If we would satisfy ourselves, therefore, concerning the nature of that evidence, which assures us of matters of fact, we must enquire how we arrive at the knowledge of cause and effect.

I shall venture to affirm, as a general proposition, which admits of no exception, that the knowledge of this relation is not, in any instance, attained by reasonings *a priori;* but arises entirely from experience, when we find that any particular objects are constantly conjoined with each other. Let an object be presented to a man of ever so strong natural reason and abilities; if that object be entirely new to him, he will not be able, by the most accurate examination of its sensible qualities, to discover any of its causes or effects. Adam, though his rational faculties be supposed, at the very first, entirely perfect, could not have inferred from the fluidity and transparency of water that it would suffocate him, or from the light and warmth of fire that it would consume him. No object ever discovers, by the qualities which appear to the senses, either the causes which produced it, or the effects which will arise from it; nor can our reason, unassisted by experience, ever draw any inference concerning real existence and matter of fact.

This proposition, *that causes and effects are discoverable, not by reason but by experience,* will readily be admitted with regard to such objects, as we remember to have once been altogether unknown to us; since we must be conscious of the utter inability, which we then lay under, of foretelling what would arise from them. Present two smooth pieces of marble to a man who has no tincture of natural philosophy; he will never discover that they will adhere together in such a manner as to require great force to separate them in a direct line, while they make so small a resistance to a lateral pressure. Such events, as bear little analogy to the common course of nature, are also readily confessed to be known only by experience; nor does any man imagine that the explosion of gunpowder, or the attraction of a loadstone, could ever be discovered by arguments *a priori*. In like manner, when an effect is supposed to depend upon an intricate machinery or secret structure of parts, we make no difficulty in attributing all our knowledge of it to experience. Who will assert that he can give the ultimate reason, why milk or bread is ˙proper nourishment for a man, not for a lion or a tiger?

But the same truth may not appear, at first sight, to have the same evidence with regard to events, which have become familiar to us from our first appearance in the world, which bear a close analogy to the whole course of nature, and which are supposed to depend on the simple qualities of objects, without any secret structure of parts. We are apt to imagine that we could discover these effects by the mere operation of our reason, without experience. We fancy, that were we brought on a sudden into this world, we could at first have inferred that one Billiard-ball would communicate motion to another upon impulse; and that we needed not to have waited for the event, in order to pronounce with certainty concerning it. Such is the influence of custom, that, where it is strongest, it not only covers our natural ignorance, but even conceals itself, and seems not to take place, merely because it is found in the highest degree.

But to convince us that all the laws of nature, and all the operations of bodies without exception, are known only by experience, the following reflections may, perhaps, suffice. Were any object presented to us, and were we required to pronounce concerning the effect, which will result from it, without consulting past observation; after what manner, I beseech you, must the mind proceed in this operation? It must invent or imagine some event, which it ascribes to the object as its effect; and it is plain that this invention must be entirely arbitrary. The mind can never possibly find the effect in the supposed cause, by the most accurate scrutiny and examination. For the effect is totally different from the cause, and consequently can never be discovered in it. Motion in the second Billiard-ball is a quite distinct event from motion in the first; nor is there anything in the one to suggest the smallest hint of the other. A stone or piece of metal raised into the air, and left without any support, immediately falls: but to consider the matter *a priori,* is there anything we discover in this situation which can beget the idea of a downward, rather than an upward, or any other motion, in the stone or metal?

And as the first imagination or invention of a particular effect, in all natural operations, is arbitrary, where we consult not experience; so must we also esteem the supposed tie or connexion between the cause and effect, which binds them together, and renders it impossible that any other effect could result from the operation of that cause. When I see, for instance, a Billiard-ball moving in a straight line towards another; even suppose motion in the second ball should by accident be suggested to me, as the result of their contact or impulse; may I not conceive, that a hundred different events might as well follow from that cause? May not both these balls remain at absolute rest? May not the first ball return in a straight line, or leap off from the second in any line or direction? All these suppositions are consistent and conceivable. Why then should we give preference to one, which is no more consistent or conceivable than the rest? All our reasonings *a priori* will never be able to show us any foundation for this preference.

In a word, then, every effect is a distinct event from its cause. It could not, therefore, be discovered in the cause, and the first invention or conception of it, *a priori*, must be entirely arbitrary. And even after it is suggested, the conjunction of it with the cause must appear equally arbitrary; since there are always many other effects, which, to reason, must seem fully as consistent and natural. In vain, therefore, should we pretend to determine any single event, or infer any cause or effect, without the assistance of observation and experience.

Hence we may discover the reason why no philosopher, who is rational and modest, has ever pretended to assign the ultimate cause of any natural operation, or to show distinctly the action of that power, which produces any single effect in the universe. It is confessed, that the utmost effort of human reason is to reduce the principles, productive of natural phenomena, to a greater simplicity, and to resolve the many particular effects into a few general causes, by means of reasonings from analogy, experience, and observation. But as to the causes of these general causes, we should in vain attempt their discovery; nor shall we ever be able to satisfy ourselves, by any particular explication of them. These ultimate springs and principles are totally shut up from human curiosity and enquiry. Elasticity, gravity, cohesion of parts, communication of motion by impulse; these are probably the ultimate causes and principles which we shall ever discover in nature; and we may esteem ourselves sufficiently happy, if, by accu-

rate enquiry and reasoning, we can trace up the particular phenomena to, or near to, these general principles. The most perfect philosophy of the natural kind only staves off our ignorance a little longer: as perhaps the most perfect philosophy of the moral or metaphysical kind serves only to discover larger portions of it. Thus the observation of human blindness and weakness is the result of all philosophy, and meets us at every turn, in spite of our endeavours to elude or avoid it.

Nor is geometry, when taken into the assistance of natural philosophy, ever able to remedy this defect, or lead us into the knowledge of ultimate causes, by all that accuracy of reasoning for which it is so justly celebrated. Every part of mixed mathematics proceeds upon the supposition that certain laws are established by nature in her operations; and abstract reasonings are employed, either to assist experience in the discovery of these laws, or to determine their influence in particular instances, where it depends upon any precise degree of distance and quantity. Thus, it is a law of motion, discovered by experience, that the moment or force of any body in motion is in the compound ratio or proportion of its solid contents and its velocity; and consequently, that a small force may remove the greatest obstacle or raise the greatest weight, if, by any contrivance or machinery, we can increase the velocity of that force, so as to make it an overmatch for its antagonist. Geometry assists us in the application of this law, by giving us the just dimensions of all the parts and figures which can enter into any species of machine; but still the discovery of the law itself is owing merely to experience, and all the abstract reasonings in the world could never lead us one step towards the knowledge of it. When we reason *a priori,* and consider merely any object or cause, as it appears to the mind, independent of all observation, it never could suggest to us the notion of any distinct object, such as its effect; much less, show us the inseparable and inviolable connexion between them. A man must be very sagacious who could discover by reasoning that crystal is the effect of heat, and ice of cold, without being previously acquainted with the operation of these qualities.

Part II

But we have not yet attained any tolerable satisfaction with regard to the question first proposed. Each solution still gives rise to a new question as difficult as the foregoing, and leads us on to farther enquiries. When it is asked, *What is the nature of all our reasonings concerning matter of fact?* the proper answer seems to be, that they are founded on the relation of cause and effect. When again it is asked, *What is the foundation of all our reasonings and conclusions concerning that relation?* it may be replied in one word, Experience. But if we still carry on our sifting humour, and ask, *What is the foundation of all conclusions from experience?* this implies a new question, which may be of more difficult solution and explication. Philosophers, that give themselves airs of superior wisdom and sufficiency, have a hard task when they encounter persons of inquisitive dispositions, who push them from every corner to which they retreat, and who are sure at last to bring them to some dangerous dilemma. The best expedient to prevent this confusion, is to be modest in our pretensions; and even to discover the difficulty ourselves before it is objected to us. By this means, we may make a kind of merit of our very ignorance.

I shall content myself, in this section, with an easy task, and shall pretend only to give a negative answer to the question here proposed. I say then, that, even after we have experience of the operations of cause and effect, our conclusions from that experience are *not* founded on reasoning, or any process of the understanding. This answer we must endeavour both to explain and to defend.

It must certainly be allowed, that nature has kept us at a great distance from all her secrets, and has afforded us only the knowledge of a few superficial qualities of objects; while she conceals from us those powers and principles on which the influence of those objects entirely depends. Our senses inform us of the colour, weight, and consistence of bread; but neither sense nor reason can ever inform us of those qualities which fit it for the nourishment and support of a human body. Sight or feeling conveys an idea of the actual motion of bodies; but as to that wonderful force or power, which would carry on a moving body for ever in a continued change of place, and which bodies never lose but by communicating it to others; of this we cannot form the most distant conception. But notwithstanding this ignorance of natural powers and principles, we always presume, when we see like sensible qualities, that they have like secret powers, and expect that effects, similar to those which we have experienced, will follow from them. If a body of like colour and consistence with that bread, which we have formerly eaten, be presented to us, we make no scruple of repeating the experiment, and foresee, with certainty, like nourishment and support. Now this is a process of the mind or thought, of which I would willingly know the foundation. It is allowed on all hands that there is no known connexion between the sensible qualities and the secret powers; and consequently, that the mind is not led to form such a conclusion concerning their constant and regular conjunction, by anything which it knows of their nature. As to past *Experience,* it can be allowed to give *direct* and *certain* information of those precise objects only, and that precise period of time, which fell under its cognizance: but why this experience should be extended to future times, and to other objects, which for aught we know, may be only in appearance similar; this is the main question on which I would insist. The bread, which I formerly ate, nourished me; that is, a body of such sensible qualities was, at that time, endued with such secret powers: but does it follow, that other bread must also nourish me at another time, and that like sensible qualities must always be attended with like secret powers? The consequence seems nowise necessary. At least, it must be acknowledged that there is here a consequence drawn by the mind; that there is a certain step taken; a process of thought, and an inference, which wants to be explained. These two propositions are far from being the same, *I have found that such an object has always been attended with such an effect,* and *I foresee, that other objects, which are, in appearance, similar, will be attended with similar effects.* I shall allow, if you please, that the one proposition may justly be inferred from the other: I know, in fact, that it always is inferred. But if you insist that the inference is made by a chain of reasoning, I desire you to produce that reasoning. The connexion between these propositions is not intuitive. There is required a medium, which may enable the mind to draw such an inference, if indeed it be drawn by reasoning and argument. What that medium is, I must confess, passes my comprehension; and it is incumbent on those to produce it, who assert that it really exists, and is the origin of all our conclusions concerning matter of fact.

This negative argument must cer-tainly, in process of time, become altogether convincing, if many penetrating and able philosophers shall turn their enquiries this way and no one be ever able to discover any connecting proposition or intermediate step, which supports the understanding in this conclusion. But as the question is yet new, every reader may not trust so far to his own penetration, as to conclude, because an argument escapes his enquiry, that therefore it does not really exist. For this reason it may be requisite to venture upon a more difficult task; and enumerating all the branches of human knowledge, endeavour to show that none of them can afford such an argument.

All reasonings may be divided into two kinds, namely, demonstrative reasoning, or that concerning relations of ideas, and moral reasoning, or that concerning matter of fact and existence. That there are no demonstrative arguments in the case seems evident; since it implies no contradiction that the course of nature may change, and that an object, seemingly like those which we have experienced, may be attended with different or contrary effects. May I not clearly and distinctly conceive that a body, falling from the clouds, and which, in all other respects, resembles snow, has yet the taste of salt or feeling of fire? Is there any more intelligible proposition than to affirm, that all the trees will flourish in December and January, and decay in May and June? Now whatever is intelligible, and can be distinctly conceived, implies no contradiction, and can never be proved false by any demonstrative argument or abstract reasoning a priori.

If we be, therefore, engaged by arguments to put trust in past experience, and make it the standard of our future judgment, these arguments must be probable only, or such as regard matter of fact and real existence, according to the division above mentioned. But that there is no argument of this kind, must appear, if our explication of that species of reasoning be admitted as solid and satisfactory. We have said that all arguments concerning existence are founded on the relation of cause and effect; that our knowledge of that relation is derived entirely from experience; and that all our experimental conclusions proceed upon the supposition that the future will be conformable to the past. To endeavour, therefore, the proof of this last supposition by probable arguments, or arguments regarding existence, must be evidently going in a circle, and taking that for granted, which is the very point in question.

In reality, all arguments from experience are founded on the similarity which we discover among natural objects, and by which we are induced to expect effects similar to those which we have found to follow from such objects. And though none but a fool or madman will ever pretend to dispute the authority of experience, or to reject that great guide of human life, it may surely be allowed a philosopher to have so much curiosity at least as to examine the principle of human nature, which gives this mighty authority to experience, and makes us draw advantage from that similarity which nature has placed among different objects. From causes which appear *similar* we expect similar effects. This is the sum of all our experimental conclusions. Now it seems evident that, if this conclusion were formed by reason, it would be as perfect at first, and upon one instance, as after ever so long a course of experience. But the case is far otherwise. Nothing so like as eggs; yet no one, on account of this appearing similarity, expects the same taste and relish in all of them. It is only after a long course of uniform experiments in any kind, that we attain a firm reliance and security with regard to a particular

event. Now where is that process of reasoning which, from one instance, draws a conclusion, so different from that which it infers from a hundred instances that are nowise different from that single one? This question I propose as much for the sake of information, as with an intention of raising difficulties. I cannot find, I cannot imagine any such reasoning. But I keep my mind still open to instruction, if any one will vouchsafe to bestow it on me.

Should it be said that, from a number of uniform experiments, we *infer* a connexion between the sensible qualities and the secret powers; this, I must confess, seems the same difficulty, couched in different terms. The question still recurs, on what process of argument this *inference* is founded? Where is the medium, the interposing ideas, which join propositions so very wide of each other? It is confessed that the colour, consistence, and other sensible qualities of bread appear not, of themselves, to have any connexion with the secret powers of nourishment and support. For otherwise we could infer these secret powers from the first appearance of these sensible qualities, without the aid of experience; contrary to the sentiment of all philosophers, and contrary to plain matter of fact. Here, then, is our natural state of ignorance with regard to the powers and influence of all objects. How is this remedied by experience? It only shows us a number of uniform effects, resulting from certain objects, and teaches us that those particular objects, at that particular time, were endowed with such powers and forces. When a new object, endowed with similar sensible qualities, is produced, we expect similar powers and forces, and look for a like effect. From a body of like colour and consistence with bread we expect like nourishment and support. But this surely is a step or progress of the mind, which wants to be explained. When a man says, *I have found, in all past instances, such sensible qualities conjoined with such secret powers:* And when he says, *Similar sensible qualities will always be conjoined with similar secret powers,* he is not guilty of a tautology, nor are these propositions in any respect the same. You say that the one proposition is an inference from the other. But you must confess that the inference is not intuitive; neither is it demonstrative: Of what nature is it, then? To say it is experimental, is begging the question. For all inferences from experience suppose, as their foundation, that the future will resemble the past, and that similar powers will be conjoined with similar sensible qualities. If there be any suspicion that the course of nature may change, and that the past may be no rule for the future, all experience becomes useless, and can give rise to no inference or conclusion. It is impossible, therefore, that any arguments from experience can prove this resemblance of the past to the future; since all these arguments are founded on the supposition of that resemblance. Let the course of things be allowed hitherto ever so regular; that alone, without some new argument or inference, proves not that, for the future, it will continue so. In vain do you pretend to have learned the nature of bodies from your past experience. Their secret nature, and consequently all their effects and influence, may change, without any change in their sensible qualities. This happens sometimes, and with regard to some objects: Why may it not happen always, and with regard to all objects? What logic, what process of argument secures you against this supposition? My practice, you say, refutes my doubts. But you mistake the purport of my question. As an agent, I am quite satisfied in the point; but as a philosopher, who has some share of curiosity, I will not say scepticism, I

want to learn the foundation of this inference. No reading, no enquiry has yet been able to remove my difficulty, or give me satisfaction in a matter of such importance. Can I do better than propose the difficulty to the public, even though, perhaps, I have small hopes of obtaining a solution? We shall at least, by this means, be sensible of our ignorance, if we do not augment our knowledge.

I must confess that a man is guilty of unpardonable arrogance who concludes, because an argument has escaped his own investigation, that therefore it does not really exist. I must also confess that, though all the learned, for several ages, should have employed themselves in fruitless search upon any subject, it may still, perhaps, be rash to conclude positively that the subject must, therefore, pass all human comprehension. Even though we examine all the sources of our knowledge, and conclude them unfit for such a subject, there may still remain a suspicion, that the enumeration is not complete, or the examination not accurate. But with regard to the present subject, there are some considerations which seem to remove all this accusation of arrogance or suspicion of mistake.

It is certain that the most ignorant and stupid peasants—nay infants, nay even brute beasts—improve by experience, and learn the qualities of natural objects, by observing the effects which result from them. When a child has felt the sensation of pain from touching the flame of a candle, he will be careful not to put his hand near any candle; but will expect a similar effect from a cause which is similar in its sensible qualities and appearance. If you assert, therefore, that the understanding of the child is led into this conclusion by any process of argument or ratiocination, I may justly require you to produce that argument; nor have you any pretence to refuse so equitable a demand. You cannot say that the argument is abstruse, and may possibly escape your enquiry; since you confess that it is obvious to the capacity of a mere infant. If you hesitate, therefore, a moment, or if, after reflection, you produce any intricate or profound argument, you, in a manner, give up the question, and confess that it is not reasoning which engages us to suppose the past resembling the future, and to expect similar effects from causes which are, to appearance, similar. This is the proposition which I intended to enforce in the present section. If I be right, I pretend not to have made any mighty discovery. And if I be wrong, I must acknowledge myself to be indeed a very backward scholar; since I cannot now discover an argument which, it seems, was perfectly familiar to me long before I was out of my cradle.

SECTION V

Sceptical Solution of These Doubts

Part I

The passion for philosophy, like that for religion, seems liable to this inconvenience, that, though it aims at the correction of our manners, and extirpation of our vices, it may only serve, by imprudent management, to foster a predominant inclination, and push the mind, with more determined resolution, towards that side which already *draws* too much, by the bias and propensity of the natural temper. It is certain that, while we aspire to the magnanimous firmness of the philosophic sage, and endeavour to confine our pleasures altogether within our own minds, we may, at last, render our philosophy like that of Epictetus, and other *Stoics,* only a more refined system of selfishness, and reason ourselves out of all virtue as well as social enjoyment. While we study with attention the vanity of human life, and turn all our thoughts towards the empty and transitory nature of riches and honours, we are, perhaps, all the while flattering our natural indolence, which, hating the bustle of the world, and drudgery of business, seeks a pretence of reason to give itself a full and uncontrolled indulgence. There is, however, one species of philosophy which seems little liable to this inconvenience, and that because it strikes in with no disorderly passion of the human mind, nor can mingle itself with any natural affection or propensity; and that is the Academic or Sceptical philosophy. The academics always talk of doubt and suspense of judgment, of danger in hasty determinations, of confining to very narrow bounds the enquiries of the understanding, and of renouncing all speculations which lie not within the limits of common life and practice. Nothing, therefore, can be more contrary than such a philosophy to the supine indolence of the mind, its rash arrogance, its lofty pretensions, and its superstitious credulity. Every passion is mortified by it, except the love of truth; and that passion never is, nor can be, carried to too high a degree. It is surprising, therefore, that this philosophy, which, in almost every instance, must be harmless and innocent, should be the subject of so much groundless reproach and obloquy. But, perhaps, the very circumstance which renders it so innocent is what chiefly exposes it to the public hatred and resentment. By flattering no irregular passion, it gains few partizans: By opposing so many vices and follies, it raises to itself abundance of enemies, who stigmatize it as libertine, profane, and irreligious.

Nor need we fear that this philosophy, while it endeavours to limit our enquiries to common life, should ever undermine the reasonings of common life, and carry its doubts so far as to destroy all action, as well as speculation. Nature will always maintain her rights, and prevail in the end over any abstract reasoning whatsoever. Though we should conclude, for instance, as in the foregoing section, that, in all reasonings from experience, there is a step taken by the mind which is not supported by any argument or process of the understanding; there is no danger that these reasonings, on which almost all knowledge depends, will ever be affected by such a discovery. If the mind be not engaged by argument to make this step, it must be induced by some other principle of equal weight and authority; and that principle will preserve its influence as long as human nature remains the same. What that principle is may well be worth the pains of enquiry.

Suppose a person, though endowed with the strongest faculties of reason and reflection, to be brought on a sudden into this world; he would, indeed, immediately observe a continual succession of objects, and one event following another; but he would not be able to discover anything farther. He would not, at first, by any reasoning, be able to reach the idea of cause and effect; since the particular powers, by which all natural operations are performed, never appear to the senses; nor is it reasonable to conclude, merely because one event, in one instance, precedes another, that therefore the one is the cause, the other the effect. Their conjunction may be arbitrary and casual. There may be no reason to infer the existence of one from the appearance of the other. And in a word, such a person, without more experience, could never employ his conjecture or reasoning concerning any matter of fact, or be assured of anything beyond what was immediately present to his memory and senses.

Suppose, again, that he has acquired more experience, and has lived so long in the world as to have observed familiar objects or events to be constantly conjoined together; what is the consequence of this experience? He immediately infers the existence of one object from the appearance of the other. Yet he has not, by all his experience, acquired any idea or knowledge of the secret power by which the one object produces the other; nor is it, by any process of reasoning, he is engaged to draw this inference. But still he finds himself determined to draw it: And though he should be convinced that his understanding has no part in the operation, he would nevertheless continue in the same course of thinking. There is some other principle which determines him to form such a conclusion.

This principle is Custom or Habit. For wherever the repetition of any particular act or operation produces a propensity to renew the same act or operation, without being impelled by any reasoning or process of the understanding, we always say, that this propensity is the effect of *Custom*. By employing that word, we pretend not to have given the ultimate reason of such a propensity. We only point out a principle of human nature, which is universally acknowledged, and which is well known by its effects. Perhaps we can push our enquiries no farther, or pretend to give the cause of this cause; but must rest contented with it as the ultimate principle, which we can assign, of all our conclusions from experience. It is sufficient satisfaction, that we can go so far, without repining at the narrowness of our faculties because they will carry us no farther. And it is certain we here advance a very intelligible proposition at least, if not a true one, when we assert that, after the constant conjunction of two objects— heat and flame, for instance, weight and solidity—we are determined by custom alone to expect the one from the appearance of the other. This hypothesis seems even the only one which explains the difficulty, why we draw, from a thousand instances, an inference which we are not able to draw from one instance, that is, in no respect, different from them. Reason is incapable of any such variation. The conclusions which it draws from considering one circle are the same which it would form upon surveying all the circles in the universe. But no man, having seen only one body move after being impelled by another, could infer that every other body will move after a like impulse. All inferences from experience, therefore, are effects of custom, not of reasoning.

Custom, then, is the great guide of human life. It is that principle alone which renders our experience useful to us, and makes us expect, for the future, a similar train of events with those which have appeared in the past. Without the influence of custom, we should be entirely ignorant of every matter of fact beyond what is immediately present to the memory and senses. We should never know how to adjust means to ends, or to employ our natural powers in the production of any effect. There would be an end at once of all action, as well as of the chief part of speculation.

But here it may be proper to remark, that though our conclusions from experience carry us beyond our memory and senses, and assure us of matters of fact which happened in the most distant places and most remote ages, yet some fact must always be present to the senses or memory, from which we may first proceed in drawing these conclusions. A man, who should find in a desert country the remains of pompous buildings, would conclude that the country had, in ancient times, been cultivated by civilized inhabitants; but did nothing of this nature occur to him, he could never form such an inference. We learn the events of former ages from history; but then we must peruse the volumes in which this instruction is contained, and thence carry up our inferences from one testimony to another, till we arrive at the eyewitnesses and spectators of these distant events. In a word, if we proceed not upon some fact, present to the memory or senses, our reasonings would be merely hypothetical; and however the particular links might be connected with each other, the whole chain of inferences would have nothing to support it, nor could we ever, by its means, arrive at the knowledge of any real existence. If I ask why you believe any particular matter of fact, which you relate, you must tell me some reason; and this reason will be some other fact, connected with it. But as you cannot proceed after this manner, *in infinitum,* you must at last terminate in some fact, which is present to your memory or senses; or must allow that your belief is entirely without foundation.

What, then, is the conclusion of the whole matter? A simple one; though, it must be confessed, pretty remote from the common theories of philosophy. All belief of matter of fact or real existence is derived merely from some object, present to the memory or senses, and a customary conjunction between that and some other object. Or in other words; having found, in many instances, that any two kinds of objects—flame and heat, snow and cold—have always been conjoined together; if flame or snow be presented anew to the senses, the mind is carried by custom to expect heat or cold, and to *believe* that such a quality does exist, and will discover itself upon a nearer approach. This belief is the necessary result of placing the mind in such circumstances. It is an operation of the soul, when we are so situated, as unavoidable as to feel the passion of love, when we receive benefits; or hatred, when we meet with injuries. All these operations are a species of natural instincts, which no reasoning or process of the thought and understanding is able either to produce or to prevent.

INDUCTION AS

HYPOTHESIS*

WILLIAM WHEWELL (1794–1866) was a British philosopher, scientist, and educator. Influenced by Kant, he stressed the importance of what the mind must bring to observed facts in order that inductive inferences can be made. Whewell's three volume *History of the Inductive Sciences* appeared in 1837 and his two volume *Philosophy of the Inductive Sciences* appeared in 1840. Although he is seldom read today, Whewell's theory of scientific method is much closer to the modern conception than is that of John Stuart Mill, with whom Whewell engaged in controversy during their lifetimes.

18

Deductive reasoning is virtually a collection of syllogisms, as has already been stated; and in such reasoning, the general principles, the Definitions and Axioms, necessarily stand at the *beginning* of the demonstration. In an inductive inference, the Definitions and Principles are the *final result* of the reasoning, the ultimate effect of the proof. Hence when an Inductive Proposition is to be established by a proof involving several steps of demonstrative reasoning, the enunciation of the Proposition will contain, explicitly or implicitly, principles which the demonstration proceeds upon as axioms, but which are really inductive inferences. Thus in order to prove that the force which retains a planet in an ellipse varies inversely as the square of the distance, it is taken for granted that the Laws of Motion are true, and that they apply to the planets. Yet the

doctrine that this is so, as well as the law of the force, were established only by this and the like demonstrations. The doctrine which is the *hypothesis* of the deductive reasoning, is the *inference* of the inductive process. The special facts which are the basis of the inductive inference, are the conclusion of the train of deduction. And in this manner the deduction establishes the induction. The principle which we gather from the facts is true, because the facts can be derived from it by rigorous demonstration. Induction moves upwards, and deduction downwards, on the same stair.

But still there is a great difference in the character of their movements. Deduction descends steadily and methodically, step by step. Induction mounts by a leap which is out of the reach of method. She bounds to the top of the stair at once; and then it is the business of Deduction, by trying each step in order to establish the

* From William Whewell, *The Philosophy of the Inductive Sciences* (1840), Volume II.

solidity of her companion's footing. Yet these must be processes of the same mind. The Inductive Intellect makes an assertion which is subsequently justified by demonstration: and it shows its sagacity, its peculiar character, by enunciating the proposition when as yet the demonstration does not exist; but then it shows that it *is* sagacity, by also producing the demonstration.

It has been said that inductive and deductive reasoning are contrary in their scheme; that in Deduction we infer particular from general truths; while in Induction we infer general from particular: that Deduction consists of many steps, in each of which we apply known general propositions in particular cases; while in Induction we have a single step, in which we pass from many particular truths to one general proposition. And this is truly said; but though contrary in their motions, the two are the operation of the same mind travelling over the same ground. Deduction is a necessary part of Induction. Deduction justifies by calculation what Induction had happily guessed. Induction recognizes the ore of truth by its weight, Deduction confirms the recognition by chemical analysis. Every step of Induction must be confirmed by rigorous deductive reasoning, followed into such detail as the nature and complexity of the relations (whether of quantity or any other) render requisite. If not so justified by the supposed discoverer, it is *not* Induction.

· · ·

Sect. II.—On the Logic of Induction

54

. . . The derivation of principles by reasoning from facts is performed by a process which is termed *Induction,* which is very different from the process of De-duction already noticed, and of which we shall attempt to point out the character and method.

It has been usual to say of any general truths, established by the consideration and comparison of several facts, that they are obtained by *Induction;* but the distinctive character of this process has not been well pointed out, nor have any rules been laid down which may prescribe the form and ensure the validity of the process, as has been done for Deductive reasoning by common Logic. The *Logic of Induction* has not yet been constructed; a few remarks on this subject are all that can be offered here.

55

The Inductive Propositions, to which we shall here principally refer as examples of their class, are those elementary principles which occur in considering the motion of bodies, and of which some are called the Laws of Motion. They are such as these;—a body not acted on by any force will move on for ever uniformly in a straight line;—gravity is a uniform force;—if a body in motion be acted upon by any force, the effect of the force will be compounded with the previous motion;—when a body communicates motion to another directly, the momentum lost by the first body is equal to the momentum gained by the second. And I remark, in the first place, that in collecting such propositions from facts, there occurs a step corresponding to the term "Induction," (ἐπαγωγή, *inductio*). Some notion is *superinduced* upon the observed facts. In each inductive process, there is some general idea introduced, which is given, not by the phenomena, but by the mind. The conclusion is not contained in the premises, but includes them by the introduction of a new generality. In order to obtain our inference, we travel beyond the cases we have before us; we consider them as exemplifications of, or deviations from, some ideal case in which the relations are complete and intelligible. We take a standard, and measure the facts by it; and this standard is created by us, not offered by Nature. Thus we assert, that a body left to itself will move on with unaltered velocity, not because our senses ever disclosed to us a body doing this, but because (taking this as our ideal case) we find that all actual cases are intelligible and explicable by means of the notion of forces which cause change of motion, and which are exerted by surrounding bodies. In like manner, we see bodies striking each other, and thus moving, accelerating, retarding, and stopping each other; but in all this, we do not, by our senses, perceive that abstract quantity, momentum, which is always lost by one as it is gained by another. This momentum is a creation of the mind, brought in among the facts, in order to convert their apparent confusion into order, their seeming chance into certainty, their perplexing variety into simplicity. This the idea of momentum gained and lost does; and, in like manner, in any other case in which inductive truths are established, some idea is introduced, as the means of passing from the facts to the truth.

56

The process of mind of which we here speak can only be described by suggestion and comparison. One of the most common of such comparisons, especially since the time of Bacon, is that which speaks of induction as the *interpretation* of facts. Such an expression is appropriate; and it may easily be seen that it includes the circumstance which we are now noticing;—the superinduction of an idea upon the facts by the interpreting mind. For when we read a page, we have before our eyes only black and white, form and colour; but by an act of the mind, we transform these perceptions into thought and emotion. The letters are nothing of themselves; they contain no truth, if the mind does not contribute its share: for instance, if we do not know the language in which the words are written. And if we are imperfectly acquainted with the language, we become very clearly aware how much a certain activity of the mind is requisite in order to convert the words into propositions, by the extreme effort which the business of interpretation requires. Induction, then, may be conveniently described as the interpretation of phenomena.

57

But I observe further, that in thus infering truths from facts, it is not only necessary that the mind should contribute to the task its own idea, but, in order that the propositions thus obtained may have any exact import and scientific value, it is requisite that the idea be perfectly *distinct* and precise. If it be possible to obtain some vague apprehension of truths, while the ideas in which they are expressed remain indistinct and ill-defined, such knowledge cannot be available for the purposes we here contemplate. In order to construct a science, all our fundamental ideas must be distinct; and among them, those which Induction introduces.

58

This necessity for distinctness in the ideas which we employ in Induction, makes it proper to *define,* in a precise and exact manner, each idea when it is thus brought forwards. Thus, in establishing the propositions which we have stated as our examples in these cases, we have to define *force* in general; *uniform force; compounding* of motions; *momentum.* The construction of these definitions is an essential part of the process of Induction, no less than the assertion of the inductive truth itself.

59

But in order to justify and establish the inference which we make, the ideas which we introduce must not only be distinct, but also *appropriate*. They must be exactly and closely applicable to the facts; so that when the idea is in our possession, and the facts under our notice, we perceive that the former includes and takes up the latter. The idea is only a more precise mode of apprehending the facts, and it is empty and unmeaning if it be anything else; but if it be thus applicable, the proposition which is asserted by means of it is true, precisely because the facts *are* facts. When we have defined force to be the cause of change of motion, we see that, as we remove external forces, we do, in actual experiments, remove all the change of motion; and therefore the proposition that there is in bodies no internal cause of change of motion, is true. When we have defined momentum to be the product of the velocity and quantity of matter, we see that in the actions of bodies, the effect increases as the momentum increases; and by measurement, we find that the effect may consistently be measured by the momentum. The ideas here employed are not only distinct in the mind, but applicable in the world; they are the elements, not only of relations of thought, but of laws of nature.

60

Thus an inductive inference requires an idea from within, facts from without, and a coincidence of the two. The idea must be distinct, otherwise we obtain no scientific truth; it must be appropriate, otherwise the facts cannot be steadily contemplated by means of it; and when they are so contemplated, the Inductive Proposi-

tion must be seen to be verified by the evidence of sense.

It appears from what has been said, that in establishing a proposition by Induction, the definition of the idea and the assertion of the truth, are not only both requisite, but they are correlative. Each of the two steps contains the verification and justification of the other. The proposition derives its meaning from the definition; the definition derives its reality from the proposition. If they are separated, the definition is arbitrary or empty, the proposition is vague or verbal.

61

Hence we gather, that in the Inductive Sciences, our Definitions and our Elementary Inductive Truths ought to be introduced together. There is no value or meaning in definitions, except with reference to the truths which they are to express. Discussions about the definitions of any science, taken separately, cannot therefore be profitable, if the discussion do not refer, tacitly or expressly, to the fundamental truths of the science; and in all such discussions it should be stated what are taken as the fundamental truths. With such a reference to Elementary Inductive Truths clearly understood, the discussion of Definitions may be the best method of arriving at that clearness of thought, and that arrangement of facts, which Induction requires.

I will now note some of the differences which exist between Inductive and Deductive Reasoning, in the modes in which they are presented.

62

One leading difference in these two kinds of reasoning, is, that in Deduction we infer particular from general truths; in Induction, on the contrary, we infer general from particular. Deductive proofs consist of many steps, in each of which we apply known general propositions in particular cases;—"all triangles have their angles equal to two right angles, therefore this triangle has; therefore, &c." In Induction, on the other hand, we have a single step in which we pass from many particular Propositions to one general proposition; "This stone falls downwards; so do those others;—all stones fall downwards." And the former inference flows necessarily from the relation of general and particular; but the latter, as we have seen, derives its power of convincing from the introduction of a new idea, which is distinct and appropriate, and which supplies that generality which the particulars cannot themselves offer.

63

I observe also that this difference of process in inductive and deductive proofs, may be most properly marked by a difference in the form in which they are stated. In Deduction, the *Definition* stands at the beginning of the proposition; in Induction, it may most suitably stand at or near the end. Thus the definition of a uniform force is introduced in the course of the proposition that gravity is a uniform force. And this arrangement represents truly the real order of proof; for, historically speaking, it was taken for granted that gravity was a uniform force; but the question remained, what was the right definition of a uniform force. And in the establishment of other inductive principles, in like manner, definitions cannot be laid down for any useful purpose, till we know the propositions in which they are to be used. They may therefore properly come each at the conclusion of its corresponding proposition.

INDUCTIVE GROUNDS

FOR INDUCTION*

JOHN STUART MILL (1806–1873).   See page 53.

Preliminary Observations on Induction in General

1

The portion of the present inquiry upon which we are now about to enter may be considered as the principal, both from its surpassing in intricacy all the other branches, and because it relates to a process which has been shown in the preceding Book to be that in which the investigation of nature essentially consists. We have found that all Inference, consequently all Proof, and all discovery of truths not self-evident, consists of inductions, and the interpretation of inductions; that all our knowledge, not intuitive, comes to us exclusively from that source. What Induction is, therefore, and what conditions render it legitimate, cannot but be deemed the main question of the science of logic—the question which includes all others. It is, however, one which professed writers on logic have almost entirely passed over. The generalities of the subject have not been altogether neglected by metaphysicians; but, for want of sufficient acquaintance with the processes by which science has actually succeeded in establishing general truths, their analysis of the inductive operation, even when unexceptionable as to correctness, has not been specific enough to be made the foundation of practical rules, which might be for induction itself what the rules of the syllogism are for the interpretation of induction; while those by whom physical science has been carried to its present state of improvement—and who, to arrive at a complete theory of the process, needed only to generalise, and adapt to all varieties of problems, the methods which they themselves employed in their habitual pursuits—never until very lately made any serious attempt to philosophise on the subject, nor regarded the mode in which they arrived at their conclusions as deserving of study, independently of the conclusions themselves.

2

For the purposes of the present inquiry, Induction may be defined, the operation of discovering and proving general propositions. It is true that (as already shown) the process of indirectly ascertaining individual facts is as truly inductive as that by which we establish general truths. But it is not a different kind of induction; it is a form of the very same process: since, on the one hand, generals are but collections of particulars, definite

* From John Stuart Mill, *A System of Logic* (1843).

in kind but indefinite in number; and on the other hand, whenever the evidence which we derive from observation of known cases justifies us in drawing an inference respecting even one unknown case, we should on the same evidence be justified in drawing a similar inference with respect to a whole class of cases. The inference either does not hold at all, or it holds in all cases of a certain description; in all cases which, in certain definable respects, resemble those we have observed.

If these remarks are just; if the principles and rules of inference are the same whether we infer general propositions or individual facts; it follows that a complete logic of the sciences would be also a complete logic of practical business and common life. Since there is no case of legitimate inference from experience, in which the conclusion may not legitimately be a general proposition, an analysis of the process by which general truths are arrived at is virtually an analysis of all induction whatever. Whether we are inquiring into a scientific principle or into an individual fact, and whether we proceed by experiment or by ratiocination, every step in the train of inferences is essentially inductive, and the legitimacy of the induction depends in both cases on the same conditions.

True it is that in the case of the practical inquirer, who is endeavouring to ascertain facts not for the purposes of science but for those of business, such, for instance, as the advocate or the judge, the chief difficulty is one in which the principles of induction will afford him no assistance. It lies not in making his inductions, but in the selection of them; in choosing from among all general propositions ascertained to be true, those which furnish marks by which he may trace whether the given subject possesses or not the predicate in question. In arguing a doubtful question of fact before a jury, the general propositions or principles to which the advocate appeals are mostly, in themselves, sufficiently trite, and assented to as soon as stated: his skill lies in bringing his case under those propositions or principles; in calling to mind such of the known or received maxims of probability as admit of application to the case in hand, and selecting from among them those best adapted to his object. Success is here dependent on natural or acquired sagacity, aided by knowledge of the particular subject and of subjects allied with it. Invention, though it can be cultivated, cannot be reduced to rule; there is no science which will enable a man to bethink himself of that which will suit his purpose.

But when he *has* thought of something, science can tell him whether that which he has thought of will suit his purpose or not. The inquirer or arguer must be guided by his own knowledge and sagacity in the choice of the inductions out of which he will construct his argument. But the validity of the argument when constructed depends on principles and must be tried by tests which are the same for all descriptions of inquiries, whether the result be to give A an estate, or to enrich science with a new general truth. In the one case and in the other, the senses, or testimony, must decide on the individual facts; the rules of the syllogism will determine whether, those facts being supposed correct, the case really falls within the formulæ of the different inductions under which it has been successively brought; and finally, the legitimacy of the inductions themselves must be decided by other rules, and these it is now our purpose to investigate. If this third part of the operation be, in many of the questions of practical life, not the most, but the least arduous portion of it, we have seen that this is also the case in some great departments of the field of science; in all those which are principally deductive, and most of all in mathematics, where the inductions themselves are few in number, and so obvious and elementary that they seem to stand in no need of the evidence of experience, while to combine them so as to prove a given theorem or solve a problem may call for the utmost powers of invention and contrivance with which our species is gifted.

. . .

Of the Ground of Induction

1

Induction, properly so called, as distinguished from those mental operations, sometimes though improperly designated by the name, which I have attempted in the preceding chapter to characterise, may, then, be summarily defined as Generalisation from Experience. It consists in inferring from some individual instances in which a phenomenon is observed to occur, that it occurs in all instances of a certain class; namely, in all which *resemble* the former, in what are regarded as the material circumstances.

In what way the material circumstances are to be distinguished from those which are immaterial, or why some of the circumstances are material and others not so, we are not yet ready to point out. We must first observe that there is a principle implied in the very statement of what Induction is; an assumption with regard to the course of nature and the order of the universe; namely, that there are such things in nature as parallel cases; that what happens once will, under a sufficient degree of similarity of circumstances, happen again, and not only again, but as often as the same circumstances recur. This, I say, is an assumption involved in every case of induction. And if we consult the actual course of nature, we find that the assumption is warranted. The universe, so far as known to us, is so constituted, that whatever is true in any one case, is true in all cases of a certain description; the only difficulty is, to find what description.

This universal fact, which is our warrant for all inferences from experience, has been described by different philosophers in different forms of language; that the course of nature is uniform; that the universe is governed by general laws; and the like. One of the most usual of those modes of expression, but also one of the most inadequate, is that which has been brought into familiar use by the metaphysicians of the school of Reid and Stewart. The disposition of the human mind to generalise from experience,—a propensity considered by these philosophers as an instinct of our nature,— they usually describe under some such name as "our intuitive conviction that the future will resemble the past." Now it has been well pointed out by Mr. Bailey, that (whether the tendency be or not an original and ultimate element of our nature) Time, in its modifications of past, present, and future, has no concern either with the belief itself, or with the grounds of it. We believe that fire will burn to-morrow, because it burned to-day and yesterday; but we believe, on precisely the same grounds, that it burned before we were born, and that it burns this very day in Cochin-China. It is not from the past to the future, as past and future, that we infer, but from the known to the unknown; from facts observed to facts unobserved; from what we have perceived, or been directly conscious of, to what has not come within our experience. In this last predicament is the whole region of the future; but also the vastly greater portion of the present and of the past.

Whatever be the most proper mode of expressing it, the proposition that the course of nature is uniform is the fundamental principle, or general axiom, of Induction. It would yet be a great error to offer this large generalisation as any explanation of the inductive process. On the contrary, I hold it to be itself an instance of induction, and induction by no means of the most obvious kind. Far from being the first induction we make, it is one of the last, or at all events one of those which are latest in attaining strict philosophical accuracy. As a general maxim, indeed, it has scarcely entered into the minds of any but philosophers; nor even by them, as we shall have many opportunities of remarking, have its extent and limits been always very justly conceived. The truth is, that this great generalisation is itself founded on prior generalisations. The obscurer laws of nature were discovered by means of it, but the more obvious ones must have been understood and assented to as general truths before it was ever heard of. We should never have thought of affirming that all phenomena take place according to general laws, if we had not first arrived, in the case of a great multitude of phenomena, at some knowledge of the laws themselves; which could be done no otherwise than by induction. In what sense, then, can a principle, which is so far from being our earliest induction, be regarded as our warrant for all the others? In the only sense in which (as we have already seen) the general propositions which we place at the head of our reasonings when we throw them into syllogisms ever really contribute to their validity. As Archbishop Whately remarks, every induction is a syllogism with the major premise suppressed; or (as I prefer expressing it) every induction may be thrown into the form of a syllogism by supplying a major premise. If this be actually done, the principle which we are now considering, that of the uniformity of the course of nature, will appear as the ultimate major premise of all inductions, and will, therefore,

stand to all inductions in the relation in which, as has been shown at so much length, the major proposition of a syllogism always stands to the conclusion; not contributing at all to prove it, but being a necessary condition of its being proved; since no conclusion is proved for which there cannot be found a true major premise.

The statement that the uniformity of the course of nature is the ultimate major premise in all cases of induction may be thought to require some explanation. The immediate major premise in every inductive argument it certainly is not. Of that Archbishop Whately's must be held to be the correct account. The induction, "John, Peter, &c., are mortal, therefore all mankind are mortal," may, as he justly says, be thrown into a syllogism by prefixing as a major premise, (what is at any rate a necessary condition of the validity of the argument), namely, that what is true of John, Peter, &c., is true of all mankind. But how came we by this major premise? It is not self-evident; nay, in all cases of unwarranted generalisation it is not true. How, then, is it arrived at? Necessarily either by induction or ratiocination; and if by induction, the process, like all other inductive arguments, may be thrown into the form of a syllogism. This previous syllogism it is, therefore, necessary to construct. There is, in the long-run, only one possible construction. The real proof that what is true of John, Peter, &c., is true of all mankind, can only be, that a different supposition would be inconsistent with the uniformity which we know to exist in the course of nature. Whether there would be this inconsistency or not, may be a matter of long and delicate inquiry; but unless there would, we have no sufficient ground for the major of the inductive syllogism. It hence appears, that if we throw the whole course of any inductive argument into a series of syllogisms, we shall arrive by more or fewer steps at an ultimate syllogism, which will have for its major premise the principle or axiom of the uniformity of the course of nature.[1]

· · ·

3

In order to a better understanding of the problem which the logician must solve if he would establish a scientific theory of Induction, let us compare a few cases of incorrect inductions with others which are acknowledged to be legitimate. Some, we know, which were believed for centuries to be correct, were nevertheless incorrect. That all swans are white, cannot have been a good induction, since the

[1] But though it is a condition of the validity of every induction that there be uniformity in the course of nature, it is not a necessary condition that the uniformity should pervade all nature. It is enough that it pervades the particular class of phenomena to which the induction relates. An induction concerning the motions of the planets, or the properties of the magnet, would not be vitiated though we were to suppose that wind and weather are the sport of chance, provided it be assumed that astronomical and magnetic phenomena are under the dominion of general laws. Otherwise the early experience of mankind would have rested on a very weak foundation; for in the infancy of science it could not be known that *all* phenomena are regular in their course.

Neither would it be correct to say that every induction by which we infer any truth implies the general fact of uniformity *as foreknown,* even in reference to the kind of phenomena concerned. It implies, *either* that this general fact is already known, *or* that we may now know it: as the conclusion, the Duke of Wellington is mortal, drawn from the instances A, B, and C, implies either that we have already concluded all men to be mortal, or that we are now entitled to do so from the same evidence. A vast amount of confusion and paralogism respecting the grounds of Induction would be dispelled by keeping in view these simple considerations.

conclusion has turned out erroneous. The experience, however, on which the conclusion rested was genuine. From the earliest records, the testimony of the inhabitants of the known world was unanimous on the point. The uniform experience, therefore, of the inhabitants of the known world, agreeing in a common result, without one known instance of deviation from that result, is not always sufficient to establish a general conclusion.

But let us now turn to an instance apparently not very dissimilar to this. Mankind were wrong, it seems, in concluding that all swans were white; are we also wrong when we conclude that all men's heads grow above their shoulders, and never below, in spite of the conflicting testimony of the naturalist Pliny? As there were black swans, though civilised people had existed for three thousand years on the earth without meeting with them, may there not also be "men whose heads do grow beneath their shoulders," notwithstanding a rather less perfect unanimity of negative testimony from observers? Most persons would answer No; it was more credible that a bird should vary in its colour than that men should vary in the relative position of their principal organs. And there is no doubt that in so saying they would be right; but to say why they are right would be impossible, without entering more deeply than is usually done into the true theory of Induction.

Again, there are cases in which we reckon with the most unfailing confidence upon uniformity, and other cases in which we do not count upon it at all. In some we feel complete assurance that the future will resemble the past, the unknown be precisely similar to the known. In others, however invariable may be the result obtained from the instances which have been observed, we draw from them no more than a very feeble presumption that the like result will hold in all other cases. That a straight line is the shortest distance between two points, we do not doubt to be true even in the region of the fixed stars.[2] When a chemist announces the existence and properties of a newly discovered substance, if we confide in his accuracy, we feel assured that the conclusions he has arrived at will hold universally, though the induction bé founded but on a single instance. We do not withhold our assent, waiting for a repetition of the experiment; or if we do, it is from a doubt whether the one experiment was properly made, not whether, if properly made, it would be conclusive. Here, then, is a general law of nature, inferred without hesitation from a single instance; an universal proposition from a singular one. Now mark another case, and contrast it with this. Not all the instances which have been observed since the beginning of the world in support of the general proposition that all crows are black would be deemed a sufficient presumption of the truth of the proposition, to outweigh the testimony of one unexceptionable witness who should affirm that in some region of the earth not fully explored he had caught and examined a crow, and had found it to be grey.

Why is a single instance, in some cases, sufficient for a complete induction, while in others myriads of concurring instances, without a single exception known or presumed, go such a very little way towards establishing an universal proposition? Whoever can answer this question knows more of the philosophy of logic than the wisest of the ancients, and has solved the problem of Induction.

. . .

[2] In strictness, wherever the present constitution of space exists; which we have ample reason to believe that it does in the region of the fixed stars.

Of the Evidence of the Law of Universal Causation

1

We have now completed our review of the logical processes by which the laws, or uniformities, of the sequence of phenomena, and those uniformities in their co-existence which depend on the laws of their sequence, are ascertained or tested. As we recognised in the commencement, and have been enabled to see more clearly in the progress of the investigation, the basis of all these logical operations is the law of causation. The validity of all the Inductive Methods* depends on the assumption that every event, or the beginning of every phenomenon, must have some cause, some antecedent, on the existence of which it is invariably and unconditionally consequent. In the Method of Agreement this is obvious; that method avowedly proceeding on the supposition that we have found the true cause as soon as we have negatived every other. The assertion is equally true of the Method of Difference. That method authorises us to infer a general law from two instances: one, in which A exists together with a multitude of other circumstances, and B follows; another, in which A being removed, and all other circumstances remaining the same, B is prevented. What, however, does this prove? It proves that B, in the particular instance, cannot have had any other cause than A; but to conclude from this that A was the cause, or that A will on other occasions be followed by B, is only allowable on the assumption that B must have some cause; that among its antecedents in any single instance in

* Editors' note: Formulations of the five Inductive Methods or Canons: Agreement, Difference, Joint Method of Agreement and Difference, Residues, and Concomitant Variation, can be found on pages 289–290.

which it occurs, there must be one which has the capacity of producing it at other times. This being admitted, it is seen that in the case in question that antecedent can be no other than A; but, that if it be no other than A it must be A, is not proved, by these instances at least, but taken for granted. There is no need to spend time in proving that the same thing is true of the other Inductive Methods. The universality of the law of causation is assumed in them all.

But is this assumption warranted? Doubtless (it may be said) *most* phenomena are connected as effects with some antecedent or cause, that is, are never produced unless some assignable fact has preceded them; but the very circumstance that complicated processes of induction are sometimes necessary, shows that cases exist in which this regular order of succession is not apparent to our unaided apprehension. If, then, the processes which bring these cases within the same category with the rest require that we should assume the universality of the very law which they do not at first sight appear to exemplify, is not this a *petitio principii?* Can we prove a proposition by an argument which takes it for granted? And if not so proved, on what evidence does it rest?

For this difficulty, which I have purposely stated in the strongest terms it will admit of, the school of metaphysicians who have long predominated in this country find a ready salvo. They affirm that the universality of causation is a truth which we cannot help believing; that the belief in it is an instinct, one of the laws of our believing faculty. As the proof of this, they say, and they have nothing else to say, that everybody does believe it; and they number it among the propositions, rather numerous in their catalogue, which may be logically argued against, and perhaps cannot be logically proved, but which are of higher authority than logic, and so essentially inherent in the human mind, that even he who denies them in speculation shows by his habitual practice that his arguments make no impression upon himself.

Into the merits of this question, considered as one of psychology, it would be foreign to my purpose to enter here; but I must protest against adducing, as evidence of the truth of a fact in external nature, the disposition, however strong or however general, of the human mind to believe it. Belief is not proof, and does not dispense with the necessity of proof. I am aware that to ask for evidence of a proposition which we are supposed to believe instinctively is to expose oneself to the charge of rejecting the authority of the human faculties; which of course no one can consistently do, since the human faculties are all which any one has to judge by; and inasmuch as the meaning of the word evidence is supposed to be something which, when laid before the mind, induces it to believe; to demand evidence when the belief is ensured by the mind's own laws is supposed to be appealing to the intellect against the intellect. But this, I apprehend, is a misunderstanding of the nature of evidence. By evidence is not meant anything and everything which produces belief. There are many things which generate belief besides evidence. A mere strong association of ideas often causes a belief so intense as to be unshakeable by experience or argument. Evidence is not that which the mind does or must yield to, but that which it ought to yield to, namely, that, by yielding to which, its belief is kept conformable to fact. There is no appeal from the human faculties generally, but there is an appeal from one human faculty to another; from the judging faculty to those which take cognisance of fact, the faculties of sense and consciousness. The legitimacy of this appeal is admitted whenever it is allowed that our judgments ought to be conformable to fact. To say that belief suffices for its own justification is making opinion the test of opinion; it is denying the existence of any outward standard, the conformity of an opinion to which constitutes its truth. We call one mode of forming opinions right and another wrong, because the one does and the other does not tend to make the opinion agree with the fact—to make people believe what really is, and expect what really will be. Now a mere disposition to believe, even if supposed instinctive, is no guarantee for the truth of the thing believed. If, indeed, the belief ever amounted to an irresistible necessity, there would then be no *use* in appealing from it, because there would be no possibility of altering it. But even then the truth of the belief would not follow; it would only follow that mankind were under a permanent necessity of believing what might possibly not be true; in other words, that a case might occur in which our senses or consciousness, if they could be appealed to, might testify one thing and our reason believe another. But in fact there is no such permanent necessity. There is no proposition of which it can be asserted that every human mind must eternally and irrevocably believe it. Many of the propositions of which this is most confidently stated great numbers of human beings have disbelieved. The things which it has been supposed that nobody could possibly help believing are innumerable; but no two generations would make out the same catalogue of them. One age or nation believes implicitly what to another seems incredible and inconceivable; one individual has not a vestige of a belief which another deems to be absolutely inherent in humanity. There is not one of these supposed instinctive beliefs which is really inevitable. It is in the power of every one to cultivate habits of thought which make him independent of them. The habit of philosophical analysis, (of

which it is the surest effect to enable the mind to command, instead of being commanded by, the laws of the merely passive part of its own nature), by showing to us that things are not necessarily connected in fact because their ideas are connected in our minds, is able to loosen innumerable associations which reign despotically over the undisciplined or early-prejudiced mind. And this habit is not without power even over those associations which the school of which I have been speaking regard as connate and instinctive. I am convinced that any one accustomed to abstraction and analysis, who will fairly exert his faculties for the purpose, will, when his imagination has once learnt to entertain the notion, find no difficulty in conceiving that in some one, for instance, of the many firmaments into which sidereal astronomy now divides the universe, events may succeed one another at random without any fixed law; nor can anything in our experience, or in our mental nature, constitute a sufficient, or indeed any, reason for believing that this is nowhere the case.

Were we to suppose (what it is perfectly possible to imagine) that the present order of the universe were brought to an end, and that a chaos succeeded in which there was no fixed succession of events, and the past gave no assurance of the future; if a human being were miraculously kept alive to witness this change, he surely would soon cease to believe in any uniformity, the uniformity itself no longer existing. If this be admitted, the belief in uniformity either is not an instinct, or it is an instinct conquerable, like all other instincts, by acquired knowledge.

But there is no need to speculate on what might be, when we have positive and certain knowledge of what has been. It is not true as a matter of fact that mankind have always believed that all the successions of events were uniform and according to fixed laws. The Greek philosophers, not even excepting Aristotle, recognised Chance and Spontaneity as among the agents in nature; in other words, they believed that to that extent there was no guarantee that the past had been similar to itself, or that the future would resemble the past. Even now a full half of the philosophical world, including the very same metaphysicians who contend most for the instinctive character of the belief in uniformity, consider one important class of phenomena, volitions, to be an exception to the uniformity, and not governed by a fixed law.

2

As was observed in a former place, the belief we entertain in the universality, throughout nature, of the law of cause and effect, is itself an instance of induction, and by no means one of the earliest which any of us, or which mankind in general, can have made. We arrive at this universal law by generalisation from many laws of inferior generality. We should never have had the notion of causation (in the philosophical meaning of the term) as a condition of all phenomena, unless many cases of causation, or, in other words, many partial uniformities of sequence, had previously become familiar. The more obvious of the particular uniformities suggest, and give evidence of, the general uniformity, and the general uniformity, once established, enables us to prove the remainder of the particular uniformities of which it is made up. As, however, all rigorous processes of induction presuppose the general uniformity, our knowledge of the particular uniformities from which it was first inferred was not, of course, derived from rigorous induction, but from the loose and uncertain mode of induction *per enumerationem simplicem;* and the law of universal causation, being collected

from results so obtained, cannot itself rest on any better foundation.

It would seem, therefore, that induction *per enumerationem simplicem* not only is not necessarily an illicit logical process, but is in reality the only kind of induction possible; since the more elaborate process depends for its validity on a law, itself obtained in that inartificial mode. Is there not then an inconsistency in contrasting the looseness of one method with the rigidity of another, when that other is indebted to the looser method for its own foundation?

The inconsistency, however, is only apparent. Assuredly, if induction by simple enumeration were an invalid process, no process grounded on it could be valid; just as no reliance could be placed on telescopes if we could not trust our eyes. But though a valid process, it is a fallible one, and fallible in very different degrees: if therefore we can substitute for the more fallible forms of the process an operation grounded on the same process in a less fallible form, we shall have effected a very material improvement. And this is what scientific induction does.

A mode of concluding from experience must be pronounced untrustworthy when subsequent experience refuses to confirm it. According to this criterion, induction by simple enumeration—in other words, generalisation of an observed fact from the mere absence of any known instance to the contrary—affords in general a precarious and unsafe ground of assurance; for such generalisations are incessantly discovered, on further experience, to be false. Still, however, it affords some assurance, sufficient, in many cases, for the ordinary guidance of conduct. It would be absurd to say that the generalisations arrived at by mankind in the outset of their experience, such as these, Food nourishes, Fire burns, Water drowns, were unworthy of reliance.[3] There is a scale of trustworthiness in the results of the original unscientific Induction; and on this diversity (as observed in the fourth chapter of the present book) depend the rules for the improvement of the process. The improvement consists in correcting one of these inartificial generalisations by means of another. As has been already pointed out this is all that art can do. To test a generalisation, by showing that it either follows from, or conflicts with, some stronger induction, some generalisation resting on a broader foundation of experience is the beginning and end of the logic of Induction.

3

Now the precariousness of the method of simple enumeration is in an inverse ratio to the largeness of the generalisa-

[3] It deserves remark, that these early generalisations did not, like scientific inductions, presuppose causation. What they did presuppose, was *uniformity* in physical facts. But the observers were as ready to presume uniformity in the co-existences of facts as in the sequences. On the other hand, they never thought of assuming that this uniformity was a principle pervading all nature; their generalisations did not imply that there was uniformity in everything, but only that as much uniformity as existed within their observation, existed also beyond it. The induction, Fire burns, does not require for its validity that all nature should observe uniform laws, but only that there should be uniformity in one particular class of natural phenomena; the effects of fire on the senses and on combustible substances. And uniformity to this extent was not assumed, anterior to the experience, but proved by the experience. The same observed instances which proved the narrower truth, proved as much of the wider one as corresponded to it. It is from losing sight of this fact, and considering the law of causation in its full extent as necessarily presupposed in the very earliest generalisations, that persons have been led into the belief that the law of causation is known *à priori,* and is not itself a conclusion from experience.

tion. The process is delusive and insufficient, exactly in proportion as the subject-matter of the observation is special and limited in extent. As the sphere widens, this unscientific method becomes less and less liable to mislead; and the most universal class of truths, the law of causation for instance, and the principles of number and of geometry, are duly and satisfactorily proved by that method alone, nor are they susceptible of any other proof.

With respect to the whole class of generalisations of which we have recently treated, the uniformities which depend on causation, the truth of the remark just made follows by obvious inference from the principles laid down in the preceding chapters. When a fact has been observed a certain number of times to be true, and is not in any instance known to be false; if we at once affirm that fact as an universal truth or law of nature, without either testing it by any of the four methods of induction, or deducing it from other known laws, we shall in general err grossly; but we are perfectly justified in affirming it as an empirical law, true within certain limits of time, place, and circumstance, provided the number of coincidences be greater than can with any probability be ascribed to chance. The reason for not extending it beyond those limits is, that the fact of its holding true within them may be a consequence of collocations, which cannot be concluded to exist in one place because they exist in another; or may be dependent on the accidental absence of counteracting agencies, which any variation of time, or the smallest change of circumstances, may possibly bring into play. If we suppose, then, the subject-matter of any generalisation to be so widely diffused that there is no time, no place, and no combination of circumstances, but must afford an example either of its truth or of its falsity, and if it be never found otherwise than true, its truth cannot be contingent on any collocations, unless such as exist at all times and places; nor can it be frustrated by any counteracting agencies, unless by such as never actually occur. It is, therefore, an empirical law co-extensive with all human experience, at which point the distinction between empirical laws and laws of nature vanishes, and the proposition takes its place among the most firmly established as well as largest truths accessible to science.

Now, the most extensive in its subject-matter of all generalisations which experience warrants, respecting the sequences and co-existences of phenomena, is the law of causation. It stands at the head of all observed uniformities in point of universality, and therefore (if the preceding observations are correct) in point of certainty. And if we consider, not what mankind would have been justified in believing in the infancy of their knowledge, but what may rationally be believed in its present more advanced state, we shall find ourselves warranted in considering this fundamental law, though itself obtained by induction from particular laws of causation, as not less certain, but, on the contrary, more so, than any of those from which it was drawn. It adds to them as much proof as it receives from them. For there is probably no one even of the best established laws of causation which is not sometimes counteracted, and to which, therefore, apparent exceptions do not present themselves, which would have necessarily and justly shaken the confidence of mankind in the universality of those laws, if inductive processes founded on the universal law had not enabled us to refer those exceptions to the agency of counteracting causes, and thereby reconcile them with the law with which they apparently conflict. Errors, moreover, may have slipped into the statement of any one of the special laws, through inattention to some material cir-cumstance; and instead of the true proposition, another may have been enunciated, false as an universal law, though leading, in all cases hitherto observed, to the same result. To the law of causation, on the contrary, we not only do not know of any exception, but the exceptions which limit or apparently invalidate the special laws, are so far from contradicting the universal one, that they confirm it; since in all cases which are sufficiently open to our observation, we are able to trace the difference of result, either to the absence of a cause which had been present in ordinary cases, or to the presence of one which had been absent.

The law of cause and effect, being thus certain, is capable of imparting its certainty to all other inductive propositions which can be deduced from it; and the narrower inductions may be regarded as receiving their ultimate sanction from that law, since there is no one of them which is not rendered more certain than it was before, when we are able to connect it with that larger induction, and to show that it cannot be denied, consistently with the law that everything which begins to exist has a cause. And hence we are justified in the seeming inconsistency of holding induction by simple enumeration to be good for proving this general truth, the foundation of scientific induction, and yet refusing to rely on it for any of the narrower inductions. I fully admit that if the law of causation were unknown, generalisation in the more obvious cases of uniformity in phenomena would nevertheless be possible, and though in all cases more or less precarious, and in some extremely so, would suffice to constitute a certain measure of probability; but what the amount of this probability might be we are dispensed from estimating, since it never could amount to the degree of assurance which the proposition acquires, when, by the application to it of the Four Methods, the supposition of its falsity is shown to be inconsistent with the Law of Causation. We are therefore logically entitled, and, by the necessities of scientific induction, required to disregard the probabilities derived from the early rude method of generalising, and to consider no minor generalisation as proved except so far as the law of causation confirms it, nor probable except so far as it may reasonably be expected to be so confirmed.

CRITICISM OF MILL'S METHODS*

FRANCIS H. BRADLEY (1846–1924). See page 116.

1

We have seen that in reality there is no such thing as an inference from the particular to a fresh particular. In this chapter we approach a cognate superstition. In England, at least if we go with the fashion, we all have to believe in an Inductive Logic, which, starting from particular given facts, goes on to prove universal truths. Its processes, exact as the strictest syllogism, surrender themselves to the direction of Canons, reputed no less severe than *Barbara* and believed with reason to be far more fertile. I am afraid I may lose the reader's sympathy when I advise him to doubt the union of these qualities.

2

To question the existence or deny the efficacy of those methods of reasoning (whatever they may be), by which modern science has made its conquests, would of course be absurd. To succeed on a great scale is to prove one's title. And it is not within the scope of this work to investigate either the nature of the processes which science employs, or the amount of evidence which it accepts as proof. What I wish to assert is that, starting from particular perceptions of sense, there is no way of going to universal truths by a process of demonstration perfectly exact, and in all its steps theoretically accurate. The induction of logicians, so far as it professes to make that attempt, I shall try to show will not stand criticism.

. . .

4

. . . In the treatise which, partly from merits of its own and partly also from other causes, has threatened to fasten itself on us as a text book, we find the so-called Canons of Induction, collected and developed from other writers, and formulated with a show of rigorous accuracy. It is the illusory nature of these self-styled proofs that I wish to point out in the present chapter. We must not be afraid of the shadow of authority. The balance of authority among modern logicians is, I think, against the claim of the inductive proofs, and is not on their side. And perhaps already, from experience we have had, we may be prepared to find that Mr. Mill may at times be mistaken.

* From Francis H. Bradley, *The Principles of Logic* (1928), pp. 355–368. Reprinted by permission of The Clarendon Press, Oxford.

5

We must remember above all things throughout this discussion that the question is *not,* Can discoveries be made by the use of the Methods? They may be as efficacious in actual practice as is asserted by some, or as practically inadequate and unsuited for work as is affirmed by others. That is not the issue which we have before us. The question we have to answer here is, Are they valid ways of proof, by which we can go from facts to universals?

For that is the claim which the Canons set up. "The business of Inductive Logic is to provide rules and models (such as the Syllogism and its rules are for ratiocination) to which if inductive arguments conform, those arguments are conclusive, and not otherwise. This is what the Four Methods profess to be" (J. S. Mill, *Logic,* Bk. III. ix § 6). "In saying that no discoveries were ever made by the Four Methods, he affirms that none were ever made by observation and experiment; for assuredly if any were, it was by processes reducible to one or other of those methods" (*ibid.*). "But induction is not a mere mode of investigation." "Induction is proof; it is inferring something unobserved from something observed; it requires, therefore, an appropriate test of proof; and to provide that test is the special purpose of inductive logic" (*Logic,* III. ii. § 5). We can have now no doubt about the nature of this claim; and this claim it is that we are going to discuss.

6

I shall endeavour to show three things: first that the Four Inductive Methods can not be used if we start with mere facts, that the Canons presuppose universal truths as the material upon which the work is to be done; and that therefore, if valid, the Methods are not *inductive* at all, in the sense of generalizing from particulars. In the next place I shall briefly exhibit the real nature of the reasoning used in the above Four Methods, and shall point out that its essence is not thus inductive. And finally I shall show that not one of the Canons is a test of proof, and that by every one you can bring out what is false. None of these three positions depends on the others. If the Canons are invalid, if their essence is not inductive, or if they can not be applied to individual facts—if, in short, any one of these contentions is established, the inductive logic is certainly refuted. And I hope to establish firmly all three.

7

(I.) In the first place there is no doubt at all that the basis, from which we are to start in induction, consists primarily of particular given facts. I need cite no passages to establish this point. We naturally expect then to see on the one side the material as yet untouched by the Methods, and on the other the operation of these agents on the crude subject matter with which they must begin. This natural expectation is doomed to disappointment.

(*a*)   A suspicion of the shock which we are destined to receive may have come from the effrontery of the Method called "Residues." This estimable exemplar of "our great mental operation" comes up to us placarded as one of "the means which mankind possess for exploring the laws of nature by specific observation and experience," and then openly avows that it depends entirely on "previous inductions." Unless supplied beforehand, that is, with one or more ready-made universal propositions, it candidly declines to work at all. We enquire of "Residues" where we are then to begin, and it says,

"I do not know; you had better ask 'Difference.' " We anxiously turn to consider "Difference," and are staggered at once by the distressing extent of the family likeness. A chilling idea now steals into the mind; but we have gone too far to retreat at once, so, resolutely turning our back upon "Residues," we begin our examination.

(*b*) We look at the samples of the work produced, and we find the same thing turning up everywhere. The material supplied to be dealt with by the Methods is never facts but is always universals. Sometimes an open and professed generalization is used as a starting point. But, where this is not done, the material is never a particular fact. It has always been subjected to such previous operation that it is able at once to be taken and used as a "case" or "instance." But this means that already it is an abstract statement, ideal and not real, capable of repetition with other environment, and without doubt universal. Take the very first instance: "Let the antecedent A be the contact of an alkaline substance and an oil. This combination being tried under several varieties of circumstances, resembling each other in nothing else, the results agree in the production of a greasy and detersive or saponaceous substance" (*Logic,* III. viii. § 1). And this is the *raw material* which is supplied. Before I begin my induction I am to know already that, under certain sets of definite conditions exactly known, certain results have followed. But, if I know this, I also know that these results will *always* follow given the conditions. Every one of the instances is already an universal proposition; and it is not a particular fact or phenomenon at all.

8

It seems at first a strange obliquity of instinct to choose illustrations which *can* not illustrate. But on turning to examine the Canons themselves, our surprise gives place to another feeling. The illustrations have been selected, not according to choice, but from hard necessity. For the Canons are such that *ex hypothesi* they can not possibly work upon any material but universal propositions.

First Canon

If two or more instances of the phenomenon under investigation have only one circumstance in common, the circumstance in which alone all the instances agree, is the cause (or effect) of the given phenomenon.

Second Canon

If an instance in which the phenomenon under investigation occurs, and an instance in which it does not occur, have every circumstance in common save one, that one occurring only in the former; the circumstance in which alone the two instances differ, is the effect, or the cause, or an indispensable part of the cause, of the phenomenon.

Third Canon

If two or more instances in which the phenomenon occurs have only one circumstance in common, while two or more instances in which it does not occur have nothing in common save the absence of that circumstance; the circumstance in which alone the two sets of instances differ, is the effect, or the cause, or an indispensable part of the cause, of the phenomenon.

Fourth Canon

Subduct from any phenomenon such part as is known by previous inductions to be the effect of certain antecedents, and the residue of the phenomenon is the effect of the remaining antecedents.

Fifth Canon

Whatever phenomenon varies in any manner whenever another phenomenon varies in some particular manner, is either a cause or an effect of that phenomenon, or is connected with it through some fact of causation. (Mill, *Logic*, III. viii.)

Consider the phrases *"only one circumstance in common," "every circumstance in common but one," "nothing in common save the absence of that circumstance."* Only think for a moment and realize what they mean, and then take on the other hand a given fact of perception. The fact is *made* a particular fact by the presence of that, the absence of which is postulated beforehand by these formulas. A universal judgment is *made* universal by just those attributes which are pronounced indispensable in the material for these Methods. The moment you have reduced your particular fact to a perfectly definite set of elements, existing in relations which are accurately known, there you have left the fact behind you. You have already a judgment universal in the same sense in which the result of your "induction" is universal. Let us take once again the very first instance. The universal which you come to is "that the combination of an oil and an alkali causes the production of soap." The universals which you start with are that an oil and an alkali, if combined under conditions *bc* and *de*, in each case produce soap. But how can you deny that these latter are universals? No doubt they are impure; but the result of the "induction" is surely not quite pure. And is an impure universal no universal at all? If you assert this, you deny the efficacy of your "induction." If you will not assert it, then you admit that your "inductions" are not inductive, since

the base they start from is not individual facts. If we regard the formulas for a little steadily, we must surely see that an "instance" which is capable of being so formulated, has had already done upon it that work which we heard the Methods, *and the Methods alone,* were capable of performing. And, if so, these Methods must retire from the field or withdraw their claims. Something like a farce has been played before us, whether we consider the airs and pretences of the Canons, or remember the promises and the boasts of their patron.

9

But I may be reminded of and in fairness I must quote an instance, selected by the author himself, to show that his Methods can deal with common material. And the instance has the greater relevancy here, since he devised it expressly to meet the objection that the conditions of his formulas could not be found in facts.

"If it had been my object to justify the processes themselves as means of investigation, there would have been no need to look far off, or make use of recondite or complicated instances. As a specimen of a truth ascertained by the Method of Agreement, I might have chosen the proposition 'Dogs bark.' This dog, and that dog, and the other dog, answer to ABC, ADE, AFG. The circumstance of being a dog, answers to A. Barking answers to *a*. As a truth made known by the Method of Difference, 'Fire burns' might have sufficed. Before I touch the fire I am not burnt; this is BC; I touch it, and am burnt; this is ABC, *a*BC." (*Logic*, III. ix. 6.)

The Canons we think are not hard to content if this will satisfy them. But surely their author had forgotten them for the moment. By seeing three barking dogs I perceive that they *"have only one circumstance in common."* By standing in front of a burning fireplace, and then touching the fire and being burnt, I am to know that the two facts *"have every circumstance in common but one."* Is not this preposterous? Surely it is clear in the first case that Mr. Mill's way of arguing might prove just as well that all dogs have the mange, and in the second that every fireplace blisters. And these conclusions hardly seem to be sound.[1]

If we have succeeded so far in establishing this point, then the Methods of induction are placed in this dilemma. Because they *presuppose* universal truths, therefore they are not the only way of proving them. But if they are the only way of proving them, then every universal truth is unproved.

10

(II.) The second assertion I have now to make good, is that the process of the Methods is not *inductive*. I do not mean merely that, as we have seen, they can not be applied except to universals. I mean in addition that it is not at all of the essence of their process to bring out a conclusion more general than the premises. The process is one of elimination. By removing one part of an ideal construction you establish the remainder. And hence the result will be more abstract than the whole original *datum*, but it need not be more abstract than some of the premises; on the contrary it may be less so. If five plums, two apples, and ten nuts balance the scales against three pears, two peaches, and six grapes, when I know that the nuts weigh the same as the grapes, and the apples as the peaches, I

[1] As a test of the writer's accuracy in small points, we may notice that in the second example there is a mistake in the working of the Method. The right conclusion is "Touching burns"; for the fire is not the differential condition. It was there before I touched it, and if it was not there, then we have *two* differences and another kind of mistake.

infer that the plums and the pears are equal by an ideal process of removing the rest. But if this is "induction," then "$x + 5 - 3 = a + 4 - 2$, and therefore $x = a$," and again "A is either b or c, A is not c, and therefore it is b," will also be inductions. And if everything is induction which is not syllogism, then certainly these inferences are all inductive. But such an assumption would surely be quite erroneous. It finds its parallel in the counterpart mistake, that, because the Inductive Methods are not really "inductive," therefore they are syllogistic.

The Methods are all of them Methods of Residues or Methods of Difference, and they all go to their conclusion in the selfsame way. They fix a relation between certain wholes, and then, by the removal of parts of each, establish this relation between the remaining elements. In the Methods of Agreement and Concomitant Variations the principle is the same as it is in the rest. In the former the *data* are ABC—*def*, AGH—*dij*, AKL—*dmn*. It is then assumed that the d in *def*, *dij*, and *dmn*, can not be produced by a different cause; and hence, since BC, GH, KL are different, they do not produce d. A is the residue or difference, and therefore A is the cause. The process we shall see is vicious, but, such as it is, it is elimination. In Concomitant Variations we seem to have A^1BC—d^1ef; and then, when A^1 becomes A^2, we have A^2BC—d^2ef. From this whole take away ^1BC—^1ef, ^2BC—^2ef and the conclusion is A—d. The principle involved is the same throughout, and the apparent failure to see this, and the setting down of two or three co-ordinate axioms for the different Methods, is another sign that the writer had never got really inside his subject. The different Methods are different applications of one single process, and since the premises eliminated may be just as abstract as the conclusion left behind, this process can hardly be called "inductive."

11

Having seen first of all that the Canons will not work unless applied to universals; having seen, in the second place, that within these limits their procedure is not essentially one of generalization, we come now to the third of our objections. The Methods are vicious and the Canons are false.

(III.) I do not mean to say that, for all the purposes of discovery, the flaws in the Methods amount to serious mistakes. Such a contention would lie beyond the scope of my volume. It is certain, however, that independent logicians, such as Dr. Whewell and Professor Jevons in our own country, and Professors Lotze and Sigwart in Germany, have taken a view of the process of scientific discovery which is not favourable to the claims of the Four Methods. But whatever may be the usefulness of these Methods, the point here at issue is their validity as *proofs*.

What I wish to show is that they will not prove anything beyond this or that individual case. They pass to their more general conclusion by illegitimate assumptions.

12

I think the reader will agree that, if a method will prove a false conclusion from premises which are true, then that method must be logically vicious, and its Canon, which serves as a test, must be false. Now it is stated by Mr. Mill himself that the Method of Agreement will prove false conclusions (*Logic,* Chap. X.). The Method is "uncertain" and has an "imperfection." But it still continues to figure as a proof, and the Canon is left standing in its naked falsity. We also have "axioms" implied in this Method, which can hardly be true if the Method is false, and which yet are left exposed to the daylight. We are told

(Chap. X. § 1) that in chapters preceding false assumptions have been made, and yet the chapters with all their contents are recommended to us still as a sort of Gospel. And here I must frankly confess myself at a loss. Can the writer really have known that all his Canons were false statements? Whether he did or did not, I will not here enquire, for the discussion would not be likely to profit us. It will be perhaps convenient for the sake of argument to assume that he did not know the full vice of all his Methods.

The Method of Agreement starts from the premises ABC—*def,*[2] AGH—*dij,* AKL—*dmn:* and its conclusion is that A is the cause of *d*. The principle it goes on is (as we saw before) that whatever is different in the different cases can be eliminated. And this principle is false, since a consequence, such as *d,* need not always follow from the same antecedent. The generalization is therefore vicious, and the Canon which regulates it is false. The axioms also, given in § 2 of the same eighth chapter, are no less false. To make them true you must qualify them by adding "in this one case." But that means you must destroy their generalizing power.

13

The Method of Difference is no less vicious. From the premises ABC—*def,* BC—*ef,* it goes to the conclusion that A is the cause or an indispensable part of the cause of *d*. But this conclusion is fatally unsound. A may be here a single factor in the production of *d,* the presence of which is quite accidental. The rule may be for *d* to be produced entirely without A, and for A to be present without producing *d*. The foundation of

[2] I have *of course* altered Mill's lettering. If his letters *mean* anything, they involve a flagrant *petitio;* and if they do not, their suggestion must tend to confuse us.

the Method[3] "that whatever can not be eliminated, is connected with the phenomenon by a law" is quite false, unless we add to it *"in this one case,"* and thereby make it ineffectual for the purpose of generalizing.

The Method of Joint Agreement and Difference is essentially the same, and presents the same flaw. Its premises consist of ABC—*def*, AGH—*dij*, AKL—*dmn*, BC—*ef*, GH—*ij*, KL—*mn*. It infers from these the conclusion A—*d*. The mistake is the same as that which vitiated Difference. The right conclusion is that, *in these three cases,* A has gone to produce *d*.

In the Method of Residues the process is the same, and is bad for the same reason. From ABC—*def*, B—*f*, C—*e*, the Method goes on at once to A—*d*. But it could do so legitimately, only if it excluded the possibility of B or C, or both, having influenced, and been influenced by, A. Otherwise the conclusion like all the rest is vicious, and its Canon is false, unless qualified by the words *"in this one case."*

We come in the end to Concomitant Variations, and the principle of this has, I think, not been formulated with the desirable exactness. In the first place the words *whenever* in the Canon itself and *invariably* in the Axiom assigned to it are both ambiguous. If they mean that the groups of elements are causally connected, then this must rest upon a previous Method, and not upon mere facts. And in the second place, if we consider the process as a conclusion from these idealized premises, still it is impossible even then to demonstrate a result which will

---

[3] There is no material difference between this and what is wrongly given, in the same § 3, as different, and as the ground of the Method of Agreement; for you have postulated a connection in your premises. I have given above the real ground of the Method of Agreement.

hold beyond this or that case (or cases). The premises appear to be A^1BC—d^1ef, A^2BC—d^2ef, A^3BC—d^3ef, and the conclusion arrived at seems to be A—*d*. We have apparently to eliminate *everything* but A—*d*, which is hence left as proved. But since once again the factors are not isolated, we have the old mistake of Difference once more. The real conclusion is *"In this one case (or set of cases) without A no d."* Because the modification of A has altered the result, therefore A is relevant to *d* in *this* alteration, or series of alterations. I may add that no amount of instances and of "approximation" will suffice to *demonstrate logically*.

Should however finally the premises not have been so idealized as to be reducible to the formula we have given— if we really have nothing whatever to start with but a certain number of observed concomitances—then there literally is no conclusion at all, for the co-existence always *may* be mere chance coincidence. And, according as we understand the Canon and the Axiom, we must pronounce them to be either insufficient or false.

14

I have shown that, if used in order to generalize beyond this or that individual instance as prepared for treatment, the Methods are vicious, and their Canons false. Their eliminative process will only show that the whole antecedent has been concerned in producing the whole consequent. The attempt to go further and, by isolating the factors, to transcend the limits of the premises supplied, we have seen has broken down at all points.

In the premises ABC—*def*, BC—*ef*, you are supposed to know that *def* is connected with ABC, and *ef* with BC: what you do *not* yet know is if, in ABC, A is really a factor. For it might be irrelevant, and BC without it might produce *def*. But now, having BC—*ef,* and resting on the assumption which we call the Principle of Identity, you are sure that, if BC—*ef* is once true, it will be true for ever. And you proceed from this to argue that BC—*def* must be false. For to produce *def* B must have been altered: and since in ABC—*def* the result is produced with no possible alteration except mere A, A there must be relevant to the presence of *def.* Hence A *in this case* (of ABC—*def*) must be, directly or indirectly, relevant to *d*. But you must not go further, and try in any way to specify the connection. For you can not do that without closing possibilities, and assuming something not given in your premises.

And we must not forget that even this conclusion depends on our having assumed in the premises that, in ABC—*def*, *d* is not irrelevant. Unless we are perfectly sure beforehand that the whole *def* has been produced by ABC, we can not advance one single step. This shows once more how absurd it is to imagine that the Methods can be applied to particular facts. They depend entirely on such an artificial preparation of the material supplied, as has already reduced it to the form of an universal. It would be waste of time to dwell further on the detail of the Four (or Five) Methods, since the process in all is the same at bottom.

15

We have seen that the Methods are not "inductive," since they will not generalize beyond the given instance. They fail again of being "inductive," since they can not be applied to simple facts. They will not work unless they are supplied with universals. They presuppose in short as their own condition the result they profess alone to produce. Once more, the essence of their procedure is as much deductive as it is "inductive." The conclusion in some cases has less generality than some of the premises.

On any one of these grounds (and I hope on all of them) we may set down the Inductive Logic as a *fiasco*. And, if I am told that these flaws, or most of them, are already admitted by Inductive Logicians, I will not retract the word I have used. But to satisfy the objector I will give way so far as to write for *fiasco, confessed fiasco.*

16

If it really is the case that the Methods are not sound; if it really is the case that the Canons are not true; if it really is the case that "induction" is *not proof,* and that he has all along known this, and been well aware of it—in that case I would suggest to the Inductive Logician that he has provoked a possible harsh remark. And however mistaken that harsh judgment might be, yet I can not help thinking that it would be better if *he* were to tell the public, what they certainly do not know, and the opposite of which his too large professions have led them to believe. But if, as I suppose, the Inductive Logician himself makes the mistake which his public has accepted— if, that is, while admitting that, like all things human, his Methods have "imperfections," he has no idea that, taken as proofs, they are radically vicious—in that case I will end by expressing the hope of a final agreement. By abridging claims that will not stand criticism, and by reforming the root and principle of his fabric, he will bring no ruin to the bulk of his edifice. Even if we confined ourselves to Mr. Mill's Logic, we should find that, when his so-called Four Inductive Methods were wholly removed, and his inference from mere particulars banished as a misunderstanding, the more valuable and even the larger part of his discussions on Science would remain untouched.

THE DOCTRINE OF

NECESSITY EXAMINED*

CHARLES SANDERS PEIRCE (1839–1914).   See page 62.

· · ·

I propose here to examine the common belief that every single fact in the universe is precisely determined by law. It must not be supposed that this is a doctrine accepted everywhere and at all times by all rational men. Its first advocate appears to have been Democritus the atomist, who was led to it, as we are informed, by reflecting upon the "impenetrability, translation, and impact of matter." That is to say, having restricted his attention to a field where no influence other than mechanical constraint could possibly come before his notice, he straightway jumped to the conclusion that throughout the universe that was the sole principle of action—a style of reasoning so usual in our day with men not unreflecting as to be more than excusable in the infancy of thought. But Epicurus, in revising the atomic doctrine and repairing its defences, found himself obliged to suppose that atoms swerve from their courses by spontaneous chance; and thereby he conferred upon the theory life and entelechy. For we now see clearly that the peculiar function of the molecular hypothesis in physics is to open an entry for the calculus of probabilities. Already, the prince of philosophers had repeatedly and emphatically condemned the dictum of Democritus (especially in the "Physics," Book II, Chapters IV, V, VI), holding that events come to pass in three ways, namely, (1) by external compulsion, or the action of efficient causes, (2) by virtue of an inward nature, or the influence of final causes, and (3) irregularly without definite cause, but just by absolute chance; and this doctrine is of the inmost essence of Aristotelianism. It affords, at any rate, a valuable enumeration of the possible ways in which anything can be supposed to have come about. The freedom of the will, too, was admitted both by Aristotle and by Epicurus. But the Stoa, which in every department seized upon the most tangible, hard, and lifeless element, and blindly denied the existence of every other, which, for example, impugned the validity of the inductive method and wished to fill its place with the *reductio ad absurdum,* very naturally became the one school of ancient philosophy to stand by a strict necessitarianism, thus returning to the single principle of Democritus that Epicurus had been unable to swallow. Necessitarianism and materialism with the Stoics went hand in

* From Charles Sanders Peirce, "The Doctrine of Necessity Examined," *The Monist,* Volume II (April 1892), pp. 321–337.

hand, as by affinity they should. At the revival of learning, Stoicism met with considerable favor, partly because it departed just enough from Aristotle to give it the spice of novelty, and partly because its superficialities well adapted it for acceptance by students of literature and art who wanted their philosophy drawn mild. Afterwards, the great discoveries in mechanics inspired the hope that mechanical principles might suffice to explain the universe; and though without logical justification, this hope has since been continually stimulated by subsequent advances in physics. Nevertheless, the doctrine was in too evident conflict with the freedom of the will and with miracles to be generally acceptable, at first. But meantime there arose that most widely spread of philosophical blunders, the notion that associationalism belongs intrinsically to the materialistic family of doctrines; and thus was evolved the theory of motives; and libertarianism became weakened. At present, historical criticism has almost exploded the miracles, great and small; so that the doctrine of necessity has never been in so great vogue as now.

The proposition in question is that the state of things existing at any time, together with certain immutable laws, completely determine the state of things at every other time (for a limitation to *future* time is indefensible). Thus, given the state of the universe in the original nebula, and given the laws of mechanics, a sufficiently powerful mind could deduce from these data the precise form of every curlicue of every letter I am now writing.

Whoever holds that every act of the will as well as every idea of the mind is under the rigid governance of a necessity coordinated with that of the physical world, will logically be carried to the proposition that minds are part of the physical world in such a sense that the laws of mechanics determine everything that happens according to immutable attractions and repulsions. In that case, that instantaneous state of things from which every other state of things is calculable consists in the positions and velocities of all the particles at any instant. This, the usual and most logical form of necessitarianism, is called the mechanical philosophy.

When I have asked thinking men what reason they had to believe that every fact in the universe is precisely determined by law, the first answer has usually been that the proposition is a "presupposition" or postulate of scientific reasoning. Well, if that is the best that can be said for it, the belief is doomed. Suppose it be "postulated": that does not make it true, nor so much as afford the slightest rational motive for yielding it any credence. It is as if a man should come to borrow money, and when asked for his security, should reply he "postulated" the loan. To "postulate" a proposition is no more than to hope it is true. There are, indeed, practical emergencies in which we act upon assumptions of certain propositions as true, because if they are not so, it can make no difference how we act. But all such propositions I take to be hypotheses of individual facts. For it is manifest that no universal principle can in it universality be compromised in a special case or can be requisite for the validity of any ordinary inference. To say, for instance, that the demonstration by Archimedes of the property of the lever would fall to the ground if men were endowed with free-will, is extravagant; yet this is implied by those who make a proposition incompatible with the freedom of the will the postulate of all inference. Considering, too, that the conclusions of science make no pretense to being more than probable, and considering that a probable inference can at most only suppose something to be most frequently, or otherwise approximately, true, but never that anything is precisely true without exception throughout the universe, we see how far this proposition in truth is from being so postulated.

But the whole notion of a postulate being involved in reasoning appertains to a by-gone and false conception of logic. Non-deductive, or ampliative inference is of three kinds: induction, hypothesis, and analogy. If there be any other modes, they must be extremely unusual and highly complicated, and may be assumed with little doubt to be of the same nature as those enumerated. For induction, hypothesis, and analogy, as far as their ampliative character goes, that is, so far as they conclude something not implied in the premises, depend upon one principle and involve the same procedure. All are essentially inferences from sampling. Suppose a ship arrives in Liverpool laden with wheat in bulk. Suppose that by some machinery the whole cargo be stirred up with great thoroughness. Suppose that twenty-seven thimblefuls be taken equally from the forward, midships, and aft parts, from the starboard, center, and larboard parts, and from the top, half depth, and lower parts of her hold, and that these being mixed and the grains counted, four fifths of the latter are found to be of quality A. Then we infer, experientially and provisionally, that approximately four fifths of all the grain in the cargo is of the same quality. I say we infer this *experientially* and *provisionally*. By saying that we infer it *experientially*, I mean that our conclusion makes no pretension to knowledge of wheat-in-itself, our *alētheia*, as the derivation of that word implies, has nothing to do with *latent* wheat. We are dealing only with the matter of possible experience—experience in the full acceptation of the term as something not merely affecting the senses but also as the subject of thought. If there be any wheat hidden on the ship, so that it can neither turn

up in the sample nor be heard of subsequently from purchasers—or if it be half-hidden, so that it may, indeed turn up, but is less likely to do so than the rest—or if it can affect our senses and our pockets, but from some strange cause or causelessness cannot be reasoned about—all such wheat is to be excluded (or have only its proportional weight) in calculating that true proportion of quality *A*, to which our inference seeks to approximate. By saying that we draw the inference *provisionally*, I mean that we do not hold that we have reached any assigned degree of approximation as yet, but only hold that if our experience be indefinitely extended, and if every fact of whatever nature, as fast as it presents itself, be duly applied, according to the inductive method, in correcting the inferred ratio, then our approximation will become indefinitely close in the long run; that is to say, close to the experience *to come* (not merely close by the exhaustion of a finite collection) so that if experience in general is to fluctuate irregularly to and fro, in a manner to deprive the ratio sought of all definite value, we shall be able to find out approximately within what limits it fluctuates, and if, after having one definite value, it changes and assumes another, we shall be able to find that out, and in short, whatever may be the variations of this ratio in experience, experience indefinitely extended will enable us to detect them, so as to predict rightly, at last, what its ultimate value may be, if it have any ultimate value, or what the ultimate law of succession of values may be, if there be any such ultimate law, or that it ultimately fluctuates irregularly within certain limits, if it do so ultimately fluctuate. Now our inference, claiming to be no more than thus experiential and provisional, manifestly involves no postulate whatever.

For what is a postulate? It is the

formulation of a material fact which we are not entitled to assume as a premise, but the truth of which is requisite to the validity of an inference. Any fact, then, which might be supposed postulated, must either be such that it would ultimately present itself in experience, or not. If it will present itself, we need not postulate it now in our provisional inference, since we shall ultimately be entitled to use it as a premise. But if it never would present itself in our experience, our conclusion is valid but for the possibility of this fact being, otherwise than assumed, that is, it is valid as far as possible experience goes, and that is all that we claim. Thus, every postulate is cut off, either by the provisionality or by the experientiality of our inference. For instance, it has been said that induction postulates that, if an indefinite succession of samples be drawn, examined, and thrown back each before the next is drawn, then in the long run every grain will be drawn as often as any other, that is to say postulates that the ratio of the numbers of times in which any two are drawn will indefinitely approximate to unity. But no such postulate is made; for if, on the one hand, we are to have no other experience of the wheat than from such drawings, it is the ratio that presents itself in those drawings and not the ratio which belongs to the wheat in its latent existence that we are endeavoring to determine; while if, on the other hand, there is some other mode by which the wheat is to come under our knowledge, equivalent to another kind of sampling, so that after all our care in stirring up the wheat, some experiential grains will present themselves in the first sampling operation more often than others in the long run, this very singular fact will be sure to get discovered by the inductive method, which must avail itself of every sort of experience; and our inference, which was only provisional, corrects itself at last. Again, it has been

said, that induction postulates that under like circumstances like events will happen, and that this postulate is at bottom the same as the principle of universal causation. But this is a blunder, or *bévue*, due to thinking exclusively of inductions where the concluded ratio is either 1 or 0. If any such proposition were postulated, it would be that under like circumstances (the circumstances of drawing the different samples) different events occur in the same proportions in all the different sets—a proposition which is false and even absurd. But in truth no such thing is postulated, the experiential character of the inference reducing the condition of validity to this, that if a certain result does not occur, the opposite result will be manifested, a condition assured by the provisionality of the inference. But it may be asked whether it is not conceivable that every instance of a certain class destined to be ever employed as a datum of induction should have one character, while every instance destined not to be so employed should have the opposite character. The answer is that in that case, the instances excluded from being subjects of reasoning would not be experienced in the full sense of the word, but would be among these *latent* individuals of which our conclusion does not pretend to speak.

To this account of the rationale of induction I know of but one objection worth mention: it is that I thus fail to deduce the full degree of force which this mode of inference in fact possesses; that according to my view, no matter how thorough and elaborate the stirring and mixing process had been, the examination of a single handful of grain would not give me any assurance, sufficient to risk money upon, that the next handful would not greatly modify the concluded value of the ratio under inquiry, while, in fact, the assurance would be very high that this ratio was not greatly in error. If the true ratio of grains of quality A were 0.80 and the handful contained a thousand grains, nine such handfuls out of every ten would contain from 780 to 820 grains of quality A. The answer to this is that the calculation given is correct when we know that the units of this handful and the quality inquired into have the normal independence of one another, if for instance the stirring has been complete and the character sampled for has been settled upon in advance of the examination of the sample. But in so far as these conditions are not known to be complied with, the above figures cease to be applicable. Random sampling and predesignation of the character sampled for should always be striven after in inductive reasoning, but when they cannot be attained, so long as it is conducted honestly, the inference retains some value. When we cannot ascertain how the sampling has been done or the sample-character selected, induction still has the essential validity which my present account of it shows it to have.

I do not think a man who combines a willingness to be convinced with a power of appreciating an argument upon a difficult subject can resist the reasons which have been given to show that the principle of universal necessity cannot be defended as being a postulate of reasoning. But then the question immediately arises whether it is not proved to be true, or at least rendered highly probable, by observation of nature.

Still, this question ought not long to arrest a person accustomed to reflect upon the force of scientific reasoning. For the essence of the necessitarian position is that certain continuous quantities have certain exact values. Now, how can observation determine the value of such a quantity with a probable error absolutely *nil*? To one who is behind the scenes, and knows that the most refined comparisons of masses, lengths, and

angles, far surpassing in precision all other measurements, yet fall behind the accuracy of bank-accounts, and that the ordinary determinations of physical constants, such as appear from month to month in the journals, are about on a par with an upholsterer's measurements of carpets and curtains, the idea of mathematical exactitude being demonstrated in the laboratory will appear simply ridiculous. There is a recognized method of estimating the probable magnitudes of errors in physics—the method of least squares. It is universally admitted that this method makes the errors smaller than they really are; yet even according to that theory an error indefinitely small is indefinitely improbable; so that any statement to the effect that a certain continuous quantity has a certain exact value, if well-founded at all, must be founded on something other than observation.

Still, I am obliged to admit that this rule is subject to a certain qualification. Namely it only applies to continuous quantity. Now, certain kinds of continuous quantity are discontinuous at one or at two limits, and for such limits the rule must be modified. Thus, the length of a line cannot be less than zero. Suppose, then, the question arises how long a line a certain person had drawn from a marked point on a piece of paper. If no line at all can be seen, the observed length is zero; and the only conclusion this observation warrants is that the length of the line is less than the smallest length visible with the optical power employed. But indirect observations—for example, that the person supposed to have drawn the line was never within fifty feet of the paper—may make it probable that no line at all was made, so that the concluded length will be strictly zero. In like manner, experience no doubt would warrant the conclusion that there is absolutely *no* indigo in a given ear of wheat, and absolutely *no* attar in a given lichen. But such inferences can only be rendered valid by positive experiential evidence, direct or remote, and cannot rest upon a mere inability to detect the quantity in question. We have reason to think there is no indigo in the wheat, because we have remarked that wherever indigo is produced it is produced in considerable quantities, to mention only one argument. We have reason to think there is no attar in the lichen, because essential oils seem to be in general peculiar to single species. If the question had been whether there was iron in the wheat or the lichen, though chemical analysis should fail to detect its presence, we should think some of it probably was there, since iron is almost everywhere. Without any such information, one way or the other, we could only abstain from any opinion as to the presence of the substance in question. It cannot, I conceive, be maintained that we are in any *better* position than this in regard to the presence of the element of chance or spontaneous departures from law in nature.

Those observations which are generally adduced in favor of mechanical causation simply prove that there is an element of regularity in nature, and have no bearing whatever upon the question of whether such regularity is exact and universal, or not. Nay, in regard to this *exactitude,* all observation is directly *opposed* to it; and the most that can be said is that a good deal of this observation can be explained away. Try to verify any law of nature, and you will find that the more precise your observations, the more certain they will be to show irregular departures from the law. We are accustomed to ascribe these, and I do not say wrongly, to errors of observation; yet we cannot usually account for such errors in any antecedently probable way. Trace their causes back far enough, and you will be

forced to admit they are always due to arbitrary determination, or chance.

But it may be asked whether if there were an element of real chance in the universe it must not occasionally be productive of signal effects such as could not pass unobserved. In answer to this question without stopping to point out that there is an abundance of great events which one might be tempted to suppose were of that nature, it will be simplest to remark that physicists hold that the particles of gases are moving about irregularly, substantially as if by real chance, and that by the principles of probabilities there must occasionally happen to be concentrations of heat in the gases contrary to the second law of thermodynamics, and these concentrations, occurring in explosive mixtures, must sometimes have tremendous effects. Here, then, is in substance the very situation supposed; yet no phenomena ever have resulted which we are forced to attribute to such chance concentration of heat, or which anybody, wise or foolish, has ever dreamed of accounting for in that manner.

In view of all these considerations, I do not believe that anybody, not in a state of casehardened ignorance respecting the logic of science, can maintain that the precise and universal conformity of facts to law is clearly proved, or even rendered particularly probable, by any observations hitherto made. In this way, the determined advocate of exact regularity will soon find himself driven to *a priori* reasons to support his thesis. These received such a socdolager from Stuart Mill in his examination of Hamilton, that holding to them now seems to me to denote a high degree of imperviousness to reason; so that I shall pass them by with little notice.

To say that we cannot help believing a given proposition is no argument, but it is a conclusive fact if it be true; and with the substitution of "I" for "we," it is true in the mouths of several classes of minds, the blindly passionate, the unreflecting and ignorant, and the person who has overwhelming evidence before his eyes. But that which has been inconceivable today has often turned out indisputable on the morrow. Inability to conceive is only a stage through which every man must pass in regard to a number of beliefs—unless endowed with extraordinary obstinacy and obtuseness. His understanding is enslaved to some blind compulsion which a vigorous mind is pretty sure soon to cast off.

Some seek to back up the *a priori* position with empirical arguments. They say that the exact regularity of the world is a natural belief, and that natural beliefs have generally been confirmed by experience. There is some reason in this. Natural beliefs, however, if they generally have a foundation of truth, also require correction and purification from natural illusions. The principles of mechanics are undoubtedly natural beliefs; but, for all that, the early formulations of them were exceedingly erroneous. The general approximation to truth in natural beliefs is, in fact, a case of the general adaptation of genetic products to recognizable utilities or ends. Now, the adaptations of nature, beautiful and often marvellous as they verily are, are never found to be quite perfect; so that the argument is quite *against* the absolute exactitude of any natural belief, including that of the principle of causation.

Another argument, or convenient commonplace, is that absolute chance is *inconceivable*. This word has eight current significations. The Century Dictionary enumerates six. Those who talk like this will hardly be persuaded to say in what sense they mean that chance is inconceivable. Should they do so, it would easily be shown either that they have no sufficient reason for the statement or that the inconceivability is of a kind which

does not prove that chance is nonexistent.

Another *a priori* argument is that chance is unintelligible; that is to say, while it may perhaps be conceivable, it does not disclose to the eye of reason the how or why of things; and since a hypothesis can only be justified so far as it renders some phenomenon intelligible, we never can have any right to suppose absolute chance to enter into the production of anything in nature. This argument may be considered in connection with two others. Namely, instead of going so far as to say that the supposition of chance can *never* properly be used to explain any observed fact, it may be alleged merely that no facts are known which such a supposition could in any way help in explaining. Or again, the allegation being still further weakened, it may be said that since departures from law are not unmistakably observed, chance is not a *vera causa,* and ought not unnecessarily to be introduced into a hypothesis.

These are no mean arguments, and require us to examine the matter a little more closely. Come, my superior opponent, let me learn from your wisdom. It seems to me that every throw of sixes with a pair of dice is a manifest instance of chance.

"While you would hold a throw of deuce-ace to be brought about by necessity?" (The opponent's supposed remarks are placed in quotation marks.)

Clearly one throw is as much chance as another.

"Do you think throws of dice are of a different nature from other events?"

I see that I must say that *all* the diversity and specificalness of events is attributable to chance.

"Would you, then, deny that there is any regularity in the world?"

That is clearly undeniable. I must acknowledge there is an approximate regularity, and that every event is influenced by it. But the diversification, specificalness, and irregularity of things I suppose is chance. A throw of sixes appears to me a case in which this element is particularly obtrusive.

"If you reflect more deeply, you will come to see that *chance* is only a name for a cause that is unknown to us."

Do you mean that we have no idea whatever what kind of causes could bring about a throw of sixes?

"On the contrary, each die moves under the influence of precise mechanical laws."

But it appears to me that it is not these *laws* which made the die turn up sixes; for these laws act just the same when other throws come up. The chance lies in the diversity of throws; and this diversity cannot be due to laws which are immutable.

"The diversity is due to the diverse circumstances under which the laws act. The dice lie differently in the box, and the motion given to the box is different. These are the unknown causes which produce the throws, and to which we give the name of chance; not the mechanical law which regulates the operation of these causes. You see you are already beginning to think more clearly about this subject."

Does the operation of mechanical law not increase the diversity?

"Properly not. You must know that the instantaneous state of a system of particles is defined by six times as many numbers as there are particles, three for the coordinates of each particle's position, and three more for the components of its velocity. This number of numbers, which expresses the amount of diversity in the system, remains the same at all times. There may be, to be sure, some kind of relation between the coordinates and component velocities of the different particles, by means of which the state of the system might be expressed by a smaller number of numbers. But, if this is the case, a precisely corresponding relationship must exist between the coordinates and component velocities at any other time, though it may doubtless be a relation less obvious to us. Thus, the intrinsic complexity of the system is the same at all times."

Very well, my obliging opponent, we have now reached an issue. You think all the arbitrary specifications of the universe were introduced in one dose, in the beginning, if there was a beginning, and that the variety and complication of nature has always been just as much as it is now. But I, for my part, think that the diversification, the specification, has been continually taking place. Should you condescend to ask me why I so think, I should give my reason as follows:

1. Question any science which deals with the course of time. Consider the life of an individual animal or plant, or of a mind. Glance at the history of states, of institutions, of language, of ideas. Examine the successions of forms shown by paleontology, the history of the globe as set forth in geology, or what the astronomer is able to make out concerning the changes of stellar systems. Everywhere the main fact is growth and increasing complexity. Death and corruption are mere accidents or secondary phenomena. Among some of the lower organisms, it is a moot point with biologists whether there be anything which ought to be called death. Races, at any rate, do not die out except under unfavorable circumstances. From these broad and ubiquitous facts we may fairly infer, by the most unexceptionable logic, that there is probably in nature some agency by which the complexity and diversity of things can be increased; and that consequently the rule of mechanical necessity meets in some way with interference.

2. By thus admitting pure spontaneity or life as a character of the universe, act-

ing always and everywhere though restrained within narrow bounds by law, producing infinitesimal departures from law continually, and great ones with infinite infrequency, I account for all the variety and diversity of the universe, in the only sense in which the really *sui generis* and new can be said to be accounted for. The ordinary view has to admit the inexhaustible multitudinous variety of the world, has to admit that its mechanical law cannot account for this in the least, that variety can spring only from spontaneity, and yet denies without any evidence or reason the existence of this spontaneity, or else shoves it back to the beginning of time and supposes it dead ever since. The superior logic of my view appears to me not easily controverted.

3. When I ask the necessitarian how he would explain the diversity and irregularity of the universe, he replies to me out of the treasury of his wisdom that irregularity is something which from the nature of things we must not seek to explain. Abashed at this, I seek to cover my confusion by asking how he would explain the uniformity and regularity of the universe, whereupon he tells me that the laws of nature are immutable and ultimate facts, and no account is to be given of them. But my hypothesis of spontaneity does explain irregularity, in a certain sense; that is, it explains the general fact of irregularity, though not, of course, what each lawless event is to be. At the same time, by thus loosening the bond of necessity, it gives room for the influence of another kind of causation, such as seems to be operative in the mind in the formation of associations, and enables us to understand how the uniformity of nature could have been brought about. That single events should be hard and unintelligible, logic will permit without difficulty: we do not expect to make the shock of a personally experienced earthquake appear natural and reasonable by any amount of cogitation. But logic does expect things *general* to be understandable. To say that there is a universal law, and that it is a hard, ultimate, unintelligible fact, the why and wherefore of which can never be inquired into, at this a sound logic will revolt; and will pass over at once to a method of philosophising which does not thus barricade the road of discovery.

4. Necessitarianism cannot logically stop short of making the whole action of the mind a part of the physical universe. Our notion that we decide what we are going to do, if as the necessitarian says, it has been calculable since the earliest times, is reduced to illusion. Indeed, consciousness in general thus becomes a mere illusory aspect of a material system. What we call red, green, and violet are in reality only different rates of vibration. The sole reality is the distribution of qualities of matter in space and time. Brain-matter is protoplasm in a certain degree and kind of complication—a certain arrangement of mechanical particles. Its feeling is but an inward aspect, a phantom. For, from the positions and velocities of the particles at any one instant, and the knowledge of the immutable forces, the positions at all other times are calculable; so that the universe of space, time, and matter is a rounded system uninterfered with from elsewhere. But from the state of feeling at any instant, there is no reason to suppose the states of feeling at all other instants are thus exactly calculable; so that feeling is, as I said, a mere fragmentary and illusive aspect of the universe. This is the way, then, that necessitarianism has to make up its accounts. It enters consciousness under the head of sundries, as a forgotten trifle; its scheme of the universe would be more satisfactory if this little fact could be dropped out of sight. On the other hand, by supposing the rigid exactitude of causation to yield,

I care not how little—be it but by a strictly infinitesimal amount—we gain room to insert mind into our scheme, and to put it into the place where it is needed, into the position which, as the sole self-intelligible thing, it is entitled to occupy, that of the fountain of existence; and in so doing we resolve the problem of the connection of soul and body.

5. But I must leave undeveloped the chief of my reasons, and can only adumbrate it. The hypothesis of chance-spontaneity is one whose inevitable consequences are capable of being traced out with mathematical precision into considerable detail. Much of this I have done and find the consequences to agree with observed facts to an extent which seems to me remarkable. But the matter and methods of reasoning are novel, and I have no right to promise that other mathematicians shall find my deductions as satisfactory as I myself do, so that the strongest reason for my belief must for the present remain a private reason of my own, and cannot influence others. I mention it to explain my own position; and partly to indicate to future mathematical speculators a veritable goldmine, should time and circumstances and the abridger of all joys prevent my opening it to the world.

If now I, in my turn, inquire of the necessitarian why he prefers to suppose that all specification goes back to the beginning of things, he will answer me with one of those last three arguments which I left unanswered.

First, he may say that chance is a thing absolutely unintelligible, and therefore that we never can be entitled to make such a supposition. But does not this objection smack of naïve impudence? It is not mine, it is his own conception of the universe which leads abruptly up to hard, ultimate, inexplicable, immutable law, on the one hand, and to inexplicable specification and diversification of circumstances on the other. My view, on the contrary, hypothetises nothing at all, unless it be hypothesis to say that all specification came about in some sense, and is not to be accepted as unaccountable. To undertake to account for anything by saying boldly that it is due to chance would, indeed, be futile. But this I do not do. I make use of chance chiefly to make room for a principle of generalization, or tendency to form habits, which I hold has produced all regularities. The mechanical philosopher leaves the whole specification of the world utterly unaccounted for, which is pretty nearly as bad as to boldly attribute it to chance. I attribute it altogether to chance, it is true, but to chance in the form of a spontaneity which is to some degree regular. It seems to me clear at any rate that one of these two positions must be taken, or else specification must be supposed due to a spontaneity which develops itself in a certain and not in a chance way, by an objective logic like that of Hegel. This last way I leave as an open possibility, for the present; for it is as much opposed to the necessitarian scheme of existence as my own theory is.

Secondly the necessitarian may say there are, at any rate, no observed phenomena which the hypothesis of chance could aid in explaining. In reply, I point first to the phenomenon of growth and developing complexity, which appears to be universal, and which though it may possibly be an affair of mechanism perhaps, certainly presents all the appearance of increasing diversification. Then, there is variety itself, beyond comparison the most obtrusive character of the universe: no mechanism can account for this. Then, there is the very fact the necessitarian most insists upon, the regularity of the universe which for him serves only to block the road of inquiry. Then, there are the regular relationships between the laws of nature—similarities and comparative characters, which appeal to our intelligence as its cousins, and call upon us for a reason. Finally, there is consciousness, feeling, a patent fact enough, but a very inconvenient one to the mechanical philosopher.

Thirdly, the necessitarian may say that chance is not a *vera causa*, that we cannot know positively there is any such element in the universe. But the doctrine of the *vera causa* has nothing to do with elementary conceptions. Pushed to that extreme, it at once cuts off belief in the existence of a material universe; and without that necessitarianism could hardly maintain its ground. Besides, variety is a fact which must be admitted; and the theory of chance merely consists in supposing this diversification does not antedate all time. Moreover, the avoidance of hypotheses involving causes nowhere positively known to act—is only a recommendation of logic, not a positive command. It cannot be formulated in any precise terms without at once betraying its untenable character—I mean as rigid rule, for as a recommendation it is wholesome enough.

I believe I have thus subjected to fair examination all the important reasons for adhering to the theory of universal necessity, and have shown their nullity. I earnestly beg that whoever may detect any flaw in my reasoning will point it out to me, either privately or publicly; for if I am wrong, it much concerns me to be set right speedily. If my argument remains unrefuted, it will be time, I think, to doubt the absolute truth of the principle of universal law: and when once such a doubt has obtained a living root in any man's mind, my cause with him, I am persuaded, is gained.

THE PRINCIPLE

OF INDUCTION*

BERTRAND RUSSELL (1872–   ). See page 78.

In almost all our previous discussions we have been concerned in the attempt to get clear as to our data in the way of knowledge of existence. What things are there in the universe whose existence is known to us owing to our being acquainted with them? So far, our answer has been that we are acquainted with our sense-data, and, probably, with ourselves. These we know to exist. And past sense-data which are remembered are known to have existed in the past. This knowledge supplies our data.

But if we are to be able to draw inferences from these data—if we are to know of the existence of matter, of other people, of the past before our individual memory begins, or of the future, we must know general principles of some kind by means of which such inferences can be drawn. It must be known to us that the existence of some one sort of thing, A, is a sign of the existence of some other sort of thing, B, either at the same time as A or at some earlier or later time, as, for example, thunder is a sign of the earlier existence of lightning. If this were not known to us, we could never extend our knowledge beyond the sphere of our private experience; and this sphere, as we have seen, is exceedingly limited. The question we have now to consider is whether such an extension is possible, and if so, how it is effected.

Let us take as an illustration a matter about which none of us, in fact, feel the slightest doubt. We are all convinced that the sun will rise to-morrow. Why? Is this belief a mere blind outcome of past experience, or can it be justified as a reasonable belief? It is not easy to find a test by which to judge whether a belief of this kind is reasonable or not, but we can at least ascertain what sort of general beliefs would suffice, if true, to justify the judgement that the sun will rise to-morrow, and the many other similar judgements upon which our actions are based.

It is obvious that if we are asked why we believe that the sun will rise to-morrow, we shall naturally answer, 'Because it always has risen every day'. We have a firm belief that it will rise in the future, because it has risen in the past. If we are challenged as to why we believe that it will continue to rise as heretofore, we may appeal to the laws of motion: the earth, we shall say, is a freely rotating body, and such bodies do not cease to rotate unless something interferes from outside, and there is nothing outside to

* From Bertrand Russell, *The Problems of Philosophy*. Reprinted by permission of the Oxford University Press, London.

interfere with the earth between now and to-morrow. Of course it might be doubted whether we are quite certain that there is nothing outside to interfere, but this is not the interesting doubt. The interesting doubt is as to whether the laws of motion will remain in operation until to-morrow. If this doubt is raised, we find ourselves in the same position as when the doubt about the sunrise was first raised.

The *only* reason for believing that the laws of motion will remain in operation is that they have operated hitherto, so far as our knowledge of the past enables us to judge. It is true that we have a greater body of evidence from the past in favour of the laws of motion than we have in favour of the sunrise, because the sunrise is merely a particular case of fulfilment of the laws of motion, and there are countless other particular cases. But the real question is: Do *any* number of cases of a law being fulfilled in the past afford evidence that it will be fulfilled in the future? If not, it becomes plain that we have no ground whatever for expecting the sun to rise to-morrow, or for expecting the bread we shall eat at our next meal not to poison us, or for any of the other scarcely conscious expectations that control our daily lives. It is to be observed that all such expectations are only *probable;* thus we have not to seek for a proof that they *must* be fulfilled, but only for some reason in favour of the view that they are *likely* to be fulfilled.

Now in dealing with this question we must, to begin with, make an important distinction, without which we should soon become involved in hopeless confusions. Experience has shown us that, hitherto, the frequent repetition of some uniform succession or coexistence has been a *cause* of our expecting the same succession or coexistence on the next occasion. Food that has a certain appearance generally has a certain taste, and it is a severe shock to our expectations when the familiar appearance is found to be associated with an unusual taste. Things which we see become associated, by habit, with certain tactile sensations which we expect if we touch them; one of the horrors of a ghost (in many ghost-stories) is that it fails to give us any sensations of touch. Uneducated people who go abroad for the first time are so surprised as to be incredulous when they find their native language not understood.

And this kind of association is not confined to men; in animals also it is very strong. A horse which has been often driven along a certain road resists the attempt to drive him in a different direction. Domestic animals expect food when they see the person who usually feeds them. We know that all these rather crude expectations of uniformity are liable to be misleading. The man who has fed the chicken every day throughout its life at last wrings its neck instead, showing that more refined views as to the uniformity of nature would have been useful to the chicken.

But in spite of the misleadingness of such expectations, they nevertheless exist. The mere fact that something has happened a certain number of times causes animals and men to expect that it will happen again. Thus our instincts certainly cause us to believe that the sun will rise to-morrow, but we may be in no better a position than the chicken which unexpectedly has its neck wrung. We have therefore to distinguish the fact that past uniformities *cause* expectations as to the future, from the question whether there is any reasonable ground for giving weight to such expectations after the question of their validity has been raised.

The problem we have to discuss is whether there is any reason for believing in what is called 'the uniformity of nature'. The belief in the uniformity of nature is the belief that everything that has happened or will happen is an instance of some general law to which there are *no* exceptions. The crude expectations which we have been considering are all subject to exceptions, and therefore liable to disappoint those who entertain them. But science habitually assumes, at least as a working hypothesis, that general rules which have exceptions can be replaced by general rules which have no exceptions. 'Unsupported bodies in air fall' is a general rule to which balloons and aeroplanes are exceptions. But the laws of motion and the law of gravitation, which account for the fact that most bodies fall, also account for the fact that balloons and aeroplanes can rise; thus the laws of motion and the law of gravitation are not subject to these exceptions.

The belief that the sun will rise tomorrow might be falsified if the earth came suddenly into contact with a large body which destroyed its rotation; but the laws of motion and the law of gravitation would not be infringed by such an event. The business of science is to find uniformities, such as the laws of motion and the law of gravitation, to which, so far as our experience extends, there are no exceptions. In this search science has been remarkably successful, and it may be conceded that such uniformities have held hitherto. This brings us back to the question: Have we any reason, assuming that they have always held in the past, to suppose that they will hold in the future?

It has been argued that we have reason to know that the future will resemble the past, because what was the future has constantly become the past, and has always been found to resembly the past, so that we really have experience of the future, namely of times which were formerly future, which we may call past futures. But such an argument really begs the very question at issue. We have ex-

perience of past futures, but not of future futures, and the question is: Will future futures resemble past futures? This question is not to be answered by an argument which starts from past futures alone. We have therefore still to seek for some principle which shall enable us to know that the future will follow the same laws as the past.

The reference to the future in this question is not essential. The same question arises when we apply the laws that work in our experience to past things of which we have no experience—as, for example, in geology, or in theories as to the origin of the Solar System. The question we really have to ask is: 'When two things have been found to be often associated, and no instance is known of the one occurring without the other, does the occurrence of one of the two, in a fresh instance, give any good ground for expecting the other?' On our answer to this question must depend the validity of the whole of our expectations as to the future, the whole of the results obtained by induction, and in fact practically all the beliefs upon which our daily life is based.

It must be conceded, to begin with, that the fact that two things have been found often together and never apart does not, by itself, suffice to *prove* demonstratively that they will be found together in the next case we examine. The most we can hope is that the oftener things are found together, the more probable it becomes that they will be found together another time, and that, if they have been found together often enough, the probability will amount *almost* to certainty. It can never quite reach certainty, because we know that in spite of frequent repetitions there sometimes is a failure at the last, as in the case of the chicken whose neck is wrung. Thus probability is all we ought to seek.

It might be urged, as against the view we are advocating, that we know all natural phenomena to be subject to the reign of law, and that sometimes, on the basis of observation, we can see that only one law can possibly fit the facts of the case. Now to this view there are two answers. The first is that, even if *some* law which has no exceptions applies to our case, we can never, in practice, be sure that we have discovered that law and not one to which there are exceptions. The second is that the reign of law would seem to be itself only probable, and that our belief that it will hold in the future, or in unexamined cases in the past, is itself based upon the very principle we are examining.

The principle we are examining may be called the *principle of induction,* and its two parts may be stated as follows:

(*a*) When a thing of a certain sort *A* has been found to be associated with a thing of a certain other sort *B,* and has never been found dissociated from a thing of the sort *B,* the greater the number of cases in which *A* and *B* have been associated, the greater is the probability that they will be associated in a fresh case in which one of them is known to be present;

(*b*) Under the same circumstances, a sufficient number of cases of association will make the probability of a fresh association nearly a certainty, and will make it approach certainty without limit.

As just stated, the principle applies only to the verification of our expectation in a single fresh instance. But we want also to know that there is a probability in favour of the general law that things of the sort *A* are *always* associated with things of the sort *B,* provided a sufficient number of cases of association are known, and no cases of failure of association are known. The probability of the general law is obviously less than the probability of the particular case, since if the general law is true, the particular case must also be true, whereas

the particular case may be true without the general law being true. Nevertheless the probability of the general law is increased by repetitions, just as the probability of the particular case is. We may therefore repeat the two parts of our principle as regards the general law, thus:

(*a*) The greater the number of cases in which a thing of the sort *A* has been found associated with a thing of the sort *B,* the more probable it is (if no cases of failure of association are known) that *A* is always associated with *B;*

(*b*) Under the same circumstances, a sufficient number of cases of the association of *A* with *B* will make it nearly certain that *A* is always associated with *B,* and will make this general law approach certainty without limit.

It should be noted that probability is always relative to certain data. In our case, the data are merely the known cases of coexistence of *A* and *B.* There may be other data, which *might* be taken into account, which would gravely alter the probability. For example, a man who had seen a great many white swans might argue, by our principle, that on the data it was *probable* that all swans were white, and this might be a perfectly sound argument. The argument is not disproved by the fact that some swans are black, because a thing may very well happen in spite of the fact that some data render it improbable. In the case of the swans, a man might know that colour is a very variable characteristic in many species of animals, and that, therefore, an induction as to colour is peculiarly liable to error. But this knowledge would be a fresh datum, by no means proving that the probability relatively to our previous data had been wrongly estimated. The fact, therefore, that things often fail to fulfil our expectations is no evidence that our expectations will not *probably* be fulfilled in a given case or a given class of cases. Thus our inductive principle is at any rate not capable of being *disproved* by an appeal to experience.

The inductive principle, however, is equally incapable of being *proved* by an appeal to experience. Experience might conceivably confirm the inductive principle as regards the cases that have been already examined; but as regards unexamined cases, it is the inductive principle alone that can justify any inference from what has been examined to what has not been examined. All arguments which, on the basis of experience, argue as to the future or the unexperienced parts of the past or present, assume the inductive principle; hence we can never use experience to prove the inductive principle without begging the question. Thus we must either accept the inductive principle on the ground of its intrinsic evidence, or forgo all justification of our expectations about the future. If the principle is unsound, we have no reason to expect the sun to rise to-morrow, to expect bread to be more nourishing than a stone, or to expect that if we throw ourselves off the roof we shall fall. When we see what looks like our best friend approaching us, we shall have no reason to suppose that his body is not inhabited by the mind of our worst enemy or of some total stranger. All our conduct is based upon associations which have worked in the past, and which we there-

fore regard as likely to work in the future; and this likelihood is dependent for its validity upon the inductive principle.

The general principles of science, such as the belief in the reign of law, and the belief that every event must have a cause, are as completely dependent upon the inductive principle as are the beliefs of daily life. All such general principles are believed because mankind have found innumerable instances of their truth and no instances of their falsehood. But this affords no evidence for their truth in the future, unless the inductive principle is assumed.

Thus all knowledge which, on a basis of experience tells us something about what is not experienced, is based upon a belief which experience can neither confirm nor confute, yet which, at least in its more concrete applications, appears to be as firmly rooted in us as many of the facts of experience. The existence and justification of such beliefs—for the inductive principle, as we shall see, is not the only example—raises some of the most difficult and most debated problems of philosophy. We will, in the next chapter, consider briefly what may be said to account for such knowledge, and what is its scope and its degree of certainty.

SOME HISTORICAL NOTES ON INDUCTION*

JOHN MAYNARD KEYNES (1883–1946) was a British economist, political essayist, financier, and educator. His best known book, *The General Theory of Employment, Interest and Money* (1936) made a decisive and revolutionary change in the thinking of academic economists all over the world. The power and originality of Keynes's mind are clearly displayed in his *Treatise on Probability,* from which the present selection is taken. That book is distinguished not just for its bold innovations in probability theory, but also for its just appraisal and honest appreciation of earlier writers on the subject.

1

The number of books, which deal with inductive theory, is extraordinarily small. It is usual to associate the subject with the names of Bacon, Hume, and Mill. In spite of the modern tendency to depreciate the first and the last of these, they are the principal names, I think, with which the history of induction ought to be associated. The next place is held by Laplace and Jevons. Amongst contemporary logicians there is an almost complete absence of constructive theory, and they content themselves for the most part with the easy task of criticising Mill, or with the more difficult one of following him.

That the inductive theories of Bacon and of Mill are full of errors and even of absurdities, is, of course, a commonplace of criticism. But when we ignore details, it becomes clear that they were really attempting to disentangle the essential issues. We depreciate them partly, perhaps, as a reaction from the view once held that they helped the progress of scientific discovery. For it is not plausible to suppose that Newton owed anything to Bacon, or Darwin to Mill. But with the logical problem their minds were truly occupied, and in the history of logical theory they should always be important.

It is true, nevertheless, that the advancement of science was the main object which Bacon himself, though not Mill, believed that his philosophy would promote. The *Great Instauration* was intended to promulgate an actual method of discovery entirely different from any which had been previously known. It did not do this, and against such pretensions Macaulay's well-known essay was not unjustly directed. Mill, however, expressly

* From John Maynard Keynes, *A Treatise on Probability* (1921), Chapter XXIII. Reprinted by permission of the Trustees of the Keynes Estate, Macmillan & Co., Ltd., London and St. Martin's Press, Inc., New York.

disclaimed in his preface any other object than to classify and generalise the practices "conformed to by accurate thinkers in their scientific inquiries." Whereas Bacon offered rules and demonstrations, hitherto unknown, with which any man could solve all the problems of science by taking pains, Mill admitted that "in the existing state of the cultivation of the sciences, there would be a very strong presumption against any one who should imagine that he had effected a revolution in the theory of the investigation of truth, or added any fundamentally new process to the practice of it."

2

The theories of both seem to me to have been injured, though in different degrees, by a failure to keep quite distinct the three objects: (1) of helping the scientist, (2) of explaining and analysing his practice, and (3) of justifying it. Bacon was really interested in the second as well as in the first, and was led to some of his methods by reflecting upon what distinguished good arguments from bad in actual investigations. To logicians his methods were as new as he claimed, but they had their origin, nevertheless, in the commonest inferences of science and daily life. But his main preoccupation was with the first, which did injury to his treatment of the third. He himself became aware as the work progressed that, in his anxiety to provide an infallible mode of discovery, he had put forth more than he would ever be able to justify. His own mind grew doubtful, and the most critical parts of the description of the new method were never written. No one who has reflected much upon Induction need find it difficult to understand the progress and development of Bacon's thoughts. To the philosopher who first distinguished some of the complexities of empirical proof in a generalised,

and not merely a particular, form, the prospects of systematising these methods must have seemed extraordinarily hopeful. The first investigator could not have anticipated that Induction, in spite of its apparent certainty, would prove so elusive to analysis.

Mill also was led, in a not dissimilar way, to attempt a too simple treatment, and, in seeking for ease and certainty, to treat far too lightly the problem of justifying what he had claimed. Mill shirks, almost openly, the difficulties; and scarcely attempts to disguise from himself or his readers that he grounds induction upon a circular argument.

3

Some of the most characteristic errors both of Bacon and of Mill arise, I think, out of a misapprehension, which it has been a principal object of this book to correct. Both believed, without hesitation it seems, that induction is capable of establishing a conclusion which is absolutely certain, and that an argument is invalid if the generalisation, which it supports, admits of exceptions in fact. "Absolute certainty," says Leslie Ellis, "is one of the distinguishing characters of the Baconion induction." It was, in this respect, mainly that it improved upon the older induction *per enumerationem simplicem*. "The induction which the logicians speak of," Bacon argues in the *Advancement of Learning,* "is utterly vicious and incompetent. . . . For to conclude upon an enumeration of particulars, without instance contradictory, is no conclusion but a conjecture." The conclusions of the new method, unlike those of the old, are not liable to be upset by further experience. In the attempt to justify these claims and to obtain demonstrative methods, it was necessary to introduce assumptions for which there was no warrant.

Precisely similar claims were made by Mill, although there are passages in which he abates them, for his own rules of procedure. An induction has no validity, according to him as according to Bacon, unless it is absolutely certain. The following passage[1] is significant of the spirit in which the subject was approached by him: "Let us compare a few cases of incorrect inductions with others which are acknowledged to be legitimate. Some, we know, which were believed for centuries to be correct, were nevertheless incorrect. *That all swans are white, cannot have been a good induction, since the conclusion has turned out erroneous.* The experience, however, on which the conclusion rested was genuine." Mill has not justly apprehended the relativity of all inductive arguments to the evidence, nor the element of uncertainty which is present, more or less, in all the generalisations which they support.[2] Mill's methods would yield certainty, if they were correct, just as Bacon's would. It is the necessity, to which Mill had subjected himself, of obtaining certainty that occasions their want of reality. Bacon and Mill both assume that experiment can shape and analyse the evidence in a manner and to an extent which is not in fact possible. In the aims and expectations with which they attempt to solve the inductive problem, there is on fundamental points an unexpectedly close resemblance beween them.

4

Turning from these general criticisms to points of greater detail, we find that

[1] Bk. iii. chap. iii. 3 (the italics are mine)
[2] This misapprehension may be connected with Mill's complete failure to grasp with any kind of thoroughness the nature and importance of the theory of probability. The treatment of this topic in the *System of Logic* is exceedingly bad. His understanding of the subject was, indeed, markedly inferior to the best thought of his own time.

the line of thought pursued by Mill was essentially the same as that which had been pursued by Bacon, and, also, that the argument of the preceding chapters is, in spite of some real differences, a development of the same fundamental ideas which underlie, as it seems to me, the theories of Mill and Bacon alike.

We have seen that all empirical arguments require an initial probability derived from analogy, and that this initial probability may be raised towards certainty by means of pure induction or the multiplication of instances. In some arguments we depend mainly upon analogy, and the initial probability obtained by means of it (with the assistance, as a rule, of previous knowledge) is so large that numerous instances are not required. In other arguments pure induction predominates. As science advances and the body of pre-existing knowledge is increased, we depend increasingly upon analogy; and only at the earlier stages of our investigations is it necessary to rely, for the greater part of our support, upon the multiplication of instances. Bacon's great achievement, in the history of logical theory, lay in his being the first logician to recognise the importance of methodical analogy to scientific argument and the dependence upon it of most well-established conclusions. The *Novum Organum* is mainly concerned with explaining methodical ways of increasing what I have termed the Positive and Negative Analogies, and of avoiding false Analogies. The use of exclusions and rejections, to which Bacon attached supreme importance, and which he held to constitute the essential superiority of his method over those which preceded it, entirely consists in the determination of what characters (or natures as he would call them) belong to the positive and negative analogies respectively. The first two tables with which the investigation begins are, first, the table *essentiae et praesentiae,* which contains all known instances in which the given nature is present, and, second, the table *declinationis sive absentiae in proximo,* which contains instances corresponding in each case to those of the first table, but in which, notwithstanding this correspondence, the given nature is absent. The doctrine of prerogative instances is concerned no less plainly with the methodical determination of Analogy. And the doctrine of idols is expounded for the avoidance of *false* analogies, standing, he says, in the same relation to the interpretation of Nature, as the doctrine of fallacies to ordinary logic. Bacon's error lay in supposing that, because these methods were new to logic, they were therefore new to practice. He exaggerated also their precision and their certainty; and he underestimated the importance of pure induction. But there was, at bottom, nothing about his rules impracticable or fantastic, or indeed unusual.

5

Almost the whole of the preceding paragraph is equally applicable to Mill. He agreed with Bacon in depreciating the part played in scientific inquiry by pure induction, and in emphasising the importance of analogy to all systematic investigators. But he saw further than Bacon in allowing for the Plurality of Causes, and in admitting that an element of pure induction was therefore made necessary. "The Plurality of Causes," he says,[3] "is the only reason why mere number of instances is of any importance in inductive inquiry. The tendency of unscientific inquirers is to rely too much on number, without analysing the instances. . . . Most people hold their conclusions with a degree of assurance proportioned to the mere *mass* of the experience on which they appear to rest; not considering that

[3] Book iv. chap. x. 2.

by the addition of instances to instances, all of the same kind, that is, differing from one another only in points already recognised as immaterial, nothing whatever is added to the evidence of the conclusion. A single instance eliminating some antecedent which existed in all the other cases, is of more value than the greatest multitude of instances which are reckoned by their number alone." Mill did not see, however, that our knowledge of the instances is seldom complete, and that new instances, which are not known to differ from the former in material respects, may add, nevertheless, to the negative analogy, and that the multiplication of them may, for this reason, strengthen the evidence. It is easy to see that his methods of Agreement and Difference closely resemble Bacon's, and aim, like Bacon's, at the determination of the Positive and Negative Analogies. By allowing for Plurality of Causes Mill advanced beyond Bacon. But he was pursuing the same line of thought which alike led to Bacon's rules and has been developed in the chapters of this book. Like Bacon, however, he exaggerated the precision with which his canons of inquiry could be used in practice.

6

No more need be said respecting method and analysis. But in both writers the exposition of method is closely intermingled with attempts to justify it. There is nothing in Bacon which at all corresponds to Mill's appeals to Causation or to the Uniformity of Nature, and, when they seek for the ground of induction, there is much that is peculiar to each writer. It is my purpose, however, to consider in this place the details common to both, which seem to me to be important and which exemplify the only line of investigation which seems likely to be fruitful; and I shall pursue no further, therefore, their numerous points of difference.

The attempt, which I have made to justify the initial probability which Analogy seems to supply, primarily depends upon a certain limitation of independent variety and upon the derivation of all the properties of any given object from a limited number of primary characters. In the same way I have supposed that the number of primary characters which are capable of producing a given property is also limited. And I have argued that it is not easy to see how a finite probability is to be obtained unless we have in each case some such limitation in the number of the ultimate alternatives.

It was in a manner which bears fundamental resemblances to this that Bacon endeavoured to demonstrate the cogency of his method. He considers, he says, "the simple forms or difference of things which are few in number, and the degrees and co-ordinations whereof make all this variety." And in *Valerius Terminus* he argues "that every particular that worketh any effect is a thing compounded more or less of diverse single natures, more manifest and more obscure, and that it appeareth not to which of the natures the effect is to be ascribed." It is indeed essential to the method of exclusions that the matter to which it is applied should be somehow resolvable into a finite number of elements. But this assumption is not peculiar, I think, to Bacon's method, and is involved, in some form or other, in every argument from Analogy. In making it Bacon was initiating, perhaps obscurely, the modern conception of a finite number of laws of nature out of the combinations of which the almost boundless variety of experience ultimately arises. Bacon's error was double and lay in supposing, first, that these distinct elements lie upon the surface and consist in visible characters, and second, that their natures are, or easily can be, known to us,

although the part of the *Instauration,* in which the manner of conceiving simple natures was to be explained, he never wrote. These beliefs falsely simplified the problem as he saw it, and led him to exaggerate the ease, certainty, and fruitfulness of the new method. But the view that it is possible to reduce all the phenomena of the universe to combinations of a limited number of simple elements—which is, according to Ellis, the central point of Bacon's whole system—was a real contribution to philosophy.

7

The assumption that every event can be analysed into a limited number of ultimate elements, is never, so far as I am aware, explicitly avowed by Mill. But he makes it in almost every chapter, and it underlies, throughout, his mode of procedure. His methods and arguments would fail immediately, if we were to suppose that phenomena of infinite complexity, due to an infinite number of independent elements, were in question, or if an infinite plurality of causes had to be allowed for.

In distinguishing, therefore, analogy from pure induction, and in justifying it by the assumption of a *limited* complexity in the problems which we investigate, I am, I think, pursuing, with numerous differences, the line of thought which Bacon first pursued and which Mill popularised. The method of treatment is dissimilar, but the subject-matter and the underlying beliefs are, in each case, the same.

8

Between Bacon and Mill came Hume. Hume's sceptical criticisms are usually associated with causality; but argument by induction—inference from past particulars to future generalisations—was the real object of his attack. Hume showed, not that inductive methods were false, but that their validity had never been established and that all possible lines of proof seemed equally unpromising. The *full* force of Hume's attack and the nature of the difficulties which it brought to light were never appreciated by Mill, and he makes no adequate attempt to deal with them. Hume's statement of the case against induction has never been improved upon; and the successive attempts of philosophers, led by Kant, to discover a transcendental solution have prevented them from meeting the hostile arguments on their own ground and from finding a solution along lines which might, conceivably, have satisfied Hume himself.

9

It would not be just here to pass by entirely the name of the great Leibniz, who, wiser in correspondence and frag-mentary projects than in completed discourses, has left to us sufficient indica-tions that his private reflections on this subject were much in advance of his contemporaries'. He distinguished three degrees of conviction amongst opinions, logical certainty (or, as we should say, propositions known to be formally true), physical certainty which is only logical probability, of which a well-established induction, as that man is a biped, is the type, and physical probability (or, as we should say, an inductive correlation), as for example that the south is a rainy quarter. He condemned generalisations based on mere repetition of instances, which he declared to be without logical value, and he insisted on the importance of *Analogy* as the basis of a valid induc-tion. He regarded a hypothesis as more probable in proportion to its *simplicity* and its *power,* that is to say, to the num-ber of the phenomena it would explain

and the fewness of the assumptions it involved. In particular a power of accu-rate prediction and of explaining phe-nomena or experiments previously un-tried is a just ground of secure confidence, of which he cites as a nearly perfect example the key to a cryptogram.

10

Whewell and Jevons furnished logicians with a storehouse of examples derived from the practice of scientists. Jevons, partly anticipated by Laplace, made an important advance when he emphasised the close relation between Induction and Probability. Combining insight and error, he spoilt brilliant suggestions by erratic and atrocious arguments. His application of Inverse Probability to the inductive problem is crude and fallacious, but the idea which underlies it is substantially good. He, too, made explicit the element of Analogy, which Mill, though he constantly employed it, had seldom called by its right name. There are few books, so superficial in argument yet suggesting so much truth, as Jevons's *Principles of Science.*

11

Modern text-books on Logic all con-tain their chapters on Induction, but contribute little to the subject. Their recognition of Mill's inadequacy renders their exposition, which, in spite of criti-cisms, is generally along his lines, nerve-less and confused. Where Mill is clear and offers a solution, they, confusedly criticising, must withhold one. The best of them, Sigwart and Venn, contain criticism and discussion which is interest-ing, but constructive theory is lacking. Hitherto Hume has been master, only to be refuted in the manner of Diogenes or Dr. Johnson.